PEACEMAKING AND PEACEKEEPING FOR THE NEW CENTURY

Edited by

Olara A. Otunnu and Michael W. Doyle

With the assistance of

Chetan Kumar, Demitra Pappas,

Marc Bennett, and Elise Oliver

ROWMAN & LITTLEFIELD PUBLISHERS, INC.

Lanham • New York • Boulder • Oxford

ROWMAN & LITTLEFIELD PUBLISHERS, INC.

Published in the United States of America
by Rowman & Littlefield Publishers, Inc.
4720 Boston Way, Lanham, Maryland 20706

12 Hid's Copse Road
Cumnor Hill, Oxford OX2 9JJ, England

British Library Cataloguing in Publication Information Available

Library of Congress Cataloging-in-Publication Data

Otunnu, Olara A., 1950–
    Peacemaking and peacekeeping for the new century / Olara A.
Otunnu and Michael W. Doyle.
        p.   cm.
    Proceedings of a seminar held in March 1995 convened by the
Government of Austria and the International Peace Academy.
    Includes bibliographical references and index.
    ISBN 0–8476–8726–0 (cloth). — ISBN 0–8476–8727–9 (pbk.)
    1. United Nations—Armed Forces—Congresses.   I. Doyle, Michael
W.   II. International Peace Academy.   III. Title.
JZ6374.O88   1998
341.5'84—dc21   97–13387
                                                               CIP

ISBN 0–8476–8726–0 (cloth : alk. paper)
ISBN 0–8476–8727–9 (pbk. : alk. paper)

Printed in the United States of America

⊗ ™ The paper used in this publication meets the minimum requirements of American National Standard for Information Sciences—
Permanence of Paper for Printed Library Materials, ANSI Z39.48–1984.

To the Peacekeepers

Contents

Foreword
Nelson Mandela   vii

Preface   ix

List of Abbreviations   xiii

Introduction: Discovering the Limits and Potential of Peacekeeping
Michael W. Doyle   1

Part I: Fifty Years of Peacemaking and Peacekeeping

1   Peacemaking and Peacekeeping for the New Century
Boutros Boutros-Ghali   21

2   Communal Conflict as a Challenge to International
Organization: The Case of the Former Yugoslavia
Adam Roberts   27

Part II: Preventing Deadly Conflict

3   Preventive Action and Conflict Resolution
Gareth Evans   61

4   Preventive Diplomacy and Peacemaking: The UN Experience
Ismat Kittani   89

**Part III: Peacekeeping, Peace Enforcement,
and the Use of Force**

5   Under What Circumstances Should the UN Intervene
Militarily in a "Domestic" Crisis?
Edward Mortimer   111

6   Dabbling in War: The Dilemma of the Use of Force
in United Nations Intervention
J. M. Sanderson   145

7   Challenges of the New Peacekeeping
Kofi A. Annan   169

8   Prospects for a Rapid Response Capability: A Dialogue
     Brian Urquhart and François Heisbourg   189

                Part IV: Humanitarian Protection

9   Humanitarian Action and Peacekeeping
     Jan Eliasson   203

10   Humanitarian Responses to International Emergencies
     Sadako Ogata   215

                Part V: Regional Dimensions

11   The Failed State and Political Collapse in Africa
     Ali A. Mazrui   233

12   The OAU Role in Conflict Management
     Salim Ahmed Salim   245

13   The Contribution of Regional Organizations in Europe
     John Roper   255

                Part VI: Peacebuilding

14   A Holistic Approach to Building Peace
     Thomas M. Franck   275

Conclusion: The Peace-and-Security Agenda of the United Nations:
     From a Crossroads into the New Century
     Olara A. Otunnu   297

Index   327

About the Contributors   347

Foreword

The empowerment of the ordinary people of our world to determine their destiny freely, unhindered by tyrants and dictators, is at the very heart of the reason for the existence of the United Nations.

But it is equally true that hundreds of millions of these politically empowered masses are caught in the death trap of poverty, unable to live life to the full. Out of all this are born social conflicts that produce insecurity and instability, civil and other wars that claim lives, millions of desperate refugees, and the destruction of what little wealth poor countries are able to accumulate.

The millions across the globe who stand expectant at the gates of hope look to the United Nations to bring them peace, to bring them life, to bring them a life worth living.

Democratic South Africa salutes the United Nations organization and its member states, both singly and collectively, for joining forces with the masses of our people in a common struggle that has brought about our emancipation and pushed back the frontiers of racism.

We know well that none of us acting alone can achieve success. We must, therefore, act together as a community of nations.

As we approach the twenty-first century, we affirm our commitment to the founding ideal of the United Nations to better the life of all human beings.

The elaboration of a new world order must, of necessity, center on this world body. In it we should find the appropriate forum in which all nations can participate to help determine the shape of the new world.

The four elements that will need to be knit together in fashioning that new universal reality are the issues of democracy, peace, prosperity, and interdependence.

We must, without delay, provide leadership for the new age and bring sunshine into the hearts of billions.

As the United Nations matures into the new millennium, it is called upon to facilitate the birth of a new world order of peace, democracy, and prosperity for all.

We are confident that this book will contribute immensely to this effort.

—Nelson Mandela

Preface

Peacemaking and Peacekeeping for the New Century is a product of a special seminar that met in March 1995. The government of Austria and the International Peace Academy (IPA) convened a special high-level session of their Vienna Seminar to commemorate both the twenty-fifth anniversary of the annual Vienna Seminar and the fiftieth anniversary of the United Nations. The seminar brought together leading figures in the fields of peacekeeping and peacemaking in order to take stock of the United Nations experience of the last fifty years and to examine measures to improve and strengthen multilateral peace operations.

This volume and other studies are key parts of the policy and research agenda of the International Peace Academy. IPA is an independent, non-partisan, international institution devoted to the promotion of peaceful and multilateral approaches to the resolution of international as well as internal conflicts. IPA programs include:

- *Providing a middle ground:* IPA plays a facilitating role in efforts to settle conflicts by bringing together parties in conflict to explore—informally and often off the record—ways to promote political settlements. In the past we have played this role in relation to conflicts in Central America, southern Africa, and Cambodia.

- *Research:* The purpose of our research program is to monitor peace processes in action, with a view to assessing their effectiveness and drawing lessons for the future. In this connection, we have completed studies of the peace processes in Cambodia and El Salvador; these were published as *Keeping the Peace* (Cambridge University Press, 1997). The current phase of our research program concentrates on peacebuilding for civil conflicts. We examine ways in which states can address the root causes of war and restore or develop the institutions and capacities that prevent the recurrence of violent conflict.

- *Africa:* IPA works closely with the Organization of African Unity (OAU) to develop ways of enhancing the capacity of the OAU to respond more effectively to the dramatic situation of conflicts in Africa. These efforts have culminated in the adoption of a new OAU mechanism devoted to the prevention and management of conflicts in Africa. We are now working with the OAU Secretariat on the challenge of translating this new mechanism into an operational instrument that can make a difference on the ground.

- *Policy seminars:* From its inception, IPA played a pioneering role in organizing training seminars for peacekeeping. These have now evolved into policy seminars for senior diplomatic and military officials as well as members of the UN Secretariat. The principal objective of the policy seminars is to deepen the understanding of the participants and explore critical policy issues of the day concerning peacekeeping and peacemaking. The policy seminars have also served the related purpose of providing a setting for networking among senior officials responsible for peacekeeping in different parts of the world.

The annual Vienna Seminar, with which the special seminar that gave rise to this volume is associated, is the flagship of the IPA seminar program. The two-week seminar has been held annually in Vienna since 1970. Organized by the International Peace Academy, in cooperation with the government of Austria, the Vienna Seminar remains the premier international seminar on peacekeeping and peacemaking.

The government of Austria and the International Peace Academy convened the special high-level session of the Vienna Seminar in March 1995 with two objectives in mind. The first objective was celebratory: to commemoration the twenty-fifth anniversary of the Vienna Seminar and of IPA itself and the fiftieth anniversary of the United Nations. The second objective was intellectual: to take stock of almost fifty years of UN experience in peacekeeping and peacemaking and to examine measures necessary to strengthen multilateral peace operations in the twenty-first century.

After almost seven years of extensive engagement and experimentation, the UN is being overwhelmed by escalating demands that cannot be met, undermined by the lack of resources and capability, and perplexed by the complexity of some of these internal conflicts. As the UN prepares for the twenty-first century, there are signs that we may be entering a phase of peacekeeping and peacemaking marked by a retreat from the earlier ambition and optimism, a reduced scope of engagement, and a renewed emphasis on the imperative of preventing conflicts before they are transformed into full-scale wars. Is this a passing phenomenon, a pause in a period of profound uncertainties, or are we witnessing the wave of the future? As we look back, what in fact are the correct lessons we can draw from the first fifty years of UN experience in this field? As we look ahead, what measures will be necessary to improve and strengthen peacekeeping and peacemaking in general? And what should be the appropriate scope of the UN's mission relative to the roles of the other international actors, such as regional organizations and international civil society?

We could think of no better group before which to place this challenge than the distinguished participants who gathered at the Hofburg Palace in Vienna. Together they represented an unusual assembly of experience, expertise, and scholarship that would be difficult to match in this field, including the former UN secretary-general, Dr. Boutros Boutros-Ghali. (In 1995, IPA published a report of the deliberations of the seminar, *Peacemaking and Peacekeeping for the Next Century,* whose rapporteurs were Ameen Jan, Robert Orr, and Timothy Wilkins.) We later recruited another set of eminent authors to supplement the agenda of the seminar, including the then under-secretary-general for peace-keeping operations, Mr. Kofi Annan, who succeeded Dr. Boutros-Ghali as secretary-general in January 1997.

We as editors want to extend our thanks for the editorial assistance we received from Chetan Kumar, Demitra Pappas, Marc Bennett, Elise Oliver, Daniel David, Tyler Felgenhauer, and Scott Vesel. We also again thank Florence Musaffi for her expert and patient assistance throughout this project. We also express our deep appreciation for the strong and generous support of the government of Austria and of its foreign and defense ministries in particular. This commitment exemplifies the historic contribution of Austria to peacekeeping and the spirit of its long-standing collaboration with IPA.

—*Michael W. Doyle, Princeton, N.J.*
—*Olara O. Otunnu, New York*

Abbreviations

ANC	African National Congress
ARF	Association of South East Asian Nations Regional Forum
ASEAN	Association of South East Asian Nations
BALTBAT	Baltic Battalion
CFSP	Common Foreign and Security Policy
CIA	Central Intelligence Agency
CIS	Commonwealth of Independent States
CNN	Cable News Network
CSCE	Conference on Security and Cooperation in Europe
DHA	Department of Humanitarian Affairs
DPA	Department of Political Affairs
DPKO	Department of Peace-keeping Operations
DPRK	Democratic People's Republic of Korea
ECA	Economic Commission for Africa
ECOMOG	Economic Community of West African States Monitoring Group
ECOSOC	Economic and Social Council
ECOWAS	Economic Community of West African States
EP5	Expanded Permanent Five
FALD	Field Administration and Logistics Division
FLS	Frontline States
FRAPH	Front révolutionnaire pour l'avancement du progrès en Haiti (Revolutionary Front for the Advancement of Progress inHaiti)
FYROM	Former Yugoslav Republic of Macedonia

IAEA	International Atomic Energy Agency
IASC	Inter-Agency Standing Committee
IATA	International Air Transport Association
IBRD	International Bank for Reconstruction and Development
ICITAP	International Criminal Investigative Training and Assistance Programme
ICJ	International Court of Justice
IFOR	Implementation Force
IGADD	Intergovernmental Authority on Drought and Development
IMF	International Monetary Fund
IPA	International Peace Academy
ITU	International Telecomunications Union
JNA	Yugoslav People's Army
KEDO	Korean Peninsula Energy Development Organization
NATO	North Atlantic Treaty Organization
NGO	nongovernmental organization
NPT	Nonproliferation Treaty
OAS	Organization of American States
OAU	Organization of African Unity
ODA	Official Development Assistance
OECD	Organization for Economic Cooperation and Development
OIC	Organization of the Islamic Conference
ONUC	United Nations Operation in the Congo
ONUMOZ	United Nations Operation in Mozambique
ONUSAL	United Nations Observer Mission in El Salvador
ONUVEH	United Nations Observer Mission for the Verification of the Elections in Haiti
OPEC	Organization of Petroleum Exporting Countries
OSCE	Organization for Security and Cooperation in Europe
PDD	Presidential Decision Directive
RENAMO	Resistência Nacional Moçambicana (Mozambican National Resistance)

ROK	Republic of Korea
RPF	Rwandese Patriotic Front
SACB	Somali Aid Coordination Body
SADC	Southern Africa Development Community
SADF	South Africa Defence Force
SCANBAT	Scandinavian Battalion
SCOR	Security Council Official Records
SIPRI	Stockholm International Peace Research Institute
SWAPO	South West Africa People's Organization
UNAMIR	United Nations Assistance Mission for Rwanda
UNAVEM	United Nations Angola Verification Mission
UNCRO	United Nations Confidence Restoration Operation in Croatia
UNDP	United Nations Development Programme
UNEF	First United Nations Emergency Force
UNFICYP	United Nations Peace-keeping Force in Cyprus
UNHCR	United Nations High Commissioner for Refugees
UNICEF	United Nations Children's Fund
UNIFIL	United Nations Interim Force in Lebanon
UNIKOM	United Nations Iraq-Kuwait Observation Mission
UNITA	União Nacional para a Independência Total de Angola (National Union for the Total Independence of Angola)
UNITAF	Unified Task Force
UNOGIL	United Nations Observer Group in Lebanon
UNOSOM	United Nations Operation in Somalia
UNPREDEP	United Nations Preventive Deployment Force
UNPROFOR	United Nations Protection Force
UNSC	United Nations Security Council
UNTAC	United Nations Transitional Authority in Cambodia
UNTAG	United Nations Transition Assistance Group
UNTAT	United Nations Training Assistance Team
UNTEA	United Nations Temporary Executive Authority in West New Guinea

UNTSO	United Nations Truce Supervision Organization
UNYOM	United Nations Yemen Observer Mission
WEU	Western European Union
WFP	World Food Programme
WHO	World Health Organization

Introduction

Discovering the Limits and Potential of Peacekeeping

Michael W. Doyle

As the United Nations (UN) reached its fiftieth anniversary, retrenchment became the watchword of the day in peace operations. Unfulfilled expectations and escalating violence in Somalia, Rwanda, and Bosnia, rising costs for even the more successful peacekeeping operations—such as those that took place in Cambodia, El Salvador, and Mozambique—and a growing awareness of the complexity of intervening in ethnic and civil wars gave rise to a compelling impetus to rethink and restructure. But rethinking and restructuring, it was soon realized, are not the same as abandonment. Rational retrenchment requires that the international community assess which UN activities are successful and which are not, consider ways in which UN peace operations might be strengthened, and investigate ways to employ scarce resources more effectively. There is therefore an urgent need to examine those aspects of UN peace activities that will continue to be necessary to assure international order and justice and to explore what resources the international community should devote to international order, given the likelihood of continuing demands in the years ahead.

With these purposes in mind, the government of Austria and the International Peace Academy (IPA) convened in early March 1995 a special high-level seminar at the Hofburg Palace in Vienna to commemorate both the twenty-fifth anniversary of the annual Vienna Seminar and the fiftieth anniversary of the United Nations. Under the theme "Peacemaking and Peacekeeping for the Next Century," the seminar brought together leading figures in the fields of peacemaking and peacekeeping for three days of discussions that focused on a set of papers that were both expert and wide-ranging. The IPA then commissioned additional chapters to round out an exploration of the challenges as well as the opportunities in peacemaking and peacekeeping that the international community now faces.

The chapters of this book discuss the future in light of the mixed record of UN activity in peace and security. The striking growth in UN peace operations, especially after 1988, reflected the new credibility the organization had come to enjoy since the end of the Cold War. But the growing costs, the escalating violence in Somalia and Bosnia, the vociferous criticism from some UN member states, and the financial crisis that soon ensued all raised questions about whether the UN could or should continue to take on the active role it had come to play.

This book thus builds upon a growing concern for the future of peacekeeping that reflects the expanding and innovative role the UN undertook, the crisis in peace enforcement that ensued, and the new search for a role in a world of diminished resources and expectations.

The UN's Expanding Agenda for Peace

In the early 1990s, with the end of the Cold War, the UN's agenda for peace and security rapidly expanded. At the request of the UN Security Council Summit in January 1992, Secretary-General Boutros Boutros-Ghali prepared the conceptual foundations of an ambitious UN role in peace and security in his seminal report, *An Agenda for Peace* (1992). The secretary-general outlined five interconnected roles that he hoped the UN would play in the fast-changing context of post–Cold War international politics:

- Preventive diplomacy—action undertaken in order "to prevent disputes from arising between parties, to prevent existing disputes from escalating into conflicts and to limit the spread of the latter when they occur." Involving confidence-building measures, fact-finding, early warning, and possibly "preventive deployment" of UN-authorized forces, preventive diplomacy seeks to reduce the danger of violence and increase the prospects for peaceful settlement.

- Peace enforcement—action with or without the consent of the parties to ensure compliance with a cease-fire mandated by the Security Council acting under the authority of Chapter VII of the UN Charter. These military forces are composed of heavily armed, national forces operating under the direction of the secretary-general.

- Peacemaking—mediation and negotiations designed "to bring hostile parties to agreement" through peaceful means such as those found in Chapter VI of the UN Charter. Drawing upon judicial settlement, mediation, and other forms of negotiation, UN peacemaking initiatives would seek to persuade parties to arrive at a peaceful settlement of their differences.

- Peacekeeping—military and civilian deployments for the sake of establishing a "United Nations presence in the field, hitherto with the consent of all the parties concerned," as a confidence-building measure to monitor a truce between the parties while diplomats strive to negotiate a comprehensive peace or officials attempt to implement an agreed peace.

- Post-conflict peacebuilding—measures organized to foster economic and social cooperation to build confidence among previously warring parties; develop the social, political and economic infrastructure to prevent future violence; and lay the foundations for a durable peace.

Between 1987 and 1994, the Security Council quadrupled the number of resolutions it issued, tripled the peacekeeping operations it authorized, and increased from one to seven per year the number of economic sanctions it imposed. Military forces deployed in peacekeeping operations increased from fewer than ten thousand to more than seventy thousand. The annual peacekeeping budget accordingly skyrocketed from $230 million to $3.6 billion in the same period, thus reaching about three times the regular UN operating budget of $1.2 billion.[1] The activities of the Security Council in preventive diplomacy and sanctions, the secretariat's role in election monitoring, and above all the massive growth in peacekeeping and peace enforcement all testified to the new, expanded role that the international community wanted the UN to perform.

These initiatives, peace enforcement most striking among them, also reflected significant shifts in the international legal and political environment in which the UN operated. Member states of the UN subtly extended the acceptable scope of UN activity by altering the definition of what was considered to be essentially sovereign, national activity. Matters once legally preserved from UN intervention, such as civil conflicts and humanitarian emergencies within sovereign states, now became legitimate issues of UN concern. Gross violations of global standards of human rights were seen to override domestic sovereignty, becoming a defining issue for what was a legitimate matter of international attention. Human rights, then, were increasingly claimed to be inherently global, a proposition endorsed by the Vienna Conference on Human Rights (June 1993).[2]

The Security Council also expanded the operational meaning of the authority in UN Charter Article 2(7) to override domestic sovereignty: "threats to peace, breaches of the peace, acts of aggression." The new interpretation of UN jurisdiction soon appeared to include a wide range of what were once seen as infringements of traditional sovereignty. Indeed, "threat to the peace, etc." came to mean protracted civil wars that resisted international efforts at settlement, armed interference with humanitarian assistance in emergencies, and, in effect, whatever nine members of the Security Council (absent a permanent-member veto) said it was.[3]

These two developments had roots in the striking changes in the international system that emerged at the end of the Cold War. A new spirit of multilateral cooperation from the USSR, beginning with President Gorbachev's reforms, met a new spirit of tolerance from the United States. Together the two former adversaries broke the forty-year gridlock in the UN Security Council. Post–Cold War cooperation meant that the Security Council was now functioning as the global guardian of peace and security. The Security Council had become what it was supposed to have been since 1945—the continuation, incorporated in the design of the UN Charter, of the World War II grand alliance reestablished on a genuinely multilateral, collective basis. At the same time, there also emerged an ideological community of human rights values that gave specific content to the cooperative initiatives of these years. The Vienna Conference on Human Rights (1993) and President Gorbachev's plea before the General Assembly for "global human values" (A/43/PV72) signified that human rights were no longer merely a Western, but rather a global, principle of good governance.

Those two changes coincided with a temporary conjunction of power and will. Following the collapse of the USSR, the United States experienced a "unipolar moment" when its power eclipsed that of all other states. At the same time, the Security Council, building on the initiatives of the United Kingdom, began to evolve toward what the United States would later call a strategy of "assertive multilateralism," a strategy that flourished from the Gulf War in January 1991 until the 3 October 1993 disaster in Mogadishu, Somalia. The five permanent members of the Security Council, led by the United States, provided a degree of commitment and resourceful leadership that the UN had rarely seen before. Eschewing the national role of "globocop" in order to address a pressing domestic agenda, the Clinton administration encouraged UN Secretary-General Boutros Boutros-Ghali to take an ever more assertive role in international crises. The small dissenting minority in the Security Council, which included China on some occasions, was not prepared to resist the United States on issues that did not affect their paramount national interests.

For the enthusiasts of the moment, multilateral action seemed to be the politically available solution to a difficult dilemma. It reconciled an advocacy of collective security, universal human rights, and humanitarian solidarity overseas with the need to refocus Cold War spending on domestic reform at home. Multilateral action under the United Nations Charter was not only the prescribed legal route to world order; it also appeared to be a practical solution to global community when each nation caring a little seemed sufficient to ensure that all together cared enough. Although far from universal in its reach, the spirit of collective security was sufficient to mobilize a multilateral effort to reverse Saddam Hussein's aggression in the Gulf. The December 1992 U.S.-led rescue of segments of the Somali population from starvation heralded what appeared to be a remarkable partnership: The Security Council decreed, the United States led, and—conveniently, for the while—many other states paid and supported.

Together, these developments made the new globalism feasible and legitimate. Collective intervention by the United Nations was morally, politically, and legally acceptable where unilateral intervention was not. Because it appeared more impartial and not self-serving, the UN community was perceived to be acting as a whole, speaking for the whole community of nations. The traditional suspicion of intervention was thus allayed and the traditional moral, legal, and political restraints were lifted—perhaps, in retrospect, too readily.

Innovation through Evolution

The UN's record in peace operations—before, during, and after the assertive period we have just experienced—is long, various, distinguished by accomplishments and failures, and, most important, innovative. Indeed, it is that record of evolutionary flexibility described below and discussed at the Vienna Seminar that suggests that the UN can weather the difficulties it is currently experiencing.

Peacekeeping operations have come to encompass three distinct activities that have evolved as "generations" of UN peace operations.[4] They include not only the early activities of first-generation peacekeeping, which requires the interposition of a force after a truce has been reached, but also a far more ambitious group of second-generation operations that rely on the consent of parties and an even more ambitious group of third-generation operations that operate with Chapter VII mandates and without a comprehensive agreement reflecting the acquiescence of the parties. In today's circumstances, these operations involve less interstate conflict and more factions in domestic civil wars, not all of which are clearly identifiable and few of which are stable negotiating parties. Current peace operations thus intrude into aspects of domestic sovereignty once thought to be beyond the purview of UN activity.

In traditional peacekeeping, sometimes called *first-generation peacekeeping,* unarmed or lightly armed UN forces are stationed between hostile parties to monitor a truce, troop withdrawal, or buffer zone while political negotiations go forward.[5] They provide transparency—an impartial assurance that the other party is not violating the truce—and raise the costs of defecting from and the benefits of abiding by the agreement through the threat of exposure, the potential resistance of the peacekeeping force, and the legitimacy of UN mandates. The benefits are obvious: armed conflict is held at bay. Their price, as in the long Cyprus operation, is sometimes paid in conflicts delayed rather than resolved. Today these monitoring activities continue to play an important role in Tajikistan, Georgia, and on the border between Kuwait and Iraq.

The second category, called second-generation operations by Secretary-General Boutros-Ghali, involves the implementation of complex, multidimensional peace agreements. In addition to the traditional military functions, the peacekeepers are often engaged in various police and civilian tasks, the goal of which is a long-term settlement of the underlying conflict. Taking a substantial step beyond first-generation operations, *second-generation multidimensional operations* are based on the consent of the parties. But the nature of the consent and the purposes for which it is granted are qualitatively different from traditional peacekeeping.

In these operations, the UN is typically involved in implementing peace agreements that go to the roots of the conflict and help build a long-term foundation for stable, legitimate government. As Boutros-Ghali observed in *An Agenda for Peace* (p. 32):

> peacemaking and peace-keeping operations, to be truly successful, must come to include comprehensive efforts to identify and support structures which will tend to consolidate peace. . . . [They] may include disarming the previously warring parties and the restoration of order, the custody and possible destruction of weapons, repatriating refugees, advisory and training support for security personnel, monitoring elections, advancing efforts to protect human rights, reforming or strengthening governmental institutions and promoting formal and informal processes of political participation.

The UN has a commendable record of success in second-generation multidimensional peacekeeping operations as diverse as those in Namibia, El Salvador, and Cambodia.[6] The UN's role in helping settle those conflicts has been threefold. It served as a peacemaker facilitating a peace treaty among the parties; a peacekeeper monitoring the cantonment and demobilization of military forces, resettling refugees, and supervising transitional civilian authorities; and a peacebuilder monitoring—and in some cases organizing—the implementation of human rights, national democratic elections, and economic rehabilitation.

In Secretary-General Boutros-Ghali's lexicon, "peace-enforcing" missions—which in effect are war-making missions—are *third-generation* operations, which extend from low-level military operations to protect the delivery of humanitarian assistance to the enforcement of cease-fires and, when necessary, assistance in the rebuilding of so-called failed states. Like Chapter VII UN enforcement action to roll back aggression, as in Korea in 1950 and against Iraq in the Gulf War, the defining characteristic of third-generation operations is the lack of consent by one or more of the parties to some or all of the UN mandate.[7] Unlike traditional Chapter VII collective security, these operations focus on internal strife.

Neither Somalia nor Bosnia reflected a coherent plan to restore peace by force. Instead, both were composites of coercive restraints (no-fly zones, arms embargoes, humanitarian protection, safe areas) and broad-brushed or piecemeal local endorsements (such as the signing by many factions of the Addis Ababa accords of 26 March 1993 for Somalia).

Insightful doctrine for peace-enforcing operations appeared just as Somalia and Bosnia exposed their limitations. Recent studies have thoughtfully mapped out the logic of what it might take to succeed in this political terrain. In order to preclude an outcome based on the use of force by the parties, the UN instead uses collective force (if necessary) to persuade the parties to settle the conflict by negotiation. This strategic terrain, however, is murky. Forcing a peace depends on achieving a complicated preponderance of events in which the forces (UN and local) supporting a settlement acceptable to the international community acquire both a superiority of military might and a predominance of popular support that together permit them to impose a peace on the recalcitrant local military forces and their popular supporters.

The result of these three generations operating together in the post–Cold War world was an unprecedented expansion of the UN's role in the protection of world order and in the promotion of basic human rights in countries torn until recently by costly civil wars. Self-determination and sovereignty were enhanced, and a modicum of peace and rehabilitation was introduced in Namibia, Cambodia, El Salvador, Haiti, and Mozambique. Tens—perhaps even hundreds—of thousands of lives were saved in Somalia and the former Yugoslavia.

But in 1993 and 1994, the more ambitious elements of third-generation peace enforcement encountered many of the problems interventionist and imperial strategies have faced in the past and discovered fresh problems peculiar to the UN's global character. The UN proved itself ineffective in imposing order by force, whether it sought to disarm factions in Somalia or provide humanitarian protection in Bosnia. Instead it became complicit in a record of inadequate protection, seemingly unnecessary casualties, and Vietnam-like escalation on the one hand and 1930s-style appeasement on the other.

UN "war-making" suffered from severe disabilities, ranging from those that were a product of the organization's incapacity to others that were a product of the kinds of wars that the UN tried to address:

- Although the UN seemed to have the advantage of global impartiality, that should have (and often has) won it more local acceptance when it intervened, this was not universally the case. Israel maintained a suspicion of UN involvement dating back to the UN General Assembly's notorious anti-Zionism resolutions of the 1970s. In Somalia, Egypt's support for the former dictator, Siad Barre, seemed to taint the impartial role that Secretary-General Boutros-Ghali, a former Egyptian minister of state for foreign affairs, sought to play. And there was lingering distrust of the UN in other parts of Africa because of its role in the Congo.[8] Many smaller, non-Western states, moreover, distrusted the use of the Security Council by the great powers, and particularly the Western "permanent three" (France, the United Kingdom, and the United States), which sometimes appeared to be trying to impose a selective vision of world order on weaker states.[9]

- The UN was particularly poorly suited to interventionist strategies involving the strategic employment of coercive force. The political roots of the UN's "command and control" problems were threefold. First, countries with battalions in UN peace operations were reluctant to see their (often lightly armed) troops engaged in combat under UN direction, fearing that a UN force commander of any nationality other than their own would fail to take due care to minimize risks. Second, countries with seats on the Security Council, pressured to achieve a response to humanitarian crises and unwilling to confront the UN's ongoing resource crisis, assigned missions to UN peace operations without providing adequate means to achieve them. And third, the UN's traditional ideology, despite recent practice, was highly protective of national sovereignty. To its credit, the UN lacked the callousness or psychological distance required to inflict coercive punishment on political movements with even the smallest amount of popular support.[10] To its cost, the UN rarely planned the peacebuilding process as a comprehensive effort to reestablish (or establish) a legitimate, effective political order.

- "Peace-enforcing fatigue" afflicted the UN's contributing countries, whether new or old. States are rarely willing to invest their resources or the lives of their soldiers in war other than for a vital interest, such as oil in the Persian Gulf. But if states have a vital national interest in a dispute, they are not likely to exercise the impartiality a UN peace operation requires. Nor are they likely to cede decision-making control over, or command of, their forces to the UN. As a result, the UN found it increasingly difficult to find troops for the dangerous operations, such as Rwanda, and to supervise the delegated operations, such as the Russian operation in Georgia.

- The very act of intervention, even by the UN, can mobilize nationalist opposition against the foreign forces. In Somalia, according to some observers, UN intervention contributed to a significant growth of support for Aidid's Somali National Alliance. Aidid's supporters soon roundly condemned UN "colonialism."[11] The strategic balance is not static. Military intervention tilts two local balances, improving the military correlation of forces but often at the cost of undermining the more important political balance.

- Coercively intervening for eventual self-determination, as J. S. Mill noted over a century ago, is very often a self-contradictory enterprise.[12] If the local forces of freedom, self-determination, and human rights cannot achieve sovereignty without a foreign military intervention, then they are very unlikely to be able to hold on to power after the intervention force leaves. Either the installed forces of freedom will collapse or they will employ those very coercive methods that provoked and justified the initial intervention. In 1991 the Kurds, for example, won widespread sympathy for their resistance to Saddam Hussein and benefited from a UN-endorsed U.S.-French-British intervention in the aftermath of the war against Iraq. By 1996 the Kurdish factions were so divided that they appeared incapable of establishing law and order in their territory. Instead, three factions divided the region. None appeared capable of sustaining itself against whatever attempts to reincorporate Kurdistan Saddam Hussein would make. The international community had thus placed itself in the awkward position of either adopting Kurdistan as a long-term ward or returning it to the not-so-tender mercies of the Iraqi ruler.[13]

The United Nations, in the role of assertively multilateral peace enforcer, thus presented an almost textbook case of multiple strategic incapacity. But encountering strategic problems while intervening in ethnic and civil wars is not unique to the United Nations. The Multi-National Force in Lebanon created even larger catastrophes of misdirected, overly violent, and intrusive intervention in 1983. Even with national-quality command and control, the United States failed to impose peace in Vietnam in the 1960s, just as the Soviets failed in Afghanistan in the 1970s and 1980s. The United Nations, moreover, is essentially the collective agent of its member states. Many of the UN's organizational incapacities could be corrected by additional resources from its member states, who devote but a tiny fraction of the resources they spend on national security to collective action under the umbrella of the United Nations.

Retrenchment

The crises in Somalia and Bosnia, together with the wider limitations those crises exposed, constitute a challenge to the international community. The UN must now develop a combination of initiatives that enhances capacities, retrenches responsibilities, reviews strategies, and redefines roles.

The importance of reforming the United Nations is widely recognized. Abandonment is thus not an option. Indeed, for many, the UN has no alternative for the roles it should be playing in peace and security. Emilio Cardenas, former permanent representative of Argentina to the United Nations, expressed this well when he noted:

> The United Nations, notwithstanding its apparent decline in terms of ability to forward and maintain international security, remains the central institution in the security realm. And, in my view, it should be so. Otherwise, we will all be confronted with the "return of the strong" to the center of the world's scenario. And this is certainly not what we agreed upon in 1945.[14]

Reflecting both legal legitimacy and practical support, the United Nations holds a unique claim on legitimate authority in international peace and war.[15]

- The UN is the only international organization formally entrusted with the legal authority to preserve peace in cases other than national or collective self-defense. At the same time, as the only multipurpose universal organization, it has the authority to promote those wider political, social, and economic conditions that are conducive to preventing violent conflict and redressing the causes of conflict once it has occurred.

- The UN is again the only institution truly global in scope, where the states of the world can explore their common interests and aspirations as equal members of the international community. It allows for—indeed requires—dialogue across cultures, races, and economic systems.

- The UN is delegatee of last resort (often the scapegoat) for global conflict and hard-to-resolve disputes. For the vast majority of nations preferring to focus on domestic welfare and wishing to avoid having to become global policemen, the UN has stood ready to be the international "911." Although the UN does need to learn when to say no, it is rightly assumed to be the place where such a decision will be made on the basis of the principles of collective security, self-determination, and fundamental human freedoms.

- As described above, the UN has effectively delivered both first generation truce supervision and second-generation multidimensional peacebuilding operations. The UN has proven ineffectual at third-generation enforcement and weak at operations in the gray zone where violence disrupts peacebuilding, but these failings should not lead us to neglect the vital and effective role the UN has played in those other crucial operations. Its involvement has prevented disputes from spreading across borders and begun to address the root causes of long-lingering conflicts, such as the ones in El Salvador and Cambodia.

- The UN, moreover, is the institution that promotes and reformulates the rules that govern the growing interdependence of nations. Ranging from choosing a common language of communication for air traffic controllers (a useful convention) to protecting the forty-five million refugees around the world (a moral commitment), the organization provides the institutional foundation for the emergence of an increasingly interdependent world.

Convinced that no one initiative alone could bear the entire burden of revising the UN's peacemaking and peacekeeping role in the years to come, the participants of the twenty-fifth Vienna Seminar outlined a combination of initiatives. They sought to avoid a retreat from the responsibilities in peace and security for which the international community relies on the UN. They also identified areas for restraint and reconsideration, seeking—where they could—to suggest measures that would allow the UN to economize on scarce resources while continuing and, perhaps, even expanding the role the UN could play in effectively furthering international peace and security.

The Plan of the Book

In his keynote address to the twenty-fifth Vienna Seminar (excerpted as the first chapter of Part I), Secretary-General Boutros Boutros-Ghali outlined the multiple challenges in the past fifty years of peacemaking and peacekeeping that have given rise to the need to make hard choices. Implicitly evoking images of peacekeeping triage, he discussed ending operations that are not effective and transferring resources from less to potentially more promising operations. Faced with stark choices, political, diplomatic, academic, military, and official leaders of the United Nations community considered a variety of possible responses that could help develop, on the one hand, a more effective, less costly UN role in peace and security and, on the other hand, a variety of measures that might expand the institutional and financial resources that the international community can make available for multilateral cooperation. Impressed by the need, therefore, to focus on new ways to do more with less and design more effective peace operations, the participants explored ways to maintain the innovative record that has sustained UN activity in the difficult times of the past.

In the second chapter, Adam Roberts examines the wider context of international security in the post–Cold War world, a political environment that has come to include deadly and costly spillovers of so-called ethnic strife in civil wars, especially in the epoch-defining involvement in the former Yugoslavia. He notes that the UN was designed to contain a Nazi Germany–type threat to international security. Hence, it has faced difficulties in peacekeeping in internal conflicts and has had to adapt rapidly in order to be capable of not just containing conflicts but also resolving them.

Part II begins an exploration of what it takes to prevent violent conflict.

The importance of prevention could not be more evident. The inability to resolve the conflict that led to the Gulf War (or to deter war in the meantime) doubled the price of a barrel of oil for global consumers, produced hundreds of deaths among coalition forces (148 of them U.S.), and, most consequentially, caused the devastation in Kuwait and enormous suffering for Iraq's civilian population. Starting an exploration of how these conflicts can be avoided, Ismat Kittani, former special adviser to the secretary-general and under-secretary-general for peace-keeping operations, details the UN's record of preventive diplomacy and peacemaking in order to explore whether preventive diplomacy and negotiated solutions could reduce the heavy burden on UN security resources by preventing the emergence of violent conflicts. He describes the advantages that UN intermediaries have over other actors and suggests the UN's involvement in Bahrain in 1970 and in the Iran-Iraq war in 1987 as useful examples of the initiatives that the secretary-general can take on behalf of preventive diplomacy. He also describes the important advantages that UN preventive diplomacy has over the efforts of other peacemakers, both national and multinational.

Australian former foreign minister Gareth Evans presents a far-reaching analysis of preventive action that illustrates the importance of drawing a wide range of potential actors into prevention efforts and employing means that go beyond the diplomatic to include preventive economic and social development. Stressing the significance of very early prevention, Evans outlines a concept of "preventive peacebuilding" whereby, in order to ensure that conditions for conflict do not develop, attempts are made to meet people's crucial needs for security, a reasonable standard of living, and a sense of identity and worth. In his chapter, Evans describes various means of carrying out such preventive peacebuilding. These include international regimes that guarantee basic rights and freedoms and guard against the proliferation of weapons, the assistance of international organizations suited to alleviating those long-term social and economic developments that might threaten peace, and attempts by states themselves to provide access to resources and guarantee the basic rights of their peoples.

Edward Mortimer's chapter, which begins Part III, focuses on the use of force in the general context of retrenchment. He surveys the arguments, drawing on the classic formulations of nineteenth century British philosopher John Stuart Mill, for and against intervening militarily in the domestic conflicts that have come to characterize so much of the UN's post–Cold War agenda and urges the United Nations community to develop a principle of intervention, reexamining its fundamental purposes as a way of carefully considering the reasons why the UN, or any other international actor, should become involved in or avoid these deadly conflicts. He concludes that interventions in cases of genocide enjoy the greatest legitimacy. The most effective military interventions occur where there is a strong national interest for the intervening power, where the intervenor has the effective capacity to intervene, and where there is a clear humanitarian interest in averting or stopping a major human rights or humanitarian catastrophe.

John Sanderson, former force commander of UNTAC, takes the analysis a step further by probing whether, when, and how the UN should take the important step of deciding to use force in peacekeeping operations. Drawing on his extensive experience in force planning and his stewardship of UN forces in Cambodia, he explores the many limitations the UN faces in the employment of military force. He notes that the defection of the Khmer Rouge from the framework of the Paris Accords, and their attempts to disrupt the implementation of the peace agreement and the conduct of the elections, led to pressure being exerted upon UNTAC officials to take punitive action even though the pursuit of such options was untenable given the UN's mandate and the deployment and posture of UNTAC's military forces. Attempted peace enforcement, he adds, might have derailed the successful conduct of elections and the installation of a legitimate government that was then able to pursue punitive action against the Khmer Rouge with the assistance of the international community and the people of Cambodia.

Secretary-General Kofi Annan (the former under-secretary-general for peace-keeping operations) examines the recent changes—both doctrinal and operational—in the Department of Peace-keeping Operations, highlighting the UN's efforts to respond to the much more demanding environment in which it operates. He outlines methods to deal with the two most likely engagements for future UN peacekeeping: preventive deployments such as the one now in Macedonia, and multidimensional peacekeeping such as was successfully attempted in Namibia and El Salvador. Annan describes the development of a core of military expertise at the Department of Peace-keeping Operations that enables the department to conduct feasibility studies of the various options to be presented by the secretary-general to the Security Council and convert mandates given by the Security Council into implementable concepts of operations. The department provides strategic guidance to field units and assists the secretary-general in providing feedback to the Security Council.

Sir Brian Urquhart, former under-secretary-general for special political affairs, and François Heisbourg, former director of the International Institute for Security Studies, debate whether UN peace operations might be made more effective if the UN were provided with a rapid-reaction capability designed to head off crises before they escalate. Urquhart develops the political, financial, operational, and logistical requisites of an effective standing volunteer force. Heisbourg, on the other hand, outlines the case for an adaptation of the current plan for standby forces.

Part IV includes an assessment of the UN's role in humanitarian action. Jan Eliasson, the UN's first under-secretary general for humanitarian affairs, develops the role of humanitarian action as a preventive alternative to, reason for, and accompaniment of, peace operations. He stresses the key role that should be played by coordination between humanitarian assistance, on the one hand, and international efforts at peacemaking, peacekeeping, and peacebuilding, on the other. He explores in detail the numerous ways in which these activities support each other on the ground, suggesting, among other measures, joint training programs for relief workers and troops participating in peacekeeping operations.

UN High Commissioner for Refugees (UNHCR) Sadako Ogata explores the UN's ability to respond to humanitarian emergencies. Highlighting the extensive experience of UNHCR, she outlines how peace operations should be managed in order to achieve the needed integrated result that combines political, military and humanitarian action. She adds that emergencies that require a rapid humanitarian response are often not just political but also economic, social, cultural, and environmental. She details the various characteristics of these emergencies and then, drawing upon the experience of the UNHCR, describes organizational and operational innovations that might lead to more integrated and effective humanitarian action. She also notes the costs and benefits of military involvement in humanitarian activities.

In Part V, focusing on the regional dimension of international conflict, John Roper, director of the Institute for Security Studies of the Western European Union, picks up on a theme introduced by the secretary-general that could assist with the retrenchment process: the possibility of a division of labor between the UN and regional organizations. He assesses whether the regional organizations, particularly those of Europe, can assume some of the burdens that the UN now carries on its own. Roper explores the relative merits and demerits of the role of regional organizations in conflict management. Drawing upon the recent experience of European countries, he also explores the security roles of regional organizations other than in peacekeeping, in particular the creation of "security communities" and the stabilization of neighboring regions, as with NATO's Partnership for Peace program in Eastern Europe.

Professor Ali Mazrui discusses the security environment that has emerged in Africa in the post–Cold War era and draws our attention to a crisis in the viability of the African state. He argues that where populations with two strong ethnic identities are intermixed, violence is especially likely unless innovative schemes of power-sharing are developed. Mazrui provides suggestions regarding how power could be sustainably shared in countries characterized by severe internal divisions and prone to violent conflict. He diagnoses societies characterized by ethnic duality, but without an accompanying territorial duality, as being particularly prone to conflict. Examples of such societies are Rwanda and Burundi, which are characterized by conflict between the Hutus and Tutsis but not by a territorial division between the two groups. Mazrui critically explores several power-sharing options that have been suggested for pluralistic societies in Africa, including the "diarchy" model that was proposed by Nigeria's Nnamdi Azikiwe and the "no-party" system that is being attempted in Uganda, as well as several suggestions of his own for power-sharing in internally divided societies.

Salim A. Salim, OAU secretary-general, considers how the OAU is responding to the security crisis in Africa and outlines various innovations the OAU has made to cope with the crisis. He pays special attention to two developments: the changes in doctrine (the willingness to engage in what before were seen as solely domestic conflicts) and organizational capacity (the development of a special mechanism within the OAU) that marked the new activism evident in African approaches to peaceful settlement. He outlines principles on which partnerships between the UN and regional organizations should be based, including a more comprehensive understanding of security that goes beyond the traditional notions of security between states and an acceptance by regional organizations of their primary responsibility for dealing with conflicts within their regions.

In Part VI, dedicated to an exploration of peacebuilding, Professor Thomas Franck offers an extensive exploration of the UN's role in building peace that is sufficiently firm that it will preclude the next rounds of violent conflict. He highlights the importance of stretching our vision to include the need for long-term institutional development and increased investment in international security and recommends the establishment of a permanent cadre dedicated to peacebuilding and the design of enhanced sources of direct revenue. This cadre would be raised directly from the individuals and corporations in the international community who benefit from the security and order that the UN promotes.

In the conclusion to the volume, Olara Otunnu, president of the International Peace Academy, brings together the contributions made in the preceding chapters to address the central issue of retrenchment and discusses the important lessons that the past fifty years of UN peacemaking and peacekeeping can offer for the next fifty years. He traces a range of views that run from sober and constrained assessments of the present difficulties to lofty visions of the UN's fundamental purposes and the hopes those visions embody. Otunnu articulates the vitality and commitment with which the UN community is prepared both to persevere in the face of costly reverses and to innovate in the hope of a growing public realization of the essential role that the UN can and must play to preserve peace. He takes up both the near-term challenges and more distant opportunities of peacemaking and peacekeeping in the UN's next fifty years.

Notes

1. Boutros Boutros-Ghali, *Supplement to An Agenda for Peace: Position Paper of the Secretary-General on the Occasion of the Fiftieth Anniversary of the United Nations,* A/50/60;S/1995/1, 3 January 1995, 4.

2. *Vienna Declaration and Program of Action* (draft reference number: A/CONF. 157/23).

3. For a discussion of the traditional Cold War interpretations of "threat to the peace," etc., see Leland M. Goodrich, E. Hambro, and Anne Simons, *Charter of the United Nations* (New York: Columbia University Press, 1969), 293–300. But it should be recalled that post–Cold War expansiveness is not unprecedented. Even during the Cold War, the severe and prolonged violations of human rights associated with racial apartheid led to Chapter VII–mandated sanctions against the Republic of South Africa.

4. It is worth recalling that the time line of evolution has by no means been chronologically straightforward. The most extensive "third-generation" operation undertaken by the UN was ONUC in the then Congo between 1960 and 1964, which preceded the spate of "second-generation" operations that began with UNTAG in Namibia in 1989.

5. "Traditional peacekeeping" is a shorthand term that describes many, but by no means all, Cold War peacekeeping missions (the most notable exception being the Congo operation). For a cogent analysis of different types of peacekeeping, see Marrack Goulding, "The Evolution of United Nations Peacekeeping," *International Affairs* 69, 3 (July 1993).

6. Before the UN became involved, during the Cold War when action by the Security Council was stymied by the lack of consensus among its five permanent members, the international community allowed Cambodia to suffer an autogenocide and El Salvador a brutal civil war. Indeed, the great powers were involved in arming, funding, and training the factions who inflicted some of the worst aspects of the violence the two countries suffered. We should keep this in mind when we consider the international community's more recent difficulties in Somalia and Bosnia.

7. Other recent categories include "preventive deployments" deployed with the intention of deterring a possible attack, as in the former Yugoslav Republic of Macedonia today. There the credibility of the deterring force must ensure that the potential aggressor knows that there will be no easy victory. In the event of an armed challenge, the result will be an international war that involves costs so grave as to outweigh the temptations of conquest. Enforcement action against aggression (Korea or the Gulf), conversely, is a matter of achieving victory—"the decisive, comprehensive and synchronized application of preponderant military force to shock, disrupt, demoralize and defeat opponents"— the traditional zero-sum terrain of military strategy. See John Mackinlay and Jarat Chopra, *A Draft Concept of Second Generation Operations* (Providence, R.I.: Watson Institute, 1993); and John Ruggie, "The United Nations Stuck in a Fog between Peacekeeping and Peace Enforcement," McNair Paper 25 (Washington: National Defense University, 1993).

8. Recently this distrust has given way to a sense of urgency about Africa's conflicts, in which UN involvement is seen as necessary. See *The OAU and Conflict Management in Africa,* Report of a Joint OAU/IPA Consultation, Addis Ababa, May 1993.

9. See the panel discussion among UN permanent representatives at the UNHCR/IPA Conference on Conflict and Humanitarian Action, reported in *Conflict and Humanitarian Action* (UNHCR/IPA, 1994) by Michael Doyle and Ian Johnstone, rapporteurs.

10. An added problem is that the use of force in civil wars frequently causes casualties among civilians, opening the UN and its members to accusations of neocolonialism and brutality. Adam Roberts, *The Crisis in Peacekeeping* (Institutt for Forsvarsstudier, 2/1994), 24.

11. Mr. Abdi Hassan Awale, an Aidid adviser in Mogadishu, complains that "the UN wants to rule this country. They do not want a Somali government to be established. The UN wants to stay and colonize us." *New York Times,* 2 March 1994.

12. For a classic discussion of these problems, see J. S. Mill, "A Few Words on Nonintervention" (1859), in *Essays on Politics and Culture,* ed. Gertrude Himmelfarb (Gloucester: P. Smith, 1973).

13. Chris Hedges, "Quarrels of Kurdish Leaders Sour Dreams of a Homeland," *New York Times,* 18 June 1994, p. A1.

14. As quoted in Tommie Sue Montgomery, rapporteur, *Multilateral Approaches to Peacemaking and Democratization in the Hemisphere,* a report of the North-South Center (University of Miami, 1996), 19.

15. For a penetrating discussion of the value of the UN to U.S. foreign policy, see Edward Luck, "The United Nations, Multilateralism, and U.S. Interests," in *U.S. Foreign Policy and the United Nations System,* ed. C. William Maynes and Richard S. Williamson (New York: W. W. Norton, 1996), 27–53.

Part I

Fifty Years of Peacemaking

and Peacekeeping

———

I

Peacemaking and Peacekeeping
for the New Century

Boutros Boutros-Ghali

Peacemaking and peacekeeping activities in the post–Cold War period have increased in terms of both the number and the variety of operations conducted. The active involvement of the UN in preventive diplomacy and peacemaking, for example, has increased from eleven cases in 1988 to thirteen in 1992 to thirty in 1995. Similarly, the number of peacekeeping operations increased from five in 1988 to eleven in 1992 to sixteen that are currently under way. This increase in peacemaking and peacekeeping activities has generated similar increases in the number of military and civilian personnel deployed, with the annual budget for peacekeeping rising from $230 million in 1988 to $3.6 billion in 1995.

Qualitative changes in peacemaking and peacekeeping during the same period have been even more striking. A majority of conflicts in the world today are intra- rather than interstate, involve irregular forces instead of national armies, and result in high civilian causalities, sometimes accompanied by the collapse of state institutions. These new characteristics place a much greater demand upon the United Nations and impel it to respond in a variety of ways that go beyond traditional peacekeeping. UN involvement includes demobilization of troops, promotion of national reconciliation, the organization and monitoring of elections, restoration of effective government, and long-term economic and social assistance programs. As a result, UN peace efforts have become more expensive, more complex, and more dangerous.

Various Forms of Cooperation between the UN and Other Actors

These new imperatives require the United Nations to cooperate with various other actors, including groups of states and regional organizations and arrangements. Different methods of implementing such cooperation have been tried. One method involves mounting a peacekeeping operation in two phases. In the first phase, an ad hoc mandate is given by the UN Security Council to a regional organization or grouping of states to conduct an operation that usually entails securing a safe environment for further activities. The second phase involves handing over the operation to a UN force. Two examples of such an operation are Somalia and Haiti. A different method of cooperation involves a division of labor between United Nations and multinational forces. The first variation of this model entails giving multinational operations command over military aspects of a mission, with the United Nations overseeing its civilian aspects, while the second involves command of different types of forces by the multinational and UN command. Examples of this first variation are Georgia and Liberia, where troops from the respective regional organizations are coupled with United Nations observers. The former Yugoslavia provides an example of the second variation, with NATO having responsibility for providing close air support for the United Nations and the UN being responsible for ground forces.

There are two major problems with both kinds of cooperative arrangements. The first is the issue of unified command. There is no agreement on a definitive method for determining who holds operational command in cases where multinational and United Nations forces are acting concurrently. One possible solution was tried in the operation in the former Yugoslavia, where a "double key" approach was employed, that is, securing an agreement by both NATO and the UN on the use of air power. The principle of joint agreement by both organizations was an extremely important one.

The second major problem involves giving a United Nations mandate to a regional or multinational grouping to intervene when such intervention could be used to serve the purely political interests of the multinational group. Despite this drawback, such an arrangement is an effective fallback position for the United Nations when an emergency situation exists in a theater where the Security Council is not willing to act but where a smaller number of countries are in a position to respond. Rather than do nothing, in such a case the Security Council can mandate a group of countries to conduct an operation, if not in the name of the United Nations, then at least with some sort of official UN authorization.

Withdrawal from Peacekeeping Operations

In certain cases, the United Nations can be forced to withdraw its troops from a peacekeeping operation without having achieved its objectives.

This can happen in three distinct circumstances. The first involves the unilateral withdrawal of troops by a country or countries in a particular theater of operations. Since countries contribute troops to UN peacekeeping operations on a purely voluntary basis, they are at liberty to withdraw their troops at will and can decide to do so for various political reasons. This happened in Somalia, where the United States decided to withdraw its troops following an incident in which several U.S. servicemen were killed. Similarly, in the former Yugoslavia, a number of countries, including France, the United Kingdom, Canada, and Russia, indicated that they would immediately withdraw their forces from the ground if the arms embargo on Bosnia-Herzegovina were lifted.

A second circumstance is one in which the UN is unable to mount a peacekeeping operation or is forced to withdraw from a theater of operations for financial reasons because of nonpayment of dues by member states to the peacekeeping budget of the organization. Because of its inability to reimburse in a timely fashion member states that contributed troops, the UN confronts a reluctance from potential troop-contributing countries to engage in peacekeeping operations. Potential reductions in the U.S. contribution to the United Nations further threaten the cash flow of the organization. A related issue is the high cost of sustaining certain peacekeeping operations, particularly those lasting a long time, as in Cyprus. In this connection, it is important to ask whether the cost of a long-term presence in places like Cyprus and the Golan Heights is less than the cost of potential confrontations there. Peacekeeping expenses can, in this sense, be compared to long-term insurance costs for maintaining nonviolent situations.

A problem may also arise when a peacekeeping operation is unable to achieve its objectives and is terminated without a resolution of the conflict and while the confrontation is still going on. This was the case in Somalia, where no political will existed among the various factions to end the war. It was also the case in the former Yugoslavia, where the president of Croatia demanded that UN troops begin to leave his country by 31 March 1995. As a result, the UN had to consider whether to withdraw troops from Bosnia-Herzegovina or Croatia, or both, by assessing the relative risks of keeping troops in the two states.

The security of withdrawing troops is threatened in such cases because the various factions or parties are involved in a struggle for control of equipment being left behind and of strategic positions previously occupied by the United Nations. Accordingly, large numbers of additional troops are required to protect the withdrawal, which also takes considerable time because equipment has to be removed under hostile conditions.

There are also ethical problems that have to be considered when the

United Nations decides to withdraw from a peacekeeping operation without achieving its objectives. However, if there is no political will, the United Nations cannot impose peace, since the UN does not have the capacity to conduct real enforcement. The role of the United Nations is to help maintain peace. A second ethical consideration is the cost of maintaining a large peacekeeping operation in theaters where the political will to make peace does not exist. Doing so means, in effect, that funds are more limited for mounting peacekeeping operations in other parts of the world, for example, Afghanistan or Tajikistan, where there may be greater political will for a settlement. In practice, the solution to such problems rests on political rather than ethical grounds, but the ethical dilemma exists.

A New Approach to Withdrawal
When a Peacekeeping Operation "Fails"

The withdrawal of troops from a peacekeeping operation while war is continuing must not be considered a failure. Rather, it is an act that recognizes that the UN cannot impose a solution in the absence of political will among protagonists. But by maintaining a political, diplomatic, and humanitarian presence in the country and continuing to work towards achieving a peace settlement, the UN can again send troops to that theater to keep the peace and to assist the protagonists to overcome their differences once they have demonstrated sufficient political will. This, for example, was the case in Angola, where the UN maintained a political presence after the troops withdrew following the refusal of one of the protagonists to accept the results of the elections there. It eventually succeeded in concluding an agreement, the Lusaka Protocol. As a result, peacekeeping forces were redeployed in Angola and expanded on a step-by-step basis in the ensuing months, relying on the continuing cease-fire.

Discussion

Withdrawal from the Former Yugoslavia

In response to a question, the secretary-general clarified that because of the links among the situations in the various former republics of Yugoslavia, if UN forces were compelled to withdraw from Croatia, their presence in Bosnia-Herzegovina could become "impossible." Although efforts were made both from his office and on the part of other countries to persuade President Franjo Tudjman to reconsider his demand that UN troops withdraw from Croatia, NATO prepared three scenarios for the withdrawal of UN troops from Croatia, from Bosnia-Herzegovina, or from both. The secretary-general hoped, however, that UN troops would not have to withdraw from either country, as such a withdrawal could spell a disaster for the former Yugoslavia. He noted, however, that his role was limited to creating a necessary awareness of the implications of withdrawal and that the decision lay in the hands of the various member states of the UN.

UN Mandate in Croatia

In response to a question on the Security Council's lack of adequate resolve in backing its decision to place the UN forces in Croatia under a Chapter VII enforcement mandate, which was seen as a dangerous precedent, the secretary-general clarified that UN troops in Croatia were operating under a Chapter VI mandate. Although the Security Council could decide to change the mandate to Chapter VII, thereby avoiding having to withdraw UN forces from Croatia according to President Tudjman's demand, this was not feasible for two reasons. First, certain technicalities, such as the lack of agreement of troops on the ground, insufficient equipment, and insufficient numbers, did not allow changing the mandate from Chapter VI to Chapter VII. Second, the present Security Council mood did not make likely a new Chapter VII mandate for UN forces in Croatia.

United Nations Reform

In response to a question about UN reform, the secretary-general noted that this is a continual process and that recent developments, including the creation of new institutions, such as the Commission on Sustainable Development, and of new posts, such as the high commissioner for human rights and the inspector general, posed additional challenges. The streamlining process had succeeded in eliminating sixteen top UN posts and 13 percent of the entire staff of the organization. He highlighted the importance of coordination among the various bodies of the UN system. However, the real problem was not the coordination of multilateral aid to developing countries through the United Nations system, which provided only 20 percent of such assistance, but better coordination of bilateral assistance, which accounted for the other 80 percent. Relations between industrialized and developing countries also needed to be improved.

UN Inaction in Lebanon and Nigeria

The secretary-general noted, in response to a question about the Israeli blockade of Southern Lebanon, that the UN cannot act in any way regarding the blockade without a complaint first being brought by the government of Lebanon to the UN Security Council. In response to a similar question about the UN's role in preventive action in Africa, with particular reference to Nigeria, the secretary-general reiterated that the United Nations is not able to intervene politically or militarily in a country without the agreement of that country.

2

Communal Conflict as a Challenge to International Organization: The Case of the Former Yugoslavia

Adam Roberts

In the former Yugoslavia from 1991 to 1995, the UN grappled with one of the most difficult crises in its history, involving the largest and most expensive UN peacekeeping operation. The events surrounding the Dayton accords of November 1995, which did not entirely end either the conflicts in former Yugoslavia or the UN's involvement there, afford an opportunity to take stock of the UN's strengths and weaknesses in handling conflict with a communal dimension.

Conflicts of nationalities in the Balkans have haunted efforts at European and world organization in both the nineteenth and the twentieth centuries. Fear of such conflicts played a fateful part in the early years of the League of Nations. Towards the end of World War I, when allied leaders were considering the future structure of what was to become the League of Nations, Jan Christian Smuts of South Africa wrote:

> The animosities and rivalries among the independent Balkan States in the past, which kept that pot boiling, and occasionally boiling over, will serve to remind us that there is the risk of a similar state of affairs on a much larger scale in the New Europe, covered as it will be with small independent States. In the past the Empires kept the peace among the rival nationalities; the League will have to keep the peace among the new States formed from these nationalities. This will impose a task of constant and vigilant supervision on it.[1]

In 1918 and 1919, there was much heated discussion as to whether membership in the League of Nations would require heavy commit-

This is a revised, edited, and updated version of an article that appeared in *Review of International Studies* 21, no. 4 (October 1995); and in *International Perspectives on the Yugoslav Conflict*, ed. Alex Danchev and Thomas Halverson (London: Macmillan, 1996). Copyright © Adam Roberts 1996.

ment in the Balkans. This discussion was especially intense in the United States, whose geographical isolation and strong anticolonial traditions militated against accepting distant and debatable responsibilities of this kind. President Woodrow Wilson said on 8 January 1918 in his Fourteen Points address that the relations of the Balkan states should be "determined by friendly counsel along historically established lines of allegiance and nationality."[2] In his passionate but doomed advocacy of the League, he naturally denied that membership would involve the United States in endless policing of troubled regions. As he said in a speech in September 1919, "If you want to put out a fire in Utah you do not send to Oklahoma for the fire engine. If you want to put out a fire in the Balkans . . . you do not send to the United States for troops."[3] The fear of involvement in the Balkans was among the factors that made the U.S. Senate oppose joining the League of Nations.

Thus, once before in this century, the question of how to tackle ethnic/communal conflict, notably in the Balkans, dealt a crippling blow to an attempt at global political organization. Now, three-quarters of a century later, such conflict has posed a challenge to the United Nations, and to regional institutions, that is every bit as serious as the one posed to the League of Nations so many years ago.

Ethnic/communal conflict can have several consequences. It can cause, or at least hasten, the collapse of states and other political entities; lead to an almost ineradicable habit of violence in certain societies; result in the formation of new states; spread across national boundaries, especially where one ethnic group is distributed among several neighboring states; trigger foreign interventions, sometimes competitive ones; and cause major interstate wars.

This short survey of communal conflict in general, and the conflict in the former Yugoslavia in particular, focuses on the challenge posed to international organizations, mainly the United Nations. It glances at the language used in connection with such conflict, outlines a few different national and intellectual perspectives, and draws attention to the special problems posed by the collapse of the communist federations of Yugoslavia and the Soviet Union. It then considers some of the UN's techniques for addressing this type of conflict and examines their strengths and weaknesses. It takes into account the November 1995 Dayton accords and the aftermath up to March 1996. It is largely limited to responses to conflicts after they have broken out and only touches tangentially on preventive action.

Questions of Terminology

The words used to characterize a conflict matter deeply. They often imply the type of interpretation to be directed at it and even the policy prescription to be followed. For example, calling the conflict in former Yugoslavia a case of "ancient ethnic hatred" and "civil war" has often been code language for recommending a policy of partial or total nonintervention, while calling it a case of "aggression" and defense of a multiethnic Bosnia has been associated with support for a more militant outside response. Two terms that are used remarkably loosely are "ethnic conflict" and "nation."

Ethnic v. Communal Conflict

In the history of conflict, ethnicity has been a central and fateful factor. However, there are hazards in labeling a conflict ethnic. To characterize an entire conflict in this way is to imply that the adversaries are biologically distinct peoples who are at war with each other purely because of such "objective" factors as different racial origins, skin colors, and languages. In many conflicts, even those to which the word "ethnic" is commonly applied, such a view is too simple. It may involve accepting too easily the semimythological but nonetheless powerful belief of particular groups that they have a common ancestry distinct from that of their adversaries.[4] Some conflicts occasionally labeled as ethnic, far from being between rival ethnic groups, are between people of common ethnic origin. The civil war in Somalia has been for the most part a conflict of clans, not of distinct ethnic groups; indeed, Somalia is more ethnically homogeneous than most states. In former Yugoslavia, some of the most bitter fighting has been between groups—most notably Bosnian Serbs and Bosnian Muslims— that have largely common ethnic origins but that centuries ago adopted different faiths identifying them with different outside powers.

"Communal conflict" is often a better term for hostilities between peoples who live in close proximity but have different allegiances and strong mutual fears. The term was familiar in Britain in the days of the empire and has been commonly applied to Northern Ireland. It has its faults: it has a superior and world-weary sound and does not completely capture the international complexities of at least some of these conflicts nor their significance in the process of state formation. Yet it does better encompass not just ethnic, but also linguistic, regional, class, and religious divisions.

A problem with all such terms is that they pigeonhole conflicts that may have many dimensions. As the Slovene ambassador to the UN put it in an address to the Security Council in January 1995, there were "ethnic and religious elements in many conflicts of the past and other nonethnic and nonreligious elements in present military conflicts, including those described as ethnic. As a matter of fact, it is possible to speak of an ethnic coefficient in most military conflicts in human history. What is really necessary is a careful identification of actors in each conflict and their actual agendas. Only if this is done can one hope that the response by the United Nations and other international mechanisms will correspond to the actual needs."[5]

In the conflicts in Croatia and Bosnia-Herzegovina, undoubtedly, communal aspects of conflicts have been overlaid with other elements, including the involvement of the Yugoslav army in support of local Serbs in a role that has often been seen as a case of international aggression. While the case for characterizing these wars as communal conflicts remains strong, for some purposes it may be more accurate to refer to the communal (or ethnic) factor (or coefficient) in such conflicts.

Nation v. State

What is a nation? Like so many abstract terms in common use in international politics, it means different things to different people. The term is used here mainly to refer to a large group of people who share a significant number of attributes: history, language, ethnic origin, religion, political belief, fear of the same adversaries. In short, a nation may be defined as "a community that is, or wishes to be, a state."[6] In sharp contrast, the term "state" is used here to mean an independent sovereign country, whether or not it consists of one "nation" as defined above. In many cases "nations" (e.g., the Scots) are simply one part of a larger sovereign state, while in other cases it may be argued that there is one nation (e.g., the Arabs) divided among several different sovereign states.

The disjunction between nation and state has been among the major causes of practically every war this century. Yet the language habitually used in international relations actually conceals the disjunction. The frequent use of such terms as "nation-state" to refer to virtually all states, however mixed their ethnic composition, is misleading. So is the media habit of calling states or countries "nations," a habit that seems to be growing and that needs to be actively discouraged as a barrier to understanding.

There is a long tradition of distinguished works, mainly by historians, on the place of nationalism and national self-determination in the troubled politics of the European continent and the world.[7] Some of these have dealt particularly with Yugoslavia.[8] Such works have been widely known and taught in departments of international relations in the United Kingdom, and their themes have been taken up by many scholars in the field.

Some American writers who have stressed the importance of group identity and so-called ethnic conflict have felt that they were swimming against the intellectual tide in their country.[9] Undeniably, many of their colleagues, including some leading international relations theorists, have neglected a wide range of problems associated with nationalism and ethnic identity. Hans Morgenthau's *Politics among Nations* follows the common American practice of using the term "nation" uncritically, as if it were synonymous with existing states, their boundaries, and their inhabitants. The potential of nationalism as a divisive force that could lead to the breakup of existing states is badly underestimated.[10]

Part of the explanation for this American usage arises from the unique character and experience of the U.S. federal system. Americans use the word "nation" to refer to a country because in their political lexicon the word "state" refers to the states of the union. As Louis Henkin has put it:

> Throughout I frequently refer to "nations" even where, strictly, the lawyer and the political scientist would insist on "states." . . . (This is common usage, and avoids confusion between the states of international society and the states of the United States.)[11]

The usage in another great federal republic, the former Yugoslavia, was the exact opposite and was closer to the definitions offered above. In the Socialist Federal Republic of Yugoslavia, the term "nation" referred to each of the major national groups that formed Yugoslavia, and the federation was the "state." As article 1 of the 1974 constitution put it, "The Socialist Federal Republic of Yugoslavia is a federal state having the form of a state community of voluntarily united nations and their Socialist Republics."

Today, the language used in much journalistic, political, and sometimes even academic discourse treats "nation" and "state" as identical and fails to comprehend that each term means different things in different societies. The deplorable conflation of the terms is built into such basic terms as "international relations" and indeed the "United Nations." Such linguistic confusion, which is an impediment to understanding many contemporary conflicts, cannot be eliminated, but attempts can be made to contain it.

Some Perspectives on Communal Conflict and on the Former Yugoslavia

Different individuals, states, and regional bodies have fundamentally diverging perceptions of communal conflict in general and of particular crises involving such conflict, including in the former Yugoslavia. There are notable differences on such key questions as whether such conflict is a widespread threat or one confined to particular situations and countries; whether it is susceptible to integrative solutions or requires the surgery of secession; and whether outside powers, individually or collectively, can play a useful part in helping to end it, and if so at what stage and by what means. The perspectives of countries and individuals are shaped by their own attitudes and experiences: those with recent experience of civil war and communal conflict often view matters differently from those that have been more preoccupied with interstate problems.

Reactions to the Yugoslav conflict illustrate all too well the general truth that people in different states see the world differently. For example, Russia has naturally had much sympathy with the Serbian cause, or causes. This is not only for the reasons commonly advanced (traditionally close ties with Serbia and fear of Western encroachments) but also because Russia and Serbia have shared the trauma of collapse of a communist federation. Similarly, if for different reasons, Greece has been much more favorable to Serbia than any of its NATO allies. Many Muslim states and those with substantial Muslim minorities have identified closely with Bosnia. Germany has renewed old connections with Croatia and has shown only limited understanding of the messy complexities of communal conflict.

The various perspectives on the former Yugoslavia have not been well articulated. There have been short statements and sound bites galore, but no Western political leader has made a major statement analyzing in depth the causes and character of the war and the policy options for outside powers. There have been obvious reasons for this, but there have also been costs, not least the elements of incomprehension in much international, including transatlantic, debate.

The UN Secretary-General

Senior figures in the UN Secretariat did not want the organization to be saddled with the problems attendant upon Yugoslavia's breakup. They rightly perceived the problems as extremely difficult, and the UN's possible involvement as hazardous. Today, UN officials sometimes hint that, but for the terrible intrastate conflicts with which the organization has had to deal (of which Yugoslavia is the main example), the UN might have realized at least part of the optimistic vision, widespread in 1991 and 1992, of its post–Cold War role.

In many statements at the UN, including those by leading members of the Secretariat and Security Council, nationalism, warlordism, and ethnic conflict have been treated as modern versions of original sin, to be deplored and to be restrained and controlled from outside. UN Secretary-General Boutros Boutros-Ghali addressed the subject of ethnic/communal conflict in a number of documents and statements. He said in 1992 in *An Agenda for Peace* that "the cohesion of States is threatened by brutal ethnic, religious, social, cultural or linguistic strife."[12] This presents communal strife exclusively as a threat to the cohesion of states rather than (as sometimes happens) as part of a process of state formation.

In a speech in 1993, Boutros-Ghali discussed ethnic conflict at some length, including the key question of whether, or when, it constitutes a threat to the peace calling for action under the UN Charter: "All ethnic conflict is deplorable. But not all ethnic conflict threatens world peace. The United Nations cannot and should not try to solve every such problem." However, another passage in the same speech, using a biological analogy, presented ethnic conflict as a general threat:

> [E]thnic conflict poses as great a danger to common world security as did the cold war. The character of the challenge and the time frame involved are not the same—but the threat to security is no less real. No country today, and particularly multi-ethnic countries, can afford to ignore ethnic conflict. Borders and oceans can no longer insulate people at home from the consequences of such violence abroad. . . . Just as biological disease spreads through a body, and as an epidemic spreads geographically, so also a political disease can spread through the world. When one State is endangered by ethnic conflict, others will be endangered as well.[13]

Boutros-Ghali called ethnic conflict a "new reality."[14] While it is indeed new in some areas and forms, it is basically an old phenomenon, one that has often been viewed by outside powers nervously, as something in which to avoid direct involvement. One of the UN's problems in respect to such conflicts, including in the former Yugoslavia, has been this sense of nervousness: states have been able to use the UN as a means of limiting their own direct involvement.

Some Western States and Organizations

In the early stages of the war, many Western leaders underestimated the depth and seriousness of the Yugoslav crisis. The hubris of a regional organization in claiming to be able to handle a tragic conflict without outside help was exemplified by the remark of Jacques Delors, president of the European Commission, in the summer of 1991, when fighting broke out in Yugoslavia: "We do not interfere in American affairs. We hope they will have enough respect not to interfere in ours."[15]

The U.S. policy in the crucial year, 1991, illustrates the difficulty of resisting the tide of nationalist events. In respect to Yugoslavia, even after Croatia and Slovenia had adopted declarations of independence in June 1991, the U.S. policy remained one of supporting whatever unity of the country could be salvaged—which was not a lot. Similarly, in respect to the equally ailing Soviet Union, President George Bush, speaking in the Ukrainian capital in August 1991 in what was to be dubbed his "chicken Kiev" speech, warned the Ukrainian people of the dangers of "suicidal nationalism" and stated that his administration intended to "maintain the strongest possible relationship with the Soviet government of Mikhail Gorbachev." The fate of these policies suggests that, however flawed the doctrine of national self-determination may be, to resist it as a matter of general principle is not an option for the international community.

Following the outbreak of the wars in the former Yugoslavia, official speeches by Western leaders generally described the conflict in terms of ancient hatreds unleashed and of a cauldron of hot liquid that boils over when the lid is removed. In August 1992, President Bush said that Balkan strife grew out of "age-old animosities." Therefore, Bush went on to say, "let no one think there is an easy or a simple solution to this tragedy . . . whatever pressure and means the international community brings to bear."[16] A similar view was offered in what is arguably the fullest statement of American policy on the former Yugoslavia—that by Warren Christopher on 10 February 1993. His image of the war was summed up in this statement:

> The death of President Tito and the end of communist domination of the former Yugoslavia raised the lid on the cauldron of ancient ethnic hatreds. This is the land where at least three religions and a half-dozen ethnic groups have vied across the centuries. It was the birthplace of World War I. It has long been a cradle of European conflict, and it remains so today.[17]

Warren Christopher's interpretation of the Yugoslav conflict contained much truth. It is indisputable that there have long been deep and exceptionally bitter ethnic divisions in Yugoslavia; indeed, these have been noted by countless writers. Yet the suggestion that Tito's death led directly to disaster distracts attention from the fact that a decade elapsed between Tito's death in 1980 and the outbreak of war in 1991. Further, the imagery of a cauldron of ancient ethnic hatreds obscures evidence of extensive ethnic coexistence (including widespread intermarriage) over a period of decades and even centuries. It was this very coexistence, with different communities living in the same areas, that made the breakup of Yugoslavia so peculiarly difficult and its mismanagement so tragic.

The "ancient ethnic hatreds" view of ex-Yugoslavia predominated for a long time in much U.S. foreign policymaking, but was it too pessimistic to capture the high ground in American political and public debate. There, another compelling framework of thought held sway: that which saw international problems in terms of (Serb) aggression versus (Bosnian) defense and was quick to condemn European powers for their alleged selfishness, weakness, and general incapacity. This perspective led naturally to "lift and strike"—that is, opposition to the UN arms embargo on the former Yugoslavia so that Bosnia could defend itself better—and advocacy of that traditional U.S. long-distance and low-risk instrument, bombing. This perspective also shaped the implementation in 1995 of a strategy to curb the Bosnian Serb forces and thus made a significant contribution to the conclusion of the Dayton accords.

Propositions about ancient ethnic hatreds and claims that this is a war of aggression are not complete or convincing explanations of the causes and character of the wars in the former Yugoslavia. A third perspective sees these wars as the outcome of the machinations of corrupt politicians who have exploited ethnic rivalries to further their own political ambitions. This perspective is compatible with elements of the other two, but stresses particularly the responsibility of certain individuals, the failure of the international community to understand and manage the process of breakup, and the real possibilities that existed to avert tragedy.[18]

In light of the existence of many different views on the Yugoslav conflict, only a few of which have been mentioned here, it is remarkable that any international organization, including the UN Security Council, has been able to reach any agreement on action at all, and it is not surprising that the action recommended has often been only a limited and partial response to a peculiarly difficult challenge.

The End of Empires and Federations

The central feature of many post–Cold War conflicts, including ones that have engaged the UN, is not so much the nature of the contending groups as the complete collapse of an existing system of government. The original causes of the collapse may involve many factors besides ethnic/communal issues. The process of collapse, however, may exacerbate communal tensions. All kinds of groups—ethnic, religious, territorial, and linguistic—may have their own ideas and folk memories of who their friends are, who their enemies are, what kind of state they aspire to create, and within what frontiers they will create it.

Yugoslavia and the Soviet Union are not normal cases of imperial dissolution. They are disintegrations of large and complex socialist-cum-federal states that had been akin to empires, albeit in socialist colors and with some special features. Some of the internal borders of these two great states did not follow clear ethnic, economic, or strategic lines and were not well suited to be possible international frontiers. Their previous regimes' official nationalities policies had for better or for worse emphasized nationality as one basis of political units, had patronized ethnic cultures, and at the same time had sought to constrain and discredit serious ethnic claims. When the chance came to break with the old communist order, its only half-real suborder of republics and ethnic groups suddenly became the main surviving foundation for political construction. The theoretical right to secession became actual, and the steadying hand of the old communist system was no longer there to hold centrifugal tendencies in check. The old communist political language of absolute right and wrong was transferred catastrophically to an ethnic framework.

Once the breakup of the Soviet Union and Yugoslavia became inevitable, the international community, and some local political forces, sought to accept the existing republics of the federation as the successor states. This meant accepting the internal frontiers of the federation, however artificial or arbitrary, as the international frontiers of these new or reconstituted states.[19] In both cases, the federal collapse took place so quickly that the republics had little or no time to prepare for independent statehood. Many of the new states thus formed contained significant sectors of the population that were reluctant to come under their rule. The biggest and most populous units (Russia and Serbia, respectively) of these old federations had large numbers of fellow nationals in nearby republics but also faced potential for further fission because of the existence within them of republics or autonomous provinces with distinctive populations and good reason to fear domination and desire independence. The Russian Federation includes twenty Autonomous Republics and eleven Regions containing an impressive variety of language groups and populations in almost every possible proportion and combination.

In many parts of the former Soviet Union, much effort was devoted to preventing the outbreak of ethnic conflict and to trying to build new states "on the basis of co-citizenship and on the policy of cultural pluralism."[20] Despite such effort, it is not surprising that many wars began there: in Armenia and Azerbaijan, Moldova, Georgia, Tajikistan, and within the Russian Federation itself, in Chechnya. In ex-Yugoslavia, wars broke out in Slovenia, Croatia, and Bosnia. There was fear of conflict in Macedonia and also in Vojvodina and Kosovo, both of which are within Serbia.

The rapid moves toward national self-determination in the former socialist world in the 1990s have not had the dubious benefit of any Lenin- or Woodrow Wilson–style advocacy. As indicated above, in 1991 the United States was notably cautious, even conservative, with respect to the breakup of both Yugoslavia and the Soviet Union. In Russia there were some exponents of national self-determination as a general principle, including, notably, Dr. Galina Starovoitova, who in 1992 was a member of the Russian parliament and an adviser on ethnic matters to President Boris Yeltsin. However, there has been little international political debate on the merits and defects of self-determination as a basis for order. It is as if, after the collapse of communist empires and their ideologies, national self-determination was the default position—the principal remaining basis for political organization. It has largely ceased to be a theory for international order, but it remains an effective battle cry for ambitious local leaders and their followers.

Techniques for Addressing Ongoing Conflicts

International institutions can respond to conflicts involving ethnic/communal dimensions with a wide variety of action. Boutros-Ghali has listed four: "education, economics, human rights, military."[21] The order is interesting, and the first approach deserves more attention than it has received. Five types of action are discussed here: mediation, population exchange, peacekeeping, international administration, and sanctions. All these are types of action that have been applied in cases of ongoing conflicts; preventive action—a partly separate, larger, and more rewarding field—is not covered here.

Mediation

Attempts at interethnic mediation by international bodies have taken many forms and have been the subject of much interesting advocacy.[22] Two of the most common have been proposals for partition to enable hostile communities to live in separate states and proposals for federal arrangements within a single state.

The UN has been continuously and deeply involved in attempting to mediate in conflicts with an intercommunal dimension, but with only limited results. Its efforts at mediation in various phases of the Middle East conflict, whether through international conferences or the "good offices" function of the secretary-general, have been less productive than those of other mediators, especially the U.S. The longest-running "good offices" effort of the secretary-general—the attempt since 1964 to get a confederal structure of government in Cyprus—has served many useful functions but has not yet succeeded in its central purpose. Similarly, the joint efforts under European Community, UN, and Contact Group auspices to mediate in the Yugoslav conflicts have repeatedly run into difficulties.[23]

International attempts to mediate in communal conflicts frequently revolve around efforts at territorial management, in which recognition of distinct zones, even of separate states, is seen as the basis of a solution.[24] UNSCOP (the UN Special Committee on Palestine) tried to create separate units in 1947. The resulting UN partition plan for Palestine, approved by the General Assembly on 29 November 1947, would have created an Arab state and a Jewish state, each composed of three separate parts. As Avi Shlaim has written: "The borders of these two oddly shaped states, resembling two fighting serpents, were a strategic nightmare."[25]

Similarly, with respect to the former Yugoslavia, the Vance-Owen mission in its various incarnations and the international Contact Group that largely succeeded it proposed complex schemes for partition, albeit within the framework of a loose federal Bosnian state. A principal problem is that such mediation proposals involve setting up under international auspices a series of zones that may reflect (albeit imperfectly) existing ethnic distributions of population, the interests of major outside powers, or the current state of the battlefield, but also have built-in faults. Such arrangements often lack territorial contiguity and in an extreme form are sometimes likened to leopard spots. They are often criticized on the basis that the proposed units fail to meet important aspirations of the embattled belligerents, make little economic sense, and fail to provide defensible territory and a sense of security for the inhabitants. The desire for security, which is at the heart of many communal conflicts, militates against the acceptance of any patchwork solution that leaves a group with frontiers that are vulnerable and hard to defend.

It is hard to see what else mediators can do when circumstances make interethnic cooperation within a single political unit hard to achieve. They point out that the belligerents themselves often produce complicated patchwork plans. International mediators, representing not just the individual countries of the international community but also the principles to which those countries subscribe, simply cannot propose the vast population expulsions or violent changes in existing states and frontiers that would be necessary to create ethnically homogeneous and militarily defensible states. If they were to advocate such a course, they would, with good reason, incur heavy criticism. Sometimes it even seems—and not only to some of the belligerents directly involved—that despite the terrible costs, the fortunes of war can have a better chance of yielding defensible territorial units than the machinery of international diplomacy.[26]

There are good reasons why, in mediation as in other matters, international bodies do not necessarily trump individual states. International bodies are often constrained from departing from well-known fixed positions—by their fundamental principles, by their record on the issue at stake, and by the need to maintain whatever agreement there is among their member states. Yet the resolution of conflicts with an ethnic dimension, whether in the matter of Israel-Palestine or the former Yugoslavia, almost always involves making departures from key principles, including that of the nonrecognition of any changes of frontiers by force. Such resolution also frequently involves working on limited agreements with limited numbers of parties. This is something that universal bodies such as the UN are often reluctant to do, as it implies a departure from the principles of universality and impartiality.

In the former Yugoslavia from 1994 onwards, the mediatory roles of individual governments (principally the United States) were more decisive than those of the various international bodies. Two important deals were concluded in March 1994. First, a series of agreements in February-March 1994, largely brokered by the United States, helped to bring about the fragile peace between the Bosnian government and Bosnian Croats. In particular, agreements on the creation of a federation of the Bosnian Muslim and Croat areas and on the eventual establishment of a confederation between the Bosnian Republic and Croatia were signed in Washington in mid-March 1994. Second, both the United States and Russia played key roles in the negotiations that led to the short-lived Zagreb agreement between the Croatian government and the Serbian rebel forces (Republic of Serb Krajina) signed on 29 March 1994. This accord broke down in 1995 when the government of Croatia, impatient with the lack of progress towards a political solution, intervened militarily to restore its control in most of the Serb-held areas.

It was largely a U.S. mediation effort that led to the Dayton accords on Bosnia and Herzegovina that were concluded on 20 November 1995 and formally signed in Paris on 14 December. These accords reflected a change in the local balance of power. In summer 1995, Croat forces had not only overrun most of the Serb-held areas of Croatia but also had extended their military campaign into Bosnia and Herzegovina. Further, atrocities committed by Serb forces in the "safe area" of Srebrenica, which they overran on 22 July, led to a sustained NATO bombing campaign in August and September against the Serb military infrastructure in Bosnia. U.S. diplomacy was poised to take advantage of these developments by pressing for a settlement in which the Bosnian Serbs would get much less territory than they had previously demanded and would have to accept other conditions not to their liking.

There is much to be said in criticism of the U.S. role in mediation over Bosnia. The United States was unhelpful at earlier points, including in May 1993, when its constructive involvement might have strengthened the chances of getting agreement roughly along the lines of what eventually emerged at Dayton. The Muslim-Croat alliance, brokered in March 1994, may have prepared the ground for later Serb concessions, but it was and remains fragile. The Dayton accords of November 1995 are even more vulnerable. Their central political plank is that the Republic of Bosnia and Herzegovina will remain an effective overarching state containing two entities: the Federation of Bosnia and Herzegovina (i.e., the Muslim-Croat federation) and the Republika Srpska (i.e., the Serb-held areas of Bosnia). This elaborate structure is not likely to work. The fiction (if that is what it is) of an effective state of Bosnia and Herzegovina may have been maintained partly for the sake of international and U.S. opinion, which is particularly reluctant to accept the ideas that frontiers can be changed by force and that new states can be based on ethnic criteria. Yet the reality will probably be that the Serb areas will gravitate toward closer links with Serbia, the Croat areas will gravitate toward Croatia, and Bosnia will have at best a truncated existence. In short, Dayton may end up being one of the many peace agreements of the post-1945 era whose military provisions are largely implemented but whose political provisions remain more or less a dead letter.

The U.S.-led mediation effort in respect to the former Yugoslavia was, of course, far from being purely unilateral. The United States operated within a framework of principles and pressures (including the sanctions on Serbia) established by the UN Security Council. NATO's use of force against the Bosnian Serbs in August and September 1995 and the establishment of the NATO-based Implementation Force (IFOR) in December acquired legitimacy from UN resolutions. The picture of a decisive United States succeeding where a dithering UN had failed is far too simple. The failure of senior UN figures to vigorously contest this picture is surprising, and may reflect a degree of unease about the U.S. seizure of the initiative in the second half of 1995.

The fact remains that the United States showed more capacity to develop an overall strategy for ending the war (and knocking heads together) than did the UN and European Union through their various multinational mediation efforts. Even if the political provisions of Dayton come unstuck, it is conceivable that what will ensue is not full-scale war but rather political and military rivalry between three entities, with some of the borders between them following roughly the lines indicated at Dayton.

What general conclusions emerge? Efforts at mediation of conflicts with an ethnic or communal dimension have to be made, if only to satisfy demands in the international community for action of some kind. Such efforts can open up possibilities for peace. Yet they always involve hovering around the very fine line between the containment of conflict and its exacerbation. Attempts to force hostile parties into federations they do not want are unlikely to succeed. There are no quick fixes, and no possibility of imposing a diktat from outside. Since mediation efforts necessarily involve reassuring threatened communities, they require local knowledge and readiness for the long haul.[27]

Population Exchange

Where efforts to protect minority rights seem doomed to failure, exchange of populations is sometimes proposed as the only way of preventing the continuation of a conflict. The exchange of populations between Greece and Turkey starting in 1912 is a leading example. Mass flights of Greeks from Turkey largely preceded the convention of 30 January 1923, which sought to regulate the exchange process. The convention, widely denounced at the time as inhumane, may well have been "the best policy in the unhappy circumstances."[28] The League of Nations Council was deeply involved in the implementation of the convention and in the various controversies that arose.

Population exchanges, even those accompanied by "ethnic cleansing," have become a sadly common aspect of state creation or consolidation. They occurred in eastern Europe after World War II, especially in Czechoslovakia with the expulsion of the Sudeten Germans. They also occurred in several cases of European decolonization, most notably in the partition of India in 1947. While creating much tragedy, such exchanges may sometimes result in the creation of relatively defensible borders with fewer "leopard spots" than the original distribution of population might have indicated.

Within the UN system, especially in UNHCR, forced population exchange is a taboo subject. The appalling practices associated with ethnic cleansing in the former Yugoslavia have compelled UNHCR and other organizations to help move threatened people, mainly Bosnian Muslims. This has led to occasional accusations that they are actually assisting ethnic cleansing. In 1994 and 1995, UNHCR conducted internal studies of forced exchange but remained very strongly opposed to the practice.

Transfers of populations have a terrible momentum of their own and are very hard to reverse. In the Agreement on Refugees and Displaced Persons, part of the November 1995 Dayton accords, article 1 begins: "All refugees and displaced persons have the right freely to return to their homes of origin." In subsequent months, there was no sign of any general return of those refugees who had been expelled from their homes. On the contrary, the transfer of populations continued, most notably with the mass departures of Serbs from those suburbs of Sarajevo that were handed back to Bosnian government control in March 1996.

Peacekeeping

All significant UN peacekeeping operations in the first three decades after 1945 related to territory and people recently freed from colonialism.[29] In practically all these cases there was some element of communal conflict, often combined with dispute about some of the territorial arrangements left by departing colonial powers. In many of these cases the interposition of lightly armed UN peacekeeping forces worked reasonably well. There was usually some willingness by the parties involved to stick to an agreed cease-fire, to give consent to the presence of a UN peacekeeping force, and to respect its impartial and neutral character.

The conflicts that have erupted in the former Yugoslavia and former Soviet Union have—because of their violence, their terrible effects on civilians, their creation of refugee flows, and their tendency to spread— created strong and natural demands in the international community for action. Where it has materialized at all, such action has taken the form of peacekeeping or some variant thereof. However, peacekeeping has been made particularly difficult by eight characteristics of these conflicts:

1. the involvement of a large number of belligerent parties, including both governments and nonstate groups, making peace negotiations difficult

2. lack of willingness or ability on the part of the leaders of the principal groups involved to stick to the terms of agreed cease-fires

3. widespread use of hastily assembled armed forces, often with little

professional training and an uncertain command structure; and wide dispersion of light weapons. These factors make the forces involved hard to bring under control as part of a cease-fire, peace, or partial disarmament agreement.

4. rejection by some parties of certain existing borders (including international ones in some cases), and a complex, widely dispersed pattern of military activities, making cease-fire lines hard to establish and monitor

5. the existence of numerous points of friction between the parties involved, arising from the fact that communities at war with each other live in the same regions, sometimes even in the same towns and villages

6. desire to carry out policies—forcible border changes, expulsion or killing of members of an ethnic group, massive resettlement of occupied areas with members of another ethnic group—that by their very nature are contrary to basic principles of international law in general and the laws of war (international humanitarian law) in particular

7. the creation of human disasters with which the belligerents cannot cope, thus drawing peacekeeping forces into humanitarian activities that result in their dispersion and their dependence on the cooperation of the warring parties

8. a tendency to endure for decades, even generations, thus severely testing the patience and staying power of outside peacekeepers[30]

These features of recent conflicts have forced UN peacekeeping away from its traditional character, and they have cruelly exposed its limits. The case of the UN operations in an ongoing war in the former Yugoslavia illustrates the point. Established in February 1992, the UN Protection Force (UNPROFOR) in the former Yugoslavia became the largest UN peacekeeping operation ever. By the end of 1994 it had some 40,000 personnel, which is more than any previous UN peacekeeping operation, and it was costing $1.6 billion a year, nearly half the cost of all seventeen peacekeeping operations in place around the world at that time.[31] Its mandates, based on over sixty Security Council resolutions, were more complex than those of any previous UN force.[32] On 31 March 1995, following a crisis over the renewal of the mandate in Croatia and prolonged negotiations, the UN Security Council resolved to transform UNPROFOR in the former Yugoslavia into three separately named forces in the three successor states that were the theater of its main operations: the UN Confidence Restoration Operation in Croatia (UNCRO); the UN Preventive Deployment Force (UNPREDEP) in Macedonia; and, keeping its old name, the UN Protection Force (UNPROFOR) in Bosnia and Herzegovina.[33]

What UN peacekeeping forces attempted in the former Yugoslavia—a major international presence in the midst of unresolved conflicts and ongoing wars—was historically unprecedented. Their initial and fundamental task, laid down in 1992, was "to create the conditions of peace and security required for the negotiation of an overall settlement of the Yugoslav crisis."[34] In their operations, especially the two key tasks of attempting to implement cease-fires in Croatia and in Bosnia, they have encountered extreme difficulties. It was probably a mistake that contributed to inflated expectations for UNPROFOR to carry the name "protection force" and to be classified as a "peacekeeping force." In Croatia, UN peacekeeping forces did monitor a cease-fire between the government and the Serb-held areas. However, President Franjo Tudjman of Croatia, hostile to the de facto emergence of a state within a state comparable to that in northern Cyprus, repeatedly threatened to refuse consent to a renewal of UNPROFOR's mandate, and in May and August 1995 he defied the UN by recapturing western Slavonia and Krajina.[35] Meanwhile, in Bosnia, UNPROFOR helped monitor and implement local cease-fires, including one between the Muslims and Croats, but it could not stop the Muslim-Serb war. Its most effective performance was in assisting the delivery of humanitarian aid, including aid to besieged areas. For example, getting 12,951 sorties to Sarajevo in the three-and-a-half years of the UNHCR airlift was an impressive achievement.[36]

UNPROFOR's humanitarian role in itself posed a problem: it required forces to be widely dispersed and to operate with the permission of the dominant forces in the area, in many cases the Bosnian Serbs. Hence it became very difficult for the UN forces to take, or encourage NATO to take, tough action against the parties—at least until the summer of 1995, by which time Serb action had virtually halted the humanitarian effort and had led to a withdrawal of UN personnel from vulnerable positions. Until that point, critics could plausibly argue that, in a communal conflict, a peacekeeping and humanitarian role tends at best to buttress the military status quo.

The perceived weaknesses of the UN peacekeeping efforts in the former Yugoslavia help to explain the determination of the U.S. government in 1995 to replace the UN with a more forceful entity. The United States and the other powers involved had little difficulty in agreeing on the desirability of having the implementation of the military provisions of Dayton monitored by IFOR, which took over from UNPROFOR in December 1995. This new entity had UN authorization but was not under UN control.

The peacekeeping aspect of the war in Bosnia and Herzegovina involved a curious paradox. For the long years of the war, there was a peacekeeping force even though there was no peace. Then, after the war, when there was a formal agreement between the warring parties and something more nearly like a traditional peacekeeping task to be performed, there was a more highly armed international force. This eschewed the label "peacekeeping," even though it did incorporate some UNPROFOR units, which were duly rehelmeted and relabeled. All this is a reflection on the perceived inadequacies of UN peacekeeping in a long-running and violent conflict with a strong communal dimension.

International Administration

The UN has been notably reluctant to take over responsibility for government in a quasi-trustee role in divided societies, including Bosnia and the UN-protected areas of Croatia. However, there were important civil affairs and police components in the work of UNPROFOR. In addition, in Bosnia-Herzegovina there was the office of the UN special coordinator for Sarajevo, established in April 1994 to help restore essential public services in the Bosnian capital; and the European Union administrator for Mostar, who assumed his responsibilities on 23 July 1994. These outside officials in Sarajevo and Mostar have had limited but very different administrative roles. In both cases the experience has been difficult and the achievements modest. Neither these nor any other administrative arrangements, including the International Police Task Force (IPTF) established by the UN in Bosnia and Herzegovina in the wake of the Dayton accords, constitute anything like a prospective government.

The historical record of trusteeship systems under international auspices is not encouraging; indeed, the problems of some divided societies, including Palestine, Iraq, and Ruanda-Urundi (now Rwanda and Burundi), may well have been made worse in the period of the League of Nations mandate system. Except in cases of regional hegemony, old-fashioned forms of the direct exercise of dominance are out of fashion.[37]

The contemporary importance of the question of administration has been well identified by Boutros-Ghali:

> Another feature of such [intrastate] conflicts is the collapse of state institutions, especially the police and judiciary, with resulting paralysis of governance, a

breakdown of law and order, and general banditry and chaos. Not only are the functions of government suspended, its assets are destroyed or looted and experienced officials are killed or flee the country. This is rarely the case in inter-state wars. It means that international intervention must extend beyond military and humanitarian tasks and must include the promotion of national reconciliation and the re-establishment of effective government.[38]

What is emerging in the post–Cold War era is not a formal doctrine of trusteeship but rather a modest, tentative, and pragmatic international involvement in aspects of government in many countries, in collaboration with local and national authorities and often in connection with an on-going UN peacekeeping operation. If unavoidable, this seems also to be an inadequate role for international organizations when faced with the extreme challenge of the genocidal state (as in Rwanda in 1994), the failed state (Somalia in 1992), and the deeply divided state (Bosnia and Herze-govina from 1992 on).

The absence of any serious drive for a UN-based system of trusteeship strengthens the possibility that it may be left to regional powers, whether acting on their own or with some degree of international blessing, to per-form some trustee-like functions in failed states. The roles of France in its former African colonies, Nigeria in Liberia, Russia in Tajikistan, and Syria in Lebanon indicate some of the possibilities and areas of controversy.

Economic Sanctions and Arms Embargoes

At least in theory, global international organizations have a special capacity to organize economic sanctions and arms embargoes, which gen-erally need to be near universal if they are to be effective. The UN has imposed nonforcible sanctions under Article 41 of the Charter in several cases of conflict where there has been an ethnic or communal dimension. There have been general economic sanctions against Rhodesia (1966–79), and Serbia and Montenegro (1992–). There have also been embargoes on the supply of arms to South Africa (1977–94), the former Yugoslavia (1991–), Somalia (1992–), Liberia (1992–), and Rwanda (1994).

In the former Yugoslavia, such measures have been imperfectly imple-mented, and their results have, at best, been mixed. The general economic sanctions against Serbia and Montenegro may have been one factor in the progressive diminution of Serbia's support for Serb forces in Bosnia and Croatia in 1994–95, and the prospect of their being ended was evidently an inducement to Belgrade to consider changing course. On the other hand, being a plainly partisan measure aimed at one side only, the sanc-tions reinforced Serb doubts about UN impartiality.

The effects of the arms embargo against the countries of the former Yugoslavia have been more controversial. With the exception of the short war in Slovenia in 1991, the conflicts in the former Yugoslavia have been prolonged by the general availability of weapons and the large number of people trained in their use. The Yugoslav system of General People's Defense, which had been implemented in 1969, had always involved a risk of misuse in internal conflict. In 1976, I wrote: "The Yugoslav defense system rests on fragile social and political foundations. If those foundations fail, the idea of General People's Defense might be quickly forgotten; or, worse, it might be perversely misused for civil war."[39] Although the wide availability of arms was indeed a problem from 1991 onward, so was the arms embargo. The Yugoslav experience confirms that embargoes on the supply of arms tend to favor one side—in this case the well-armed Serbs. This resulted in the increasingly strong calls for Bosnia to be enabled to defend itself. There was also evidence of blind eyes being turned to numerous violations of the arms embargo, not only with respect to Bosnia. Like other aspects of the international response, the arms embargo was perceived as ineffective, yet far from impartial.

Dilemmas of Recognition Policy

Diplomatic recognition, whether by individual states or by international institutions, is an important and controversial issue in ethnic/communal conflicts. Acts of recognition have had several consequences. The prospect of recognition can force the pace of state creation by putting pressure on would-be states to get their claims in while the music of recognition is being played. An act of recognition implies a degree of obligation on the part of states and international organizations to maintain respect for the newly recognized state and its international borders, even if there has not always been deep determination to act on this. Once recognized, a state may feel entitled to insist on retaining all its territory, however strongly it is disputed. Above all, recognition can have the effect of transforming other states' legal and political perceptions of a conflict: what was previously a civil war or communal conflict may come to be viewed as an international war. A state trying to recover its old territory may suddenly be seen as an aggressor.

Lord Carrington and Javier Pérez de Cuéllar warned in December 1991 of the hazards of early and selective diplomatic recognition of some of the Yugoslav republics in advance of an overall settlement. As Lord Carrington put it in a letter to Hans van den Broek:

There is also a real danger, perhaps even a probability, that Bosnia-Herzegovina would also ask for independence and recognition, which would be
wholly unacceptable to the Serbs in that republic in which there are something like 100,000 JNA [Yugoslav People's Army] troops, some of which
have withdrawn there from Croatia. Milosevic has hinted that military
action would take place there if Croatia and Slovenia were recognized. This
might well be the spark that sets Bosnia-Herzegovina alight.[40]

There can be no question of attributing the ensuing tragedy in Bosnia
entirely to the acts of recognition that took place in January 1992. However, recognition was politically explosive in the states being recognized.
Recognition of a new entity is especially controversial where, as in former
Yugoslavia, the old state still exists, at least in rump form, and has not
accepted its own collapse; where there are large minorities that adhere to
an outside state and reject the borders, or even the existence, of the new
entity in which they find themselves; and where promises by emergent
states in the field of human rights are not backed up by performance. Yet
it is understandable that states sometimes see a strong case for early
recognition of new entities. In an unstable situation in which the central
state or imperial power has collapsed, there is a need to keep some control over events. Where recognition is conditional upon certain commitments (for example, about human rights, treatment of minorities, or
respect for frontiers), it can have special attractions. With respect to Croatia, there was a serious belief that the process of European Community
recognition, which finally took effect on 15 January 1992, even before
Croatia had met EC conditions for protection of minorities, might actually
assist the process of concluding and implementing the cease-fire between
Croatia and Serbia. This cease-fire accord, concluded on 2 January, was
indeed better implemented than its fourteen predecessors, although its
implementation was inadequate.

Should there be a reversion to old and well-established criteria for
diplomatic recognition? Principal among these are some coherence as a
political and social entity and a capacity for self-defense. The experience
of European decolonization, in which the successor states achieved recognition and UN membership reasonably smoothly, contributed to a relative
decline of these older criteria. The EU and UN experience with the former
Yugoslavia raises doubts about whether international institutions are necessarily better at making judgments on these matters than individual
states. The traditional criteria for recognition need to be revived, perhaps
with some changes, including more emphasis on human rights and
minority protection.

Attempts to Develop Criteria for Involvement

As great powers tire of heavy commitments to distant and puzzling conflicts, it is likely that the Security Council's attitude will become more parsimonious. Since 1991, the council has in fact limited its involvement in a number of conflicts with an ethnic dimension, including several in the former Soviet Union. Already in 1992, *An Agenda for Peace* indicated an interest in placing a greater part of the burden of peacekeeping onto regional powers and organizations.[41] In May 1994 the council specified six criteria that must be taken into account when a new operation is under consideration. These were the existence of a threat to international peace and security, readiness of regional bodies to assist, the existence of a cease-fire, a clear political goal that can be reflected in the mandate, a precise mandate, and reasonable assurances of the safety of UN personnel.[42] Several of these criteria would be hard to satisfy in many communal conflicts, including that in the former Yugoslavia. An even stronger note of caution was struck at about the same time in the Clinton administration's unveiling of Presidential Decision Directive (PDD) 25, on "multilateral peace operations."[43] PDD 25 raised questions as to whether, had it applied earlier, many existing UN operations would have been undertaken or would have secured U.S. participation. As Mats Berdal has said, "Strict adherence to the criteria of 'no open-ended commitments' and continuing public support are bound to limit the scope for UN action in a world where domestic, religious and ethnically motivated hatreds are the major sources of conflict."[44] Since PDD 25 appeared, the United States has moved still further away from support for UN peacekeeping. The new Republican majorities in the House and Senate are the inheritors of a long-standing American distrust of any mode of overseas military involvement other than the quick victory based on overwhelming force. The proposals of the Senate Budget Committee, announced in February 1995, threatened even more serious cutbacks in support for UN peacekeeping than those previously discussed.[45] After Dayton, the NATO-based IFOR could get congressional approval only because it was seen as very different from traditional peacekeeping forces in its level of armament, its mandate, and its system for authorizing the use of force.

Conclusions

The conflicts of the post–Cold War era, not least their communal conflict aspects, present exceptionally difficult challenges to the international community and its institutions, especially the UN. How are those challenges to be understood, addressed, and acted upon, especially in light of the Yugoslav disasters?

First, the international community has faced periods of such conflict before, including, in this century, in the Balkans around the time of the two world wars and in former European colonies around the time of decolonization. The international system managed to endure these periods of conflict, sometimes with great difficulty and cost, and to prevent intensely disruptive regional phenomena from leading to a general process of fission.

Second, the historical record suggests that the management of communal conflicts is inherently difficult, whether it is attempted by states, empires, or regional or global organizations. The UN should not be judged harshly merely for running into difficulties similar to those encountered by other bodies.

Third, the UN system was not designed to address problems of communal conflict, but instead the very different challenge of the excessively well-organized and aggressive state exemplified by Nazi Germany. However, this does not in principle make it impossible to address such problems effectively: the UN's history is replete with innovations. The UN has in fact spent a great deal of its existence dealing with this very issue, including in Kashmir, in the Israel-Palestine conflict, and in Cyprus. It has accumulated a great deal of experience in such conflicts. It has been more effective in limiting their spread than in actually resolving them.

Fourth, the performance of the UN in tackling such conflicts suggests that it does not trump individual states and alliances and has some institutional defects:

1. The collective character of UN decision-making is not necessarily appropriate to the management of complex and fast-moving situations. States differ in their views on, and interests in, specific conflicts, and may vote for all kinds of resolutions, for a variety of reasons, in ignorance or indifference. While decisions for specific immediate action may be possible, especially if it is of an essentially impartial or humanitarian character, it is more difficult to get agreement on long-term goals and strategy.

2. States providing personnel for multilateral peacekeeping in such conflicts may not always have sufficient interest, determination, and local knowledge to take risks, accept sacrifices, and stay involved in dangerous and expensive operations over the long term. National contingents may reflect diverging policies and prac-

tices, and there may even be ethnic tensions within and between them, hampering efficiency. For such reasons, UN forces are often seen as ineffectual compared to those of determined local parties.

3. The UN's Charter and past practices drive it to respond to crises in one of two basic ways: either by taking sides in a Chapter VII enforcement operation, or by resorting to its more normal modes of operation—impartiality, cease-fires, mediation, and peacekeeping. Yet complex communal conflicts, as in Yugoslavia, Somalia, Angola, and Rwanda, may require elements of both approaches: for example, the simultaneous use of sanctions against Serbia and maintenance of a supposedly impartial peacekeeping operation in various parts of the former Yugoslavia. The combination of the two, and especially the transfer from peacekeeping to enforcement mode, has proved difficult.

4. Whereas the UN is bound by its Charter and other principles, including the non-acquisition of territory by force, the settlement of communal conflicts sometimes involves deals between parties that, in greater or lesser degree, conflict with some of those principles.

5. The UN lacks a strong tradition of analysis and debate, reinforcing the difficulty of addressing such problems.

Fifth, as compared to regional organizations and individual states, the UN does have some significant advantages in addressing conflicts with a communal dimension:

1. Its reputation for impartiality, however tarnished, makes it a possible interlocutor and provider of services.

2. Notwithstanding such cases as Cyprus and Lebanon, a UN presence has some capacity to discourage competitive national interventions in a conflict and may have assisted that purpose in former Yugoslavia.

3. It has, in the Security Council, clearer and more effective decision-making machinery than that of many international bodies.

4. It can bring huge resources to bear.

5. There is only one UN, and it is often more acceptable to refer a problem to it than to a regional body.

Sixth, in several ongoing conflicts, and most strikingly in the former Yugoslavia, the UN has become involved in a historically novel response: maintaining a large presence—partly to support humanitarian assistance, and partly to assist the negotiating process—in the middle of a continuing war. Somalia, Angola, and Rwanda offer parallels. This radical departure from traditional peacekeeping is caused by the difficulty of getting lasting cease-fires in communal conflicts. In these conflicts, the UN has faced a cruel dilemma in the 1990s. If it takes little or no action, it risks being accused of ineffectiveness or of unjustifiable selectivity in choosing which problems to tackle. If it does get more deeply involved in military action, it risks falling prey to hostage-taking, accusations of colonial oppressiveness, and the imposition of an unbearable burden on contributing states. UN forces may sometimes be able to do little more than reduce the number of casualties, assist victims, help broker cease-fire accords (often local rather than general), and limit the likelihood of the conflict spreading to other states. To the extent that their presence is based on consent of the parties, they are perpetually vulnerable to pressure for their missions to be changed and their mandates modified. In the Balkans and elsewhere, UN forces end up in unheroic if still important roles. It is not surprising that there is much dissatisfaction with the UN's role in such ongoing conflicts and a belief that it must be possible to find better answers than those found so far.

Seventh, as the limits of the UN Security Council's capacity to provide effective overall direction of operations relating to communal conflicts are exposed, there is bound to be pressure on the UN to establish systems of delegated authority to individual states or regional bodies in the management of UN peacekeeping operations. To a modest extent, as much by drift as formal decision, and with many difficulties and denials along the route, this has begun to happen in several recent cases, not least the former Yugoslavia.

Eighth, partly because of its responsibilities in communal conflicts, the UN is in danger of severe overcommitment. The very universality of the organization makes it hard to refuse involvement, and the scope of problems in Yugoslavia and elsewhere led to a requirement for forces of substantial size. The various methods for limiting involvement—devising general criteria, encouraging regional action, and being prepared to cut losses when UN efforts fail—have not prevented an accretion of responsibilities. The main limit is a crude and unsatisfactory one: the reluctance of states to provide the money and the troops needed for operations. There is a widespread perception that the former Yugoslavia had massive (if still inadequate) resources devoted to it and that the UN has not succeeded in maintaining a proper balance between the various crises that demand its attention.

Ninth, because of the pressures on the existing system of obtaining troops for UN action, it is natural that there are several proposals for UN rapid-reaction forces—whether composed of individual volunteers or of national contingents held on a genuinely standby basis for participation in UN operations. The main intention behind such proposals is to enable the UN to intervene quickly in developing crises. However, such proposals should not feed illusions that all the UN needs if it is to tackle all major crises is faster mobilization and more muscle. Nor should these proposals deflect attention from the fundamental requirement for the UN to find some means of being selective and decisive about its involvements.

Ironically, when a UN rapid reaction force was established as part of UNPROFOR in Bosnia-Herzegovina in June-August 1995, it assumed a form and purpose quite different from what had previously been advocated: it operated in one country only, and its main function was to assist a process that would enable the UN to get out of a costly conflict in which UN peacekeepers had been engaged for too long. This was very different from the function of rapid engagement in new and incipient crises envisaged by proponents of the standby concept.

Tenth, the need for the UN to be selective about its commitments reinforces the pressures for regional powers to handle problems of communal conflict more or less independently of the UN, whether acting unilaterally or through regional organizations. There may even be a revival of certain notions of "spheres of influence"—always a contested concept in international relations.

Eleventh, there remains the question of whether ethnic and communal conflict could be the undoing of the UN. The UN's record in such conflicts, including in Rwanda and the former Yugoslavia, is easy to criticize. Its combination of denunciatory resolutions and ineffective actions is reminiscent of the conduct of democracies before the outbreak of World War II. Its reputation could crash like that of the League of Nations. It has been perennially faced with the unenviable choice between continuing a presence perceived as ineffectual and staging a withdrawal perceived as humiliating. Yet the UN has proved to be a more robust organization than the League, with an astonishing capacity to survive setbacks, including in its management of communal conflict. It has begun to develop some capacity for careful examination of its own modes of action. It deserves continued support, not just because of the sheer difficulty of the problems of communal conflict, but also because it has achieved some results and may yet achieve more.

In Yugoslavia the UN was the victim of inflated expectations that the organization itself may have helped to encourage. Its performance was far below what many had expected after the rhetoric of new world orders and agendas for peace. The UN peacekeeping force should not have been called a protection force. Yet there were some solid achievements. The UN's assistance of humanitarian relief work saved countless lives. Its legitimation of the use of armed force, especially in defense of "safe areas," did in the end help to lay the foundations for the peace settlement, imperfect as it certainly is, concluded at Dayton. The UN's spokesmen have sometimes made too little of their real achievements and their key role in establishing conditions for Dayton.

In the matter of communal conflict, as more generally, the UN needs to avoid creating false expectations of a new era of collective security. If the summoning of distant brigades by the UN is perceived as the rule rather than the exception—and if the states involved in running such operations do not have a common strategic appreciation and a serious commitment to the operations—the UN is not likely to be effective in addressing communal conflict. There are rare occasions when, to put out a fire in Utah, it is necessary to go to Oklahoma for the fire engine. However, this cannot become routine, and when it does happen, it may sometimes involve letting the Oklahoma fire chief take temporary charge. The UN can play a role in the management of conflicts with a communal dimension, but it does not have a monopoly in this any more than in other security crises.

Notes

1. Jan Christian Smuts, *The League of Nations: A Practical Suggestion* (London, 1918), 25.

2. Part of the eleventh of the Fourteen Points in President Wilson's address to the two Houses of Congress, Washington, 8 January 1918. *Foreign Relations of the United States,* 1918, Supplement 1, *The World War,* vol. 1, p. 15. The statement was quoted by E. H. Carr in the interesting chapter "The Crisis of Self-Determination" in his *Conditions of Peace* (London, 1942), 41–42.

3. Cited in Robert D. Schulzinger, *American Diplomacy in the Twentieth Century* (New York, 1984), 121.

4. See esp. Benedict Anderson, *Imagined Communities: Reflections on the Origin and Spread of Nationalism* (London, 1983).

5. Dr. Danilo Türk, Permanent Representative of Slovenia to the UN, Security Council Official Record, 3492d meeting, 19 January 1995, 7–8.

6. Alfred Cobban, *The Nation State and National Self-Determination,* rev. ed. (London, 1969), 108.

7. Apart from other works cited in this text, in the United Kingdom this tra-

dition includes E. H. Carr's *Nationalism and After* (London, 1945); Cobban, *Nation State*; Elie Kedourie, *Nationalism in Asia and Africa* (London, 1971); and Hugh Seton-Watson, *Nations and States: An Enquiry into the Origins of Nations and the Politics of Nationalism* (London, 1977).

8. See esp. R. W. Seton-Watson, *The Southern Slav Question and the Habsburg Monarchy* (London, 1911), 46–47. This book carries the hopeful printed inscription: "To that Austrian Statesman who shall possess the genius and the courage necessary to solve the Southern Slav question, this book is respectfully dedicated." In the copy in the Bodleian Library, Oxford, a reader has handwritten here: "Marshall Tito." Alas!

9. See, e.g., Daniel Patrick Moynihan, *Pandaemonium: Ethnicity in International Politics* (Oxford, 1993); and Walker Connor's collected articles from several decades in his *Ethnonationalism: The Quest for Understanding* (Princeton, N.J., 1994).

10. Hans J. Morgenthau, *Politics among Nations*, 4th ed. (New York, 1967), 97–158: this is part 3, "National Power." See also his discussion of nationalism on pp. 321–24. The equivalent passages in the 6th ed. are at pp. 117–83 and 349–52.

11. Louis Henkin, *How Nations Behave: Law and Foreign Policy*, 2d ed. (New York, 1979), 1n.

12. Boutros Boutros-Ghali, *An Agenda for Peace: Preventive Diplomacy, Peacemaking, and Peace-keeping* (New York, 1992), para. 11.

13. Boutros-Ghali, statement in opening a seminar on ethnic conflict at National Defense University, Washington D.C., 8 November 1993, UN doc. SG/SM/5152 (New York, 1993), 3, 5.

14. Ibid., 5.

15. Cited in Owen Harries, "`The Collapse of 'The West,'"*Foreign Affairs* 72, no. 4 (September/October 1993): 49.

16. Quoted in Andrew Rosenthal, "Bush Urges UN to Back Force to Get Aid to Bosnia," *New York Times*, 7 August 1992, 1, 8; cited in a chapter by Jack Snyder that is severely critical of the "ancient hatred" view, "Nationalism and the Crisis of the Post-Soviet State," in *Ethnic Conflict and International Security*, ed. Michael E. Brown (Princeton, N.J., 1993), 79.

17. Warren Christopher, "New Steps toward Conflict Resolution in the Former Yugoslavia," opening statement at a news conference, Washington, D.C., 10 February 1993; published in *U.S. Department of State Dispatch* 4, no. 7 (15 February 1993): 81.

18. For a fine exposition of this perspective, see Susan L. Woodward, *Balkan Tragedy: Chaos and Dissolution after the Cold War* (Washington, D.C., 1995).

19. For a critical evaluation of the European Community and U.S. record on self-determination with respect to the former Yugoslavia, and of the work of the Badinter Commission, see Kamal S. Shehadi, *Ethnic Self-Determination and the Break-up of States*, Adelphi Paper 283 (London, December 1993), 28–31.

20. For an account of such efforts, see esp. a paper by Professor Valery Tishkov, who was in charge of the nationalities issues in the Yeltsin government from February through October 1992 as chairman of the State Committee for Nationalities Policy, "The Burden of the Past: Experiences with Ethnic Mediation

and Governance in the Former Soviet Union," *Ethnic Conflict and International Security,* ed. Anthony McDermott (Oslo, 1994), 70–83.

21. Boutros-Ghali, statement at seminar on ethnic conflict, Washington D.C., 8 November 1993, 3.

22. For a discussion of economic and legal pressures by outsiders to help mediate ethnic tensions within states, see Jenonne Walker, "International Mediation of Ethnic Conflicts," in *Ethnic Conflict,* ed. Brown, 165–80.

23. For a succinct account of the UN secretary-general's efforts over Cyprus, see Thomas M. Franck and Georg Nolte, "The Good Offices Function of the UN Secretary-General," in *United Nations, Divided World: The UN's Roles in International Relations,* 2d ed., ed. Adam Roberts and Benedict Kingsbury (Oxford, 1993), 155–57. They also refer to the difficulties encountered in the Middle East (163–64) and the former Yugoslavia (169–72).

24. For a useful general survey, see John Coakley, ed., *The Territorial Management of Ethnic Conflict* (London, 1993). Cases considered include Belgium, Canada, Czechoslovakia, Pakistan, the former Soviet Union, Sri Lanka, and Tanzania.

25. Avi Shlaim, *The Politics of Partition: King Abdullah, the Zionists, and Palestine, 1921–1951* (Oxford, 1990), 101. See also the map of the UN Partition Plan, 102.

26. These conclusions are echoed in IISS, *Strategic Survey 1993–1994* (London, May 1994), 99. It describes the complex ethnic patchwork proposal for Bosnia, painstakingly constructed in early 1993 by the UN mediators, as "a piece of laboured artificiality, a construct imposed from the outside."

27. These points are all made in John Chipman, "Managing the Politics of Parochialism," in *Ethnic Conflict,* ed. Brown, esp. 261. The chapter has a notably *de haut en bas* managerial tone, opening (237) with a reference to "overindulgence in the domestic and international politics of parochialism."

28. The view expressed in C. A. Macartney et al., *Survey of International Affairs 1925,* vol. 2 (London, 1928), 258.

29. The exception that proved the rule was DOMREP, the Mission of Representative of the Secretary-General in the Dominican Republic, 1965–1966. It consisted of two persons, or at a generous count four.

30. Many of the above points can be found in Boutros Boutros-Ghali, *Supplement to An Agenda for Peace,* UN doc. A/50/60 of 3 January 1995, e.g., paras. 12, 13.

31. At 31 December 1994, UNPROFOR had 39,789 military and civilian police personnel, plus over 4,000 civilian personnel. It had suffered 131 fatalities since it had commenced operations in March 1992. Figures from UN Department of Public Information, New York, January 1995.

32. From 25 September 1991 to 31 December 1994 there were eighty-one UN Security Council resolutions on the former Yugoslavia. Some, however, dealt with separate matters (e.g., admission of new members and establishment of the War Crimes Tribunal) and were not directly part of the mandate of UN peacekeeping forces.

33. SC Res. 981 of 31 March 1995, establishing UNCRO in Croatia and defining its mandate in very broad terms, which left detail to be added in further dif-

ficult negotiations; SC Res. 982 of 31 March 1995, extending UNPROFOR's mandate in Bosnia and Herzegovina and deciding that "all previous resolutions relating to UNPROFOR shall continue to apply"; and SC Res. 983 of 31 March 1995, renaming UNPROFOR within Macedonia as UNPREDEP and reaffirming its mandate.

34. SC Res. 743 of 21 February 1992, establishing UNPROFOR.

35. Franjo Tudjman wrote to Boutros Boutros-Ghali on 12 January 1995 informing him "that the UNPROFOR mandate is hereby terminated in Croatia effective March 31, 1995." Copy on file with author. As noted above, on 31 March 1995 a revised mandate for the renamed UN force, UNCRO, was approved by the Security Council. It had been the subject of prolonged and difficult negotiation, in which the U.S. government played the lead role.

36. The figures refer to the entire period from the start of the humanitarian airlift on 30 June 1992 up to its end on 5 January 1996. Source: communication to author from UNHCR, Geneva, 12 February 1996.

37. For general discussions, see Gerald B. Helman and Steven R. Ratner, "Saving Failed States," *Foreign Policy*, no. 89 (Winter 1992–93): 3–20; and Peter Lyon, "The Rise and Fall and Possible Revival of International Trusteeship," *Journal of Commonwealth and Comparative Politics*, no. 31 (March 1993): 96–110.

38. Boutros-Ghali, *Supplement to An Agenda for Peace*, para. 13.

39. Adam Roberts, *Nations in Arms: The Theory and Practice of Territorial Defence* (London, 1976), 217. See also p. 136. When a Serbo-Croat edition of the book was proposed, these were among the passages that Yugoslav colleagues indicated would have to be cut. I was not able to agree to these cuts, and the project never went ahead.

40. Letter from Lord Carrington, chairman of the Conference on Yugoslavia, writing from London to Hans van den Broek, minister of foreign affairs of the Netherlands (at that time president of the European Community Council of Ministers), 2 December 1991. On 10 December 1991, UN Secretary-General Javier Pérez de Cuéllar wrote in similar vein to Hans van den Broek. Remarkably, it was Hans-Dietrich Genscher, vice-chancellor and minister for foreign affairs of the Federal Republic of Germany, who responded, in a short letter to Pérez de Cuéllar of 13 December. Pérez de Cuéllar, in a letter of 14 December, sent a strong and detailed response reiterating that "early selective recognitions could result in a widening of the present conflict." Copies on file with author.

41. Boutros-Ghali, *Agenda for Peace*, paras. 11, 16, 27, 60–65.

42. Statement by the president of the Security Council, UN doc. S/PRST/1994/22, 3 May 1994.

43. *The Clinton Administration's Policy on Reforming Multilateral Peace Operations*, U.S. Department of State Publication 10161 (Washington, D.C., 1994). This document was unveiled on 5 May 1994. This and the UN Security Council presidential statement mentioned in the preceding note are briefly summarized and discussed in Adam Roberts, "The Crisis in UN Peacekeeping," *Survival* 36, no. 3 (Autumn 1994): 108–9.

44. Mats Berdal, *Whither UN Peacekeeping?* Adelphi Paper 281 (London, October 1993), 74.

45. Overall, the Senate draft report proposed to reduce U.S. spending on international affairs from about $21 billion a year to about $17.5 billion. Peacekeeping was one of the major targets for such cuts. Eric Pianin and Thomas W. Lippman, "Republicans Float Proposal to Slash Foreign Spending," *International Herald Tribune*, 17 February 1995, 2, Paris edition.

Part II

Preventing Deadly Conflict

3

Preventive Action and Conflict Resolution

Gareth Evans

It might have been possible, during the years of the Cold War, to dismiss as foolish idealism the idea that the international community might work together to prevent disputes from becoming violent. For more than four decades, the strategic and ideological rivalry of two nuclear-armed camps permeated all aspects of international life and dominated all other issues of global management. In such an environment, the effective practice of cooperative, peace-oriented multilateral and regional diplomacy was made ineffective—and, to be fair, also often unnecessary—by the fierce reality of global strategic competition between dominant superpowers.

The end of the Cold War, however, has shifted many aspirations out of the realm of the unattainable or theoretical into that of the merely ambitious or difficult. Preventive action is one such aspiration. Disputes themselves will continue to arise, of course, and there is already evidence that they will do so with greater frequency and in more complex formulations, as the recent rapid growth of intrastate disputes suggests. But in addressing these disputes, there can be little doubt that the least complex, the most humane, and the most cost-effective path for the international community to take is preventive action—and *early* preventive action. The challenge is to translate that general precept into practical strategy.

The Scope of Preventive Action

Preventive action combines strategies of maintaining peace with those of building peace. "Peace maintenance" strategies are those designed to resolve, or at least contain, particular disputes (and some kinds of emerging threats) and prevent them from escalating into armed conflict. They include preventive deployment—the use of military resources for containment purposes—and also embrace a variety of strategies, best described collectively as preventive diplomacy, that rely on diplomatic and similar methods rather than military ones. Included here is the full range of "peaceful means" described in Article 33 of the UN Charter, that is, "negotiation, enquiry, mediation, conciliation, arbitration, judicial settlement, resort to regional agencies or arrangements, or other peaceful means of their own choice," all of which are described in detail in the *Handbook on the Peaceful Settlement of Disputes between States,* prepared by the UN Secretariat and welcomed unanimously by the General Assembly in 1991. There is particular scope for the further development of preventive diplomacy—particularly in the UN's mediation role—and it is this subject to which I devote most attention in this chapter.

"Peacebuilding" strategies are those that seek to address the underlying causes of disputes, conflicts, and crises: to ensure either that problems do not arise in the first place, or that if they do arise, they will not recur. In his 1992 report, *An Agenda for Peace,* the secretary-general focused his attention on nonrecurrence—what he described as "post-conflict peacebuilding." But peacebuilding has a strongly preventive character as well. If the foundations are properly laid by efforts, among other things, to create fair systems of rules and fair ways of distributing scarce resources and to meet basic human needs for survival and dignity, then the chances are that many potential problems, whether international or internal, will remain manageable.

At the heart of the notion of peacebuilding is the idea of meeting needs: for security and order, for a reasonable standard of living, and for recognition of identity and worth. Conflict, whether cross-border or in-country, typically begins, and continues, when important interests or needs of one or more parties are frustrated or threatened or remain unfulfilled. Preventive diplomacy and peacemaking are built around this same approach, of identifying needs and interests and seeking as far as possible to accommodate and reconcile them. But whereas the focus there is on resolving a particular dispute or conflict, here it is more general: on creating the conditions that will ensure that problems needing such attention will not occur, or recur, at all.

To a large extent, peacebuilding involves doing exactly the sorts of things that a civilized international community, and the states that make it up, should be doing anyway—that is, putting in place effective international rules systems, dispute-resolution mechanisms, and cooperative arrangements; meeting basic economic, social, cultural, and humanitarian needs; and rebuilding societies that have been shattered by war or other major crises. But too often in the past these things, while seen as worthwhile in their own right, have not been identified clearly enough as absolutely integral to the achievement and maintenance of peace and security, and as a result they have been given less than the attention they deserve. If we are to achieve just and durable peace in the post–Cold War world, it is crucially important that the international community not continue to make that mistake. The secretary-general made the necessary connection in *An Agenda for Peace,* but his message should be given even wider application by applying it to pre-conflict as well as post-conflict situations.

The Concept of Preventive Diplomacy

As signatories to the UN Charter, member states are under an obligation—made express in Chapter VI, Article 33 of the Charter—to resolve their disputes peacefully. The Charter, however, gives members a choice of the dispute-resolution method that they will employ. When it deems necessary, the Security Council may also call upon members to resolve their disputes peacefully and even recommend a particular method that they should use. In practice, however, peaceful methods of dispute resolution can be effective only if the parties consent to participate in this process. For this reason, approaches that allow the parties more control over the process, and that seek to address their interests, are more likely to be attractive to disputants and more likely to be used. This explains why methods such as negotiation and mediation have been used with much greater frequency than those such as arbitration and judicial settlement.

The difficulty of resolving disputes peacefully, however, suggests that disputing parties may sometimes need assistance from a third party in order to comply with their obligations under Chapter VI of the Charter. Increasingly, the international community is looking to the UN to assist in this regard. My primary focus here is on outlining ideas for strengthening the preventive diplomacy activities of the UN, both at its headquarters and in the field; a central theme is that preventive action, as early as possible, is the least complex, the most humane, and the most cost-effective path for the international community to take in resolving disputes.

There are two quite different approaches to preventive diplomacy, which might be called "late prevention" and "early prevention," respectively. The difference is not between tardiness and timeliness but rather between different time perspectives and different goals. The distinction has considerable implications for how preventive diplomacy is implemented.

Under a late-prevention approach, the UN would monitor situations around the globe, doing little until it is fairly certain that a particular dispute was about to cross the threshold into armed conflict. If and when this early warning system indicated a problem, the UN would become involved in an attempt to persuade the parties to desist. By this stage, the Security Council would be likely to be the best UN organ for carrying out preventive action, since significant pressure or leverage may well be needed to modify behavior. Preventive action that the council might employ could include fact-finding missions (in accordance with the 1991 Declaration of Fact-Finding), preventive deployment, recommendation of a specific dispute settlement procedure (Article 36), or a resolution calling upon the parties to desist and warning them of further council action.

Late-prevention action relies heavily on adequate intelligence information, such as the monitoring of troop movements or refugee flows, to indicate that a situation is about to move to a new level of violence. Proposals for obtaining this information have included making arrangements with member states, establishing a UN satellite, converting UN Information Centers into political offices, and improving procedures for alerting the Security Council. Had the UN had an effective system of late prevention in place before Iraqi troops crossed the border into Kuwait, it would likely have been able to provide better information, and therefore early warning, that Iraqi troops were massing on that border: more such information might have allowed the council to meet and take action before, rather than after, the invasion.

The last minute, however, will rarely be the optimal time to intervene in a dispute: in fact, the point at which a dispute is just about to erupt into conflict is close to being the most difficult at which the international community could seek to intervene. The dynamics of escalation are usually so strong at this point that it is very difficult to stop or reverse the situation.

A more promising approach to preventive diplomacy is one that involves the UN's having the ability to offer, in effect, an early dispute resolution service to its members to assist them in complying with their obligations under Chapter VI of the Charter. The goal would be to provide skilled third-party assistance through good offices and mediation as early as possible in a dispute, when the opportunity for dispute resolution is most ripe.

International disputes rarely develop into full-blown conflicts overnight, at least for those who understand the situation and have been following its development. In many of the situations that have become the object of recent UN efforts, the presence of a serious dispute was well known to the international community far in advance, even if in some cases, such as the dispute over Falklands/Malvinas Islands, few were paying attention. In the case of the Persian Gulf crisis, knowledge of the existence of a border dispute between Iraq and Kuwait was long-standing. It was also well known for months ahead of time, from rhetoric emanating from Baghdad, that Iraq was becoming increasingly aggrieved and belligerent. Of course, in this case, it is possible that preventive diplomacy of either the early- or late-prevention type would not have been effective, since the actors might not have cooperated. We will never know, since neither type was seriously mobilized before Kuwait was invaded.

Late-prevention and early-prevention approaches are not mutually exclusive, but giving priority to early prevention has a number of significant advantages, namely:

- *Motivation.* Parties are more likely to accept assistance while issues are still specific and before grievances accumulate and the desire for retribution becomes paramount.

- *Effectiveness.* Prevention is more likely to be effective before issues have generalized, issues and parties have multiplied, positions have hardened, and actions have turned into ever more hostile reverberating echoes of threat and counterthreat.

- *Completeness.* Since the goal of early prevention is resolution rather than containment, it is more likely that the dispute will be resolved and will not recur.

- *Cost.* Early prevention is likely to be more cost-effective in both financial and human terms.

Preventive Diplomacy in Action

Recent examples of preventive diplomacy at work in resolving traditional interstate disputes include a long series of UN secretary-general's special envoy fact-finding and good-office missions, such as that involving Cyrus Vance in the dispute between Greece and the former Yugoslav Republic of Macedonia (FYROM). Efforts to resolve territorial claims to the Spratly and Paracel Islands in the South China Sea have involved both "first track" (i.e., involving governments directly) preventive diplomacy, in the lead-up to, and at, the Brunei (1995) meeting of the ASEAN Regional Forum, where China and the ASEAN claimants stepped back from an increasingly tense situation; and "second track" (i.e., more broadly based) efforts, with the Indonesian-sponsored workshops since 1990. The Beagle Channel dispute involving Argentina and Chile was successfully mediated by the Vatican, while Libya and Chad agreed to submit their dispute over the Aouzou

Strip to the International Court of Justice (ICJ) for adjudication.

Preventive diplomacy applied to intrastate disputes include the recent efforts in Burundi by the United Nations, the Organization of African Unity (OAU), and African leaders in their personal capacity to find a formula to keep an extremely volatile situation from exploding there. The Organization on Security and Cooperation in Europe (OSCE) High Commissioner on National Minorities has likewise been active in addressing European minorities' issues in Albania, Latvia, FYROM, Hungary, and Slovakia. FYROM, in particular, stands out as an example of how skilled negotiations can defuse tensions and bring about compromises and agreements in an environment widely considered intractable.

Preventive diplomacy has also proved useful in avoiding some of the potential disputes associated with the breakup of states. These hybrid inter- and intrastate cases include the Czech and Slovak Republics; the future of the Crimea in Russia and Ukraine; Ethiopia and Eritrea; and the role of the OSCE in defusing some post-breakup issues (e.g., the rights of Russian-language speakers in Estonia). The agreement between the Czech and Slovak Republics over ownership of territory and resources so soon after the collapse of the Soviet empire in Eastern Europe was illustrative of what could be achieved in resolving the many disputes in that region that were a legacy of Soviet rule. The Carter Center's pivotal role in the resolution of the Ethiopia-Eritrea conflict shows the important role that can be played by a nongovernmental organization in preventive diplomacy.

Within this framework it is useful to assess two recent crises to develop lessons about the applicability and success rate of preventive diplomacy. Both the following examples are drawn from post–Cold War experience. Both are examples of interstate disputes, but while the first involves a traditional form of dispute—a border dispute that degenerated into war— the second involves a dispute about the internal policies of a state that, by reference to internationally agreed standards, were judged to have threatening repercussions for the security of the region and the globe and that were negotiated away without recourse to violence.

Iraq's Invasion of Kuwait: A Failure to Use Preventive Diplomacy

The Problem

There had been a long-standing but mostly dormant border dispute between Iraq and Kuwait. Iraq's failure to gain access to the Persian Gulf through its eight-year war with Iran revived an interest in past claims to Kuwait's Warba and Bubiyan Islands in the Gulf. Iraq also claimed that Kuwait had been pumping oil from the Iraqi side of their shared Rumaila oil field. Iraq's war with Iran had been financed by loans from Saudi Arabia and the Gulf States, and some of these states were prepared to forgive the loans in return for the bulwark that Iraq provided against Iran. Kuwait, however, refused to forgive its Iraqi war debt. Short of cash, the Iraqis faced a declining oil market—where Kuwait was helping keep the price down by overproducing on its OPEC quota.

The Response

In the months leading up to the conflict, Iraqi demands escalated. Both sides became less able to back down. Iraq feared loss of face, and Kuwait did not want to give in to intimidation. In modern times no Arab state had invaded another; this caused Kuwait and the international community to discount the possibility of an Iraqi invasion, and this misreading meant a failure to match Iraqi threats with appropriate countersignals. In late July 1990, Kuwait suggested to the UN secretary-general that an Arab committee examine the Iraq-Kuwait border issue, and other Arab states stepped up diplomatic activity for a peaceful solution. These efforts—and a UK suggestion, to which other permanent members were unreceptive, that the border issue be looked at by the Security Council—were overtaken by events when Iraq invaded Kuwait on 2 August. The Arab League condemned the invasion (in a split decision) but rejected Kuwait's call to have its defense pact collective self-defense activated. The international community—including the Arab states, the United States, France, and the former Soviet Union—engaged in various peacemaking efforts over the next six months. Iraq rejected these overtures, and the UN Security Council eventually resorted to peace enforcement, with coalition forces beginning military operations on 16 January 1991.

The Lessons

Although there were long-standing disagreements between Iraq and Kuwait, there were no real attempts to resolve them. Failure to resolve this issue earlier led to later problems.

In the months leading up to the conflict, there were few concerted efforts to address the specific issues in dispute—the oil pricing issue, the Rumaila oil field issue, the Warba and Bubiyan Islands issue, and the debt issue—before tensions escalated. Underlying all of these issues was the

68

major Iraqi concern about trying to keep its economy from worsening in the aftermath of the ruinous Iran-Iraq war. In the absence of another solution, invading Kuwait appeared to be an attractive answer to Iraq's financial problems. Early attention to more specific issues might have kept the dispute from escalating to this stage.

From July 1990, the international community misread Iraqi intentions because they did not take Iraq's threats seriously: threats should be considered to be an important early warning indicator.

Mixed and confusing messages from the international community aggravated the situation: clear messages are needed in response to threats.

Member states with satellite reconnaissance failed to provide the UN with early warning: members possessing relevant information should draw it to the attention of the Security Council.

Neither the council nor the secretary-general proved able to respond to mounting evidence that a dispute was rapidly escalating: member states should consider exercising Article 35 more readily, and the secretary-general should feel less inhibited in using Article 99 to bring escalating disputes to the attention of the council.

Nuclear Weapons Development on the Korean Peninsula: Early and Successful Preventive Diplomacy

The Problem

Concern about the Democratic People's Republic of Korea (DPRK) nuclear activities goes back to the early 1980s. The DPRK acceded to the nuclear Nonproliferation Treaty (NPT) in 1985, in the face of concerted international pressure, and in early 1992 signed the required safeguards agreement with the International Atomic Energy Agency (IAEA). The DPRK might have expected these steps to bring some of the political and economic benefits it needed to address its growing isolation and deteriorating economic situation. Instead, when IAEA safeguards inspections later that year revealed evidence that the DPRK had secretly produced enough plutonium for a nuclear weapon—in violation of its obligations to declare all plutonium production to the IAEA—Pyongyang faced mounting international condemnation and demands that it declare the full extent of its nuclear program. Its position hardened; it refused IAEA demands for access to two undeclared sites at its Yongbyon nuclear complex and in March 1993 announced its intention to withdraw from the NPT. By about June, there was a real risk of a serious escalation of the dispute, triggered by the possible imposition of UNSC economic sanctions. This could have led quickly to hostilities—military forces on both sides of the peninsula were on a heightened state of alert throughout most of 1993. The issue had the potential to dramatically alter strategic relationships in North Asia and threatened the emergence of a regional nuclear arms race.

The Response

International responses to the DPRK's actions through 1992 and early 1993 centered on demands that it act in accordance with its treaty obligations under the NPT and its safeguards agreement with the IAEA. The Security Council resolution of May 1993 foreshadowed further action in the absence of DPRK compliance, and preliminary discussion began among the five permanent members of the Security Council on options for a sanctions package. At the same time, the major players—including particularly the United States and China—ensured that avenues for dialogue with the DPRK were not closed. Crisis talks between the United States and the DPRK in June 1993 led to agreement on terms for further negotiations, involving conditional security assurances from the United States and agreement by the DPRK to "suspend" its withdrawal from the NPT and to accept IAEA safeguards. The subsequent U.S.-DPRK dialogue, which was supported and encouraged by other regional players, including China, the Republic of Korea (ROK), Japan, and Australia, enabled the DPRK to outline what it expected in return for meeting international demands that it abandon its weapons-related nuclear activities and remain within the framework of the NPT.

Trust in the negotiating process was assisted by a more open and transparent approach to the negotiations, in which the full range of reciprocal undertakings for both sides was dealt with as a package. Former U.S. president Jimmy Carter assisted at a crucial stage in the negotiations by acting as a mediator in talks with then DPRK president Kim Il-Sung. The bilateral negotiations led ultimately to the conclusion of the agreed framework, under which the DPRK has agreed to abandon its sensitive nuclear activities and comply fully with its NPT and IAEA safeguards obligations in return for political recognition, security assurances, and a package of energy and economic assistance.

The Lessons

The ability of IAEA safeguards verification measures to detect treaty noncompliance was critical in enabling early international action.

Reference to international standards provided the justification and the means for international leverage over the internal policies of a state.

The preparedness of the international community to take firm action against treaty noncompliance was critical in establishing the relevance of treaty norms and the political and legal authority for later preventive action. It also protected the credibility of treaty arrangements.

Concerted action at a multilateral level, through IAEA Board and UN Security Council resolutions, meant the DPRK was getting clear signals about what was expected of it.

Avenues for dialogue were not closed off, despite gradually increasing multilateral pressure and DPRK brinkmanship. When talks resumed, it was important to ensure that the DPRK understood that its concerns would be seriously addressed and that it also fully appreciated the resolve of the international community.

Although the United States was the main player in the negotiations, it did not exclude the other key parties—China, the ROK, and Japan. So they also had confidence in the process and ensured that the DPRK was getting generally consistent messages. It was also important that the wider multilateral machinery, particularly the IAEA, was acting in a manner supportive of the negotiating process.

An open and transparent approach to negotiations—"laying the cards on the table"—was critical to overcoming suspicion between the parties. The "package" approach gave the DPRK confidence that its wider political, economic, and security concerns would be addressed and persuaded it of the benefits of remaining engaged.

A legitimate and useful role can be played by outside mediators in resolving negotiating deadlocks and building trust between the parties.

It can be important to separate the main elements of a dispute from other problems that, while important in themselves, might serve only to complicate resolution of the dispute at hand. Thus while the U.S.-DPRK-agreed framework provides a basis for dealing with the DPRK nuclear issue and meets some of the DPRK's political and economic needs, it does not attempt to deal in a central way with problems like DPRK missile exports, its human rights record, or broader problems of security on the peninsula.

Continued international support for the terms of the agreed framework, both political and practical, has been essential to its sustainability. Australia's early commitment of a $5 million contribution for energy assistance to the DPRK through the Korean Peninsula Energy Development Organization (KEDO), though small in absolute terms, was important in generating this wider international support for KEDO and the agreed framework.

Players and Methods in Preventive Diplomacy

Preventive diplomacy can operate on a number of different tracks, with the UN, regional organizations, and nongovernmental organizations (NGOs) all playing a role. Indeed, it is likely to remain well beyond the capacity of the UN to identify and monitor, let alone manage, all the disputes that might lead to international friction or otherwise endanger international peace and security.

The United Nations

There is no doubt that, in a great many cases, disputes both can and should be satisfactorily managed and resolved without recourse to the UN, through cooperation at the bilateral, subregional, or regional level. Local solutions offer such advantages as familiarity of all parties with the parties to the dispute and their interests and sensitivities. Bringing differences before a wider body, and ultimately before the UN membership, can itself be an escalation of a dispute that lessens the margin for its resolution. So, in the area of prevention, the UN's role would often be complementary to more localized efforts and in many cases would be secondary to them. All that said, there are still many problems where a preventive response by the UN would be warranted—either because the governments or parties concerned call for it, or because the magnitude of the problem and the absence of any other effective response cry out for it. There remains enormous scope for the UN to do better in assisting the resolution of disputes, both those in which it plays a primary role and those where it can assist in a secondary role through quietly providing expert assistance and experience.

In one sense, preventive diplomacy can be seen as a continuous behind-the-scenes feature of the UN system, as the secretary-general and his staff, as well as the diplomatic community, engage in preventive efforts in many different situations through conversations and consultations with a wide range of interlocutors. However, a more systematic and institutionalized approach, the outlines of which have gradually emerged in recent years, is needed to assist members in implementing their obligations under Chapter VI of the Charter.

The first significant, although still insufficient, attempt at setting up a preventive diplomacy mechanism in the UN Secretariat occurred in 1987 with the establishment of the Office of Research and the Collection of Information. This was established to meet a number of objectives, but among its various sections were two small geographic units, with a total of six professional staff, set up to collect and analyze information, to provide early warning, and to suggest options to the secretary-general.

A second boost for preventive diplomacy came in January 1992, when the Security Council met at the level of heads of state and government to consider how the UN could better meet the peace and security challenges of the post–Cold War world. At that meeting there were repeated calls for the United Nations to develop its role in preventive diplomacy, and the secretary-general was invited to offer his ideas about how this should be done. For the first time, the growing consensus that had been developing about preventive diplomacy—a consensus influenced by the lessons of the failure to use preventive diplomacy before Iraq's invasion of Kuwait—was being expressed at the highest levels.

Shortly after Boutros Boutros-Ghali became secretary-general in January 1992, he acted to initiate a widespread restructuring process intended, among other things, to enhance the secretariat's capacity to carry out preventive diplomacy and peacemaking, in particular through geographic divisions set up in the Department of Political Affairs (DPA). These new divisions have provided the basis for a more viable system, but resource shortages and systemic constraints have meant that these reforms are still less than adequate to the task. Even with these initial steps, and even though preventive diplomacy is beginning to be almost universally acknowledged as the most cost-effective approach available, it has remained a vastly underdeveloped cooperative security response. UN staff are only just beginning to be trained in dispute-resolution techniques; UN information-gathering procedures are cumbersome; there is little research assistance; there are inadequate computing and communication capabilities; and there is insufficient funding for travel to the hot spots where preventive diplomacy is most needed.

A promising development has been the recent decision taken at the Fiftieth General Assembly of the UN in December 1996 to double the financial resources of the DPA, although this has been offset by a reduction in the amount set aside for the Department of Peace-keeping Operations (DPKO). The move does show that the UN is seriously grappling with the challenge of preventive diplomacy, in moving to shift its focus from peacekeeping to prevention. However, financial resources are not sufficient in themselves. It is vitally important that the UN upgrade its capacity to the point where it can offer both an effective early warning system and a dispute-resolution service to its members, providing low-profile, skilled, third-party assistance through good offices, mediation, and the like.

Regional Organizations

Regional organizations have a special role to play in preventive diplomacy. Being close to the conflicts in question and with obvious interests in their resolution, they may in some circumstances be better placed to act than the UN. In *An Agenda for Peace* the UN secretary-general called for greater involvement of regional arrangements and agencies in the UN's peace-related activities, including preventive diplomacy, a call reinforced by the Security Council in January 1993. But neither the secretary-general nor the council has made any attempt to prescribe which arrangements or agencies should be so involved. Some of the regional organizations not part of the UN system already have a linkage with it, formal or informal, usually in relation to peace and security matters. A number of regional bodies have a standing invitation to participate in the General Assembly's work. One of the newest is the South Pacific Forum, which was admitted as a General Assembly observer after the beginning of the Forty-ninth General Assembly of the UN. Others, such as the Organization of African Unity (OAU), the Organization of American States (OAS), the Organization of the Islamic Conference (OIC), and the Arab League have worked closely with the Security Council on peace and security matters. All but the OAS have entered into framework agreements with the UN. These organizations have an express mandate to address and respond to security issues or, in the absence of such a mandate, have developed the necessary functions through practice or need.

But there are many existing regional arrangements and agencies with the potential to become involved in the UN's peace-related activities, including preventive diplomacy, that currently do not have any formal or informal links with the United Nations. In practice, most regional organizations embody agreements among geographically concentrated groups of states for cooperative action on issues of mutual interest (for example, the OAU, the OAS, and the Arab League). Others are brought together by shared experience only partly related, if at all, to geography (for example, the OIC). All are bound internally by perceived common interest. Yet each is different from the other in mandate, scope, and composition and in inclination and capacity to take on the functions envisaged under Chapter VIII, whether alone or in cooperation with the UN.

The UN Charter does not define the manner and extent to which regional organizations should develop their security role. Article 52 stipulates that "local disputes" are to be addressed in the first instance by regional organizations, if at all possible, but does not elaborate further on what matters are appropriate for regional action. It is for each regional organization to determine what the parameters of this role should be. In practice, this seems to mean that issues are appropriate for regional action when regional states deem them to be so. This might be because a threat or dispute has multilateral dimensions, with several states involved (for example, the South China Sea dispute) or with regional implications going beyond the immediate disputants (for example, in the case of Cambodia). In other circumstances, states may conclude that there is no longer scope or reason to pursue their local dispute by bilateral means and may wish to place the matter on the regional agenda.

There are relatively few documented cases of practical cooperation on the ground between the UN and regional organizations in preventive approaches, and there is no fixed practice as to whether the UN or a regional organization should take the lead in a dispute resolution. The most important point is that any cooperative arrangement between the UN and regional organizations must be sufficiently adaptable to meet each situation as it arises. In some cases, it may be best for the regional organization to take the lead and carry out preventive diplomacy with consultation and backup by the UN; in other cases, it may be more advantageous for the UN to carry out the function with consultation and backup from regional organizations. In still other instances, both parties acting together may provide the most powerful approach, underlining to protagonists the unanimity of the international community. Coordination of efforts is, of course, essential in order to avoid the diffusion of responsibility that can occur when both the UN and the regional organization think that the other should be handling a given situation. A good example of successful cooperation between the UN and regional players has been the DPRK nuclear-activity issues, where the U.S.-DPRK dialogue following the June 1993 crisis talks was supported and encouraged by regional players, including China, the ROK, Japan, and Australia.

Nongovernmental Organizations

Many of the quiet successes of preventive diplomacy have come from nongovernmental organizations. The Quakers have a long history of quiet mediation around the world. The Carter Center has played a helpful role in the resolution of the Ethiopia-Eritrea conflict and in easing the North Korean nuclear impasse. Another example may be found in the visits to Senegal and Zambia by South African business leaders to meet African National Congress (ANC) representatives organized in the late 1980s by the prominent white opposition figure Dr. Frederik van Zyl Slabbert. These meetings were an important prelude to the South African government's change of course on apartheid in 1990. In some cases, a single actor may have more influence than the international community as a whole. If preventive diplomacy is truly to succeed, it will be important for the international system to use all its resources toward this end. Close cooperation with the UN and relevant regional organizations is, however, very desirable in this situation.

NGOs play an important role in preventive diplomacy in a variety of ways. They are especially good at early warning of emerging threats or crises, including the outbreak of hostilities, famine, human rights abuses, refugee flows, and the like. Moreover, NGOs are often successful in their attempts to make such threats salient to an overstretched international community, as they have been, in particular, with successive crises on the African continent. As well, NGOs often help to promote problem solving and constructive dialogue between groups.

Multitrack diplomacy efforts also provide an important part of the spectrum of dispute resolution. A number of "second track" diplomacy efforts (between influential parties, not necessarily officials, from both sides of a dispute) are under way, sponsored by a variety of governments and unofficial bodies. Such efforts break down enemy image perceptions, open up channels of communication, and help all sides to think about new options for old problems. To the extent that such efforts target opinion leaders, they may build a momentum from below for later dispute-resolution efforts.

New Approaches to Skills Training for Diplomats

Traditionally, preventive diplomacy has relied on backroom rather than front-of-house performances: being able to move quietly between the parties, testing propositions whose premature disclosure would invite immediate rejection. But this is becoming even harder to achieve. The problem is that, not only does it become impossible for the better-known players to go anywhere or do anything without scrutiny and demand for comment, but also previously less well known actors get precipitated into the limelight. And excessive visibility can lead to slips by diplomats who are not media-battle-prepared: "no comment," for some people, is the hardest phrase in the language to utter.

The reverse is also true: there is a problem of *invisibility*. The problem with preventive diplomacy (and indeed any preventive action) is that it succeeds when things do not happen: if it works, nobody notices. In that regard, it transgresses the iron law of government, national and international, that everyone likes to be seen to be doing something. The notion that it might be worthwhile to allocate resources and effort at an early stage, before disputes and threats are particularly noticeable, as insurance premiums to avoid bigger payouts later tends to be foreign to the political psyche.

These constraints can be minimized in part through new approaches to skills training. Traditional diplomatic training has focused on reporting and representational skills and bilateral problem solving as issues arise or sensitivities are addressed with a particular country. The assumption was that diplomats on the ground would have reasonable freedom of action to proceed in implementing objectives set by home governments. Multilateral diplomacy meant negotiating the occasional treaty and playing word games with resolutions in annual sessions of the UN and the like, and not much else. There was no real training in handling the media, either defensively or proactively, as a useful diplomatic tool.

The context has changed dramatically, but it is not clear that skill training has been keeping up with it. Much more multilateral diplomatic activity is occurring, addressing a huge range of specific problems, not least in the context of the new dialogue forums, which provide new kinds of opportunities but also place new kinds of demands upon diplomats. There is much more central government control and direction of diplomatic activity, with specialized teams working on specialized tasks, as compared with the older greater reliance on generalists. There is more demand for negotiation, dispute and conflict resolution, and problem-solving skills of a kind that can, at least partially, be taught. Much more needs to be known about how to handle the media—both the traps and the opportunities.

In the same way, if early prevention is to be practiced effectively, it will be necessary to develop not only better early warning systems but also better appraisal and reaction skills. Improved intelligence of, for example, pre-conflict troop movements can be acquired through improved technology and organization. But at least as important as what we know is what we do about what we know—and getting this right requires improving the human skills of assessment, judgment, and communication.

Much of this applies to diplomats at the official level. But it is perhaps also a matter of skill training for ministers. Ministers are called on to be closely involved in, for example, the regional dialogue bodies that are now widely being formed; their personal skills can be crucial not only in promoting the interests of their governments but also in determining whether the regional dialogue forum itself survives and succeeds.

Discussions of preventive diplomacy tend to concentrate heavily on questions of process. But preventive diplomacy is only a means to an end, and it would be useful if we devoted more resources and analytical effort to organizing and documenting the experiences of the past and thinking about new kinds of solutions for new kinds of problems (e.g., in preventing conflict within states between ethnic, national, or religious groups, we need to think more about options for power sharing through proportional division of key offices, mutual veto rights, representational concessions by stronger parties, and the like). One of the tasks for those practicing preventive diplomacy should be the constant refining of this methodology through the systematic study of the factors that have evidently promoted or inhibited progress in dispute resolution. Adopting an analytical approach to past and present experience and evaluating how pitfalls might be avoided in the future could teach valuable lessons that would improve the practice of future dispute settlement.

Giving Higher Priority, and Better Resources, to Preventive Diplomacy

Political commitment and available resources are always likely to fall short of aspirations—and have certainly done so in the aftermath of what have been widely, if unfairly, seen as United Nations failures in Bosnia, Somalia, and Rwanda. The costs and complexities involved in seeking to resolve full-blown conflicts make it obvious that we should concentrate more effort on preventing conflicts than on trying to restore peace after the event.

There is scope for the UN to be much more engaged in coordinating available resources of a preventive character from around the world, thereby enhancing the quality of service available. Regional groupings and NGOs have expertise and skills that can be integrated into a system of worldwide preventive diplomacy. Better organization of all the available resources will strengthen linkages and assist in the promotion of preventive diplomacy as a key international habit rather than just another security response, thereby ensuring that a problem like the Iraq-Kuwait border dispute is tackled at the early stage of prevention.

Minimizing such problems of coordination could well be one of the more important benefits derived from the creation of regionally based, expertly staffed peace and security resource centers—regionally focused preventive diplomacy teams or units, staffed by senior professionals expert in dispute resolution and familiar with the disputes on which they work. Such units could contribute to dispute resolution in a number of different ways, acting as resource and referral sources, as well as providing direct services. Where disputes are uncomplicated, it may be a matter simply of tracking the progress of negotiation by the parties themselves. In other instances, the staff might offer its own services as an impartial third party that could facilitate the initial contacts between disputing parties, assist in beginning a dialogue, establish "talks about talks," or become involved in structuring or guiding talks.

Such an approach could be based on newer problem-solving methods of negotiation rather than on traditional negotiation strategies. The goal would be to reconcile the parties' differing interests through innovative solutions rather than through adversarial bargaining over positions. Using such an approach, the UN intermediaries could encourage and facilitate the discussion of the issues and interests that lie behind parties' positions, encourage and suggest the development of a range of innovative options, study and propose objective criteria or principles of fairness or precedent that might serve as a basis for settlement, package proposals to meet parties' concerns, and rally influential third parties as sources of support.

Through such a process, the aim of the preventive diplomacy team would be to carefully manage the mediation exercise, provide a neutral site, keep emotions under control, encourage acts of goodwill, and exclude audiences—recognizing always that mediation efforts can sometimes have a chilling effect on negotiations and that it is crucial that the parties retain full power over the negotiating process and its outcomes. Preventive diplomacy units could also assist parties in making full use of the UN system for resolving their disputes. In some instances, preventive-diplomacy teams might refer disputants to another third-party intermediary for assistance. They might, for example, assist the parties in approaching a regional organization or NGO that can help in resolving the dispute.

Such centers would represent a more formalized delivery of existing preventive-diplomacy services in the UN system, in the Middle East (as part of the Arms Control and Regional Security multilateral track), and in the Asia Pacific (as a possible exercise for the ASEAN Regional Forum). The idea is really just to be more organized and focused in the application of familiar preventive-diplomacy activity, with the same basic rules: be informal, low key, nonbinding, nonjudgmental, noncoercive, and confidential. One can have no illusions about the sensitivity of this sort of exercise for many countries, and it is not something that can be achieved overnight. But we should be able to do better than the extreme "ad hocery" that has hitherto characterized preventive-diplomacy efforts.

There can be no doubt about the financial benefit if such enterprises can succeed, at least partially, in preventing disputes from becoming conflicts. The cost of keeping one hundred preventive-diplomacy practitioners in the field for a year would be not much more than $20 million. Compare that with the current annual peacekeeping budget of around $3.7

billion—and the cost of the six-week Gulf War peace enforcement coalition of more than $70 billion!

The Concept of Preventive Deployment

Preventive deployment is a new concept for the UN, given prominence by the secretary-general's advocacy in *An Agenda for Peace* and by its application—for the first, and so far only, time—in the former Yugoslav Republic of Macedonia. The essence of this strategy is that it is a preventive military, rather than diplomatic, response involving, in the clearest case, the positioning of troops, military observers, and related personnel on one or both sides of a border between entities that are in dispute (or where there is an emerging threat of conflict), with the primary object of deterring the escalation of that situation into armed conflict. Associated objectives may be to calm communities in the area by monitoring law and order and general conditions and to render other forms of assistance to local authorities.

In the case of FYROM there was a concern (in the context of the deteriorating situation in the former Yugoslavia generally, and its own continuing dispute with Greece) that if the neighboring Kosovo area of Serbia were to erupt in a conflict between the Serbs and Albanian Muslims, FYROM—with a quarter of its own population Albanian—could be drawn rapidly into a conflict, with other powers possibly also becoming involved: a clear "emerging threat" situation. In December 1992 the Security Council authorized the deployment of a small force of seven hundred, plus military observers and civil police, to monitor FYROM's borders and report developments that could signify a threat to its territory; this force was augmented in July 1993 by three hundred troops. The forces deployed in FYROM were clearly too small on their own to handle any actual armed conflict that might erupt in the area. The "deterrent" here lay in the fact that the Security Council demonstrated its interest in the situation, all the relevant parties were under close international scrutiny, and there was at least an implication of willingness to take further action if there were any resort to violence.

How credible such a deterrent is will depend essentially on the weight that potential transgressors give to international opinion and their assessment of the likelihood in practice of a strong Security Council reaction. A rather clear deterrent would exist in an overtly "trip wire" deployment, that is, where a small number of military personnel are ranged along a line the crossing of which would mobilize a larger and more capable "strike" force held in reserve or out of theater, clearly armed with both Chapter VII enforcement powers and the capability and will to exercise them.

As already stated, the clearest preventive deployment situation involves a border between disputing entities. The clearest case of such a border, in turn, is an international one between sovereign states. However, the concept of preventive deployment is equally applicable to notional borders *within* states, in situations where lines of one kind or another have been drawn in the context of a dispute—for example, one concerning a minority enclave—the crossing of which would escalate the situation into an armed conflict. One can also envisage cases where preventive deployment might be contemplated but no immediate "border" question is involved at all, for example, where a dispute is not between immediate neighbors and where the threatened action against which troops are preventively deployed is an air strike. The essence of preventive deployment, then, goes not so much to *where* troops are deployed as to *why* they are deployed, namely, to contain the dispute or emerging threat and prevent it from turning into an armed conflict.

In *An Agenda for Peace,* the concept of preventive deployment is taken a little further still, to apply to situations of internal national crisis where, at the request or with the consent of the government or all parties concerned, military personnel are sent in to give humanitarian assistance or create secure conditions. But it might help avoid further complications in this already somewhat confused debate if these situations were not regarded as ones of preventive deployment. It is suggested, rather, that if the use of any kind of force is contemplated (other than in self-defense), the deployment is better treated as a form of peace enforcement. And if what is being talked about is in-country help being given by military personnel, in circumstances where the use of force is not contemplated, then that is best treated as a form of peacebuilding.

The legal basis for preventive deployment by the UN, given that no use of force is involved, is Chapter VI of the UN Charter. Such deployment would be authorized by the Security Council. In cases of interstate disputes, consent would be needed from both governments concerned if the deployment were to be on both sides of a border, but a deployment could proceed with the consent only of the requesting country if that country were able to persuade the Security Council that this was desirable to deter hostilities. For intrastate situations where the Security Council felt able to intervene, intervention presumably again would occur only with the consent of the government or all parties concerned; the secretary-general put it in these terms in *An Agenda for Peace.*

A preventive deployment force has similar tasks to early warning observers, but by deploying in greater strength, it performs a greater symbolic role. While the primary object of such a force is deterrence, its task may also include some or all of the following:

- monitoring, observing, and reporting on developments that could undermine confidence or stability (e.g., arms flows) in the vicinity of a contested border or more generally

- assisting and monitoring local authorities in the maintenance of law and order, including the protection of threatened minorities or other vulnerable populations

- assisting and monitoring local authorities in the maintenance of essential services (water, power, and the like)

- assisting local authorities, UN agencies, or nongovernmental organizations in the provision of humanitarian assistance.

The Concept of Peacebuilding

Peacebuilding strategies fall into two broad groups, which may be described, respectively, as "international regimes" and "in-country peacebuilding." The former refers to strategies that by their nature are general in application, embracing more than one country; the latter refers to efforts, whether internationally assisted or not, to build the conditions for peace within particular countries. Each group of strategies has both preventive and post-conflict dimensions. In the case, for example, of most of the legal regimes described below, the regime has been designed to prevent disputes from arising, but there will also be provisions within the same regime for the resolution of disputes if they occur.

International Regimes

"International regimes" are defined here as international laws, norms, agreements, and arrangements—global, regional, and bilateral—designed to minimize threats to security, promote confidence and trust, and create institutional frameworks for dialogue and cooperation. They can fall into three broad categories: legal regimes and dispute-resolution mechanisms, arms control and disarmament regimes, and dialogue and cooperation arrangements.

There is already in place today a substantial framework of legal regimes and dispute-resolution mechanisms permeating every facet of international relations. They operate at the global, regional, and bilateral levels. They tend to operate habitually and, for the most part, invisibly. They cover virtually every field of interstate activity, including diplomatic relations, maritime affairs, and international environmental, trade, and communications issues. Without these regimes, much of contemporary international intercourse—and its routine and orderly nature—would be inconceivable.

International legal regimes can offer security benefits not only to the parties to an agreement but also to the international community in general. The Antarctic regime, for example, has ensured that Antarctica has remained a demilitarized zone. The treaty, moreover, provides parties with a framework for consultation and exchange of information. It is one of the earliest examples of "anywhere, anytime" on-site inspections in response to possible or emerging threats to the treaty's integrity.

Since its establishment under the UN Charter in 1945, the International Court of Justice, or World Court, has been very much *the* judicial organ of the international community. But it lacks compulsory jurisdiction. Less than a third of member states have submitted voluntarily to its jurisdiction, and when they have done so, in many instances their submission has been subject to highly restrictive conditions. And to the extent that the court does have jurisdiction, it has been conspicuously underutilized. Secretary-General Boutros-Ghali, in *An Agenda for Peace,* made a series of recommendations about taking greater advantage of the court, including its advisory jurisdiction. These recommendations should be wholeheartedly endorsed by the international community.

Arms control and disarmament regimes have a particular and powerful role in peacebuilding. The very process of their negotiation can have a highly beneficial impact on international peace and security as states agree, and are seen to agree, on the elimination of, or lower limits and controls on, armaments—in short, as they cooperate for peace. In their operation over time, these regimes build confidence further as their restraints on arms procurement or military holdings begin to stick and as on-site verification measures ensure transparency of state behavior. As a method of security enhancement, arms control and disarmament measures have been this century—and particularly since 1945—a regular feature of the international community's efforts to respond to technological developments that have potential or actual military applications. They must remain so, with efforts to achieve, not merely the stabilization and reduction, but also the actual elimination of nuclear weapons being the preeminent focus in the post–Cold War world.

It is not only formal legal regimes and institutions with a specifically defined dispute-resolution function that have an international peace-building role in the sense being discussed here. Important foundations for peace are also regularly laid around the world in the innumerable bilateral, regional, and global-scale arrangements that bring countries together for dialogue and cooperation. What is important, for present purposes, about these arrangements is not so much the specific outcomes that may be the product of such meetings and exchanges but the sense of familiarity, comfort, and understanding that tends to flow, other things being equal, from the mere fact of their occurrence. It would be naive to overstate this point, but wrong to ignore its significance.

States and nonstate actors in different geographical areas should be encouraged to look beyond purely national concerns and work for the gradual development of broad, regional agendas for economic and social growth, mutually reinforcing confidence-building measures, and mechanisms for the nonviolent resolution of conflict. Contrast, for example, the inconceivability of armed conflict among the member states of the European Union with the conflict and instability that has marked the collapse of an arbitrary and oppressive regional arrangement in Eastern Europe. Robust regional economic and political institutions in turn become important building blocks in the evolution of effective global institutions, just as robust, peaceable states help to reinforce good global governance.

In-Country Peacebuilding

Preventive peacebuilding within states, in which both the international community and individual states themselves have mutually supportive roles to play, should aim to achieve progress in reducing the gap between rich and poor, to extend basic human rights to all people (including minorities), to promote sustainable development, and to advance a just and fair society that does not discriminate on grounds of gender and race. Preventive peacebuilding at this level also seeks to promote adherence by states to the established standards of good international citizenship. Good internal government is the necessary foundation of good global governance.

Peacebuilding through National Effort. At the national level appropriate preventive peacebuilding techniques include social and economic development, democratization, observance of fundamental human rights, the elimination of all forms of gender or racial discrimination, and respect for minorities. Many states spend disproportionate amounts of their scarce resources for military purposes, thus depriving their populations of vital economic and social infrastructure benefits that would be, in general, far more effective in enhancing their national security and well-being. In all regions of the world—and this is just as true of developed as of developing countries—the conversion from defense industry and expenditure to civilian programs and the adoption of disarmament and arms control measures could, if appropriately managed, result in substantial economic benefits.

That said, a great many states simply do not have the physical or financial capacity by themselves to deliver material well-being to their people; to do so involves not just goodwill and sound priorities but resources, and those are often in desperately short supply. What every state does have the capacity to deliver to its people, however, is distributive justice (ensuring, through taxation and related policies, that gross inequalities of wealth and income are minimized) and also political and civil rights—in particular, giving to all a direct say in how they are governed and a capacity to think, talk, and act freely subject only to reasonable respect for the rights of others.

Democracy and human rights issues these days are acknowledged much more widely to be everybody's business. Secretary-General Boutros-Ghali put the point with absolute clarity in *An Agenda for Peace:*

> The authority of the United Nations system to act in this field would rest on the consensus that social peace is as important as strategic or political peace. There is an obvious connection between democratic practices—such as the rule of law and transparency in decision making—and the achievement of true peace and security in any new and stable political order.

It is much remarked that, as a matter of evident historical fact, democracies have not gone to war against one another. It would seem, for this reason alone, to be in everyone's interest to safeguard and extend democratic processes, individual and collective rights, and the interests of minorities—and to ensure that authoritarian societies are encouraged to move in a democratic direction. A good recent example of a country dealing constructively with a potentially explosive minority human rights issue was Romania's agreement in July 1993 to a package on language and related measures sought by its Hungarian minority.

It is essential, in all these respects, that states protect and promote the independence of the judiciary; underline the primacy of the rule of law; and periodically review their compliance with international humanitarian, human rights, refugee, economic, and social agreements. Where national laws or practices contradict or diverge from international agreements, states should seek to, and be urged to, bring domestic practices into line with international standards. States should periodically review the extent to which national policy and practice conform to international standards and should be encouraged to become parties to the key human rights conventions, in particular the International Covenants on Civil and Political Rights and on Economic, Social and Cultural Rights; the Conventions on the Elimination of All Forms of Discrimination Against Women, and of Racial Discrimination; the Convention against Torture and Other Cruel, Inhuman or Degrading Treatment or Punishment; and the Convention on the Rights of the Child. Importantly, all these conventions have mechanisms for the regular examination by expert tribunals of the practices of states party to the conventions.

Peacebuilding with International Support. The United Nations system has a strong supportive role to play in promoting peacebuilding within states in some of the areas just mentioned. The secretary-general's conviction that the UN has both the authority and the responsibility to act in the fields of democracy and human rights has already been mentioned. One recent manifestation of that commitment, which is much to be applauded, is the establishment of an electoral assistance unit within the Department of Political Affairs. The UN Center for Human Rights in Geneva can provide expert advice and technical assistance on the establishment of national institutions to promote and protect human rights and thereby to further democracy generally.

International development assistance and the promotion of cooperative development projects, especially in areas of potential dispute, are important to economic peacebuilding within states. Projects aimed at bringing adjoining states together around joint agricultural development projects and transportation, water, and electricity utilization schemes are important confidence-building measures in their own right and should be encouraged. An example is the ability of the Interim Mekong Committee to foster development-related cooperation even while post–Vietnam War hostilities continued in the area.

UN economic and technical assistance can relieve many of the social and economic tensions underlying disputes. It is important here to ensure that the UN does not lose sight of the fact that peace and security involves the security of peoples and societies as much as it does that of states and that the promotion of popular, as well as state, well-being should be a criterion for determining resource allocation. The Economic and Social

Council (ECOSOC) could play a role in accordance with Article 65 of the Charter of the UN in alerting the Security Council to economic and social developments that threaten international peace and security. This role should be aimed in the first instance at better coordination of those UN organizations and agencies devoted to economic and social progress.

There is a particular need to strengthen the coordination of UN humanitarian emergency assistance, to improve its capability in prevention and in preparedness for natural disasters and other emergencies, particularly those involving food. Improving the UN early warning capability for potential humanitarian emergency situations, including the involvement of national institutions, is an important peacebuilding function that can avert destabilizing situations. In responding to such emergencies, one option—with the consent of the government of the country concerned, or of all relevant parties—is for military personnel from other member states to be deployed to give urgent assistance;this is described in *An Agenda for Peace* as a form of "preventive deployment," but "peacebuilding" may better capture the flavor of what is involved.

More generally, there is a need for much more integration of activities within the whole UN system, so that the pursuit of peace and security is seen to include the satisfaction of basic human needs as well as the prevention, containment, and settlement of violent conflict. This will inevitably require linkages between visions of a more peaceful world and greater integration within the system, particularly in relation to program planning, the application of resources, and the development of smooth-functioning coordination mechanisms.

The secretary-general, as chief administrative officer of the UN and chairman of the Administrative Committee on Coordination, has the major responsibility in this regard. There is a case for establishing a new section within the secretariat—possibly in the Department of Political Affairs or the Department of Humanitarian Affairs—to assist in this regard, stimulating and coordinating peacebuilding processes across the whole UN system.

Delivering Preventive Action

All the clear thinking in the world about appropriate responses to different kinds of problems will not count for much if the strategies thus devised are flawed in their execution. The UN itself has, in all circumstances, performed quite remarkably in adapting to the surge in new demands made upon it for cooperative security action in the post–Cold

War period. And there are many instances where regional organizations have played their own part, particularly in preventive diplomacy, or show a clear capacity—with more resources and more encouragement—to do more. Similarly, individual states and combinations of states, as well as a variety of nongovernmental actors, have all played useful niche roles from time to time in contributing to the resolution of particular problems.

Overwhelmingly, however, one is left with a sense that the international community could be doing much better in tackling these issues, particularly at the preventive peacebuilding stage. And while there will continue to be a major, and growing, role for regional organizations—both the long-established formal ones and the emergent new dialogue forums—overwhelmingly the major responsibility for doing better is going to have to be borne by the UN, the only fully empowered cooperative security body with global membership that we have.

The ideal of nations and communities living and working together in peace and security, enjoying, in the words of the UN Charter, "better standards of life in larger freedom," should be closer now to realization than at any previous time in modern world history. There are some signs of a culture of cooperation emerging to replace the culture of conflict that has prevailed so long, but what has to happen now is for that mood to be systematically tapped and translated into effective institutional structures and processes. That kind of adjustment is never easy to achieve. It depends partly on achieving a measure of intellectual consensus among decision makers as to the applicable principles and partly on there being a clearly defined set of widely supported practical proposals for change.

But what major change *also* needs is commitment, and stamina, from the governments and individuals who, at the end of the day, have to make it happen. Member states of the UN, when they accede to its Charter, commit themselves to cooperating both with other states and with the organization itself to achieve both international peace and security, and—through economic and social cooperation—the conditions of stability and well-being necessary for peaceful and friendly relations with and among nations. The fiftieth anniversary of the UN in 1995 was the occasion for renewing that formal commitment. But what is also now necessary is a renewed practical determination to make it all happen.

4

Preventive Diplomacy and Peacemaking: The UN Experience

Ismat Kittani

Preventive diplomacy and peacemaking have become priority activities for the United Nations—as important as, but perhaps less publicized than, peacekeeping. Action before a conflict breaks out or, once it has broken out, to resolve it peacefully is clearly more cost-effective than major peacekeeping and peace enforcement operations, in terms both of money saved and of human suffering prevented. Moreover, in the current climate of austerity, these activities are likely to become even more prominent among the UN's instruments for the maintenance of peace.

Unfortunately for those who are frustrated by the relative lack of media attention devoted to UN successes, preventive diplomacy and peacemaking tend to be most effective when least well known. By necessity, these efforts are often quiet and behind the scenes—only the failures appear on television and the front pages of newspapers.

Prevention and peacemaking have been undertaken by the UN since the earliest days of the organization, but the end of the Cold War has greatly expanded the opportunities, both in inter- and intrastate conflicts. In the *Supplement to An Agenda for Peace*, the secretary-general stated that during 1994, the United Nations was actively involved in preventive diplomacy or peacemaking in twenty-eight disputes, a figure that grew by one or two cases in 1995. If one adds humanitarian action, human rights missions, and electoral assistance, all of which can have a preventive or peacemaking dimension, plus numerous goodwill missions of the secretary-general (in addition to the twenty-eight mentioned above), the intensity of UN activities in this sphere becomes apparent. Yet translating opportunities into successes has not been easy. Various constraints, some old and some new, stand in the way of the UN's realizing its full potential for conflict prevention and resolution.

This chapter begins with some definitions and a description of the principal actors engaged in preventive diplomacy and peacemaking. Although the focus is on the United Nations, the contributions of other entities that are active in this field, either alone or in collaboration with the UN, are also discussed. Some examples of preventive action and peacemaking during the Cold War years are then described, followed by an overview of recent developments within the UN system designed to take advantage of the growing opportunities. The chapter then examines some of the practical constraints and political obstacles to a more active UN preventive and peacemaking role, followed by discussion of several current cases to illustrate the opportunities and constraints. It concludes with a number of lessons for future efforts in this dynamic field.

Definitions and Principal Actors

Preventive diplomacy is defined in *An Agenda for Peace* as "action to prevent disputes from arising between parties, to prevent existing disputes from escalating into conflicts and to limit the spread of the latter when they occur."[1] In addition to quiet and not-so-quiet diplomacy, preventive action may entail the deployment of small political teams, human rights observers, civilian police, military observers, or even troops to forestall disputes from escalating into armed conflict. In the 1995 *Annual Report on the Work of the Organization,* the secretary-general of the UN lists humanitarian action and peacebuilding as having a conflict-prevention potential as well. The definition in *An Agenda for Peace* would also encompass support for activities like local dialogues, education programs, and balanced media reporting.

Peacemaking is defined as action to bring hostile parties to agreement, essentially through such peaceful means as those foreseen in Chapter VI of the Charter. Article 33 of Chapter VI lists negotiation, inquiry, mediation, conciliation, arbitration, judicial settlement, and resort to regional agencies or arrangements as peacemaking techniques. To these should be added the good-offices role of the secretary-general, which has developed steadily throughout the history of the United Nations. Although the use of military force is included in the peacemaking section of *An Agenda for Peace,* the term is used here to mean diplomatic and other noncoercive activity.

Within the United Nations, responsibility for preventive diplomacy and peacemaking rests principally with the Security Council and the secretary-general and to a lesser extent with the General Assembly. The authority of the Security Council derives from its primary responsibility for the maintenance of international peace and security. The council can act on its own, as it has by sending missions to Somalia, Western Sahara, Burundi, and elsewhere at critical moments. More commonly, it authorizes or approves action by the secretary-general; examples include the dispatch of a special representative and small advisory team to Burundi and the appointment of a Special Envoy for Sierra Leone.

The secretary-general's authority, however, is not entirely dependent on specific mandates from the Security Council or General Assembly. On the basis of the power under Article 99 of the Charter to bring any matter to the attention of the Security Council that in the opinion of the secretary-general may threaten international peace and security, along with the general language of Article 33, successive secretaries-general have carved out a comparatively independent role for the office. As far back as 1946, when the Security Council was considering whether to send a commission of inquiry to investigate alleged infiltration across Greece's northern frontier, Trygve Lie announced:

> I hope the Council will understand that the Secretary-General must reserve his rights to make such inquiries or investigations as he may think necessary, in order to determine whether or not he should consider bringing any aspect of this matter up to the attention of the Council under the provisions of the Charter.[2]

Thomas Franck and Georg Nolte, in their study of the office of the secretary-general, explain how subsequent secretaries-general interpreted and executed their good-offices role.[3] Dag Hammarskjöld was the boldest in this regard, beginning with a number of diplomatic initiatives in the Middle East, including a decision on his own authority to enlarge the UN Observer Group in Lebanon (UNOGIL) in 1958, after which he told the Security Council, "were you to disapprove, I would of course accept the consequences of your judgment."[4] Subsequent secretaries-general have carried on the tradition of relative independence, including Boutros Boutros-Ghali, who has sought to maximize the leverage of his office by actively seeking opportunities to intervene diplomatically when all parties indicate a desire for UN involvement.

The UN does not have or claim a monopoly on preventive action or peacemaking, as the secretary-general said in the *Supplement to An Agenda for Peace,* although the international community is turning increasingly to the UN for these activities. Regional organizations, ad hoc coalitions, national envoys, and private actors have also become more involved.

The comparative advantages of these various actors suggest that all can be effective, depending on the circumstances. The UN has unparalleled experience and may be better able to engage in sustained mediation than representatives of governments, simply because the tenure of UN officials and special representatives is less subject to the vicissitudes of electoral politics. "Distance" from the conflict is also an advantage for UN intermediaries because, emanating from an international body, they are more likely to be perceived as impartial and lacking in ulterior motives. Thus, while the Economic Community of West African States has taken the lead in Liberia, it is clear that the additional presence of the UN Special Representative and a UN observer mission has made some of the Liberian factions more comfortable with the idea of third-party involvement. Regional and subregional actors, on the other hand, often have greater familiarity with the dynamics of local disputes and greater interest in preventing or resolving violent conflict in their neighborhoods. Ad hoc groupings and national envoys may be able to offer incentives or bring to bear pressure that neither the UN nor regional organizations can muster. And private actors—either eminent persons like former U.S. president Jimmy Carter or nongovernmental organizations—can often act with greater flexibility and discretion than governmental or intergovernmental representatives.

Thus there is no formula for identifying the appropriate entity to undertake preventive diplomacy or mediation. Indeed, often the mutually supporting efforts of more than one actor are the most effective, as long as there is a clear division of responsibility and good coordination.

Cold War Cases

One of the least well known cases of preventive diplomacy—until Sir Brian Urquhart published his biography of Ralph Bunche—was the intervention of Secretary-General U Thant and Ralph Bunche to avert a crisis over Bahrain, a British protectorate until 1970 but claimed by Iran as its fourteenth province. When the British were departing the Middle East in the late 1960s, there was a threat of serious conflict over the future of Bahrain. Many months of secret negotiations led by Ralph Bunche produced an agreement between Britain and Iran to allow the secretary-general to send a personal representative to ascertain the wishes of the people of Bahrain. The Bahrainis eventually concurred, and Vittorio Winspeare Guiccardi was assigned the task. He undertook inquiries and concluded in April 1970 that a majority of the people preferred independence. Although the procedure fell short of the initial demand of the Iranian government for a full plebiscite, it provided the shah with a face-saving way of giving up Iran's historic claim, which he did. The Security Council welcomed the solution and praised all the participants for what Sir Brian Urquhart called a "textbook example of settling a dispute by quiet diplomacy before it degenerated into conflict."[5]

An example of peacemaking by the secretary-general and the Security Council concerns the Iran-Iraq war. I had direct experience in the negotiations that led to the end of the war, events that are well documented by Cameron Hume in his book *Iran, Iraq, and the United Nations: How Peacekeeping Changed.* In 1986, as developments in the former Soviet Union began to revolutionize the superpower relationship, Secretary-General Pérez de Cuéllar called on the Permanent Five to revive the Security Council as an instrument for the maintenance of peace and security. Shortly thereafter, in a January 1987 press conference, he suggested that the Iran-Iraq conflict could be the starting point for this revival, since it was not a by-product of the Cold War. A series of meetings among the Permanent Five members of the Security Council ensued, which I, as the permanent representative of Iraq, followed very closely, keeping Baghdad informed about the progress being made. The talks led to agreement on what became Security Council Resolution 598, which mandated a cease-fire under Chapter VII of the Charter. This continuous dialogue with the Permanent Five facilitated Iraq's immediate acceptance of the resolution upon its adoption in July 1987. Iran followed suit a year later, when the military conflict turned decisively against it. Iraq then insisted on tying the cease-fire to direct negotiations between the two parties, which Iran had persistently refused. Thanks to the good offices of the secretary-general, a compromise was found and adopted by the Security Council, setting the cease-fire date and providing for negotiations under the auspices of the secretary-general.

This case illustrates the power of initiative of the secretary-general and the complementarity of his peacemaking role and that of the Security Council. In intractable conflicts, the good offices of the secretary-general alone may not suffice to produce a settlement, and there were many situations during the Cold War when diplomatic intervention by the secretary-general would have been fruitless. But by the late 1980s the permanent members of the council began to act in concert on major conflicts, opening the door to a host of opportunities for UN preventive diplomacy and peacemaking. Following the success of the Permanent Five in the Iran-Iraq dispute, concerted action among them became the rule rather than the exception—although in recent years consensus has been more difficult to achieve.

An important feature of the Bahrain and Iran-Iraq examples is that in both cases the parties were looking for a way out of the conflict. In 1970, Iran had no interest in waging a war with Britain, and vice-versa. Similarly, by 1987, continued fighting between Iran and Iraq could well have led to the collapse of both states. Diplomatic intervention, it seems, is most constructive when the parties are ready to make peace—or avoid a war—but are incapable for political reasons of dealing with each other directly. The challenge for the peacemaker is to keep abreast of potential or ongoing conflicts so that when the time is ripe for intervention, he or she can seize the opportunity by proposing solutions that the parties find acceptable but are not in a position to propose themselves.

Modalities

Developments within the UN

Although preventive diplomacy and peacemaking have long been important activities of the UN, now more than in the Cold War days the UN actively searches for opportunities where diplomatic intervention by the secretary-general, Security Council, General Assembly, or other bodies might be useful.

Various developments within the UN have made it easier for the secretary-general and the secretariat to pursue this proactive approach. First, in 1992, all political functions were consolidated in the Department of Political Affairs (DPA), initially under the leadership of two under-secretaries-general and then further streamlined under just one. This helped rationalize the political work of the UN, which before 1992 was divided among five departments and offices.

Under-Secretary-General Marrack Goulding has organized the new department into regional divisions whose primary functions are preventive diplomacy and peacemaking. Every country in the world is covered by a desk officer who is charged with monitoring developments in his or her area of responsibility and providing political advice on actions the secretary-general might take. Thus, while preventive diplomacy and peacemaking were in the past mainly the preserve of the Executive Office of the Secretary-General, there is now an effective infrastructure within the secretariat to support these expanding efforts.

As explained in the 1995 *Annual Report of the Secretary-General on the Work of the Organization,* the Department of Political Affairs has five main responsibilities in support of preventive action and peacemaking:

- To monitor, analyze, and assess political developments throughout the world. The information the department relies on comes from governments, the media, the academic community, and nongovernmental organizations.

- To identify actual or potential conflicts with respect to which the UN could play a useful preventive or peacemaking role. Because early warning of political crises is not a mechanical exercise, the desk officers in the United Nations do not rely on a formal set of criteria in performing their functions. Such developments as border tensions, troop movements, breakdowns in power-sharing arrangements, massive violations of human rights, civil or political unrest, and massive arms purchases would naturally put the desk officers on alert. The Department of Humanitarian Affairs, it should be noted, has compiled a list of factors in assessing potential humanitarian crises—for example, a worsening economic situation, food insecurity, social cleavages, and population movements—that could lead to violent conflict.[6]

- To prepare recommendations to the secretary-general about the specific form of that role.

- To execute the approved policy when it is of a diplomatic nature.

- To assist the secretary-general in carrying out political activities decided by him and/or mandated by the General Assembly and Security Council.

Within the UN system, the Department of Political Affairs works closely with other departments in pursuit of conflict prevention and resolution. Peacemaking often precedes or occurs in parallel with peacekeeping, requiring close cooperation with the Department of Peace-keeping Operations (DPKO). When humanitarian or human rights issues are involved, the department coordinates with the Department of Humanitarian Affairs (DHA), the UN High Commissioner for Refugees, the UN High Commissioner for Human Rights, and other relevant bodies. The Office of Legal Affairs is also actively involved, particularly when commissions of inquiry and tribunals are established in the context of preventive or peacemaking efforts. Finally, the expertise of the Bretton Woods institutions may be relied upon in complex negotiations, such as those between the government of Guatemala and URNG, whose financial assistance can be used as an incentive to make peace.

To develop coordinated strategies, the Task Force on Peace Operations meets weekly. Composed of all under-secretaries-general and assistant secretaries-general who deal with these matters, including the special advisers of the secretary-general, the task force meets to discuss major issues and provide policy guidance to envoys and chiefs of mission in the field.

Below the level of this task force, a "framework for coordination" has been established to institutionalize staff-level consultations and improve coordination among DHA, DPA, and DPKO in cases of complex emergencies in the field and to formulate joint recommendations for possible action. Other departments, programs, and agencies are also invited as appropriate. In addition, interdepartmental working groups are convened as necessary to deal with particular issues or operations. And desk officers in all the relevant departments have networks of contacts with responsible officials in other UN agencies, permanent missions to the UN, and nongovernmental organizations.

Another important development within the UN system is the more direct role the Security Council has undertaken in preventive diplomacy and peacemaking. Article 29 of the Charter authorizes the Security Council "to establish such subsidiary organs as it deems necessary for the performance of its functions." An increasingly useful manifestation of this power is the dispatch by the council of a number of its members to trouble spots on fact-finding or goodwill missions. Thus, for example, the Security Council dispatched a fact-finding mission to Bujumbura in February 1995, the second in six months. These visits can have an immediate impact by demonstrating the concern and attention of the international community. They can also contribute in the longer term by allowing the council to obtain firsthand information to enable it to make appropriate recommendations. The mission to Burundi recommended, inter alia, the establishment of an international commission of inquiry into the attempted coup of 1993 (which led to the death of the president) and the massacres that followed. After several months of consultations by the secretary-general on what form the commission would take, it was established and dispatched to the country in November 1995.

These ad hoc bodies, it should be noted, need not be composed of Security Council members alone, nor must they necessarily undertake field missions. Any grouping of states with special knowledge or influence can potentially monitor a situation and report to the council, either formally or informally. One form these groupings take is the device known as "Friends of the Secretary-General." Thus in El Salvador the peacemaking and peacekeeping efforts of the UN were supported by Colombia, Mexico, Spain, and Venezuela, often joined by the United States, in a formula that came to be known as the "four plus one." Variations on the theme include the "Friends of Haiti" (Argentina, Canada, France, the United States, and Venezuela), the "troika" of Observer States in Angola (Portugal, Russia, and the United States), and the Contact Group for the former Yugoslavia (France, Germany, Russia, the United Kingdom, and the United States—occasionally joined by Italy because of its membership on the Security Council).

These "friends" can assist either the secretary-general, as was the case in El Salvador, or the Security Council directly. In the post–Cold War world, where the council is more able to act in concert but can be overwhelmed by the sheer volume of information, such groupings of states can be important sources of ideas and influence. Of course, the Security Council does not typically conduct negotiations as a body nor vote on proposals put before the parties to a conflict.[7] Rather, it reinforces the efforts of individual mediators by signaling its concern about a particular dispute and its willingness to intervene if necessary.

UN Collaboration with Other Actors

Other actors are involved, either directly or indirectly, in almost every preventive or peacemaking activity of the UN. Nowhere is this more true than in the former Yugoslavia. Initially, the main negotiating forum was the International Conference on the Former Yugoslavia, a joint effort of the UN and the European Union. The five-nation Contact Group then took over the lead role in Bosnia-Herzegovina, and the so-called Zagreb Four became active in Croatia. A high-profile trip by former U.S. president Jimmy Carter led to the Bosnian cease-fire agreement of December 1994, and the combination of UN mediator Thorvald Stoltenberg and U.S. ambassador Peter Galbraith produced the November 1995 agreement on Eastern Slavonia. Finally, the Bosnia agreement struck in Dayton, Ohio, was the result of a U.S.-led peace initiative that built on its predecessors.

At least four types of collaborators with the UN can be identified:

- formal regional organizations, like the Organization of African Unity and the Organization of American States

- ad hoc groupings, such as "friends" of the secretary-general or contact groups

- national envoys appointed by governments that may have a special interest in the dispute

- nongovernmental organizations and individuals

The support of such countries, organizations, and individuals is generally welcomed by the UN, although more is not always better. A proliferation of mediators can, if not well coordinated, duplicate efforts and lead to "crossed wires." More seriously, parties to a conflict can play the mediators off against each other—for example, by withholding agreement to a proposal from one in the hope that another will propose a better deal. Proper coordination, therefore, is critical, as is a clear division of labor. Typically, it is best for one mediator to take the lead and all others to commit to playing a supporting role. The Friends of the Secretary-General for El Salvador all had independent influence over the parties but were careful not to take initiatives that could undermine the effectiveness of the UN as lead intermediary. Similarly, the UN has been only too happy to take a back seat to regional organizations such as the Organization for Security and Cooperation in Europe (OSCE), whose efforts in resolving the Armenia-Azerbaijan dispute the UN supports wholeheartedly.

Preventive Humanitarian Action and Peacebuilding

So far this chapter has focused on political efforts to prevent or resolve conflicts, but humanitarian and peacebuilding activities can also support preventive diplomacy. Regarding humanitarian action, the United Nations High Commissioner for Refugees recently announced that her organization would begin to take a more "preventive and proactive approach" to the problem of refugees. The focus would be on conditions in potential refugee-producing states, as well as countries of asylum, with the goal of assisting desperate people before they began flowing across borders. When one considers the impact on neighboring states of the over 3 million refugees from Bosnia-Herzegovina, the 2.6 million from Afghanistan, the 2.3 million from Liberia, and the 1.8 million from Rwanda, it is clear that refugee emergencies can be a major source of political instability, and therefore preventing them can help prevent violent conflict.

Similarly, disarmament, demilitarization, the control of small arms, institutional reform, improved police and judicial systems, the monitoring of human rights, electoral reform, and social and economic development are peacebuilding tools that can contribute to conflict prevention.[8] At a minimum, these activities can build confidence and help create conditions conducive to the negotiated settlement of a simmering dispute. More profoundly, they can alleviate the root causes of a potential conflict. Economic disparities, political exclusion, and systematic human rights abuses, if left to fester, can generate violent conflict.

The Security Council endorsed this view in the statement by its president on the *Supplement to An Agenda for Peace:*

> Social and economic development can be as valuable in preventing conflicts as in healing the wounds after conflicts have occurred. The Council urges States to support the efforts of the United Nations system with regard to preventive and post-conflict peacebuilding activities and, in this context, to provide necessary assistance for the economic and social development of countries, especially those which have suffered or are suffering from conflicts.[9]

Care should be taken, however, not to define the concept of preventive action too broadly. Although social and economic development can help prevent conflict, the causal relationship is not automatic—in fact, if the fruits of development are not spread equitably and accompanied by political freedoms, development can exacerbate internal tensions. Moreover, if preventive diplomacy is defined to encompass every activity of the UN, it loses practical value. To illustrate the point, if human rights promotion, social and economic development, and civic institution building are all understood as preventive action, how can the secretary-general make a reasonable budget proposal to the General Assembly for that line item? Certainly the contingency fund of $25 million per biennium for preventive diplomacy and peacemaking proposed in the *Supplement to An Agenda for Peace* would not go very far.[10]

Practical Constraints

The rhetorical commitment to more active preventive diplomacy and peacemaking by the UN, therefore, is strong. Nevertheless, turning words into deeds faces a number of practical constraints. Before discussing those constraints, one myth should be dispelled. The UN does not suffer from a lack of information. An immense amount of data is available from governments, the media, academic sources, and nongovernmental organizations. Moreover, field offices of UN programs and agencies are a source of information on humanitarian crises or social breakdowns that may lead to conflict. One of the primary functions of desk officers in the substantive departments is to monitor those developments, and the situation center in DPKO was established partly to ensure that reliable information—both public and confidential—is received and disseminated on a timely basis. The UN, therefore, does not need its own intelligence service.

What it needs is the capacity to manage and use effectively the information it receives. The sheer volume of information, capable of instantaneous transmission through on-line networks and other products of the computer age, creates problems of management. Moreover, indicators of a threat to peace can come in forms other than political tension: systematic repression, mass movement of populations, deprivation of basic needs, ethnic tension, and environmental degradation are examples. Synthesizing, analyzing, and acting on these indicators is a challenge. Major powers have thousands of officials devoted to this task, in capitals and in embassies around the world. The UN's Department of Political Affairs has only fifty-nine professionals working on preventive diplomacy and peacemaking, along with the political staff in the secretary-general's office and a handful of political advisers attached to peacemaking and peacekeeping missions.

In an effort to enhance its analytical capabilities, the Department of Political Affairs has established a policy analysis team composed of one member of each of the substantive divisions. The team, which meets approximately every two weeks, provides policy advice and recommendations to senior department officials and ultimately to the secretary-general. This arrangement ensures that the routine "information management" work of the divisions does not overwhelm the need for medium- and long-range analysis and planning.

Another constraint, cited in the *Supplement to An Agenda for Peace,* is the lack of distinguished diplomatic or political personalities for preventive diplomacy and peacemaking. Often secretariat officials undertake good-offices missions, but because of the increasing number of requests, the secretary-general must sometimes appoint outsiders. Those who are able, willing, and permitted by their governments to bring their own experience and prestige to the process are not many. Moreover, these efforts often require sustained activity and a presence in the field. Thus, while there is no shortage of senior persons with the required skills, they often find it difficult to make the full-time, long-term commitment required. The secretary-general brought this problem to the attention of member states, and the Security Council requested them to provide the names of persons who might be considered for such posts. Meanwhile, following a request from the General Assembly for member states to provide the secretary-general with any assistance he may need to exercise his functions in this field,[11] the United Kingdom and France announced a joint initiative that resulted in their sending, in April 1994, a list of personalities, experts, and resources that could be made available. Other governments soon followed suit. The Department of Political Affairs has been tasked with maintaining a roster of such persons, now totaling several hundred. While it is an important step forward, matching names with need is a difficult exercise, given the constraints of availability, language, nationality, and other factors, both political and personal, that determine suitability for a task.

A third problem is financial. While preventive diplomacy and peace-making are less expensive than peacekeeping or peace enforcement, they do entail costs. Even the work of special envoys is enhanced if continuity can be assured by the presence on the ground of a small support mission.[12] Funding for these missions can be difficult to obtain; it is easier for governments to respond after a crisis erupts, when the implications are plain for all to see. The reaction of member states to the secretary-general's proposal to establish a contingency fund of some $25 million per biennium or to enlarge the existing fund for unforeseen and extraordinary activities has been mixed, although the Security Council as a body expressed the view that "adequate resources must be made available within the UN system for these actions," including the deployment of small field missions for preventive deployment and peacemaking.[13]

Political Obstacles

In addition to these practical constraints, all of which are surmountable, a number of political objections to proactive prevention and peacemaking are sometimes heard. These objections, because they are based on principle, may be more difficult to overcome.

First, there is continued resistance to the idea of a "mini-foreign ministry" in the secretariat. The notion of information being provided to headquarters by UN agency and other field offices is seen as particularly objectionable.

Second, while it is possible for the UN to detect an impending crisis and formulate recommendations, action requires the consent of the parties to the conflict. This constraint obtains in internal conflicts especially, because governments are often reluctant to "internationalize" disputes with insurgent groups by inviting UN involvement. Thus the Indonesian government has accepted the good offices of the secretary-general to help resolve what it perceives as its bilateral dispute with Portugal over East Timor, but it has not accepted direct negotiations with the East Timorese under UN auspices. It should be pointed out, as the East Timor case illustrates, that the concern about "internationalization" sometimes favors low-key involvement by the secretary-general as an alternative to high-profile Security Council or General Assembly consideration of a matter.

Third, beyond formal consent, effective preventive diplomacy and mediation require the willingness of parties to negotiate in earnest. A risk for the secretary-general is that his good offices can create the illusion of action, providing a convenient smokescreen for intransigent parties and an excuse for inaction by the Security Council and General Assembly.[14]

Fourth, preventive diplomacy and peacemaking can draw the UN into more expensive and risky observer or peacekeeping operations. If it is not clear that the Security Council or General Assembly is willing to provide the necessary support come what may, diplomatic efforts can be doomed from the start.

Finally, the complex and evolving relationship between the secretary-general, the Security Council, and the General Assembly affects the prospects of particular preventive or peacemaking missions. In some respects, the independence of the secretary-general is more constrained now than in the Cold War years, because the deliberative organs are more capable of acting. In other words, the gap filled by the secretary-general's good offices when the Security Council and the General Assembly were paralyzed has become narrower. As the secretary-general stated in *An Agenda for Peace,* although the mediator's effectiveness is enhanced by strong support from the political organs and relevant member states, "the good offices of the secretary-general may at times be employed most effectively when conducted independently of the deliberative bodies."[15] Close consultation to develop a common strategy is, of course, the ideal arrangement, but reducing the secretary-general to the role of "letter carrier" can damage the credibility of his good offices.[16]

Recent Cases

The stationing of military units in the former Yugoslav Republic of Macedonia has become almost legendary as a case of successful preventive deployment. The concept, first proposed by the secretary-general in *An Agenda for Peace,* was taken up by the Security Council in 1992, when it authorized the deployment of one thousand U.S. and Nordic peacekeepers on the borders with Albania and the Federal Republic of Yugoslavia. The purpose of the deployment, which has been met so far, was to contain threats facing the country and prevent a wider Balkan war.

Efforts to apply the model elsewhere have been less successful. The secretary-general has repeatedly called for the preventive deployment of troops either in, or on the border of, Burundi, as a deterrent and in order to react quickly in the event of a crisis. To date, Burundian authorities have been reluctant to accept a military presence on their territory, and the

Security Council has not authorized the deployment of troops across the border, in Zaire, for example.

Burundi is a case, however, where the combined diplomatic resources of the international community have been successful in containing—at least until this chapter was written—a potential catastrophe. Shortly after the October 1993 coup in which the president was killed, the secretary-general appointed a special representative, supported by a small political team, to defuse tension and promote national reconciliation. The Security Council later sent two fact-finding missions of its own, the first following reports that the security situation was deteriorating in the wake of the plane crash killing the presidents of Burundi and Rwanda in April 1994. The Organization of African Unity dispatched a small group of observers and in February 1995 organized a conference, with the UN High Commissioner for Refugees, to address refugee concerns throughout the region. Human rights experts sent by the UN High Commissioner for Human Rights are in Burundi to provide technical assistance to the government. Meanwhile, the countries of the region have held two summit meetings, and the secretary-general has been exploring the possibility of a broader UN-sponsored summit on peace and security in the region. The UNHCR, World Food Programme, and other intergovernmental agencies are active in the country, with programs geared to humanitarian relief, but which hopefully have a stabilizing influence as well. Numerous bilateral visits have been made by concerned governments, and various non-governmental actors are actively helping in the search for a solution. The Carter Center, for example, organized a regional conference involving Burundi, Rwanda, Tanzania, Uganda, and Zaire in late November 1995.

There is no guarantee that this flurry of activity will stave off the feared explosion, but it is clear that international attention and the tireless efforts of the special representative of the secretary-general have helped to contain the situation thus far. Moreover, the case of Burundi illustrates that lack of attention or ideas is not the main obstacle to preventive action. If an explosion does occur, it will not be because the international community was caught unaware.

I shall conclude with another example of peacemaking with which I was directly involved on behalf of the secretary-general. For many years, the secretaries-general have been using their good offices with the governments of Portugal and Indonesia on the question of East Timor. Thus far, Secretary-General Boutros-Ghali has conducted six rounds of talks with the foreign ministers, the last one in July 1995. The pace of progress in the first four rounds was slow, but at the fifth round, after a tough day of negotiations, movement occurred on two fronts. First, the communiqué issued at the end of the meeting, in a fine example of constructive ambiguity, "noted positively" the secretary-general's intention "to facilitate and offer the necessary arrangements for the convening of an all-inclusive intra–East Timorese dialogue." The secretariat moved quickly, and the date for the dialogue was set. A phone call to the permanent representative of Austria produced the offer of facilities forty-eight hours later. Twenty-six participants were selected by the UN, although dissatisfaction over the list and the mode of UN participation threatened until the last moment to derail the event. The dialogue eventually took place in Burg Schlaining, a location chosen for its lack of easy media access. At the three-day meeting, the participants, who had never sat around a table together and some of whom had been sworn enemies for twenty years, managed to reach agreement on an eight-point consensus declaration and a lengthy annex. Although the dialogue was not a parallel negotiating track to the ministerial meetings between Indonesia and Portugal and did not address the political status of East Timor, it provided an opportunity for some of the key players to exchange views and develop personal relationships away from the glare of publicity.

In parallel with this encouraging development, the ministers agreed at the fifth round that substantive issues identified by the secretary-general— but not enumerated in the communiqué—would be considered at the next set of talks. Discussions along those lines began at the sixth round and continued in New York with the permanent representatives of Portugal and Indonesia. The discussions were exploratory, and I viewed my role as one of facilitator, on the assumption that the basic positions of the parties were still too far apart for the UN to begin putting proposals on the table, although sets of "ideas" were suggested to stimulate the discussions.

My personal involvement ended there, when the demands of my new assignment as under-secretary-general for peacekeeping made it impossible to devote adequate time to the East Timor issue. Fortunately, an advantage of mediation by the UN is that personalities can change without the loss of institutional memory and with minimal interruption in continuity. My successor as special adviser to the secretary-general, Yasushi Akashi, took over my role without missing a beat, and being only one floor away, I have remained available for consultation.

Conclusions

No two conflicts are alike, and there is no ready-made formula for success in preventive diplomacy and peacemaking. Some recurring features in post–Cold War conflicts are elements of unfinished decolonization; ethnic, cultural, or religious tension; systematic human rights abuses; competition over resources or territory; and socioeconomic disparities. The secretary-general or other intermediaries can learn from experiences in dealing with past conflicts, but there is no model that can be applied to all cases. The unique features of each must be examined carefully and adjustments in strategy made throughout the process, which is invariably complex and sensitive.

Some general lessons about UN activities in this field, however, can be drawn from past experience. First, preventive action must be understood broadly to include humanitarian relief and peacebuilding, as well as traditional preventive diplomacy, but the concept should not be defined so broadly as to encompass all activities of the United Nations. While development, democratization, and the promotion of human rights are all worthy goals and can all contribute to political stability, they do not necessarily constitute preventive action. It is the context and purpose of the activities that matter, that is, whether they are implemented as part of a deliberate strategy to prevent the outbreak of violence.

Second, no third-party intervention can succeed in either preventing a conflict or resolving it unless there is some political will among the parties. The political will need not exist among all the protagonists—in fact it rarely does—but there must be some moderate leadership with whom the intermediary can interact. The challenge for the mediator in those circumstances is to draw out the moderates without making their position vis-à-vis the hardliners untenable.

Third, timing is critical for both preventive action and peacemaking. It is important for the UN to have the infrastructure and expertise to seize opportunities as they arise. The signs of an impending conflict are usually obvious to anyone paying attention, but the observer must have the analytical skills to make timely recommendations and the institutional channels to ensure that the recommendations are considered by authorities in a position to take action. Similarly, a potential peacemaker must follow a conflict closely to know when the situation is ripe for timely diplomatic intervention and to know how to intervene in a sensitive and constructive way. The centralization of these functions in the Department of Political Affairs has gone a long way toward consolidating the UN's institutional capacity for preventive action and peacemaking. The $25 million per biennium increase in resources recommended in the *Supplement to An Agenda for Peace* would further strengthen that capacity.

Fourth, the efforts of the secretary-general in preventive diplomacy and peacemaking can usefully be supplemented by ad hoc groupings of states for diplomatic and other support. Whether the groups are called "the Friends of the Secretary-General" or something else, their value lies in their capacity to offer incentives and bring to bear influence that the UN alone cannot muster. They can also help coordinate and legitimize the otherwise disjointed efforts of bilateral actors.[17] The process works best when one mediator takes the lead and all others commit to playing a supporting role. Without such a commitment, the "friends" and the lead mediator open themselves to being played off against one another by competing parties.

Finally, preventive diplomacy and peaceful dispute settlement cannot be imposed by the UN on recalcitrant parties. Success, therefore, requires patience and a keen sense of knowing when the moment is ripe—that is, when the parties are ready to give up the option of war but need help in finding the terms on which to make peace. Recognizing that moment and acting quickly and creatively when it arrives is the art of the peacemaker. There is no lack of opportunities for failure, but resilience, resourcefulness, and a good measure of luck can improve the chances of success. The rest, of course, is up to the parties.

Notes

1. Boutros Boutros-Ghali, *An Agenda for Peace* (New York: United Nations, 1992), 11.

2. Security Council Official Records (SCOR), 1st year, 70th meeting, 20 September 1946, 404.

3. Thomas M. Franck and Georg Nolte, "The Good Offices Function of the UN Secretary-General," in *United Nations, Divided World*, 2d ed., ed. A. Roberts and B. Kingsbury(Oxford: Clarendon Press, 1993), 143–82.

4. SCOR, 13th year, 837th meeting, 22 July 1958, 4. Quoted in Franck and Nolte, *United Nations, Divided World*, 145. For an insightful review of Dag Hammarskjöld's years as secretary-general and his impact on the office, see Brian Urquhart, *Hammarskjöld* (New York: Harper & Row, 1972).

5. Brian Urquhart, *Ralph Bunche: An American Life* (New York: Norton, 1993), 429.

6. See *Humanitarian Early Warning System (HEWS): List of Indicators*, United Nations Department of Humanitarian Affairs, May 1995.

7. Alvaro de Soto, letter to the editor, *Foreign Affairs* 74, no. 1 (January/February 1995): 185–87.

8. Boutros Boutros-Ghali, *Supplement to An Agenda for Peace* (New York: United Nations, 1995), para. 47.

9. Security Council Presidential Statement (S/PRST)/1995/9, para. 3.

10. I would like to thank Pierre Van Hoeylandt, D.Phil. candidate at Oxford University, for making this point in a thoughtful paper he prepared while an

intern in the Department of Peace-keeping Operations, "Preventive Diplomacy: Conclusions from Recent Debate," December 1995.

11. General Assembly Resolution 47/120.

12. Boutros-Ghali, *Supplement to An Agenda for Peace,* para. 31.

13. S/PRST/1995/9, para. 2.

14. Franck and Nolte, *United Nations, Divided World,* 158.

15. Boutros-Ghali, *An Agenda for Peace,* 21–22.

16, See Franck and Nolte, *United Nations, Divided World,* for a good discussion of this issue.

17. See Michael W. Doyle, Ian Johnstone, and Robert Orr, "Strategies for Peace: Conclusions and Lessons," chap. 15 in *Keeping the Peace: Multidimensional UN Operations in Cambodia and El Salvador,* ed. Doyle, Johnstone, and Orr (London: Cambridge University Press, 1997).

Part III

Peacekeeping, Peace Enforcement,

and the Use of Force

5

Under What Circumstances Should the UN Intervene Militarily in a "Domestic" Crisis?

Edward Mortimer

Two False Dawns

1945

At the end of World War II the United Nations was set up, in the opening words of its Charter, "to save succeeding generations from the scourge of war." It was hoped that states would act together, through the new organization, to prevent further conflicts.

The unstated assumption was that such conflicts were most likely to be caused by aggression of one state against another, as had happened in the 1930s, and that aggression could in future be deterred by perpetuating the coalition of antifascist powers that had just defeated Germany and Japan. This coalition was institutionalized in the Security Council, with China, France, the Soviet Union, the United Kingdom, and the United States as permanent members.

Chapter V of the Charter laid down the composition, functions, and procedures of the council, which was given "primary responsibility for the maintenance of international peace and security," all members agreeing that "in carrying out its duties under this responsibility the Security Council acts on their behalf" (Article 24.1). Its specific powers were laid down in Chapters VI (Pacific Settlement of Disputes), VII (Action with Respect to Threats to the Peace, Breaches of the Peace, and Acts of Aggression), VIII (Regional Arrangements), and XII (International Trusteeship System).

Of these, Chapter VII was the most important because it allowed the council to "determine the existence of any threat to the peace, breach of the peace, or act of aggression" and to take action to "maintain or restore international peace and security" (Article 39), including if necessary "action by air, sea or land forces" (Article 42). All member states were supposed to make armed forces and other assistance available to the council for this purpose (Article 43), under the "strategic direction" of a Military Staff Committee, composed of the chiefs of staff of the permanent members or their representatives (Article 47). Members retained, however, their "inherent right of individual or collective self-defense" in the event of an armed attack "until the Security Council has taken measures necessary to maintain international peace and security" (Article 51).

In the event, the system never functioned as intended, partly because the Cold War made it impossible for the permanent members to agree on joint action and partly because many of the conflicts that erupted after 1945 were not classic wars between states but were based on ethnic, social, or ideological divisions that cut across state boundaries. It was seldom possible to reach consensus on who was the aggressor and who was the victim, and when the conflict was raging mainly within a member state, it was usually considered to be outside the Security Council's terms of reference. Article 2.7 of the Charter laid down that "nothing contained in the present Charter shall authorize the United Nations to intervene in matters which are essentially within the jurisdiction of any state." True, it did go on to say that "this principle shall not prejudice the application of enforcement measures under Chapter VII," but this was understood as referring to measures taken in response to a breach of the *international* peace, not as legitimizing interference in a purely domestic conflict.

On only one occasion during the Cold War did member states combine to resist aggression under the UN flag. This was the aggression by North Korea against South Korea (neither of them UN members at the time) in 1950. The UN action was not under the strategic direction of the Military Staff Committee but under a commander appointed by the president of the United States. It was in fact an action by the United States and its allies, bitterly opposed by the Soviet Union and communist China. Its approval by the Security Council was something of a fluke, because at the time the Soviet Union was boycotting the Security Council in protest against the nonrecognition of communist China.

The Soviet Union took care not to repeat this mistake. For the remainder of the Cold War the Security Council was unable to agree on any action that either superpower thought might bring some advantage to the other, and Chapter VII remained virtually a dead letter. The UN's role in international security became confined to helping negotiate cease-fires or other agreements in disputes where superpower interests were not directly at stake—many of them were conflicts that arose in the aftermath of decolonization. In the course of playing this role, the UN gradually developed a new kind of military activity, not mentioned in the Charter, but known as "peacekeeping": the deployment, in conflict zones, of lightly armed but highly visible neutral forces, with white-painted vehicles and blue helmets or berets bearing the UN crest. These forces were deployed with the consent of the parties to a conflict, under the terms of a cease-fire agreement, and their role was to help both parties observe the cease-fire by giving each of them confidence that the other could not violate its provisions (for instance, by moving men or equipment into a demilitarized zone) without being observed. This did not in itself, of course, resolve the substance of any conflict. Indeed, in some cases (Cyprus is often cited) it reduced the pressure on one or both of the parties to reach agreement on substance, allowing them instead to prolong the existing military stalemate. Thus several of the forces so deployed found themselves kept in place decade after decade. But at least their presence helped prevent further bloodshed, allowing civilians in the area to pursue or to resume a more or less normal life. In other cases UN peacekeepers had to be withdrawn (Sinai, 1967) or to watch impotently as conflict resumed (Lebanon, 1982) when one of the parties decided it could improve its position by a further round of fighting.

In general, the UN's contribution to world peace during the Cold War fell far short of what had been hoped in 1945. Many third-world countries were ravaged by wars in which superpower rivalries exacerbated the conflicts left behind by retreating colonialism. The UN could do little about this except make its "good offices" (which came to include peacekeeping) available to be used by the parties at such time as neither saw any immediate advantage in continuing military operations. Elsewhere, peace was kept by alliances and other arrangements (such as the European Community) made outside the UN framework.

1990

In the late 1980s, the end of the Cold War aroused widespread hopes that the UN, and in particular the Security Council, might at last be able to fulfill the hopes vested in it in 1945. Beginning with Resolution 598 (20 July 1987), which eventually helped end the eight-year war between Iraq and Iran, the five permanent members began to cooperate actively with each other in attempts to restore and maintain international peace, acting in accordance with the spirit, if not always the letter, of the Charter. Hitherto intractable conflicts—in Afghanistan, Angola, Cambodia, El Salvador, Eritrea, Namibia, Nicaragua—came within sight of negotiated settlements, as the superpowers stopped confronting each other by proxy and instead put pressure on their respective protégés to negotiate and compromise. In many of these negotiations the UN Secretariat played an important role, and UN peacekeepers—hitherto used mainly to preserve cease-fires—found themselves assigned more ambitious and complex tasks under the terms of political agreements: demobilizing and disarming combatants, resettling refugees, training and supervising police forces, monitoring or even organizing elections.

A new phase was reached with the Kuwait crisis of August 1990. For the first time, the Security Council took enforcement action under Chapter VII to deal with a classic case of aggression by one member state against another. The president of the United States, George Bush, declared that one of the objectives of this action was "a new world order. . . . A world where the rule of law supplants the law of the jungle. A world in which nations recognize the shared responsibility for freedom and justice. A world where the strong respect the rights of the weak."[1] After imposing stringent economic sanctions on the aggressor, the council proceeded to authorize military action by member states, under the euphemism of "all necessary means" (Resolution 678 of 30 November 1990).

This was not the precise form of military action envisaged by the Charter, which provides for the council to take action itself, using the armed forces of member states under the "strategic direction" of the Military Staff Committee. As in the Korean War, action was taken by an ad hoc coalition of member states under U.S. leadership—and this time not even under the UN flag. But this time the Soviet Union supported the enabling resolution, and communist China voluntarily refrained from vetoing it. The action appeared to fulfill the intention of the authors of the Charter more effectively than any previous one. Misgivings were provoked less by the form it took than by the fact that, with the weakening of the rival superpower, the United States appeared so strong that it could almost dictate the council's decisions.

Immediately after the expulsion of Iraqi forces from Kuwait, there were large-scale uprisings against the regime of Saddam Hussein in both southern and northern Iraq. These were suppressed with extreme brutality, and hundreds of thousands of Iraqi citizens fled across the frontiers, mainly into Iran and Turkey. This drew attention to the fact that many of the most violent and brutal conflicts—involving violations of international instruments such as the Universal Declaration of Human Rights, the 1949 Geneva Conventions Relating to the Protection of War Victims, and sometimes even the Convention on the Prevention and Suppression of Genocide—occur not between states but within them. In Resolution 688, of 5 April 1991, the Security Council described the Kurdish refugee crisis, caused by the Iraqi government's oppression, as a "threat to international peace and security," thereby implicitly bringing Iraq's domestic crisis within the scope of Chapter VII of the Charter. Three of the council's permanent members (Britain, France, and the United States) then proceeded, in an action whose legality is still disputed, to send forces into northern Iraq to enable the Kurdish refugees to return home by giving them protection against their own government.

In its turn, this unprecedented action aroused expectations among some northern elites, and in some nongovernmental groups in the third world, that henceforth "world order" could be enforced by international action, not only in cases of aggression by one state against another but also in cases of civil conflict or gross violations of human rights occurring within a state's boundaries. President François Mitterrand, for instance, hailed the passage of Resolution 688 by proclaiming that "for the first time, non-interference has stopped at the point where it was becoming failure to assist a people in danger."[2] And a few weeks later the deputy general secretary of the Sudan Council of Churches was quoted as saying:

> The whole question of sovereignty needs to be addressed for Sudan as in Iraq. If a regime has proved absolutely intransigent, has used food as a political weapon, and is incapable of feeding its own people, the option of the international community should not be abdication and indifference, but intervention. The precedent set in Iraq should be applied to Africa, where the situation is more grave.[3]

In the years since then, such expectations have been cruelly deflated. The Iraqi precedent was applied to Africa, not in the Sudan (where no external power has been willing to confront the "intransigent" government), but in Somalia, where the problem was not an intransigent government but the absence of any effective government at all. In Resolution 794 of 3 December 1992, the Security Council explicitly authorized action under Chapter VII. U.S. troops went into Somalia in a spirit of genuine humanitarian idealism, but in less than a year it all went sour. The United States became engaged in a grotesque trial of strength with a local Somali warlord, General Farah Aidid, in circumstances that became harder and harder to explain to the American public. In October 1993, after an incident in which two U.S. helicopters were shot down, eighteen U.S. Rangers killed and seventy-five wounded, and one of the bodies dragged through the streets of Mogadishu in full view of television cameras, President Bill Clinton announced that all U.S. troops would be out by 31 March 1994. In less than a year after that, the rest of the UN force was also pulled out, leaving behind a country as anarchic as the one it had found. (See "The

New World Order: Somalia," p. 131 in this chapter.)

Meanwhile, the international community has proved unable or unwilling to prevent large-scale "ethnic cleansing" in the former Yugoslavia, or even wholesale genocide in Rwanda. The Soviet Union, which President Bush saw as an indispensable partner in the construction of his New World Order, has fallen apart, leaving many conflicts within and between its successor states. At the end of 1994 the largest of these, the Russian Federation (which inherited the Soviet seat in the Security Council), embarked on the brutal suppression of a separatist movement in Chechnya. Other powers might deplore this, but they did not dream of intervening militarily to safeguard the Chechen population, any more than they would intervene to make Tibet a "safe haven" from Chinese oppression.

When, if ever, should liberals acquiesce in, or indeed advocate, military intervention by outsiders in the domestic conflicts of sovereign states? And what should the objective of such intervention be: to halt conflicts once they have started, or to prevent them? Should it be restricted only to the most extreme circumstances, such as genocide, or can it have a broader mission to promote humanitarian causes? The aim of this study commissioned by the John Stuart Mill Institute is, if not to answer such questions, at least to illuminate them by examining, first, what Mill himself had to say in his essay *A Few Words on Non-Intervention*,[4] and, second, how his principles can be applied to a number of actual interventions since 1945. I hope in the process to throw some light on the kind of "new world order" we can reasonably aspire to, and in particular on the role that armed force might play in securing it.

John Stuart Mill and Nonintervention

The doctrine of nonintervention is, of course, much older than the United Nations. It has its origin in the self-interest of states, just as the doctrines of the inviolability of the person and of the sanctity of private property have their origin in the self-interest of individuals. States have an interest in their own sovereignty. They do not wish to be interfered with by other powers. They therefore have an interest in proclaiming a general doctrine of noninterference—and in following it at least so far as will encourage other states to do likewise.

Can one distinguish between the interest of a state and the interest of the people residing in it, governed by it, or purportedly represented by it? It is on this question that the contemporary debate about nonintervention hinges. Historically, however, most military interventions in the domestic affairs of a state have been carried out by the armed forces of another state, and those who advocated, ordered, or defended such interventions have usually invoked as their primary motive the national interest of their own people, rather than that of the people in whose domestic affairs they were intervening. There are two reasons for this:

First, intervention involves expenditure of one's own national resources and, in the nature of things, also involves some risk to one's own citizens—certainly to those serving in the intervening force, often to others as well. National governments are assumed to exist primarily for the benefit of their own nations. They therefore feel an obligation to show that their own nation will derive some net benefit from the expenditure and can expect some advantage to justify the risk.

Second, a policy of intervening in other states "for their own good" is liable to provoke anxiety and hostility among other governments beyond the state directly concerned. This is less likely to happen if the intervening state justifies its intervention by reference to specific circumstances that threaten its own national interest. An intervention justified on grounds of national interest is thus, however paradoxically, less threatening to international order than one justified by reference to a global interest. This point is recognized, albeit in more restrictive form, by the UN Charter (Article 51) when it allows self-defense against armed attack as "the one remaining completely unambiguous justification for states using force."[5]

Traditional justifications for nonintervention were, therefore, based not so much on asserting an identity of interest between the state whose sovereignty was violated and its people as on emphasizing the risks and costs incurred by the state or states tempted to intervene. It was arguments of this traditional type that Mill sought to refute in 1859. Writing as a citizen of the greatest naval power of the time, one much given to interventions that, in his view, were in fact disinterested and motivated by high principle (notably the suppression of the slave trade), he deplored the propensity of British ministers to justify their nonintervention in the war of Italian unity on the grounds that "we ought not to interfere where no English interest is concerned."

Mill was addressing a public opinion that evidently anticipated the UN Charter in believing that one should not go to war "without having been ourselves attacked, or threatened with attack." He conceded that "to go to war for an idea, if the war is aggressive, not defensive, is as criminal as to go to war for territory or revenue; for it is as little justifiable to force our ideas on other people, as to compel them to submit to our will in any other respect." But he went on to argue that intervention was permissible, and sometimes even an obligation, when a "civilized" government found itself alongside "barbarous" neighbors. "Barbarians," he suggested, "have no rights as a *nation*, except a right to such treatment as may, at the earliest possible period, fit them for becoming one." The civilized government sooner or later "either finds itself obliged to conquer them, or to assert so much authority over them, and so break their spirit, that they gradually sink into a state of dependence on itself: and when that time arrives, they are indeed no longer formidable to it, but it has had so much to do with setting up and pulling down their governments, and they have grown so accustomed to lean on it, that it has become morally responsible for all evil it allows them to do," and thus incurs an obligation toward their subjects.

Mill was thinking about relations between the British Empire and the "native states" in India. His reasoning is a classic exposition of the argument for imperial expansion. Yet it is also revealingly close to today's arguments for "humanitarian intervention" in "failed states," such as Somalia, Liberia, and Sierra Leone in Africa or Georgia and Tajikistan in the former Soviet Union. The "failure" of such states is often blamed on assistance previously given by great powers or international institutions to despotic and incompetent governments.

When dealing with "civilized peoples, members of an equal community of nations, like Christian Europe," by contrast, Mill believed that intervention was only justified to help "a people struggling against a foreign yoke, or against a native tyranny upheld by foreign arms." In such cases he warned against intervening "when the contest is only with native rulers, and with such native strength as those rulers can enlist in their defense," because "there can seldom be anything approaching to assurance that intervention, even if successful, would be for the good of the people themselves." People would only make a success of "popular institutions" (or, as we should now say, democracy) if "they, or a sufficient portion of them to prevail in the contest, are willing to brave labor and danger for their liberation."

Mill was thus clear that Britain would have been right to intervene on the side of the Hungarian revolution of 1848–49 once Russia had intervened against it. But "it might not have been right" to intervene before that, "although the Austrian Government in Hungary was *in some sense* a foreign yoke" (italics added). His uncertainty on this point should strike a chord with us today. In many contemporary conflicts, the question whether the issue is domestic or international—in Mill's terms, whether the rulers are "native" or "foreign"—is precisely what is in dispute. Accepted practice is for outsiders to treat a conflict as "domestic" so long as they have not recognized any of the parties as separate states. For instance, the conflict in the former Yugoslavia was officially regarded as a domestic one when it broke out in 1991. Yet it was rapidly apparent that new states would sooner or later be recognized, and outside bodies (notably the European Community) attempted to use the timing and conditions of recognition as levers to bring the conflict under control. This tactic may perhaps have helped to bring about a cease-fire in Croatia in January 1992 (the point is disputed). It certainly failed to avert, and may well have precipitated, the outbreak of war in Bosnia-Herzegovina.

The authorities in the new states assumed (perhaps not unnaturally, in the immediate aftermath of the Gulf War) that international recognition and UN membership would internationalize the conflicts in progress on their territory and so entitle them to expect assistance against what they saw as external aggression. It turned out, however, that the international community was quite unable to agree on any such straightforward interpretation. The precise degree of continuing Serbian involvement in Croatia and Bosnia since those states were recognized and admitted to the UN remains a matter of intense dispute, but it is clear that these are not international conflicts in the classic sense. Politically, if not legally, they come in a special category, which we may call "wars of federal secession." In such wars the borders, if not the existence, of new states are contested by some of their inhabitants, with a degree of support from other states that were formerly part of the same federation. External intervention in such conflicts, whatever its legal justification, is liable to pose many of the same moral and practical problems as intervention in a purely domestic crisis.

Mill treats as a special case "that of a protracted civil war, in which the contending parties are so equally balanced that there is no probability of a speedy issue" or in which neither side could hope to hold down the other without "severities repugnant to humanity, and injurious to the permanent welfare of the country" (what we should now call "gross violations of human rights"). In such cases, he writes, "it seems now to be an admitted doctrine, that the neighboring nations, or one powerful neighbor with the acquiescence of the rest, are warranted in demanding that the contest shall cease, and a reconciliation take place on equitable terms of compromise." Interestingly, the examples he gives are mostly of secessionist struggles in which the external intervention resulted in recognition, de jure or de facto, of a new independent state (Greece, Belgium, Egypt).

Mill's analysis is relevant today partly because, even since the creation of the UN, most actual interventions in domestic crises have been the work of one state, most often a neighbor, acting on its own authority; and not all of these have attracted general condemnation. The 1970s produced three strikingly effective unilateral interventions: those of India in East Pakistan

(1971), Vietnam in Cambodia (1978), and Tanzania in Uganda (1979). None of these was authorized by the UN. All, indeed, were in more or less transparent violation of the Charter, though the intervening states justified their action as self-defense under Article 51. But all three were largely approved by world public opinion as having put an end to regimes guilty of very large-scale human rights violations. In the first case, India behaved much like the European powers of Mill's time, and the UN actually admitted a new member state (Bangladesh) whose establishment was a direct result of the intervention. In the third case (Uganda), the international community accepted Idi Amin's overthrow without protest—indeed, for the most part, with relief. Only in the second case (Cambodia) did the UN refuse recognition to the new regime installed by the intervening power, and even then, many of the states voting to deny recognition were careful to disclaim any desire to restore the regime that had been ousted. A roughly parallel case occurred in the early 1980s: the U.S. intervention in Grenada (1983). This was generally condemned outside the immediate region where it occurred but welcomed by the population of Grenada itself. There, too, the results have been allowed to stand. No one has advocated restoration of the regime that the United States intervened to remove only days after it had itself seized power in a military coup.

Among the points made by Mill, or deducible from his argument, the following would seem to be at least potentially applicable to our contemporary debate:

- The moral case for intervention does not depend on the authorization, or even existence, of an international organization. Where intervention is justified, the moral responsibility lies with those who have the power to undertake it.

- Intervention is generally justified to counter another intervention. It is unlikely to be effective in a purely domestic conflict.

- It will not, however, always be easy to say whether a given conflict is purely domestic or not. That very fact is often at issue between the parties, especially, of course, in wars of secession or of "federal succession."

- An exception to the principle of nonintervention may also arise in the case of states so weak ("barbarian" in Mill's terms) that stronger states cannot avoid a degree of responsibility for their internal misrule. This would appear to apply to the category now known as "failed states."

The UN and Nonintervention: Behind Article 2.7

A contemporary of Mill's, W. E. Gladstone, combined support for "the principle of non-intervention in the domestic affairs of other countries" as the basis of British national policy with advocacy of "coercion by the united authority of Europe" as the right way to bring about "better government" in Turkey.[6] That distinction has been inherited by many of today's internationalists. They would condemn intervention by a single great power but argue for a right or even a duty of the United Nations to intervene in certain types of domestic crises.

We must ask, then, why the UN Charter includes Article 2.7, which is clearly intended to prohibit such interventions. The simple and obvious reason is that the UN was founded by the governments of sovereign states that intended to stay sovereign. Their object was to reduce, and if possible eliminate, the risk of conflict between them by setting up a body that would assume, in relations between states, some of the functions performed by a government and police force in relations between the citizens of a single state. But each of them assumed itself competent to continue performing those functions for its own citizens and had no intention of legitimizing external interference in its affairs by offering to share that responsibility with others.

Such is the historical *explanation*. What has been or can be said by way of *justification*? The main point must be that the UN is not a world government and that there are as yet no practicable or credible proposals to turn it into one.

The maintenance of public order within a given society requires a civil power wielding an overwhelming preponderance, if not a monopoly, of physical force. In some societies the consent of the governed results directly from that preponderance: people obey the civil power primarily out of fear. In other societies it is the other way round: the civil power enjoys a monopoly of force, without having to exercise it very often, because most of the citizens accept it as legitimate. Clearly those who advocate world government want it to be legitimate in this sense.

But how is such legitimacy acquired? Historically the most common process has been a gradual development from the first type of society to the second. With the passage of time and of generations, fear becomes habit, and power once regarded as arbitrary comes to be seen as normal and therefore legitimate. Sometimes this process is rationalized ex post facto with notions such as the implicit "social contract" between governors and governed. This in turn can be made explicit, when the constitution of a state or its existence, or the adherence of a given territory to a larger state, is confirmed by popular vote, and when rulers are elected by the ruled. Such forms of legitimation, under the broad heading of "democracy," have in the present age come to be widely if not universally regarded as the only valid ones—at least in theory. (Practice is often rather different.)

This historical process would be repeated on a global scale if one power succeeded in imposing its rule on the whole of the human race, if this rule in due course came to be generally accepted as legitimate (presumably because de facto it maintained world peace) and if, at a later stage, the people actually exercising the power were chosen by the majority of the world's population and used their power to enforce laws passed by globally representative institutions. This could only be accomplished over several generations. In the first stage, the world government would be widely regarded as arbitrary and illegitimate. It could be established only by war; and no modern political theory would regard its establishment as an object justifying war. No one, as far as I know, is proposing that the UN should be turned into a world government by such means.

The only alternative method would be for the peoples of the world, acting presumably through their representatives in the General Assembly, voluntarily to invest the UN with the power and responsibility to maintain order within states as well as between them. Such a cession of sovereignty would be of very dubious validity so long as the representatives in question (i.e., the governments of the existing UN member states) were not freely chosen by the people whom they purport to represent. Even if the day comes when all of them are so chosen, it seems very unlikely that they would take such a decision. It might also be less necessary for them to do so, since freely chosen governments are less likely to resort to, or to tolerate, large-scale abuses against the populations by whom they are chosen.

Generally speaking, the experience of this century has undermined faith in projects of large-scale centralized organization and has vindicated "Whig" theories that put a premium on the discretion of individuals and small groups in managing their own affairs. It has hardly been notable for the successful resolution of local conflicts by megalithic politicomilitary bureaucracies, with headquarters remote from the scene of action. Such exceptions as can be adduced were usually the work of one state acting in an imperial or neo-imperial mode: France in sub-Saharan Africa; Britain in Malaya, Kenya and Oman; the United States (perhaps) in various central American and Caribbean countries; Russia (perhaps) in Tajikistan.

In short, the doctrine enshrined in Article 2.7 should not be seen as purely cynical or self-serving. It can be justified on the grounds that the

UN lacks the competence, in the practical as well as the legal sense of the term, to intervene effectively in domestic crises; that it is hard to imagine it acquiring such competence; and that in many cases its intervention would be likely, on balance, to make things worse rather than better.

Intervention in Theory: A Typology

Before taking the discussion any further, it may be helpful to distinguish among different categories of international action, all or most of which are from time to time included under the broad heading of "intervention."

1. Conflict prevention/resolution: Diplomatic and other noncoercive activity aimed at settling disputes by negotiation and avoiding the use of force (if it has not yet occurred) or (where conflict is already in progress) at ending it, or at least preventing the escalation of violence. This is a virtually automatic response to conflict once it starts or is clearly imminent. Preventive diplomacy by third parties is rarer at an earlier stage, though that is when it is probably most effective. The point is difficult to demonstrate because, as one senior UN official said when a television company asked where it could film preventive diplomacy in action, "If you can film it, it probably isn't working." But one may cite the work of the high commissioner on national minorities of the Organization for Security and Cooperation in Europe (OSCE) and the Stability Pact framework devised by the European Union for resolving bilateral disputes among central and east European countries.

2. Peacekeeping (classic model): Positioning of lightly armed forces as neutral observers in a conflict zone, with the consent of the parties to the conflict, as a confidence-building measure to help them maintain a cease-fire (examples: Sinai, Golan). This does not solve the conflict but is intended to facilitate a solution by allowing a decrease in tension and giving time for negotiations. It can, however, help to freeze the conflict, allowing whichever party has the upper hand at the time of the cease-fire to consolidate its gains (example: Cyprus).

3. Preventive deployment: Same as the classic peacekeeping model, but undertaken before actual conflict has broken out (example: Macedonia).

4. Peacekeeping (end-of-Cold-War model): Extended version of classic peacekeeping, introduced as part of a negotiated political solution. Here the responsibilities of peacekeepers may include weapons collection, resettlement of refugees and/or disarmed combatants, election monitoring, police training and supervision, assistance in integrating former rebels into state armed forces, provision of accurate, unbiased information to the population, and other temporary administrative tasks (examples: Namibia; Cambodia, 1992–93; El Salvador; Mozambique). Note that some cases, such as the UN forces in Lebanon and Croatia, are borderline between preventive deployment and the end-of-Cold-War peacekeeping model.

5. *Enforcement:* Use of armed force to:

- reverse aggression (examples: UN in Korea, 1950; UN member states authorized by Security Council in Kuwait, 1991)

- impose a settlement on parties that have not consented to it (example: Syria in Lebanon, 1976)

- restore a legitimate government that has been deposed by force (example: United States authorized by the Security Council in Haiti, 1994)

- protect a population against genocide or other abuse (examples: India in East Pakistan, 1971; Vietnam in Cambodia, 1978; Tanzania in Uganda, 1979; United States in Grenada, 1983; United States and others in northern Iraq, 1991)

- prevent weapons from reaching one or more parties to a conflict (example: NATO and Western European Union (WEU) on behalf of the UN in the former Yugoslavia since 1991; United States against Nicaragua in the 1980s)

- enforce economic sanctions against one or more parties to a conflict (examples: the United Kingdom on behalf of UN in Rhodesia; NATO and WEU on behalf of the UN against Serbia and Montenegro since 1992)

- enforce "no-fly zones" in areas of conflict (examples: United States and United Kingdom in northern Iraq since 1991 and southern Iraq since 1992; NATO on behalf of the UN in Bosnia-Herzegovina since 1993)

- sustain or reimpose friendly regime against internal/external threat (examples: USSR in Hungary, 1956, Czechoslovakia, 1968, Afghanistan, 1979; United States in the Dominican Republic, Guatemala, Vietnam, etc; France in various African states; United Kingdom in Oman; and the UN in the Congo)

Among these categories, the most important dividing line falls between the end-of-Cold-War peacekeeping and enforcement models.

The first four all presuppose the consent of the parties to the conflict or potential conflict.[7] In this chapter the primary focus is on enforcement. That is not intended to belittle the importance of the other categories. Other things being equal, it is certainly preferable to avoid the use of force, to reach negotiated solutions, and above all to prevent conflicts from reaching the stage of large-scale violence in the first place, wherever that can be done. Undoubtedly, international organizations and their member states should devote more of their resources to these activities than they do at present: by doing so, they could save much money as well as many lives. But it is enforcement that raises the main issue of principle: when and in what manner do outsiders have a right or a duty to intervene, in the sense of interfering in a conflict where one or more of the parties want outsiders to keep out?

That issue, it is important to note, may very well arise even when the "intervention" is invited or requested by the government of the state concerned. Whereas states may be entitled to expect assistance when they are the object of external aggression, it is by no means clear that a government has a right to seek external military assistance, or that any external party has the right to render it such assistance, in resolving a domestic crisis. That right has often been asserted, and exercised, by states or groups of states. But it has almost always been contested, internationally as well as domestically. Why? Because it assumes that the sovereignty of a state is the exclusive property of its government, or rather of whatever body is recognized as being its government by another state that is willing to render military "assistance." Yet the very existence of a domestic crisis that cannot be resolved without recourse to such assistance implies a situation where a government's hold on power is tenuous and its legitimacy very seriously contested within the country.

In such circumstances one cannot assume an identity of interest between government and people. There is obviously room for an alternative view of the matter, in which sovereignty belongs to the whole people of a state, and the government is merely one of the parties to a domestic crisis or conflict, so that whoever assists it is intervening (in the sense of interfering) just as much as whoever assists its opponents. As Mill put it in his 1859 essay:

> Assistance to the government of a country in keeping down the people, unhappily by far the most frequent case of foreign intervention, no one writing in a free country needs take the trouble of stigmatizing. A government which needs foreign support to enforce obedience from its own citizens, is one which ought not to exist; and the assistance given to it by foreigners is hardly ever anything but the sympathy of one despotism with another.[8]

In short, even when external military forces enter a state at the invitation, or with the consent, of the government, so long as their arrival is opposed by other parties to the domestic conflict or crisis, we should still consider the action as an intervention.

Any of the above types of intervention may be undertaken with a humanitarian motive; indeed, we may well argue that none of them can be justified unless their effect is humanitarian in the broad sense of resulting in a net diminution of suffering. But the phrase "humanitarian intervention" is also used to describe actions whose objectives are limited to the *direct relief of suffering* among the civilian population, without—ostensibly at least—attempting to influence the political outcome of a conflict. Such actions may be treated as a separate category that, however, should be subdivided into two clearly distinct types:

6(a). Action by unarmed civilians: This can in some circumstances be undertaken without the consent of the state on whose territory it occurs. See UN General Assembly Resolutions 43/131 (8 December 1988) and 46/182 (19 December 1991) (example: "Operation Lifeline Sudan").

6(b). Action by armed forces: This may be undertaken to protect unarmed civilian intervenors, or the armed forces themselves may provide relief (examples: Bosnia, Somalia).

Action by unarmed civilians presupposes at least the passive consent of those who would be in a position to obstruct relief operations if they so chose. It is thus on the near side of the line dividing end-of-Cold-War peacekeeping from enforcement. Action by armed forces, by contrast, is problematic precisely because it too often blurs this dividing line. As Charles Dobbie, the British army's leading theoretician on the subject, explains, consent "is unlikely ever to be more than partial."[9] Lack of consent at the "operational" level (the senior level of command within the theater of operations) can be compensated for by its presence at the local level. More frequently the opposite is the case: the consent of political authorities and senior military commanders allows peacekeepers to "call the bluff" of local commanders (i.e., operate without their full or explicit consent). Thus, a degree of force can sometimes be used to override obstruction of relief operations without compromising the overall context of consent in which the operations are being conducted. But these are very fine judgments for peacekeepers to make. They have to navigate between the Scylla of outright hostility from one or more of the parties on the ground (which would catapult them from peacekeeping into enforcement) and the Charybdis of public opinion "back home"—that is, in countries with a decisive influence on their mandate—which may expect them to move into an enforcement mode, without understanding what that requires in the way of much larger and more heavily armed forces, as well as quite different rules of engagement. It is in this area above all that greater clarity of thought is needed on the part of those who take decisions on international action about the precise type of action they intend to take.

Intervention in Practice: The UN Experience

In this section I shall look in slightly greater detail at some specific crises where the UN may be said to have intervened, in the above sense of interfering, in the domestic affairs of its member states, that is, enforcement operations, or at least humanitarian intervention by armed forces.

The Congo: A Cold War Aberration

Such interventions are widely held to be an innovation of the post–Cold War era, but in fact there is at least one precedent from the time of the Cold War itself. In the Congo crisis of 1960–64 the UN did intervene quite dramatically—and successfully, inasmuch as the Katanga secession was thwarted and the country's territorial integrity preserved.

This was done by a kind of unintentional sleight of hand, or what would now be called "mission creep." The crisis began immediately after the former Belgian Congo (later renamed Zaire, and now Democratic Republic of the Congo) was proclaimed independent in 1960, when Congolese soldiers mutinied against their Belgian officers. To protect European residents, Belgian troops then deployed out of their bases and took over the airport of the capital Léopoldville (now Kinshasa). This was done without the permission of the Congolese government, which responded by requesting UN military assistance to repel Belgian "aggression." The UN force (ONUC) was accordingly deployed, with the government's consent and indeed at its invitation. But initially the force was prohibited from becoming a party to any internal conflict, from enforcing any specific political solution, and from seeking to influence the balance of political power. It was authorized to use force only in self-defense.

Only after ONUC had been deployed in the country for seven months, and after the murder of the deposed Congolese prime minister, Patrice Lumumba, did the Security Council urge the secretariat to take all appropriate measures to prevent civil war, including the use of force if necessary—thereby transforming a "nonthreatening" peacekeeping force into an enforcement agency authorized to intervene in what was essentially a domestic crisis. Belgian involvement in the secessionist province of Katanga (where Lumumba was murdered) provided an "international" context for the council's action; yet the council never identified Belgium as an aggressor nor authorized any enforcement action directly against it. (Any proposal to do so would have been vetoed by Britain and France.) Thereafter the force intervened directly: first to prevent the white-mercenary-led Katanga gendarmerie from crushing its opponents; then—backed by a new Security Council resolution—to apprehend and deport mercenaries and other foreign "advisers"; and finally, in response to repeated attacks and provocations, to establish full control of Katanga and put an end to its secession.[10]

The operation was a success. It prevented the breakup of the Congo, thereby probably helping prevent the disintegration of other newly independent African states and limiting the effects of the Cold War on Africa. But it also involved significant casualties among the UN force—including the secretary-general himself, Dag Hammarskjöld, who was killed in an air crash—and there were repeated and acrimonious clashes between the Secretariat and four of the five permanent members (the Soviet Union, the United States, France, and Britain), all of which had strong and divergent views about what should and should not be done in the Congo, though all five were deliberately excluded from contributing their own troops. In short, it was a traumatic experience for everyone involved.

With hindsight it was clear that an ad hoc military force, taking its orders from a tiny staff in New York and composed of units from many different states, was hardly the ideal body to reimpose law and order in a vast country that had dissolved into chaos—even in times when states were on the whole more tolerant of casualties among their armed forces in such operations than they are today. It became an axiom that the experience should not be repeated.

Cambodia: The End of the Cold War

Indeed, it was not until 1992—in Cambodia, the former Yugoslavia, and Somalia—that the UN again became involved in operations at all comparable to that in the Congo. Cambodia was perhaps the closest parallel. As the name of the UN mission, UN Transitional Authority in Cambodia (UNTAC), implied, its political mandate went much further than that of ONUC. It did not, in fact, fully take over the administration of the country, but it did provide many services while organizing elections for a constituent assembly. On the other hand, UNTAC did not emulate ONUC in the actual use of force. As in the Congo, the UN became involved in Cambodia's domestic crisis because of its international dimension—the legacy of the 1978 Vietnamese invasion—but without identifying Vietnam as an aggressor or having any mandate to use force. It went in on the basis of an agreement that supposedly ensured the consent of all parties, but it actually found itself having to implement the agreement in the face of bitter opposition from one of parties, the Khmer Rouge, and considerable non-compliance from another, the Vietnam-backed Phnom Penh government.

Yet, almost miraculously, it succeeded in its mission without having to use force. "The operation was conducted entirely within Chapter VI of the Charter, i.e. through persuasion and the consent of the parties, with no coercive or military enforcement measures in the mandate."[11] It thus perhaps fell just short of being a full-scale intervention, in the sense defined above. Indeed, its success has been attributed precisely to the fact that— in the words of its force commander[12]—UNTAC resisted pressure from "people both within and outside the United Nations" to engage in offensive operations against the Khmer Rouge.

The Cambodian operation was the result of years of negotiations. Undoubtedly the conclusion of these was facilitated by the end of the Cold War. Great powers were less distrustful of each other, the Security Council found it easier to agree on resolutions, and expectations of the UN were raised by its involvement in the solution of various international conflicts from 1988 onwards, most notably the independence of Namibia. By contrast, the settlement in Cambodia was probably not affected much by the Persian Gulf crisis of 1990–91, which occurred while the Cambodian settlement was already in gestation.

The New World Order: Northern Iraq

That crisis did, however, have a profound effect both on the worldwide image of the UN and on the debate about military intervention in domestic crises. The success of the coalition authorized by the Security Council in reversing Iraq's aggression against Kuwait led to greatly enhanced expectations of the UN's ability to enforce international order in post–Cold War conditions—expectations encapsulated in George Bush's "new world order" rhetoric. The subsequent Operation Provide Comfort—undertaken by a small group of member states in northern Iraq to secure an area in which Iraqi Kurds would be protected against the repression of their own government—was clearly a military intervention in a domestic crisis. It was unprecedented in being carried out not by any of Iraq's neighbors but by a group of powers that included three permanent members of the Security Council and in being justified explicitly on humanitarian grounds. This, too, led to expectations (and fears) that Article 2.7 was now a dead letter and that the new world order would be one in which sovereignty could be forcibly overridden in the name of universal principles such as human rights.

Whether it can properly be described as a UN intervention is debatable. It was preceded by Security Council Resolution 688, which called on Iraq to cease its oppression and "insisted" that it allow access by humanitarian organizations. The resolution, however, did not authorize any enforcement action, and in its preamble it explicitly recalled Article 2.7 as well as reaffirming the commitment of all member states to Iraq's sovereignty, territorial integrity, and political independence. It did also describe the Kurdish refugee crisis as a "threat to international peace and security." The U.S. government has argued that this brought the situation within the scope of Resolution 678—the enabling resolution for the military action to liberate Kuwait—since that resolution authorized the use of "all necessary means" to restore international peace and security in the region. (Most international lawyers regard this assertion as very dubious, especially since Resolution 688 does not refer to Resolution 678 or any of the previous Gulf crisis resolutions.) Without making this explicit link, the British and French governments have also stated or implied that Resolution 688 authorized their intervention in northern Iraq. President Mitterrand of France, in particular, made the statement, quoted in the introduction to this chapter, that "for the first time, non-interference has stopped at the point where it was becoming failure to assist a people in danger."

Mitterrand did not explain exactly how one identifies "a people" in this sense. Nor did he make explicit what form of assistance he had in mind. His phraseology contained an echo, no doubt conscious, of the French penal code, which contains an offense of "failure to assist a person in danger." The internationalization of this concept, substituting "people" for "person," was the work of Bernard Kouchner, founder of the charity Médecins sans Frontières and in 1991 minister for humanitarian affairs in the French government.

Kouchner also coined the phrase *devoir d'ingérence* (duty to interfere). In its original form this applied to the role of humanitarian organizations. The right, or duty, of such organizations to ignore state frontiers in carrying out relief work had been widely canvassed, particularly in the context of Sudan, since the mid-1980s, and it achieved a degree of recognition from the UN General Assembly in Resolutions 43/131 of 8 December 1988 (adopted after the earthquake in Armenia) and 46/182 of 19 December 1991. Both of these sought to articulate the right of people in desperate situations to receive humanitarian aid, and the right of international bodies to provide it, while still paying full respect to state sovereignty. But Kouchner, and implicitly Mitterrand, went well beyond the General Assembly's intentions in applying this concept to military intervention.

If Operation Provide Comfort established a precedent, it may be that it is not a precedent for UN intervention but for a general right or duty of humanitarian intervention, to be exercised by any state or states that are in a position to do so—a concept that would find its strongest legal support in the Convention on the Prevention and Punishment of the Crime of Genocide. That convention, adopted by the General Assembly as long ago as 1948 and accepted as of September 1994 by 114 states, puts all its signatories under an obligation to "prevent and punish" genocide, which is thus an offense against international law—Article 2.7 notwithstanding—even when directed by a state against its own citizens.[13] The convention defines genocide as any of the following acts committed with intent to destroy, in whole or in part, a national, ethnic, racial, or religious group, as such:

- killing members of the group

- causing serious bodily or mental harm to members of the group

- deliberately inflicting on the group conditions of life calculated to bring about its physical destruction in whole or in part

- imposing measures intended to prevent births within the group

- forcibly transferring children of the group to another group[14]

A strong prima facie case could be made against Iraq under several of these headings. However, none of the powers involved in Operation Provide Comfort invoked the convention.

The New World Order: Somalia

A clearer example of UN intervention for humanitarian motives occurred in December 1992, when the Security Council explicitly authorized action in Somalia under Chapter VII of the Charter. This was perhaps the most purely humanitarian military intervention ever undertaken or authorized by the UN, in the sense that it is very hard to discern any broader political objective than relief of suffering within Somalia. It is now, however, generally accounted a failure.

This is probably to be attributed to confusion about its scope. The initial view of the United States, which provided the intervention force

(UNITAF), was that the scope should be confined to securing the delivery of food. By contrast, the secretary-general took the view that the intervention force could do no lasting good unless it disarmed the militias whose activities were the direct cause of the famine. At a later stage the United States appeared to come round to this view, or something close to it. After handing over in May to a UN peacekeeping force (UNOSOM II), of which it took effective command through the secretary-general's representative, a retired American admiral, the United States engaged in a trial of strength with a local warlord, General Farah Aidid, who refused to be disarmed and launched attacks on UN troops. This culminated in the incident referred to in the introduction in which the body of a U.S. Ranger was dragged through the streets—an episode that could be said to mark the end of the "New World Order," since it turned much of the American public against the UN and "peacekeeping" in general and thereby severely damped the enthusiasm of even the Clinton administration, let alone the Republican opposition. The U.S. troops were withdrawn from Somalia in March 1994, and UNOSOM II itself followed a year later, leaving the country still without any effective government.

On one level it was grossly unfair for Americans to turn against the UN because of the bungling of one UN mission by the United States itself. Yet it might have been right to conclude that military intervention offers no solution to a situation like that in Somalia, where the state had completely collapsed into clan warfare, unless the intervention is part of a long-term, quasi-colonial program of trusteeship and "nation-building," a program for which the American body politic has little appetite even in a country in its immediate vicinity like Haiti—of which more in a moment—let alone in one as far away and mysterious (to Americans) as Somalia.

The New World Order: Bosnia

A similar conclusion might apply to Bosnia-Herzegovina. There too the UN deployed forces with a humanitarian mandate in the midst of fighting and then authorized them to use force for certain limited purposes. There, however, U.S. forces were not involved on the ground but only in an enforcement role on the sea and in the air. Another important difference is that external observers, especially in the United States, found it much easier to take sides in the conflict, identifying the Bosnian government and its mainly Muslim constituency as victims and Serb forces (whether Bosnian or from Serbia proper) as aggressors. Moreover, the mandate was a hybrid one, which the Security Council was constantly adapted by passing new resolutions in response to developments on the ground. While the overall objective of these resolutions remained humanitarian, the forms of action envisaged were increasingly forceful, and in some cases were clearly incompatible with impartiality. This applies particularly to the resolutions passed in the spring and summer of 1993 that established "safe areas," supposedly under UN protection, without specifying that the areas in question—all of them at that time under Bosnian government control—should be demilitarized. Yet UN force commanders on the ground did not have sufficient forces or suitable equipment to intervene directly in the war, and they knew that most of the troops under their command had been sent by their home governments as peacekeepers, not to fight a war. They therefore continued to interpret their mandate as a purely humanitarian one and strove to maintain an impartial attitude toward the warring parties, discouraging the use of NATO air power against the Serbs for fear of reprisals against their troops, many of whom were deployed with only light arms in the midst of Serb forces that could easily take them hostage. This attitude, however rational, made the UN appear cowardly and ineffective, further alienating much of the American public.

Once again, much of the U.S. criticism was unfair in detail. But it is not clear that the UN military operation—which certainly contained elements of an intervention, given the lack of suitable preconditions for normal peacekeeping—ever made any strategic sense. As in Somalia, it may well be that the only sensible use of force would have been to impose a UN trusteeship for a period of years, preventing and where necessary reversing "ethnic cleansing" and preventing further bloodshed while confidence was built or rebuilt between ethnic communities and political structures acceptable to all of them were worked out. This is approximately what the international community has been trying to do in Bosnia since 1995, with Security Council authorization but no longer acting mainly through the UN.

The Post–New World Order:
A Return to Spheres of Influence?

At least the situation in Bosnia could with some plausibility be identified as a "threat to the peace" of a wider region. But in Haiti (1994), as in Somalia (1992), the Security Council recognized an almost entirely fictitious threat to the peace in order to authorize intervention by the United States in a purely domestic crisis—in this case the overthrow of the elected Haitian president by the Haitian armed forces. This was a slow-motion crisis: three and a half years elapsed between the coup and the military intervention. It was abundantly clear that U.S. concern arose not from the absolute gravity of the human rights abuses occurring but from the proximity of Haiti and the problem posed to the United States itself by the flow of Haitian refugees. In fact, although blessed by the Security Council, in most respects this intervention continued the tradition of U.S. unilateral interventions in its Caribbean and Central American "backyard." Like them, it had token backing from a regional body, the Organization of American States. It follows an age-old pattern already referred to: that of states that intervene when their own interests or security seem to be threatened, through the generation of refugees or otherwise, by the domestic conflicts of their neighbors.

A significant and perhaps rather sinister feature of the buildup to intervention in Haiti was that Russia withheld its support for the "authorizing" resolution until agreement was reached on a similar resolution legitimizing its own peacekeeping role in one of its own newly "independent" neighbors, Georgia. On the face of it, this was not an intervention in the sense we are discussing here, since by 1994 the Russian presence was welcomed by the Georgian government as well as the Abkhazian separatists. But it was an open secret that this welcome had been secured only after the Abkhazians, with backing from a Russian garrison across the border, had driven Georgian troops out of their region and after the Georgian state had all but collapsed. In exchange for Russian help in defeating the forces of his predecessor and rival, Zviad Gamsakhurdia, Georgian head of state Eduard Shevardnadze had agreed to join the Russian-dominated Commonwealth of Independent States and to permit Russian military bases on Georgian territory. This certainly constituted a military intervention by Russia in a Georgian domestic crisis even if, as in the former Yugoslavia, the "domestic" and "international" aspects of events in the former Soviet Union are difficult to disentangle. The quid pro quo in the Security Council in July 1994 over Georgia and Haiti came ominously close to recognizing "spheres of influence" for two of the permanent members in which they are free to intervene with the implicit authority of the UN.

Had the criterion for intervention been genuinely humanitarian, rather than the concern of great powers to control and "stabilize" their immediate neighborhoods, the council would surely have taken swift and decisive action to deal with the unmistakable, organized genocide that occurred in Rwanda in April and May 1994 in which at least half a million, and probably nearer a million, people died. A UN "assistance mission" (UNAMIR) of about twenty-five hundred military personnel, as well as a civilian police unit, was already on the spot as part of a peace agreement negotiated between the Hutu-dominated Rwandan government and the mainly Tutsi Rwandese Patriotic Front (RPF) the previous August. When ten Belgian soldiers were killed, along with the Rwandan prime minister to whose protection they had been assigned, the Security Council decided to withdraw most of the remaining soldiers rather than order them to intervene to stop the killing and reinforce them appropriately.

On 17 May, nearly six weeks after the massacre began, the council decided to establish "secure humanitarian areas" to provide security for relief operations and to expand UNAMIR to fifty-five hundred troops, who, however, would still be permitted to use force only in self-defense. But a further six weeks elapsed before a single one of these soldiers appeared on the ground.[15] As the secretary-general later complained, "not one of the 19 Governments that at that time had undertaken to have troops on stand-by agreed to contribute."[16] Meanwhile, in the middle of June, the French government suddenly decided that the situation demanded immediate action. By then the RPF was close to defeating the government responsible for the genocide and was strongly opposed to intervention by a country with a long record of support for its opponents. But France obtained Security Council authorization for its action (with ten favorable votes and five abstentions) and proceeded to occupy the southwest of the country. Once again, the council had implicitly assigned to one of its permanent members responsibility for the maintenance of peace and security within a regional sphere of influence, in this case francophone Africa.

France's action undoubtedly saved thousands, if not tens of thousands, of lives; but it also covered the retreat of the defeated government forces, among whom were most of the organizers and perpetrators of the genocide. Many of them regrouped in refugee camps in Zaire, where, fed by a UN relief operation, they made preparations for renewing the war (and very likely the genocide as well).

Our Global Neighborhood

The Security Council obviously lacks any clear set of criteria for deciding on intervention. It is drifting into a cynical and self-serving practice whereby its permanent members—who have no need to fear intervention by anyone else, however barbarically they act within their own borders—can, without too much difficulty, obtain "authorization" to intervene to ensure "stability" in their immediate neighborhood or in a region where they have a traditional influence.

Under the Charter as it stands, the council has effectively absolute discretion to "determine," in the terms of Article 39, that a domestic crisis

constitutes a "threat to the peace." Once it has done that, it is free to intervene or to authorize intervention by member states. In his letter of 29
November 1992 to the president of the Security Council suggesting the
use of force in Somalia, the secretary-general appeared to treat Article 39
as a matter of pure form. "At present," he wrote, "no government exists
in Somalia that could request or allow such use of force. It would therefore be necessary for the Security Council to make a determination under
Article 39 of the Charter that a threat to the peace exists . . . and to decide
what measures should be taken to maintain international peace and security."[17] The council duly made the required determination.

The Commission on Global Governance, in its report *Our Global Neighbourhood*, published in January 1995, seeks to relieve the council of the
need for such transparent hypocrisy:

> We are all for enlarging the capacity of the Charter by enlightened interpre-
> tation, but when that reading strains credulity, it may be unsustainable.
> There is an even more serious consideration, however. When the interna-
> tional community is dealing with an issue this sensitive, clarity is needed on
> both the nature and the limits of the authority to act. We believe a global
> consensus exists today for a UN response on humanitarian grounds in cases
> of gross abuse of the security of people. But if we seek to find a foothold for
> intervention, what will limit such intervention save a self-denying ordi-
> nance of the Security Council itself? What, then, if it decides—under pres-
> sure from powerful members, for example—that there should be interven-
> tion in cases of human rights abuses or undemocratic practices or for other
> reasons but without there being a clear and generally acknowledged threat
> to the security of people?[18]

With the phrase "the security of people," the commission makes a
praiseworthy attempt to broaden the concept of global security "beyond
the protection of borders, ruling elites, and exclusive state interests."[19] It
proposes to expand the provision in the Convention on Genocide that
allows contracting parties to "call upon the competent organs of the United
Nations" to take action for the prevention and suppression of acts of genocide by amending the Charter to include a "right of petition," enabling nonstate actors (individuals and organizations) to bring "threats to the security
of people" to the Security Council's attention and allowing the council to
intervene, or authorize intervention, in a state's internal affairs in "cases
that constitute a violation of the security of people so gross and extreme
that it requires an international response on humanitarian grounds."[20]

This formulation is intended to be restrictive. The commission wishes
to limit intervention "strictly to cases in which the international consen-

sus deems the violation of the security of people too gross to be toler-ated." That leaves open the question of how an international consensus is to be identified. The commission admits that "the line separating a domestic affair from a global one cannot be drawn in the sand" but adds, rather lamely, "we are convinced that in practice virtually all will know when it has been crossed." It suggests that the Security Council should ask itself whether a given situation has "deteriorated to the point where the security of people has been violated so severely that it requires an international response on humanitarian grounds."[21] But this is tautologi-cal. It amounts to saying that the council should only intervene where it believes that intervention is justified, leaving it to decide at its discretion what degree of grossness and extremity requires an international response. In the end, one falls back on the same "self-denying ordinance of the Security Council itself" that the Commission considers an inade-quate safeguard under the Charter as it stands; and the commission has to rely on an enlarged council membership, with five new, non-veto-wielding standing members and three extra rotating ones, to reflect the international consensus that it seeks.[22]

It seems safe to predict that agreement on reform of the Security Coun-cil will not be reached quickly and that agreement on precise criteria for intervention will be even more elusive. Certainly there is unlikely to be consensus on the desirability of intervening in circumstances less drastic than those defined as constituting genocide by the convention quoted above, under which (as the Commission on Global Governance points out) contracting parties already have the right to "call upon the competent organs of the United Nations to take such action under the Charter of the United Nations as they consider appropriate for the prevention and sup-pression of acts of genocide." Ideally, one might wish that the Charter were amended to make it clear that Article 2.7 does not preclude intervention in such cases and that the Security Council has both the right and the duty to intervene when acts are committed that will have the *effect* of destroying "in whole or in part, a national, ethnic, racial or religious group," without having to prove that such is the *intent* of the perpetrators. But it would be a great advance on current practice if the UN and its member states were to act on the genocide convention even as it now stands.

Conclusions

The conclusions of this study can only be discouraging to those who believed or hoped that a new and more moral world order in which an impartial international authority could be relied on to deter all gross violations of human rights was just around the corner. But a number of points emerge that may help clarify future discussion of these issues.

First, some of today's arguments for intervention may fairly be called "neo-imperialist." They bear a striking similarity to those of a nineteenth-century writer such as J. S. Mill. It is all the more important, then, to recall Mill's view that a "civilized" people should not need to be liberated from a *domestic* yoke by outside intervention, and indeed *would not benefit* from outside intervention in such a case. Mill's lesson for us today is that intervention may be necessary to deal with the problems of "failed states" (analogous to his "barbarians") but may not be an effective way to deal with tyrannies, unless the tyranny itself is clearly imposed by an external power. But, alas, it will not always be obvious—as it was not to Mill himself in the case of Hungary's revolt against Austria—whether a tyranny is external or not.

Second, in discussing UN military intervention in this paper, I have deliberately included not only actions by UN forces under the control of the secretariat—or, hypothetically, of the Military Staff Committee—but also action by member states authorized by the Security Council. As the secretary-general recognized in his *Supplement to An Agenda for Peace* (1995),[23] the latter formula is likely to remain the norm for enforcement action for the foreseeable future, since "neither the Security Council nor the Secretary-General at present has the capacity to deploy, direct, command and control operations for this purpose, except perhaps on a very limited scale." He believed it desirable "in the long term" that the UN develop such a capacity but conceded that "it would be folly to attempt to do so at the present time when the Organization is resource-starved and hard pressed to handle the less demanding peacemaking and peacekeeping responsibilities entrusted to it."

It appears therefore that for the foreseeable future the only decisive UN military interventions will be those carried out by one or more member states acting with authority from the Security Council. In such cases there is clearly a risk that they will intervene on what many will regard as the "wrong" side (as France did, with the council's blessing, in Rwanda), or will use disproportionate force, or will become caught in a Vietnam-style quagmire. Indeed, they may easily combine all three of those errors.

Third, intervention may also occur when UN forces are involved initially in a peacekeeping role or with a mandate only to ensure the delivery of relief to the civilian population but come to play an interventionist role or to call in intervention by member states, as they find themselves obstructed or attacked by the parties on the ground. While the consent of the parties is a crucial factor distinguishing peacekeeping from enforcement, it is important to note that consent given at the beginning of an operation does not guarantee the maintenance of consent all the way through it. Consent can crumble, or turn out to be insincere.

Also, public opinion often fails to understand the importance of consent. Once UN troops are on the ground, they tend to be blamed for failing to prevent actions by the parties, even though they may have neither the mandate nor adequate resources to do so. This happened in 1967 to the UN Emergency Force (UNEF I) in Sinai, which was blamed for withdrawing at the Egyptian government's request, though its presence had always been quite explicitly dependent on that government's consent. It happened in 1982 to the UN Interim Force in Lebanon (UNIFIL), which was blamed first for not preventing the firing of rockets into Israeli territory from places outside its area and then for not resisting the Israeli invasion. More recently, as we have seen, it has happened in Bosnia and in Rwanda.

In the Congo in the early 1960s, a peacekeeping force was turned into an intervention force by decision of the Security Council in reaction to events on the ground. The ultimate outcome was successful, but the transition was hair-raising, especially for those directly involved. It seems very unlikely that the council would have agreed to intervene in this way if it had not already had troops in the country for a different purpose. Clearly the council needs to consider carefully, before sending a peacekeeping force to a country, whether the consent of the parties is likely to hold. If consent fails, any attempt to beef up a traditional peacekeeping operation with elements of enforcement is fraught with problems and dangers. The entire history of UNPROFOR in Bosnia can be read as a cautionary tale illustrating this point. In most cases, if a shift to enforcement is desired, it will be preferable to withdraw the peacekeeping force and replace it with an entirely different force with a new mandate (part of which should be to cover the peacekeepers' withdrawal).

It is vital at all times to keep in mind the fact that intervention is a form of war and that war and peacekeeping are intrinsically different. The public needs to be educated about this difference, so that it does not expect from peacekeeping operations results that only war could produce. But the governments represented in the Security Council themselves also need to be more clearly aware of the distinction, so that in future they can avoid drafting mandates for UN forces that do not fall clearly into one or another category.

Fourth, in this chapter I have deliberately avoided using the phrase "humanitarian intervention," because it too often generates confusion. If the UN is to intervene militarily in a domestic crisis, I believe it should always do so for a humanitarian *motive*—"to assist a people in danger," as President Mitterrand put it or, in the words of the Commission on Global Governance, to deal with a threat to "the security of people." But an effective military intervention cannot confine itself to purely humanitarian *action* in the sense of directly relieving suffering. This category, in the typology of interventions in this chapter, is a snare and a delusion. Effective intervention needs to be clearly political, involving the use of force to neutralize whoever or whatever is threatening "the security of people."

If we confine military forces to protecting relief workers or to themselves carrying out relief work in a violent environment, we entrust them with an impossible mission, because it will never be clear how much force they are supposed to use in order to carry out this mandate. That error has been the root of failure in Somalia and the source of intense acrimony in Bosnia—and those two operations between them have overshadowed all the UN successes in other parts of the world. Indeed, they have so alienated the main troop-contributing countries that it is now becoming very difficult to assemble a credible UN force for *either* peacekeeping *or* intervention.

Fifth, we have to face the fact that, historically, most effective interventions have been unilateral either in fact or in name; they have been operations carried out by a neighboring state that saw a national as well as a humanitarian interest in stabilizing the situation. If one has the power to prevent the deaths of millions of people, does one have the right, let alone the obligation, to refrain from doing so simply because the killers have a powerful friend on the UN Security Council? Whatever the correct legal answer to that question (and lawyers disagree about it), the practical answer is that where a strong humanitarian case is combined with both national interest and, above all, the *power* to intervene effectively, intervention is going to happen with or without UN sanction.

Most of us would prefer to see such interventions legitimized by the UN, because we feel uneasy about giving states an implicit right to intervene whenever and wherever they feel like it. But we should be careful not to reduce the legitimization to a rubber stamp, accorded quasi-automatically to great powers acting within their respective spheres of influence. It may be better in some cases to let states take responsibility for their own actions and let history judge, rather than compromise the authority of the UN by associating it with their decisions.

Sixth, the case where intervention is most clearly justified is that of genocide. Most states (all those that have ratified the genocide convention) have accepted an obligation to "prevent and punish" this most heinous of all crimes. Article 8 of the convention says that the contracting parties "may call upon the competent organs of the United Nations to take such action under the Charter . . . as they consider appropriate." This clearly implies that the UN should be prepared to intervene and thereby puts genocide beyond the scope of Article 2.7: it is an international crime, not something "essentially within the jurisdiction of any state."

The main limitation in the convention is that it defines genocide by intent as well as by specific acts. But the intent in question is "to destroy, in whole or in part, a national, ethnic, racial or religious group." One could argue that killing even one member of a group constitutes destroying it in part. That, perhaps, would be reductio ad absurdum. The convention's definition is, however, certainly broad enough to embrace Saddam Hussein's treatment of the Kurds in Iraq, as well as the massacre of the Tutsi in Rwanda in 1994. There is a prima facie case that genocide has also occurred in Bosnia. In all three of these cases, one can legitimately wish that there had been a robust and *timely* military intervention, with UN blessing, by whichever states were able and willing to do it.

Finally, there is the issue of "failed states": as has already been noted, the case for intervention here is strong, but it is important to be clear what this involves. By intervening, the international community is effectively offering to substitute itself for the state that has failed. In other words, it should be prepared to set up a quasi-colonial government—presumably some sort of trusteeship—and to maintain it in place for a long period, while the institutions of the failed state are rebuilt and its civil society has a chance to heal. One problem with this approach is that even among today's most successful states, few if any wish to undertake such imperial responsibility. Yet it may be that they will come to accept it, if they realize (as the old imperialists did) that failed states are a kind of security black hole, which, left unfilled, will in time become a threat to their neighbors as well as to their own inhabitants.

We should also realize that genocidal tyranny and the failed state are not always opposite ends of a spectrum. A state that resorts to or permits genocide may well be close to failure. If we intervene to halt or prevent genocide, we may not find a ready-made "civilized" government to which authority can be entrusted once the instigators of genocide have been removed. So, even if we limit intervention to cases of genocide, the trusteeship question may still have to be faced. The ideal prototypes for such interventions should be the occupation and reconstruction of Germany and Japan after World War II.

The post–Cold War world is proving a much more complicated and violent place than many hoped it would be. Conflicts between principles, as well as between people, are as much a feature of it as they were of its predecessor. Difficult calculations still have to be made about ends and means. Idealism still stubs its toe on awkward reality. General or global interests still have to be reconciled with particular or national ones. State sovereignty may be less absolute than it once was, but peoples—not least those of small and/or newly independent states—remain attached to it. The willingness of peoples in general to make sacrifices and take risks for the sake of universal principles, where their own national interest is not directly or obviously involved, must be assumed to be limited. Certainly it is so assumed by their leaders.

The much invoked "international community" proves, on closer inspection, to be a nebulous concept. Sometimes used as a mere synonym for the UN, at others the phrase seeks to suggest the existence of something more authoritative behind that battered institution—a descendant, perhaps of the nineteenth-century "Concert of Europe." But if the community is to be judged by the effectiveness of its actions, it can only be said to have manifested itself in one brief spasm in 1990–91, after which it relapsed into nonexistence. And there are still states—no doubt there always will be—big and powerful enough to feel confident that no one will "enforce" good behavior on them, however bad their behavior may be.

These seemingly permanent features of the world order—or disorder—cannot simply be wished away by those of us who define ourselves as liberals, proclaiming the defense of individual rights as our first political principle. Nor, however, can we accept the artificial model of an international order composed of equally sovereign states with equal rights and obligations, irrespective of their internal character, external influence, or size of population. Such an order is sometimes called "Westphalian," after the treaties that marked the end of the great ideological convulsion of Europe in the sixteenth and seventeenth centuries and inaugurated an era of unashamed raison d'état; and it is theoretically affirmed in Article 2.1 of the UN Charter, which states that "the Organization is based on the principle of the sovereign equality of all its members." But that principle is not consistently maintained in the rest of the Charter, let alone in subsequent UN practice. The Westphalian model was never an adequate description of actual international relations, and it has even less to do with the reality of today.

In the 1990s—and one may guess that this will be even truer of the twenty-first century—interstate relations form only a tiny fraction of the daily contacts between peoples. Many of these now occur electronically and are all but impossible for states to monitor, let alone control. States still do their best to control the physical movement of people across their borders, but the very desperation of such efforts bears witness to the increasing difficulties involved. In any case, liberals would betray their defining principle—the defense of individual rights, including the right of free association, against external constraints—if they accepted the fiction whereby individuals are represented in the international order only by the states of which they happen to be subjects or citizens, irrespective of the way those states treat them and the nature of the states' authority over them. Liberals have an obligation to formulate, and as far as possible to act on, general principles governing their conduct, and the conduct they expect of their governments, in the international arena. And those principles cannot be limited to, even if they should include, respect for the sovereignty of other states.

Notes

1. George Bush, speech to both houses of the U.S. Congress, 11 September 1990.
2. François Mitterand, quoted in *Financial Times*, 20–21 April 1991, 7.
3. *Financial Times*, 8 May 1991.
4. J. S. Mill, *A Few Words on Non-Intervention*, published in 1859 and reprinted in *Dissertations and Discussions*, vol. 3 (2d ed., 1875), 153–78.
5. Adam Roberts, "Humanitarian War: Military Intervention and Human Rights," *International Affairs* 69, no. 3 (July 1993): 433.
6. W. E. Gladstone, quoted by Roberts, "Humanitarian War," 432.
7. For an elaboration of this crucial point, see Charles Dobbie, *A Concept for Post–Cold War Peacekeeping* (Oslo: Norwegian Institute for Defence Studies, 1994), chaps 1 and 9; and the British army field manual *Wider Peacekeeping*, chap. 2.
8. Mill, *A Few Words*, 172.
9. Dobbie, *Post–Cold War Peacekeeping*, 16–17.
10. See Anthony Parsons, *From Cold War to Hot Peace: UN Interventions 1947–1994* (London: Penguin Books, 1995), 77–93.
11. Parsons, *From Cold War to Hot Peace*, 164. See also William Shawcross, *Cambodia's New Deal* (Washington, D.C.: Carnegie Endowment, 1994), 12–23.
12. J. M. Sanderson, "Dabbling in War: The Dilemma of the Use of Force in United Nations Interventions," chap. 6 in this volume.
13. Nagendra Singh, "The UN and the Development of International Law," in *United Nations, Divided World*, ed. Adam Roberts and Benedict Kingsbury (Oxford: Oxford University Press, 1993), 393–95.
14. N. J. Rengger, *Treaties and Alliances of the World*, 5th ed. (Harlow, Essex: Longman Current Affairs, 1990), 74.
15. Parsons, *From Cold War to Hot Peace*, 261.

16. Boutros Boutros-Ghali, *Supplement to An Agenda for Peace,* UN doc. A/50/60-S/1995/1, 3 January 1995, 11.

17. UN doc. S/24868 of 30 November 1992, p. 3.

18. *Our Global Neighbourhood,* report of the Commission on Global Governance, (Oxford, 1995), 89–90.

19. *Global Neighbourhood,* 81.

20. *Global Neighbourhood,* 90, 261.

21 *Global Neighbourhood,* 91.

22. *Global Neighbourhood,* 91, 240–41.

23. Boutros-Ghali, *Supplement to An Agenda for Peace,* 18.

6

Dabbling in War: The Dilemma of the Use of Force in United Nations Intervention

---

J. M. Sanderson

The Emerging Global Context

The resolution of conflict is one of the most immediate international issues of our time. We are living in a period of great change. Powers decline while others emerge as the world moves to a new strategic accommodation. During this century, the strategic shifts have been marked by the two world wars and the Cold War. Each unleashed its own set of dynamics that led to the confrontations that followed.

While the current strategic shift has seen the threat of global nuclear war recede, the end of the Cold War has also weakened the influence of the superpowers on their client states and proxies, which, for most of the fifty years since the end of World War II, seemed to contain many of the deep ethnic, religious, and cultural tensions that have plagued modern history.

The collapse of the Soviet Union's capacity to pursue a global strategy led to the disintegration of the Soviet bloc and the fragmentation of the Soviet Union itself. The world's remaining superpower, relieved of the security burdens imposed by its former adversary and denied the crystalline certainty of its role as the defender of freedom, is itself divided. It moves toward a new role only with uncertainty, while burgeoning domestic problems cast a doubt over its ability to sustain a coherent international commitment.

In this global flux, concerns about national and cultural survival, often manipulated by emerging power elites, have led to extreme responses. Brutality and suffering on a scale unprecedented since the major conflicts of this century deaden the senses, despite a universal awareness of events made possible by new information technologies. The cost in lives and infrastructure, along with the diversion of finances to arms and military capabilities, continues to detract from prosperity and the social progress needed to alleviate the causes of conflict. The common humanity of peoples demands that an escape be found from this vicious cycle of violence, before the nations are drawn into a maelstrom of war.

In many respects, the post–Cold War world is an extension of the postcolonial world. The problems of divided ethnic, cultural, religious, and economic groups are now emerging anew. These conflicts often occur within imposed boundaries that have never really encompassed sovereign states. Allegiances are frequently astride, rather than within, frontiers, and, as in centuries past, the conflicts risk drawing in other powers whose political interests are seen to lie with peoples of shared identity in other countries. The enormous advances in information transfer across international boundaries compound these problems of transnational identity.

The internal nature of these conflicts challenges the international conflict resolution machinery designed for the essential purpose of preventing conflict between states. With its emphasis on sovereignty within recognized boundaries, the United Nations Charter has deliberately denied the reality that most international conflicts have occurred as a result of internal conflicts over economic or cultural prerogatives. The challenge facing the emerging order is whether a new strategic accommodation can be arrived at without major conflict. The massive power of modern weapons and the fragility of much of the environment make the acceptance of this challenge an imperative.

The need for responsible international leadership is clear. Unfortunately, the United Nations, itself still in the process of emerging from its Cold War torpor, has been found wanting in its capacity to assume the full moral authority established in its origins.

The Conflict Resolution Dilemma

The specter of war is *the* major challenge to our capacity for international collective action. Despite the advances in cooperation, the very nature of conflict makes it inherently difficult to resolve. While the international community gives preference to conflict resolution by peaceful means, such as negotiation and mediation, peaceful approaches often seem a weak weapon against the political forces that have led to the conflict. The effectiveness of our international efforts largely depends on the leadership of the combatant parties and of those nations that sense real or potential prejudice to their interests. The ability to generate confidence in, and commitment to, international conflict resolution processes depends on their willingness to compromise entrenched positions in the interests of the greater good.

We are also dependent on the extent of the control these leaders exercise over their followers. In some circumstances (such as in many guerrilla or terrorist organizations), control is loose. Much of the decision making is left to commanders or individuals who are not ready to accept constraints on their operations. Problems also arise with armed groups of civilians who operate outside an identifiable command framework. In Rwanda in 1994, for example, the worst excesses of the conflict were perpetrated, not by professional soldiers, but by machete- and club-wielding civilians, drafted into militias and driven by the ethnic passions of generations.

In an international system based on sovereign states, how does an organization made up of those states intervene in a way that is consistent with its collective interest? How does it do so in situations where this fundamental concept has been cast into question?

The United Nations Charter

Fifty years ago, at the end of the most disastrous war the world has known, the representatives of fifty sovereign states signed the Charter of the United Nations. Those representatives were also able to recall the devastating effects of the earlier Great War. They were resolved that the United Nations would transcend the incapacity of the League of Nations to prevent conflict during the interwar years.

The United Nations Charter is a mighty document, which does great credit to those who drafted it. Its spirit is reflected in its opening statement that:

> We the peoples of the United Nations determined
>   to save succeeding generations from the scourge of war which twice in our lifetime has brought untold sorrow to mankind, and
>   to reaffirm faith in fundamental human rights, in the dignity and worth of the human person, in the equal rights of men and women and of nations large and small, and
>   to establish conditions under which justice and respect for the obligations arising from treaties and other sources of international law can be maintained, and
>   to promote social progress and better standards of life in larger freedom.

The Charter is a framework for reconciliation. Its drafters sought to use wartime cooperation to build confidence between nations. Through the united strength of member states, they hoped to provide defense against threats to the concepts of sovereignty within recognized frontiers, as well as to advance those rights and benefits the deprivation of which was seen to be the cause of wars.

But in many parts of the globe, these concepts are not well understood, or if understood, are an incitement to action to gain, for particular groups, the benefits that accrue to nation-state status. What is certain is that the massive human rights violations, hunger, disease, and refugee flows caused by conflicts and friction cannot be ignored. The central issue is how to intervene in a way that holds the prospect of resolution of a crisis, while remaining within the framework of the United Nations Charter.

If there is to be any chance of arriving at comprehensive solutions, it is essential to view the world in the light of the emerging global flux, rather than simply of the past. Importantly, the approaches taken to resolve these crises must hold out the potential to set in train dynamics that could establish a pattern for enduring international conflict resolution, and cooperation generally, in the next century and perhaps even the centuries to follow.

One means of directing these dynamics toward a civilized course is through the Charter itself. Its strength comes from its moral authority, whose source lies in the obligation of its signatories to serve the peoples of the United Nations.

Strategic Objectivity and United Nations Intervention

In the contemporary world, the deployment of peacekeeping forces has become the most visible face of the United Nations and is among its most important conflict resolution tools. Peacekeeping operations were never envisaged in the United Nations Charter. Nevertheless, they are an appropriate mechanism within the framework of Chapter VI, "The Pacific Settlement of Disputes." Specifically, they come under Article 33, which provides for "other peaceful means" among a range of peaceful options. Consent of the parties in conflict is the key issue here.

Operations that come under Article 42 in Chapter VII of the Charter, "Threats to the Peace, Breaches of the Peace and Acts of Aggression," are not peacekeeping. The purpose of Chapter VII is, in essence, collective defense against an expansionist military power, such as the Axis forces of World War II. Article 42 legitimizes international violence against offending parties to this end (which is otherwise proscribed by Article 2). The Korean War of 1950–53 and the Gulf War of 1991 provide the only clear examples of Article 42 action. These were conducted by war-fighting international coalitions led by the United States and sanctioned by the Security Council.

Although Chapter VI and Chapter VII operations are both political acts, they are dependent on the moral authority of the Charter, to which all member states have indicated their consent. As with any binding document, the application of the Charter must remain objective and independent of specific national interests in order to sustain the collective consent of the nations. In this process it must be recognized that the generation of political consensus in support of any international resolution will normally involve compromise to accommodate diverse political goals. But if the political purpose is allowed to become ambiguous, is subject to frequent change, or is of questionable morality, then consent is likely to prove illusory and the capacity for success to be gravely prejudiced.

By way of example, the U.S.-led intervention in Somalia in 1992 and the French intervention in southern Rwanda in 1994 are both ostensibly Chapter VII actions sanctioned by Security Council resolutions. However, both introduced the contradictory state that plagues modern international policymaking: having Chapter VI and Chapter VII actions parallel in an internal conflict. This fails to recognize that while some actions under Chapter VII can resemble those normally associated with peacekeeping, their jurisdictional base is quite different, and the implied capacity for violence is contrary to the pacific nature of Chapter VI. The confusion that surrounds these issues has had a corrosive effect on the moral authority of the United Nations. While not unfamiliar to former colonial powers, this contradiction is at odds with the spirit of the Charter.

The Dynamics of Force

In an environment of excesses and obstacles, the use of force as a preventive measure, to impose a settlement on recalcitrant parties or to establish order over lawless groups, emerges as an apparent necessity. Experiences in the United Nations Transitional Authority in Cambodia (UNTAC) from 1992 to 1993 and more recent public commentary suggest that many see enforcement by peacekeepers as an option. The issues involved are not well understood, and in many peacekeeping operations this confusion over the necessary constraints on the use of force can make effective command impossible.

From the perspective of a military commander, the use of force is essentially a command and control problem. Unlike the laws of physics, in which every action has an equal and opposite reaction, actions in war are likely to be magnified severalfold as passions are compounded by the fatal consequences of conflict. In these circumstances, an escape from the vicious cycle of violence is likely to remain distant until one or more sides bleed themselves to exhaustion. This terrible reality seems to be little understood in many quarters.

This is why the essence of a successful conflict-resolution strategy includes, at its core, absolute discrimination in the use of force. It should not occur haphazardly in a climate of passion and raw politics. Nor should the use of force occur as a result of decisions made purely in the glow of television screens. It needs to be borne in mind that enforcement implies that someone does not agree to the role of the enforcer and is therefore likely to resist in a way that quickly moves affairs into a state of reciprocating violence. Force has to be directed only toward the achievement of legitimate political objectives. Where control is loose, force is free to generate its own dynamic. Discrimination is even more critical in the case of enforcement action.

Anyone who thinks he can bluff his way through these things with a mandate and troops designed for peacekeeping has little understanding of the nature of conflict and the consequences of the use of force. He is also likely to compromise the neutrality of the United Nations and. with it, its credibility and capacity to act as an honest broker in other conflicts. There are significant lessons to be learned in this respect from United Nations experiences in the former Yugoslavia.

Enforcement in Context

This is not to suggest that there are no enforcement options. But force has to be lawful. It is difficult to argue that anyone has the right to kill or injure people in their own country without proper sanction under either international or domestic law. How can a mandate that draws its authority from a Charter designed to defend the sovereignty of states and to promote and encourage respect for human rights authorize hostile intervention against any party or individual within a state? And if responses are not firmly based within the framework of the Charter, how can the United Nations commander issue lawful and sustainable orders to soldiers of another member state or, indeed, of his own country? Where does that leave the soldier who might have to make the choice between obeying and disobeying those orders and bear the consequences of that decision?

In Cambodia, there was no legitimate authority to engage in offensive operations, since all the parties to the Paris Agreements had not acceded to it. The enforcement of law and order was their responsibility, consistent with the human rights provisions to which Cambodia had agreed. The appropriate response was the one taken, namely, in the context of a peace-keeping operation, to fulfill the mandated responsibility of establishing a recognizable legitimate authority that was capable of exercising sovereign jurisdiction.

Moreover, offensive operations impose significantly greater demands than peacekeeping. In Cambodia, a force several times larger than the one provided by the United Nations would have been required: one structured, equipped, and trained for a protracted conflict, and at a significantly greater cost. Such an operation would have spelt doom for the Cambodian peace process, even if it had been given wide international support. Many years of diplomatic effort and a huge expenditure of international funds would have been wasted.

Enforcement is, after all, *war* by another name. It is only if there is almost universal consent that a particular party is in the wrong that international support for enforcement will follow. Universal consent does not mean simply the views of some journalists or commentators. Often members of the media are encumbered by baggage from the past, or their views are obscured by the horror and passion of more immediate events. Interests of great magnitude must be at stake before the consensus within the contributing countries will reach the necessary fervor to provide the forces and funds for war-fighting and possibly to accept casualties on a significant scale. A critical issue in such considerations is sustainment. Can a coalition response be sustained once it comes under stress?

There are those, of course, who are prepared to make bold suggestions about enforcement, but often there is not even domestic consensus for it in their own nation, let alone in the multinational array of countries that contribute to a modern-day peacekeeping force.

Anyone who joins a conflict without the means or the intention of winning is betraying those who will be called on to make the sacrifices. And the pressure on a force commander in an environment where there is active debate about transition from Chapter VI peacekeeping to Chapter VII enforcement operations very quickly raises the conclusion that most of the force is ill prepared for such a transition, and the wavering international support for whatever new objectives are chosen will make the command weak and vulnerable. It is no way to go to war!

Nothing could spell out this essential fact more clearly than the results of selective NATO offensive action in Bosnia. Successive commanders, aware of the vulnerability of those under their command, have been reluctant to authorize any form of enforcement action, despite the urging of those who, more secure and less responsible, have been extravagant in their judgment of the deficiencies of United Nations command.

Objective judgment will determine whether Chapter VI or Chapter VII action is warranted, what form it should take, and the resources required. While consensus can be more readily generated in support of peacekeeping, if Chapter VII action is required, peacekeeping cannot be used as a substitute.

The Peacekeeping Ethos

Peacekeeping is based on international consent and that of all the parties involved, including the peacekeepers. This requires, for their own protection, an overt display of impartiality on the part of peacekeepers to establish their credentials as "honest brokers" in the process. This display is totally different from the display required for enforcement, which is warlike and concentrated to establish seriousness of intent.

Peacekeeping operations seek to resolve disputes on the basis of an agreement between the parties to a conflict while impartially seeking to generate the climate for compliance with that agreement. The fundamental building block for diplomatic responses (outlined under Article 33) that can be most readily agreed is the peaceful intent of the operation. Article 2 obliges this, and Chapter VI provides the legitimate framework for United Nations action.

Member states deploy an international peacekeeping force to facilitate a settlement or to inhibit escalation of a conflict. It matters little whether the agreement of the parties in conflict is due to diplomatic pressure, economic sanctions, or exhaustion. The opposing factions want resolution of the conflict, or at least its suspension while diplomacy proceeds. The peacekeepers are legally protected by the agreement; their legitimate purpose is confidence building, and there are clear limits to what they can do while retaining consent.

A peacekeeping force gains and retains its acceptability because it is impartial. The peacekeepers' impartiality gives them their unity and their strength. They are constrained to limit the use of force to self-defense. If peacekeepers exceed their jurisdiction and move beyond their inherent right of self-defense, experience shows us that they will almost inevitably compromise their neutrality and become another party to the conflict. When this occurs, their unity is shattered, they are stripped of their strength, and, because of their nature, they are without the protection of the array of combat and support systems that any able commander will seek to support his forces in the achievement of their assigned military objectives. Peacekeepers are instruments of diplomacy, not of war.

Defending a Peacekeeping Mandate

With the extension of United Nations intervention into the area of peace-building, peacekeeping operations have become finely balanced affairs, involving the need for harmonization of widely diverse activities and interests in environments of an increasingly dynamic nature. It is now, more than ever, essential that United Nations forces maintain their peace-keeping bona fides throughout. Force can be used *only* in self-defense if this is to be the case.

Regrettably, the confusion over these issues is exacerbated by widely differing interpretations of the meaning of self-defense among contributing countries and analysts. In UNTAC, for example, interpretations covered the full spectrum, despite clear definitions in standing operating procedures and continuous briefings. Initially, responses among UNTAC contingents ranged from some troops allowing themselves to be disarmed when threatened to others opening fire with all available weapons at the slightest provocation.

The Cambodian operation was conducted in a country that had suffered a quarter of a century of civil war, genocide, and more civil war. Despite the pledges of the parties to the Paris Agreements, the UNTAC peacekeepers and civilian components eventually deployed into a climate of escalating violence, demanding "go" or "no go" decisions, with the ability to defend the various components of the mission being a key consideration.

The key element in UNTAC's success was the readiness of the people to vote. This depended in a large part on the perceived commitment of the United Nations to that end and on the Cambodian conviction of that commitment. At the outset, the delayed start by UNTAC eroded many of the hard-won opportunities provided by the Paris Agreements, opening a new set of conflicting dynamics.

The Khmer Rouge claimed that UNTAC was not implementing the agreements fairly and that the people would reject the UNTAC process. They said that the violence in the countryside, including the massacres of innocent civilians, was a manifestation of the people's anger. On the other hand, the Phnom Penh faction claimed that UNTAC lacked the will to prevent the Khmer Rouge from subverting the peace process. How to respond was the dilemma the United Nations faced.

On a number of occasions, in response to atrocities, the force commander was called on by people both within and outside the United Nations to use the peacekeeping force to conduct operations against the Khmer Rouge. These would have been *offensive* operations—no one could draw any other interpretation. But what was most astonishing was the passion with which the use of force was espoused. Often, the most fervent advocates of violence were those who would otherwise declare their total opposition to war!

It is easy to understand the frustration of people when they cannot achieve the results they aspire to or when they see atrocities committed within their reach. But it is also deeply disturbing when they are moved in the face of this to exhort publicly the transition to enforcement by peacekeepers. Not only are such exhortations very dangerous, but also they are often counterproductive to the objective of the mission.

The difficulty here lies in ensuring that everyone understands the purpose of peacekeeping operations, why the peacekeepers are deployed to these volatile areas in the first place, their objectives, and what they are legally entitled to do. The issues of consent and jurisdiction are the key themes here. The only way to avoid the need to consider peace enforcement, with all its consequences, is to generate and maintain consensus on the steps for peaceful resolution of the conflict.

To do this, everyone has to have something at stake, and the benefit of complying with an agreement has to exceed the consequences of not complying. In this process, leaders have to be forced into considering the needs of their followers. Their actual leadership may have to be put at stake. There has to be an element of coercion in this, but there sometimes seems to be an almost compete comprehension gap about the difference between political coercion and the dynamic nature and effect of the use of force at the international level. Closely related to this is the need to understand the effects that the use of force by peacekeepers has on the activities of all United Nations personnel and nongovernmental organizations in the mission area.

In Cambodia, the civilian components had their mandated responsibilities, and humanitarian agencies and nongovernmental organizations had their programs aimed at alleviating the suffering of the people. For most, this included extensive fieldwork. In the agencies' interests, UNTAC had to avoid conflict as much as was reasonably possible. The command assessment had to be that, although there was a climate of violence, it was manageable, provided UNTAC did nothing to contribute to it while containing it to the extent possible through negotiations and moderating its effects through diplomatic efforts. The long-term objective of the mandate had to be the focus.

But at a critical point, UNTAC had to stay and defend the mandated political objective: the conduct of an election for a constituent assembly in as neutral an environment as could be created by these means. The Cambodian people expected this of UNTAC, and only the military component could provide it for them. It was a case of bluff in which the risks could be taken only where UNTAC could be relatively sure of its support and the commitment of its own people.

From the point of view of the UNTAC force commander, self-defense meant defense of anyone going about their legitimate business under the Paris Agreements. This was intended to include defense of any Cambodian who, disarmed, placed his or her trust in the United Nations by remaining in the mandated cantonment process. In the light of changed circumstances, self-defense was extended to the use of minimum force and proportionate response in defense of the electoral process.

Self-defense meant not only an individual's defense of himself alone; it also meant collective action. In some instances, company-level defensive battles had to be fought, but it is important to understand that in these engagements the use of force by peacekeepers was never offensive: only those actually using force against mandated activities were engaged, and then only to the extent necessary to provide protection. In this context, self-defense was passive; it did not actively seek combat. While the majority of the military units were eventually mentally and physically prepared to do this, it was important that their operations were seen to be conducted strictly within these constraints. It was only in the context of self-defense that this outcome could be reasonably certain.

Contributing to the confusion on these issues is an apparent unwillingness or inability on the part of the United Nations to define clearly the fact that armed and active military forces cannot be embraced by these defense mechanisms. Refugee camps such as in Rwanda or protected zones such as in Bosnia cannot be defended by the international community unless they are demilitarized. If they are not, the authority of the United Nations to secure them will be violently contested.

The Political Imperative for Self-Defense

The United Nations operation in Cambodia was brought about by unprecedented international consensus made possible by the end of the Cold War. The Paris Agreements signed in October 1991 by the four Cambodian parties and eighteen interested countries established the status of the parties and of UNTAC and the legal obligations and relationships between the signatories and between the signatories and the United Nations. The UNTAC operation was a continuation of the dynamic of diplomacy the agreements reflected. It was a step in an ongoing process.

If the mission in Cambodia was to succeed, it was critical for UNTAC to retain the peacekeeping ethos under the prevailing political circumstances. In addition to the practical and ethical issues, there were strong strategic reasons why enforcement was never an option. While the Khmer Rouge was usually seen as the recalcitrant party, there were deep divisions internationally, within the Security Council, and within UNTAC, about where the guilt lay. There was no broad consensus within UNTAC or among the international supporters of the operation for offensive action against any party. Both UNTAC and the essential international unity that had been built up behind the Cambodian peace process and scrupulously guarded would very likely have been shattered had it been tested with enforcement.

Any force, even self-defense in support of the mandate, was possible only with cohesion in the Security Council and consensus in the countries contributing troops to the peacekeeping mission. The two issues are synergistic; each depends on the other. When they are drawn together, diplomacy is concentrated to support action. This emphasizes the need for absolute discrimination in the use of force.

Strengthening United Nations Intervention

Regardless of whether the United Nations intervenes under Chapter VI or Chapter VII, the nature and timing of that intervention need to be such that it can achieve the identified political purpose. Various options have been suggested over the years to strengthen the United Nations' capacities, including creating standing armed forces in order to allow a rapid response to emerging crises. Against the background of the tragedies we have witnessed in Bosnia and Rwanda and the difficulties in obtaining sufficient forces for the tasks envisaged, this proposal has recently received support from some quarters. But the major difficulty lies in generating support among member states generally for the creation of such a force and agreement on the framework for its employment.

It is important to maintain a strategic view on this issue. Any military response by the United Nations can only ever be *part* of the solution in a range of civil-military options. Moreover, effective operations require clearly defined and achievable objectives that are properly planned for and resourced. Decisions on any use of military forces must be made in the light of detailed and carefully considered military advice that enables the full implications and risks to be assessed. Military operations also need to be commanded effectively by trained professionals conscious of the strategic context of their operations, their integrated civil-military nature, and the implications of their directions for broader international political goals.

There is general international agreement on the need for improved United Nations crisis response. But any arrangements for rapid provision of military forces may be counterproductive if the necessary command and control arrangements are not in place to allow these forces to contribute to more effective conflict prevention and resolution.

Objectivity and Command

The capacity of peacekeepers to effect their mandate impartially is sometimes constrained from the outset. This is often the result of a fundamental contradiction between the diplomatic compromises needed to gain a mandate and the essential requirement for objectivity in the development of effective military operations.

In all of this, it must be recognized that military operations cannot be an end in themselves. Commanders will always be confronted with circumstances that require action, which will in turn generate a reaction. Without objective direction, there is a strong probability that those actions will disconnect from diplomatic action, thereby corrupting the mission and causing its failure. The resulting tendency of the actors to then blame each other will affect the credibility of the structures provided by the United Nations, causing an erosion of confidence in the organization. Money and troops will be difficult to find.

The critical issue here is not who might be to blame but that peacekeepers need to be actively supported by diplomacy. That diplomatic support is likely to be gravely weakened if strategic objectivity is lacking in the initial resolution.

It is also critical that objective decisions are passed to those charged with their implementation in a way that focuses their actions. This requires an effective command structure. The military doctrine of most countries identifies three levels of command: strategic, operational, and tactical. These have different functions and natures, but all three have the common purpose of passing objective directions to subordinates and ensuring that they are empowered and resourced to do the tasks.

If one of these levels is deficient, or if their roles become merged, the capacity of the others to function effectively is severely limited. If the strategic level becomes involved with tactics, it is likely to lose its broad perspective and diminish the power of commanders on the ground. At the same time, tactical actions that are not focused can adversely affect the strategic plan. The operational level both separates and binds the strategic and tactical levels, ensuring that tactical actions are coordinated to achieve strategic objectives. For example, these levels of command were represented in UNTAC as follows:

- The strategic level was the United Nations Security Council in New York, supported by the United Nations Secretariat and the state structures of Security Council members, with their links to the national capitals of interested states and the highest-level headquarters of involved agencies of the United Nations or nongovernmental organizations.

- The operational level was the United Nations headquarters in Phnom Penh, with its links to the leadership of the Cambodian parties, the diplomatic community, and the most senior authorities of the various agencies in-country.

- The tactical level was the military units, civilian groups, and elements in the field, coordinated by regional headquarters, normally located in provincial capitals.

The key issue is that the three levels are mutually supporting and are complementary elements that form an effective whole. Each functions in the light of the realities of the others. Much of the success achieved in Cambodia was due to the operational level's ability, despite all sorts of interventions, to achieve an effective harmony between all levels and to maintain it up to the end of the mandate.

The Strategic Level

Within a nation state, the strategic level is where decisions are made about enduring relationships between elements of society: between the people and the state and between the state, other nations, international organizations, multinationals, and the like. The central issues involve adjustment of national priorities in response to changing circumstances. It is a continuum in peace and war. However, in war, the military dimension assumes higher prominence.

Because of the essentially political nature of this activity, the processes are more dialectical and less direct than those normally associated with the exercise of military command. For this reason, it is at the strategic level that the ambiguities of the political nuances have to be absorbed and focused into directives to the next level, which are at once designed to provide clarity, flexibility, and inspiration to action. This is a hugely demanding task.

In the case of the United Nations organization, the strategic focus must be even broader, involving issues of ongoing harmony between member states, groupings, and international bodies. Decisions made by member states are collective, but the purposes of pursuing and balancing the objectives of the Charter must be paramount.

The central task would seem to lie in determining the international will on issues that are raised within the context of the Charter. While the Security Council is in a position to provide a lead, its capacity for action will be limited without broad international commitment. This is especially so in peacekeeping, which requires substantial international representation. Achieving a consensus that is, at the same time, objective is clearly very difficult—more so because objectivity has many dimensions.

A central issue is the ongoing viability and credibility of the United Nations itself. It is critical that the interests of individual states, or even groups of states, do not subvert the Charter if the existence of the organization is not to be brought into question. This can occur both in the formulation of resolutions and in the conduct of operations on the ground, if those resolutions are not sufficiently objective and binding.

The Operational Level

The operational level of command is the level at which field elements are orchestrated to achieve the objectives of strategy. In military terminology, the operational level is sometimes referred to as campaign strategy, identifying the distinction between the tactical and operational levels as the responsibility of the operational-level commander for the overall outcome of the military campaign.

The key determinant of success at this level of command is the military principle of the selection and maintenance of the aim. This is the principle that connects the strategic level to the operational level of command and should therefore emerge from strategic-level analysis to which the operational-level commander must be a contributor. Key to the derivation of, and a successful conclusion to, a campaign strategy is timely and accurate intelligence in all its forms. A combination of insight and superior knowledge is most conducive to the achievement of the desired psychological effects.

At the operational level, it is unity of command that provides strength and cohesion. While the complexity of many post–Cold War peacekeeping operations usually means that they are civil-military affairs, it nevertheless remains critical that all elements engaged come under one common authority. Somebody has to be responsible for issuing clear, unambiguous directives and looking the commanders, troops, and civilian field staff in the eye before, during, and after the time that they have committed themselves to their assigned objectives. Leadership of missions must reflect this essential requirement.

The Tactical Level

The tactical level is more finite, with objectives being defined in the more material terms of boundaries, time, numbers, and resources. This is not to say that leaders at this level do not have to contend in a dynamic environment that will test their powers to bring complex factors into harmony. It is simply that they are responsible for specified outcomes in a given area rather than the overall outcome of the campaign.

In peacekeeping operations, the tactical level involves much more than military units. And in some circumstances, such as humanitarian relief that is not subject to dispute or exploitation, military forces might only play in a supporting role. The tactical level could, for example, involve electoral teams, human rights monitors, police, and monitors of the parties' administrations, as it did in Cambodia. Each had to be harmonized with the others, across the chains of command reaching up to the operational level in Phnom Penh.

No tactical-level leader can change his objectives without referral to the next higher level. In the final analysis, to do so would be to unravel the overall strategy, risking a significant shift in the relative strength of the contending factions and prejudicing the entire mission.

For this reason, it is of particular importance that tactical units do not respond to national or other chains of command on operational matters. Nor can they be allowed to develop their own interpretations outside the operational-level commander's intent, especially on critical issues such as the use of force.

Cooperating for Peace in Cambodia

The earliest forms of United Nations peacekeeping were observer missions. These were begun by the United Nations shortly after the end of

World War II and were relatively simple affairs. At the other end of the peacekeeping spectrum, complex post–Cold War operations, like UNTAC, have to be approached and managed like major operations, with the levels of command functioning in the relationship described here.

Although the Cambodian operation is acknowledged as a United Nations success, it was clear that all three levels were deficient in some way. From the outset, there was no strategic coordination in UNTAC. Each component survey team developed its own plan in isolation, lacking the benefit of even a coordinating conference beforehand to determine the strategic direction. These plans were brought together only when the secretary-general's report was prepared for the Security Council in the period January to February 1992. Few component leaders participated in this process.

The first coordination at the operational level, between those component heads who were available, occurred en route to Phnom Penh from Bangkok the day UNTAC was established. Some component heads were not available to the mission until five months later. Among them all, only the force commander had participated in the preparation of his component's plan. None of them had participated in the negotiations that had preceded the Paris Agreements on which the strategy for the United Nations mission in Cambodia was based. The initial strategic disconnect was severe.

Within the mission, harmonizing the activities of the various elements of UNTAC was always problematic. Senior staff meetings were held regularly, chaired by the special representative of the secretary-general (SRSG) or his deputy, and attended by component heads and other key senior staff. But there was a tendency for meetings to become bogged down in matters of detail that were more appropriately the concerns of the tactical level. The lack of formalized coordinating structures at lower levels almost certainly contributed to this. Rather than being solved where they belonged, problems were often simply passed upward, where the operational level was already too busy to perform its own role effectively. In many cases, the problems were not solved at all.

In the execution, coordination was achieved through component heads networking as problems arose. There was no UNTAC-wide operations center. To some extent, the civilian logistics organization assumed a directing role in the early period of the United Nations' presence. But the logistics staff, being constrained by United Nations procedural considerations, were, for the most part, deterred from focusing on outcomes. By the end of 1992, the military component's plans branch became the focal point for a planning and control alliance between the military and electoral components and information and education division for the critical voter-registration and electoral phases.

At the same time, at the tactical level, the military component's ten sector headquarters, spread throughout Cambodia, adopted the coordinating role. This eventually drew in the liaison mechanism put in place to work with the military and police of the Cambodian parties supporting the UNTAC-sponsored elections, as well as the UNTAC civilian police and the other civilian components. These cooperative arrangements were sufficient to see the UNTAC-sponsored elections of May 1993 through to their successful conclusion.

These observations are not intended to denigrate the United Nations effort in Cambodia nor to suggest that such shortfalls are not being addressed. Rather, they are intended to highlight the systemic problems of command and control that continue to plague all United Nations missions.

In fact, success in UNTAC could not have been achieved if there had not been unity at and with the strategic level. The Paris Agreements had been long in gestation and formed an objective document. Among the signatories were the main strategic supporters of the four Cambodian parties. Their legal relationships were thus redefined by this act.

In the initial absence of a comprehensive and authoritative United Nations presence, a diplomatic body, the expanded permanent five (EP5), had been set up in Phnom Penh soon after the signing of the Paris Agreements. This grouping drew around the ambassadors of the permanent five members of the Security Council those of Australia, Germany, Indonesia, Japan, and Thailand. India and Malaysia joined subsequently. The EP5 served to remind the Cambodian parties of their obligations under the Paris Agreements during the five months between their signing and the establishment of UNTAC, as the parties, and some countries, sought to exploit the new dynamics created by the agreements. The EP5 continued to support UNTAC throughout the mandate. The EP5's relationship with the SRSG and the force commander was a corporate one. They met regularly and the EP5 was briefed often.

The EP5 mirrored a grouping in New York known as the "core group." Contact between these two groups ensured coordination between the operational and strategic levels through the policy processes in the capitals of the nations concerned. This meant that Security Council resolutions on Cambodia, drafted in the face of major obstacles as the mission progressed, were achievable and reflected the realities on the ground. UNTAC could then proceed to implement its mandated responsibilities, confident of its jurisdiction.

The obstacles were overcome politically by the operational level's generating new dynamics both at the diplomatic level and in the field. This allowed the Cambodian people to be made sovereign by the electoral process, despite the conflicts between and within the Cambodian factions. This cohesion weakened after the election but held long enough to conclude the UNTAC mandate. With the United Nations' moral authority progressively diminishing as the mandate reached its culminating point, it was a race against time.

The strategic-level grouping was essential to unify and focus diplomatic support. At the same time, the operational level needed structures to concentrate its efforts on its important task of defining and refining a policy framework for the implementation of the mandate laid down by the Security Council and adjusted by subsequent resolutions according to emerging circumstances. But rather than the ad hoc arrangements in UNTAC, it would have been better if structures had been planned for and put in place at the outset.

Command, Control, and the Charter

In multinational operations of the complexity of the one in Cambodia, nothing is a set piece. International sentiment, generated by media coverage, will ensure that those responsible cannot wait for everything to be put in place. The situation will always be reactive and dynamic. Decision makers must be able and prepared to act in pursuit of the defined objectives and to account for their actions.

To discriminate in this requires a highly responsive command and control system. Responsiveness at the highest level requires a strategic headquarters that is purposefully designed to be responsive. Among other things, it requires a deep intelligence process in order to be able to make valid judgements in the light of all the issues involved. Unbiased and independent analysis is the key here. Dependence on any individual national intelligence system is likely to involve some bias that will confuse the response.

And there is another dilemma for the United Nations. It does not have a responsive command and control system. It is a simple fact that deployed operational-level commanders do not have a superior headquarters. To create one, the structure and workings of the organization have to be addressed in a fundamental way.

The problem experienced by the United Nations in Rwanda in 1994 is a case in point. Setting aside the issues of legitimacy and preventive action, the response to events lacked strategic objectivity. Enforcement action on a large scale was required to stop the genocide. But the force was capped at fifty-five hundred and given a peacekeeping mandate making it fall short of expectations that were well beyond it. A brief foray into enforcement was endorsed by the Security Council to stabilize the mass movement of refugees into Zaire, but even this action contributed to an impression of crisis decision making rather than strategic objectivity. While a glowing example of humanitarian mobilization, Rwanda has done nothing to contribute to the credibility of United Nations peacekeeping.

Significantly, the command and control systems for UNPROFOR operations have been a maze of European and United Nations prerogatives, with strategic policymaking not matching the dangerous realities on the ground. Anticipation of, and preparation for, what seem to have been predictable responses (the primary role of a strategic-level headquarters) seems to have been a foregone responsibility.

No one should be surprised when contributing countries have difficulty reconciling contributions to such missions with their existing policy. Placed on the horns of a dilemma, they are called on to accept the consequences without being able to effect a solution. Responsible national political authorities cannot function in this way. They are unlikely to commit forces in the face of such decision making.

Under Article 43, all member states undertake to make armed forces available to the Security Council for operations within the framework of the Charter. In recent times, governments of many members states have issued policy directives or guidance defining the circumstances under which they will commit forces to United Nations operations. In essence, the purpose of these has been twofold: (1) to reassure their own people that any national commitment will be justified by the realistic prospects of the potential ends justifying the risks; and (2) to signal to the United Nations organization that it must get its house in order if it expects governments to be able to generate support from their domestic constituencies.

Apart from protecting the interests of the states concerned, the definition of a framework for involvement reflects a demand for strategic objectivity on the part of the United Nations that includes a requirement for morally sustainable responses.

Mandates that are framed with objectivity and aimed at the accomplishment of realistic goals are more likely to generate sustained consensus, confidence, and commitment to provide resources, including forces. The settlement of the dispute in a way consistent with the objectives of the Charter must be the aim. To accomplish this, the structures supporting complex operations need to be at least the equivalent of those of a relatively advanced member state or, alternatively, allow formalized access to the structures of member states in a way that does not compromise the essential need for objectivity in United Nations decision making.

The best starting point in reforming these processes is the United Nations Charter itself, which has already been agreed by the member states of the United Nations. The Security Council has specific responsibilities under both Chapter VI and Chapter VII, and its central role as the strategic authority designated by the Charter must not be eroded. In this regard, it is critical that risks of perceived bias in Security Council decisions are avoided. The United Nations Secretariat has the essential role of ensuring that the deliberations of the Security Council members maintain their objectivity. Often only the secretariat can gain the necessary access to trouble spots to determine the viability of strategic options. This places the secretary-general and his staff in a position of onerous responsibility.

Regardless of this essential role, it has always been recognized that the Secretariat would not be capable of providing comprehensive military advice nor of controlling complex military operations. Many of the difficulties experienced in places such as Somalia and Rwanda can be attributed to this incapacity.

It is only under Chapter VII that, in response to "threats to the peace, breaches of the peace and acts of aggression," the Charter provides for the strategic direction of response forces to be exercised by the Military Staff Committee, made up of the chiefs of staff of the armed forces of the five permanent members of the Security Council or their representatives.[1] While it is envisaged that the chiefs or their representatives would cooperate, they would still be answerable to their own governments, which themselves would have agreed to cooperate.

The Cold War made almost any form of military cooperation, including the empowerment of the Military Staff Committee, between the permanent five impossible. But we should be very clear in our minds that the United Nations Secretariat cannot act as a substitute. It is neither structured nor equipped to act as a strategic headquarters. This is why the original role of the Military Staff Committee for advice to the Security Council was established.

Moreover, the fact that military advice to the Security Council should be provided by the structures responsible for the implementation of those operations mandated by that advice is also acknowledged in the Charter. Clearly, the Military Staff Committee needs to be empowered to perform these responsibilities for complex Chapter VI operations as well as those mandated under Chapter VII. Undoubtedly, it would require discrete secretariat services to enable it to coordinate separate national military advice to form agreed collective advice, plans, and directions. Broader representation would probably be needed to generate the necessary climate of trust in these extended activities if the Military Staff Committee were to be acceptable in this role, and this is also provided for in the Charter.

Conclusions

Reconciliation is the basis of all successful strategies. This is the underlying theme of the United Nations Charter. The United Nations brings together most of the sovereign states on earth that, by their ratification of the Charter, establish the moral authority of the organization.

When a United Nations mission is mandated, it thereby assumes a measure of the moral authority from the Charter, the extent depending on the purpose of the mission, the objectivity with which the mandate is framed, and the consensus upon which it is based. Throughout the mission, successes consistent with the mandate can contribute to that moral authority, while failures will erode it. If the initial mandate is flawed, the erosion can be rapid.

In a media environment where the membrane between the past and the future becomes thin and the passion of the moment becomes a marketable product to be flashed around the world as events unfold, successes are likely to be less obvious than failures. Sustaining an international commitment in light of this reality requires a comprehensive public relations strategy based on a firm understanding of the central place of the moral authority of the United Nations in international peace initiatives.

Moral authority resides in the great ideals of the Charter and is generated through the belief that the peoples of the United Nations have in it. That belief is variable and is the sum total of the perception of successes and failures of the United Nations at any point in time. Where the perception of success is high, so is the faith in the organization. The commitment to both its principles and its activities is therefore likely to be strengthened.

The future of the United Nations depends on its capacity to seize the full weight of the moral authority enshrined in its own Charter and to bring it to bear in the interests of its peoples. The processes for mandating and directing operations must be reinforced to this end.

Epilogue

Over 170 years ago, Carl von Clausewitz, the renowned Prussian military theorist, in his treatise *Absolute War and Real War,* stated that:

No one starts a war—or rather, no one in his senses ought to do so—without first being clear in his mind what he intends to achieve by that war and how he intends to conduct it. The former is its political purpose; the latter its operational objective. This is the governing principle which will set its course, prescribe the scale of means and effort which is required, and make its influence felt throughout, down to the smallest operational detail.

This principle applies equally to peacekeeping under the auspices of the United Nations. Proposals to support conflict resolution, including those for standby forces for United Nations intervention, must be cognizant of this fundamental fact. For the United Nations to lose a war—which would surely be the case if, once committed to enforcement, its member states were unable to sustain that commitment or if its command and control systems were ineffective—would spell doom for the organization for many years to come. Its moral authority might be destroyed forever.

Note

1. The relevant articles of the United Nations Charter read as follows:

Article 46
Plans for the application of armed force shall be made by the Security Council with the assistance of the Military Staff Committee.
Article 47
1. There shall be established a Military Staff Committee to advise and assist the Security Council on all questions relating to the Security Council's military requirements for the maintenance of international peace and security, the employment and command of forces placed at its disposal, the regulation of armaments, and possible disarmament.
2. The Military Staff Committee shall consist of the Chiefs of Staff of the permanent members of the Security Council or their representatives. Any Member of the United Nations not permanently represented on the Committee shall be invited by the Committee to be associated with it when the efficient discharge of the Committee's responsibilities requires the participation of that Member in its work.

3. The Military Staff Committee shall be responsible under the Security Council for the strategic direction of any armed forces placed at the disposal of the Security Council. Questions relating to the command of such forces shall be worked out subsequently.

4. The Military Staff Committee with the authorization of the Security Council and after consultation with appropriate regional agencies, may establish regional subcommittees.

7

Challenges of the New Peacekeeping

Kofi A. Annan

From Past to Future: The Challenges Ahead

The purpose of this paper is fourfold: (1) to analyze the nature of conflicts that are likely to challenge the organization in the early twenty-first century; (2) to define (by necessity in broad terms) the types of responses that are most promising in such cases; (3) to outline how the United Nations in recent years has greatly enhanced its capacity to implement such responses; and (4) to suggest further innovations that will be required if the organization is to be successful at the turn of the century. In an effort to see the forest, not the trees, this paper takes the long view. It does not dwell on today's immediate worries: the political and financial crises and the challenges of current operations.

The conventional wisdom, arising primarily from the difficulties encountered by two operations (in Bosnia and Somalia), is that the organization should do less peacekeeping, either by not getting involved at all in certain conflicts or by working only at their margins. Aside from the overriding fact that inaction in the face of massive violence is morally indefensible, noninvolvement is an illusory option. The illusion is due to domestic political imperatives in an age of media-driven popular awareness, as well as to international political realities. Doing nothing to respond to violent upheaval invites those affected, whether neighboring countries strained by an influx of refugees or external players with interests in the country (including, at times, rival external states with competing interests), to take matters into their own hands, whether through interdiction of refugees, support of proxies, or direct intervention.

With regard to domestic politics, member states are sometimes unable to resist popular pressure to "do something." It is a credit to the world's peoples that a declared policy of inaction in the face of genocide is not

169

always politically viable. The problem is that the "CNN factor" tends to mobilize popular pressure at the peak of the problem—which is to say at the very moment when effective intervention is most costly, most dangerous, and least likely to succeed.

In short, in our present world and into the foreseeable future, there is no such thing as international noninvolvement in violent conflicts. There is, rather, a choice between legitimate involvement and other, more ominous forms of intervention. Absent a concerted effort to strengthen the United Nations as the center for harmonizing interests and implementing the wishes of all the members, it will be only a matter of time before a great power comes to the Security Council seeking official blessing for its intervention, is denied this blessing, and takes unilateral action. This will be countered through arms transfers and other assistance by those who refused to legitimate the intervention in the first place. Some—but fortunately not all—of these elements are already apparent in parts of the world today. It does not take much imagination to envision a case in which all of these elements would be present. This would mark a return, not to the Cold War—there is no need to be unnecessarily apocalyptic—but nevertheless to an old and unpleasant, albeit familiar, way of the world.

What faces us, thus, is a need to recognize competing national interests and to explore ways to transcend them or at least to reconcile them through acceptable institutional mechanisms. This in turn will require an effective and sustainable system of collective security (one element of which would be peacekeeping) at the disposal of the Security Council. To think in terms of a system means to stop thinking of each individual case as if it existed in isolation and to begin to think of an overall framework that would preempt the need for so many new operations. An effective system of collective security would rest on three essential elements: consistent and timely response; resources; and sustained commitment.

Whether or not such a system is put into place, the council will continue to mandate challenging new operations. It is useful to focus on what these future UN operations will look like.

Types of Operations

There is no doubt that *some* of the UN's future operations will fall into two categories in which the organization has had considerable success:

1. The UN will continue to be tasked with classic UN peacekeeping operations, in which the parties share an interest in a limited settle-

ment consisting of, for example, a cease-fire and separation of forces. With the consent and cooperation of the parties, the peacekeepers monitor the implementation of the settlement. Examples would include the operations on the Golan Heights and in Cyprus. The UN will also occasionally be assigned preventive deployment operations, similar to the above except that they are deployed before conflict breaks out, as with the current operation in the former Yugoslav Republic of Macedonia.

2. The organization will be tasked with multidimensional operations to implement comprehensive settlements arrived at in good faith on the basis of a lengthy political process (e.g., in Namibia, Cambodia, El Salvador, and Mozambique). In spite of the fact that we have had tremendous successes here, it is generally recognized, within the secretariat at least, that the machinery creaked and was stretched to the limit. A number of needed improvements have since been made, as described below; others are under way. The secretariat is now equipped with most of the functional units that are required to plan and manage such operations. The challenge for the future will be to integrate these disparate parts into a more cohesive whole (and to resist pressures to dismantle some of them each time there is a lull in operations).

To face squarely a third type of UN operation that will be required in the future, it is first necessary to free ourselves from a certain amount of organizational and bureaucratic inertia. There is a temptation to rest on the laurels of past successes, restricting the organization to tried-and-true UN peacekeeping and becoming involved only where the doctrine and methods of that well-honed instrument fit the circumstances. The problem with such an approach, of course, is that in a much changed world, the prerequisites of traditional peacekeeping will not exist in the great majority of cases. If the UN has no other method at its disposal, it will become largely irrelevant. The United Nations, like a successful corporation, must periodically adapt its product line to changing demands. In the foreseeable future, the demands of peace and security will be to meet the threats posed by conflicts that are on one level internal but that have serious international implications. Have the conflicts in Bosnia and Rwanda been without such implications? Obviously not. Have they been amenable to traditional peacekeeping? Obviously not. Should the UN prepare itself constructively to address such conflicts in the future or abdicate its responsibilities in the name of "sticking to what the organization does best"? Even if the organization should prepare to abdicate—which it should not—it will not have the luxury of doing so, for the reasons described in the first part of this paper. In the absence of any realistic alternatives, a UN operation will occasionally be the least bad option available to the council for dealing with such conflicts, and soldiers under UN operational authority will be thrust into the violence to do what they can. Since this is foreseeable, there is a need to strengthen the organization's capacity to handle such operations. Otherwise, if the organization is neither doctrinally prepared nor staffed nor structured for the tasks, the least bad option on paper could easily degenerate into a fiasco on the ground.

To stand still while the world moves forward is to slide helplessly backward. The United Nations must face challenges that do not fit into a neat peacekeeping package: the volatile, so-called gray-area operations. As discussed below, this will require, first, the development of a serious capacity for the lawful gathering and analysis of intelligence, so that we understand the crisis in which we are about to intervene and are able to anticipate how it is likely to develop. On the basis of that understanding of the situation on the ground and the turns it could take, UN operations will require, second, appropriate capabilities upon deployment: the right force structure to be able to carry out the mandate and to protect the operation. If the organization fails to do this, as was the case in both Bosnia and Somalia, credibility will be eroded even further, and it will become increasingly difficult to find troop contributors.

"Inducing" Consent

What approaches seem most promising for future UN operations in volatile internal conflicts? In any given case, blue-helmeted soldiers are likely to encounter many persons who welcome the UN presence and many others who are highly resistant. In such operations, some of which will be mandated to assist societies bordering on anarchy, the old dictum of "consent of the parties" will be neither right nor wrong; it will be, quite simply, irrelevant. Only if conceived in a new light can the concept of consent be useful to future operations. That new concept, which is outlined in this section, may hold one of the keys to the success of future operations.

Much of the literature on peacekeeping treats the consent of the parties as if it were an independent variable. It is not, for the simple reason that the decision of parties to a conflict to grant consent is never taken in a vacuum. It is, rather, a function of the alternatives. If consent carries with it certain rewards and the failure to consent carries certain costs, this obviously affects the decision as to whether or not consent will be granted.

Through most of UN history, peacekeeping operations were established in cases in which external powers had considerable influence and interests. Indeed, a driving force behind peacekeeping during the Cold War was the superpowers' mutual interest in bringing an end to proxy wars before the superpowers were dragged into a direct confrontation, with all the dangers that that implied. Hence the superpowers, which were in a position to greatly increase or drastically reduce military and economic assistance, were able to induce their respective clients to consent to a peacekeeping operation and to cooperate with it.

When consent was thus secured, patrons rewarded their clients for cooperation. Foreign aid bills increased. In addition, the peacekeeping operation, once deployed, could itself build on the consent, winning the confidence of the parties, providing a climate in which reasonably normal life, including economic activity, could resume. Hence the peacekeeping operation helped to deliver a reward, namely, stability. It did not dispense punishments, at least not directly. Rather, when coercion was required, the operation reported to the Security Council, so that those with influence could (usually behind the scenes) apply the appropriate pressure.

The situation today is different. Conflicts occur in places that the great powers no longer care very much about. They do not have in such places large military or economic assistance programs that can be manipulated to reward or punish the recipients. To complicate matters, there is often a severe weakening or even breakdown of authority in these situations, with the result that ostensible political and military leaders exercise very little control over their supposed subordinates around the country.

In such situations how are consent and cooperation to be achieved? The behind-the-scenes support of the great powers, while still necessary, is not enough. It is up to the operation in the mission area to gain the consent and cooperation directly with the people they encounter, whether peasant, civil servant, warlord, or political leader. To do this, the peacekeepers must be able *in the mission area* to provide some mix of costs and rewards. At present, it is difficult for a UN operation to do either.

Inducement operations[1] are conceived for this purpose. They are intended to restore civil society where it has broken down by two methods: (1) the use of positive incentives (rewards) to induce, in the first instance, consent and cooperation with the peace operation and, beyond that, reconciliation; and (2) the threat of coercion to gain the consent and cooperation, however grudging, of those who are unresponsive to positive incentives.

Coercive Inducement

Let us deal first with the coercive aspect, whose purpose is to intimidate recalcitrants into cooperating. (This was accomplished, for example, in the case of UNITAF in Somalia, the multinational force in Haiti, and, on a more limited scale, Operation Turquoise in Rwanda.) If consent is thereby granted, then an inducement operation ensues. Such an operation takes into account that consent was granted only in the face of intimidating force and that a credible force is required if consent is to be maintained. Simultaneously, however, it operates on the basis of freely given consent on the part of much of the population and regards this as a valuable asset to be protected and nurtured. Thus the behavior of soldiers in an inducement operation must be distinctly different from what it would be in either a war-fighting or a peacekeeping operation. The purpose of an inducement operation is to build, not to destroy, even while intimidating into acquiescence those who would prevent reconciliation and the peacebuilding processes that are inherent in the restoration of civil society.

What happens if the international community gives an ultimatum, displays its coercive capacity, and one or more parties still refuse to grant consent? Given the lasting damage to credibility that results from issuing an ultimatum and then failing to follow through, bluffs should be avoided at all costs. It follows that inducement operations should be deployed with the mandate and the capacity to conduct, if necessary, offensive operations against recalcitrants. Otherwise, the intimidation factor on which their success depends will be glaringly absent, and the operations will be doomed from the beginning. The troublemakers will continue to persecute their victims, who will blame the UN for failing to bring justice. Few imaginable outcomes could be more damaging to credibility than failures of this kind.

It should be remembered that "credible coercive capacity" is a relative term, depending on circumstances, timing, and the nature of the adversary. General Romeo Dallaire, who was the UN force commander in Rwanda at the time of the crisis there, has made the compelling argument that if he had had a cohesive, mobile, brigade-size force within three weeks of the death of the presidents of Rwanda and Burundi, he could have saved hundreds of thousands of lives, albeit with some UN casualties. Rapid and decisive action, he argues, could have prevented a loosely organized and militarily unsophisticated group from wreaking havoc on elements of the local population. The key in that case would have been to establish such a presence before the situation got completely out of hand.

The Limits of Coercive Inducement

The reliance on coercion alone, however, is insufficient for three reasons. First, given that leverage is the product of carrots and sticks, it is obviously preferable, when possible, to influence parties' behavior with the former rather than the latter. Second, the intimidation factor will erode over time. Third, the most difficult operations are those in which the members of the Security Council find it necessary to provide a mandate that sounds robust, even though they cannot agree among themselves which party should be the target of decisive military force. In such circumstances there are severe constraints on the use of coercion, because the political direction and support for it is ambiguous or faint. Fourth, carrots and sticks as tools of influence are not entirely interchangeable. Some things can be achieved *only* by providing positive rewards rather than punishment. For example, while intimidation can in some (but certainly not all) circumstances clamp a lid on violence, at least for a while, it is not useful in promoting lasting reconciliation. Put simply, the underlying problems that lead to violence cannot themselves be intimidated out of existence. Justice and a lasting solution require not only stopping the violence but, crucially, taking the next step. (This was an obvious shortcoming in the UNITAF approach.)

In the context of armed conflict, a third party's (e.g., the United Nations') threat to punish factions if they fail to cooperate with their "enemy" will most likely have an effect opposite to the one intended. The faction thus threatened, naturally suspicious in view of the violence in which it is engaged, will feel "ganged up on" and will be less likely to cooperate with the third party and with its adversary except, perhaps, as a tactical and short-term measure to alleviate the pressure. This does not promote reconciliation and indeed can actually hinder it. The offer of positive incentives, in contrast, is nonthreatening and is not as likely to evince the same visceral, negative response. The steps thus taken toward reconciliation are taken willingly, which is a far better foundation on which to build lasting peace.

Positive Inducement

The provision of rewards in the mission area can be divided into two broad categories. The first is what some military establishments have called "civic action." Its purpose is limited, namely, to gain the goodwill and consequent cooperation of the population. The second, which might be termed "peace incentives," is more ambitious. It is intended as leverage to further the reconciliation process. It provides incentives—a structure of rewards—for erstwhile antagonists to cooperate with each other on some endeavor, usually a limited one at first, that has the potential for expansion if all goes well.

Providing rewards in the mission area could include any variety of activities tailored to the particular situation. These quite often seem mundane, including development assistance of various types, local infrastructure and water projects, the provision of access to small business loans, and making available (or, better yet, training people to provide) basic medical care and veterinary services. To employ rewards effectively as tools of conflict resolution requires understanding people's problems in their complexity and being able to respond at several levels simultaneously and with a certain amount of flexibility. In UN operations as currently constituted, there is neither structure, staff, nor budget for this type of activity. Hence UN operations, which have been weak on the coercive side owing in part to ambiguous mandates and the paltry means with which they have been deployed, have been similarly weak in their ability to offer rewards. This was not a grave problem in an earlier era, when great powers could provide the sticks and carrots in support of the peacekeeping operation. It is more of a problem in conflicts where the great powers themselves have few interests and thus few ties with the parties through which to exercise leverage effectively.

Civic action and peace incentives are different from humanitarian assistance, though they may sometimes appear the same and have some of the same results. The difference lies in their purpose. The primary purpose of humanitarian assistance is to provide succor to those in need. While civic action and peace incentives also help those in need, their primary purpose is to forward political objectives: to gain people's support for a UN operation and to provide leverage in favor of reconciliation. While humanitarian assistance is unconditional, peace incentives are to some extent conditional. Their continuation depends, more or less explicitly, on a certain amount of cooperation toward the objective of political reconciliation.

It should not be surprising, therefore, that experience to date has not been promising in regard to effective cooperation between humanitarian providers, on the one hand, and peacemakers and peacekeepers, on the other. They are in the field for related but distinctly different reasons. Understandably in this context, the political and security components, without a civic action budget and with no realistic alternatives to win popular support or provide incentives for reconciliation, are anxious to use the humanitarian agencies for these purposes. Just as understandably, the humanitarian agencies wish not to be used in this way but instead "to remain independent," that is, to protect their capacity to pursue humanitarian goals, assisting the affected population, regardless of whether or not warlords can be induced to cooperate with each other or the peace operation.

Civic action, in short, is neither charity nor luxury but, in the types of conflicts we have been discussing, an essential requirement for operational effectiveness that requires a line item of its own in the peace operation's budget. Peace incentives, similarly, are rewards cum leverage rather than assistance for its own sake.

Operations such as those discussed above will require the United Nations to have a more sophisticated capacity for peacekeeping than it has had in the past. The secretariat has been strengthened in recent years to handle the increasing complexity of peacekeeping. Progress in this regard will be described in the next section, as will additional improvements that have not yet been made but will prove indispensable.

Implications for Secretariat Capacity: Recent Improvements and Future Requirements

A number of steps have been taken to enhance the capacity of the Department of Peace-keeping Operations (DPKO) to plan, manage, and direct the numerous and complex field operations established by the Security Council and the General Assembly. It has been an enormous task to keep up with peacekeeping's rapid evolution, illustrated by the fact that at the end of 1991, there were some 11,500 United Nations peacekeepers in the field, a figure that rose to 80,000 in early 1994. At this writing in February 1996, there are approximately 30,000, a figure that will inevitably ebb and flow in keeping with the unpredictable and dynamic nature of violent conflicts and the world's response to them.

To meet the immediate challenges that have been presented by these dramatic changes over the last few years, in the absence of sufficient posts being established in the secretariat, many of the new activities in DPKO have been carried out by officers made available on a short-term basis by member states at no cost to the organization. The secretariat greatly appreciates this assistance, which has been essential for the organization to be able to fulfill its responsibilities. The practice, however, is only an interim solution. If the United Nations is to develop an experienced staff that can provide continuity and institutional memory, core posts are required. The organizational chart shown in figure 7.1 provides a graphic illustration of the current department, which has developed from an office

Figure 7.1

DEPARTMENT OF PEACE-KEEPING OPERATIONS

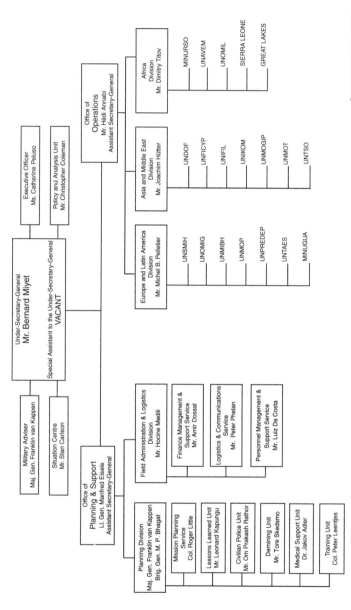

Under-Secretary-General
Mr. Bernard Miyet

Executive Officer
Ms. Catherine Peluso

Policy and Analysis Unit
Mr. Christopher Coleman

Military Adviser
Maj. Gen. Franklin van Kappen

Situation Centre
Mr. Stan Carlson

Special Assistant to the Under-Secretary-General
VACANT

Office of
Planning & Support
Lt. Gen. Manfred Eisele
Assistant Secretary-General

Field Administration & Logistics Division
Mr. Hocine Medili

Finance Management & Support Service
Mr. Amir Dossal

Logistics & Communications Service
Mr. Peter Phelan

Personnel Management & Support Service
Mr. Luiz Da Costa

Planning Division
Maj. Gen. Franklin van Kappen
Brig. Gen. M. P. Bhagat

Mission Planning Service
Col. Roger Little

Lessons Learned Unit
Mr. Leonard Kapungu

Civilian Police Unit
Mr. Om Prakash Rathor

Demining Unit
Mr. Tore Skedsmo

Medical Support Unit
Dr. Jakov Adler

Training Unit
Col. Peter Leentjes

Office of
Operations
Mr. Hédi Annabi
Assistant Secretary-General

Europe and Latin America Division
Mr. Michel B. Pelletier

UNSMIH
UNOMIG
UNMIBH
UNMOP
UNPREDEP
UNTAES
MINUGUA

Asia and Middle East Division
Mr. Joachim Hütter

UNDOF
UNFICYP
UNIFIL
UNIKOM
UNMOGIP
UNMOT
UNTSO

Africa Division
Mr. Dimitry Titov

MINURSO
UNAVEM
UNOMIL
SIERRA LEONE
GREAT LAKES

Revised 19 February 1997

of primarily political experts to an organization with the multidisciplinary expertise required to manage complex operations in dangerous settings.

In order to enable timely communications between these operations and the New York headquarters, a situation center, operating around the clock, was established in April 1993 and is still largely staffed by military officers loaned by member states. Its role is to improve and augment communications with United Nations operations around the world. It also assists other departments in discharging their responsibilities in the field. This includes the Departments of Humanitarian and Political Affairs, as well as the Office of the Security Coordinator, which is in the Department of Administration and Management and is responsible for policies and programs to ensure the safety and security of nonmilitary UN staff worldwide.

In late 1993, the nucleus of the Policy and Analysis Unit was established. The unit acts as a think tank, providing in-depth research and analysis of policy questions within the department's sphere of responsibility. It also gathers and assesses relevant studies and reports undertaken by intergovernmental, regional, and national governmental and nongovernmental organizations, maintaining liaison with counterparts from member governments and with scholars and independent policy analysts in research institutions and foundations.

As the Security Council in recent years has mandated operations in highly volatile settings where military expertise is essential, this aspect of the department has been greatly enhanced. In 1991 there was a military adviser at the rank of major-general, who was assisted by an additional three officers. That was the sum total of military personnel at New York headquarters. At the beginning of 1996, the Military Adviser's Office consisted of 4 and provided guidance to an additional 157 military officers working department-wide.

With regard to the department's overall structure, two offices, each headed by an assistant secretary-general, have been created: the Office of Operations and the Office of Planning and Support. The Office of Operations is divided into three regional divisions, each staffed with one or more political and military desk officers for each operation. This office is responsible for the day-to-day executive direction of peacekeeping operations and other field missions. This requires maintaining contact with the parties to the conflict, the members of the Security Council, countries contributing personnel to an operation, and other states having an interest in the conflict.

It is essential for the Office of Operations to provide the field with timely guidance on policy questions. To discharge this function effectively, its staff liaise closely with the Departments of Political and Humanitarian Affairs to ensure that communications with the field are coordinated, consistent, and coherent. In this regard, there have been a number of innovations. First, the secretary-general established in 1993 a high-level task force on UN operations, comprised of the under-secretaries-general of the relevant departments. Its purpose goes well beyond coordination and includes the formulation of integrated analysis and policy advice for the secretary-general. The task force has a regularly scheduled weekly meeting and convenes more frequently in a crisis. Similarly at the working level, interdepartmental working groups have been established for particular operations. Finally, the three departments have developed a framework for cooperation to ensure that information and early warning signals are shared in a timely manner and that options for action are identified when appropriate.

The Office of Planning and Support is responsible for all technical matters, including staffing, finance, logistics, and procurement, related to the planning and support of peacekeeping operations and other field missions. In addition to defining and coordinating the development of plans for peacekeeping operations and other field missions, the Office of Planning and Support is responsible for civilian police, demining, and training activities.

An important part of this office is the Mission Planning Service, established in mid-1993. It works in close cooperation with other units of the department and with specialists from other relevant departments of the secretariat, as well as with the specialized agencies and nongovernmental organizations, to design carefully integrated civilian and military plans for complex, multidimensional operations. Staff from the Mission Planning Service participate in technical missions sent in advance of an operation's establishment. The service's first major task was to prepare a detailed plan for UNAVEM III, which facilitated deployment once a political settlement had been reached and financing had been authorized. This exercise was also carried out successfully in preparing for the deployment of an expanded operation in Haiti earlier this year. This advance preparation represents a qualitative change in the UN's ability to respond quickly to assist parties to conflict to implement negotiated agreements. The concept is being further developed in concrete ways, as the department is now in the process of establishing, within the Mission Planning Service, an eight-to-ten-person nucleus of a force at headquarters. Once this team is in place, it will be involved in planning an operation. It will then be dispatched to the field to provide initial staffing in the operational headquarters and to ensure that implementation begins in a timely manner and according to plan.

A closely related function of the Mission Planning Service is the establishment and management of a system of national standby forces and other capabilities that interested member states maintain at an agreed state of readiness as a possible contribution to United Nations peacekeeping operations. As the name implies, they remain on standby in their home country. The decision as to whether or not they will be deployed in any given UN operation remains with their government.

The system of standby arrangements is still young, the concept having been developed in 1993. However, important aspects of it are now in place, and it is being enhanced continuously as more states become involved. To date, forty-seven member states have confirmed their willingness to participate in the standby arrangements system. Of these, thirty have already provided detailed lists of specific capabilities that they would like to be included in the standby arrangements database. These capabilities add up to the equivalent of five fully equipped brigades of four thousand to five thousand persons and an additional five brigades for which equipment, support services, and support units would have to be found.

To be able to make optimal use of the standby arrangements, the Mission Planning Service must have more than a list of capabilities. For planning purposes, what is required is detailed information such as the units' organizational structure, response times, air- and sealift volumetrics, as well as indications of equipment availability and requirements. This data enables the facilitation of rapid lift and deployment of these elements into a peacekeeping area. At this writing, eleven member states have provided the requisite volumetric information and technical data that make this system work, and discussions are under way with a number of others.

A very recent innovation has been the establishment in DPKO of a Lessons Learned Unit, to provide a greater capacity for in-depth study and analysis of experience whose conclusions can be applied to ongoing as well as future operations. A key element in this process is to elicit the insights of persons directly involved in operations, across the spectrum of components. Toward this end, the unit in 1995 conducted lessons-learned seminars on the United Nations Operation in Somalia (UNOSOM). The seminars brought together key personnel from UNOSOM, nongovernmental organizations active in the mission area, and personnel who had been involved in the management and support of the operation at UN headquarters in New York. In view of the usefulness of these pilot seminars, similar meetings will be organized on other major operations. The Lessons Learned Unit will also coordinate the preparation and analysis of after-action reports and relevant research.

Within its limited resources, the department works to promote standardized peacekeeping training among the many and diverse troop-contributing countries. For these tasks, a small Training Unit was established in DPKO in 1992. In addition to serving as a clearing house of information on peacekeeping training activities, this unit has developed training materials and issued them to all member states to assist them in preparing military personnel and civilian police, in accordance with agreed common standards, skills, practices, and procedures, to participate in peacekeeping operations. Some of the key elements include a United Nations military observers course and handbook, a United Nations civilian police course and handbook, a junior ranks handbook, a command and staff college training module and a peacekeeping training manual.

The Training Unit has recently established training assistance teams (UNTATs), made up of experienced peacekeepers, provided by member states as needed, to assist interested countries and regional institutions to develop training programs and train national and regional trainers. These teams are also available to train headquarters staff of United Nations peacekeeping operations. To date, such exercises have been held for the headquarters staff of the United Nations peacekeeping operations in Haiti and Angola. These have been positive experiments, assisting in the early integration of political, military, humanitarian, and administrative personnel into a cohesive team.

In addition, with significant in-kind support from a number of members, the Training Unit has recently initiated regional peacekeeping training workshops. Two were conducted in 1995 (for the Nordic countries and Latin America). On the basis of these successful pilot programs and taking into account the lessons learned from them, two additional workshops were conducted in Africa and Asia in 1996.

The role of civilian police components has become increasingly important in many operations. In order to have the expertise to provide effective headquarters management of these activities, the Civilian Police Unit was established in the department in 1993. In addition to advising the department and field missions on operational police matters, the unit is developing guidelines for the employment, conditions of service, training, and administration of civilian police in peacekeeping operations.

Mine clearance has become an operational and humanitarian problem in many countries in which there are United Nations peacekeeping operations, which often carry out demining activities both as an operational necessity and as part of their overall mission. The Demining Unit, since its establishment in 1992, has enabled the department to provide more effective headquarters management of these activities. It advises on mine-clearing activities and develops integrated plans for demining programs. Mines are now acknowledged as a major world problem, and the United Nations sets up and funds more mine clearance than any other world agency. The Demining Unit is a crucial part of this effort.

Another crucial addition to the department has been the Medical Support Unit, which advises on all medical matters related to peacekeeping operations. It provides medical support during a mission's start-up phase and during its liquidation and provides a temporary force medical officer and/or special medical adviser in cases of unforeseen events and difficulties in a mission area. The unit performs medical reconnaissance, on the basis of which it provides guidance to potential troop contributors on specific health threats to be expected in the area of operations. It processes all requests from the field for procurement of medical supplies and medical equipment.

With a view to consolidating in one department the responsibility for the direction and support of operations, the division handling field administration and logistics (formerly known as the Field Operations Division) has been moved from the Department of Administration and Management to the Department of Peace-keeping Operations. The integration of this division, renamed the Field Administration and Logistics Division (FALD), into the department's Office of Planning and Support strengthens the capacity of the United Nations to plan and manage field operations and has ameliorated problems arising from dual channels of communication between headquarters and the field.

Another significant improvement in the area of logistical support has been the establishment of an equipment depot at Brindisi, Italy. The United Nations has been able to develop at Brindisi, with assets coming out of recently closed operations, start-up kits containing basic equipment and supplies to initiate and sustain the nonmilitary components of a peacekeeping operation until its own systems are operative. To give an example of what this means in practical terms, let us look at Africa. Start-up kits and other equipment pre-positioned at Brindisi can be moved in less than three weeks to virtually any African port capable of handling ocean-going ships. This has been very valuable in the establishment of UNAVEM III in Angola.

In sum, as the number, size, and complexity of United Nations peacekeeping operations have increased, demands on the department have gone up dramatically. The department has managed a structured, prudent, and gradual expansion in order to meet these demands in a concerted and coherent manner. It began by establishing a sound skeletal structure to which, bit by bit, flesh has been added.

While the department was being strengthened, so were the channels of communication among members of the Security Council, troop contributing countries, and the secretariat. These improvements were essential. Decisions on mandates and overall policy regarding peacekeeping operations are in the competence of the Security Council, while implementation of those decisions is the purview of the secretary-general and the chief of mission. Without prejudice to the authority of any of these officials, there is a practical necessity to engage the troop contributors in dialogue in order to establish clear understandings about the mandate, strategy, and methods of the mission. The secretariat, therefore, now holds regular meetings with the troop contributors for each operation (in addition to the long-standing and natural practice of being fully accessible for informal, bilateral discussions with individual governments). These meetings are not limited to briefings about recent events but are an opportunity for substantive discussion of operational questions. More recently, at the political as opposed to the operational level, the practice has emerged of the president of the Security Council and a representative of the secretary-general cochairing meetings with troop contributors at key points in the life of a peacekeeping operation. These developments have been welcomed by all concerned.

In terms of further strengthening the UN's peacekeeping instrument for the twenty-first century, what additional capacities will be required for success? First, the military expertise of the Department of Peace-keeping Operations must be strengthened and placed on a firmer footing. This involves, first and foremost, developing a general staff in the Military Adviser's Office of DPKO. This permanent core of military expertise could be relatively lean (but not skeletal) and could be supplemented by loaned officers when faced with a need for surge capacity. The work of the general staff must be thoroughly integrated with that of the secretariat's political, humanitarian, and relevant administrative personnel. It must have a greater capacity, first, to conduct feasibility studies of achievable options for the secretary-general to present to the Security Council for its consideration; second, to translate mandates into achievable concepts of operations; third, to provide timely guidance and support to the field on military matters; and fourth, to enable the secretary-general to give timely and meaningful feedback to the council. Fulfilling these tasks responsibly will require a professional capacity for the lawful gathering, analysis, and reporting of intelligence. This will be essential to an adequate appreciation of what the operation will encounter in murky, complex situations. While much of the information already exists in the public domain and in the greater United Nations system, intelligence sharing by member states during the planning and implementation stages is essential, as is a properly staffed analytical unit at headquarters. Information without analysis is not useful. Properly analyzed, however, information is a vital tool for the planning and management of operations.

On the basis of a realistic understanding of the situation on the ground and the turns it could take, UN operations will require appropriate capabilities upon deployment: the right force structure to be able to carry out the mandate and to protect the operation. Ready access to cohesive, mobile, well-trained forces will also be crucial. The UN standby arrangements system now being developed is a step in the right direction and could be enhanced by some of the "rapid deployment" initiatives that are currently being explored by the members. Such systems, of course, are only as strong as the political will of the members to make them work.

Finally, the secretariat must have the capacity to manage the noncoercive aspects of inducement, which is a complex undertaking and which will require closer integration of different functional units of the organization. The use of limited incentives to promote conflict resolution can be effective only if the nature and complexity of the conflict are understood. Is it a deeply rooted societal conflict? Does it make sense to try to rebuild the failed state or to restore civil society under different institutions? Who are the parties? What are their interests, values, fears, strengths, and weaknesses? Most important, what do they want and need in order to move politics from the battlefield to legitimate institutions, and how can the international community best support them in that endeavor? Only on the basis of this type of information can one enunciate a coherent strategy, realistic objectives, and plan of action.

For decades if not centuries, these kinds of questions have been routinely posed by persons involved in negotiations of interstate conflicts, but in intrastate violence the answers are sometimes harder to determine. The ability to do so requires not only traditional politicomilitary and economic skills; it also requires expertise in intrasocietal politics and an ability to draw in country specialists with a detailed knowledge of local structures, values, needs, and interests. Again, a serious intelligence capacity will be required. It is as essential for the formulation and implementation of a successful political strategy as it is for the safety and effectiveness of the military component.

Conclusions

Conflict is as old as nature, and man's inhumanity to man surely predates recorded history. In the current era, unless and until a government or group of governments can be identified that is prepared to take on the role of global police, UN peace operations will in many cases be the only instrument available. This has been demonstrated repeatedly over the last few years, during which the United Nations, responding to both political and moral imperatives, has become increasingly involved in intrastate conflicts.

The organization must face this reality by adapting and learning to do things differently and by strengthening its machinery to serve the world better. None of this can be accomplished without both vision and investment.

In this partial lull that has resulted from the closure or scaling down of a few operations, we have a unique opportunity. We should take advantage of this relatively quiet period for UN peacekeeping, which will be ephemeral at best, to build on the organizational achievements of the last few years. The greatest danger is that we will do the opposite, dismantling what has been built up in the name of short-term savings. This would be penny wise and pound foolish. One need not follow world affairs very closely to understand that new and challenging operations could be on the horizon.

In the conflicts plaguing the world today and into the foreseeable future, standard requirements for success will include a reliable capacity for the lawful gathering and analysis of intelligence; credible risk and threat analysis prior to deployment; and a capacity to plan on the basis of appropriate force structures that are capable of achieving the mandate and of self-protection. The United Nations must have reliable access to such forces, adequately equipped for their task and trained to certain common standards. They must be fielded with rules of engagement that are realistic in the context of the specific mandate and mission area. They must operate within an effective command and control structure in which troop-contributing countries place a high degree of confidence. (On this latter point, the strengthening of the Department of Peace-keeping Operations, together with recent innovations to enhance opportunities for consultation among troop-contributing countries, Security Council members, and the secretariat, provides an important foundation on which to build.) UN operations must be able to utilize the appropriate mix of coercion and rewards—sticks and carrots—for managing and resolving conflicts. Finally, and crucially, they must be properly prepared to carry out the most challenging tasks in a manner that may sometimes be tough but must *always* be fair, upholding the organization's legitimacy and credibility, its indispensable assets.

Notes

This chapter was written in February 1996.

1. This term was coined by Donald C. F. Daniel and Bradd C. Hayes, whose ideas, expressed in "Securing Observance of UN Mandates through the Employment of Military Force" (*International Peacekeeping* 3, no. 4 [Winter 1996]), have contributed to part of the discussion. Their emphasis is primarily on the coercive dimension of inducement.

8

Prospects for a Rapid Response Capability: A Dialogue

Brian Urquhart and François Heisbourg

The Case for Rapid Response—*Brian Urquhart*

Since the end of the Cold War, the United Nations has been repeatedly engaged in violent situations involving human security rather than the international peace and security that the organization was set up to maintain. The member states have scarcely begun to make the changes in the organization's arrangements for peacekeeping and other activities that this fundamental change in the UN's task demands. The result has been several severely flawed operations and a serious loss of credibility and public confidence.

Until 1990, the UN's two main forms of military activity were relatively rare, large-scale enforcement actions (Korea, Kuwait) delegated to a major military power or powers by the Security Council, and peacekeeping, which included both peacekeeping forces and military observer groups. Peacekeeping was specifically nonforceful and required the consent and cooperation of the parties in conflict, as well as the willingness of member states to provide military contingents. The scope and limitations both of enforcement action and of peacekeeping were well understood.

The mood and disorder of the post–Cold War world were not anticipated at the United Nations, nor was the enormous increase in the demand for emergency operations. Because, for the first time, its permanent members were basically in agreement, it was for a brief period fashionable to believe that the Security Council had "come into its own." This belief failed to take account of two major factors: the change in the nature of the problems the council was dealing with, and the very limited capacity of the UN to engage in intensive emergency operations.

In the past four years, between traditional peacekeeping and enforcement operations, there has developed a large and uncertain range of problems—civil and ethnic wars, failed states, humanitarian and human rights disasters—for which neither peacekeeping nor enforcement, and certainly not a mixture of the two, is appropriate. Rapid and effective deployment was always a key to the success of UN operations, and in earlier years it was usually possible to deploy peacekeeping operations in a matter of days. Rapid and effective action is particularly important in preventing the current generation of civil conflict/humanitarian problems from spiraling out of control.

Paradoxically, however, as these problems have proliferated, the delays in mounting an effective UN response have steadily increased, often amounting to several months or more. Not only are governments increasingly reluctant to commit national contingents to violent and uncertain situations that are of no concern to their national security; but even when troops are eventually made available, their state of training and equipment and their suitability for the task at hand are often inadequate. Moreover, national contingents meet for the first time with commanders, staff, and other contingents in the midst of the emergency and, quite naturally, take considerable time to acclimatize themselves to each other and to the problems and conditions facing them.

Experience of recent UN operations shows that even a small, highly trained group with high morale and dedication, arriving at the scene of action immediately after a Security Council decision, would in most cases have far greater effect than a larger and less well prepared force arriving weeks, or even months, later. The failure to come to grips with a situation before it gets completely out of hand usually necessitates a far larger, more expensive, and less effective operation later on. Somalia, Haiti, and Rwanda are only three examples of this syndrome. The lesson from these and other recent cases needs to be learned and acted upon.

Options and Arguments

The solution most often proposed for the current problems of UN operations is the organization of standby forces by governments for UN service. It has been further suggested by the secretary-general that governments should train and make available standby rapid deployment units—possibly composed of volunteers—for immediate UN service. These units would be specially trained and would train periodically with each other as well.

The response from governments to the idea of rapid deployment standby units has been, at best, noncommittal, and at present the signs are not encouraging. Governments are increasingly reluctant to provide troops for violent civil conflicts in countries far removed from their region and national interest, especially for immediate deployment at the outset of a crisis. There would therefore be no certainty that—even if based on volunteers—standby national rapid deployment units would actually be available when they were needed. (Not one of the nineteen governments with peacekeeping standby agreements with the UN was willing to provide troops urgently for Rwanda in the summer of 1994.) Neither the tone nor the substance of the current debate on peacekeeping in Washington is encouraging in this respect either and may well have a considerable impact on the attitude of other governments toward participating in UN operations. In the foreseeable future, therefore, it seems likely that governmental response, even when a standby arrangement exists, cannot be taken for granted in all cases, and especially if immediate action is needed.

An alternative would be the establishment of a small, standing, highly trained volunteer rapid-response group as part of the UN itself. This is not a new idea. Something of the kind was suggested during the first Arab-Israeli war in 1948 by the first secretary-general, Trygve Lie. What is new is the increased need for a flexible rapid-response capability, reliably and immediately available for UN service.

Governmental reaction to this idea, with a few exceptions, has been extremely cautious and predominantly negative. Not unnaturally, governments are reluctant to create something that might diminish their control over, or participation in, UN operations. They fear that the ready availability of such a force might lead to its indiscriminate and unwise use. They are also apprehensive about the cost. Many countries, already wary of UN interventionism, believe that such a standing group would only encourage the Security Council to intervene more frequently.

These arguments need to be addressed. The Security Council authorizes virtually all UN operations, and without a Security Council decision a peacekeeping, enforcement, or any other type of action cannot be launched, except in the now unlikely event that the Security Council is blocked by veto and the decision is taken under the Uniting for Peace procedure by the General Assembly. If the rapid-response group is deployed by the Security Council, where the permanent members' veto provides an additional safeguard, it is hard to see why ready availability in a specifically UN force should be anything but a great improvement over the present system, where UN involvement is decided upon but is often rendered ineffective by delays in implementation and by weaknesses in performance.

As regards cost, the training and maintenance of a rapid-response group, say, ten thousand strong, would indeed be considerable. However, having to put in much larger military operations when a situation has gotten out of hand is likely to be even more costly and certainly much less effective. The inability of the UN to respond quickly in a crisis is also devastating to public confidence in the organization, quite apart from the cost in human lives and disruption in the crisis area that often results from a delay in UN intervention.

The Nature of a Ready-Response Group

To be effective and to repay the effort and expense involved, a UN ready-response group must be of the highest quality both in training and in morale, easily adaptable to different circumstances, and trained to deal expeditiously with unanticipated problems. The evolution of the right composition, training, rules of engagement, and relation to other UN activities will require much time and thought, as well as experimentation, trial, and, no doubt, some error. There is no sense in trying to force a new institution into old patterns.

A rapid-response group will not take the place of traditional peacekeeping forces, and it should be relieved as soon as possible by normal peacekeeping arrangements, should that be necessary. It will certainly not take the place of enforcement actions under Chapter VII of the Charter. Its main purpose would be to allow the United Nations to make an immediate practical response to conflict or potential conflict at a point where quite a small effort might achieve disproportionately large results. The rapid-response group would stay in an area of operations for the shortest practicable time—either until the acute phase of the crisis is over or until the group is relieved by a regular peacekeeping operation.

Possible Alternatives

The conventional approach to a rapid-reaction force is to envisage a basically military establishment. The figure of ten thousand has been mentioned as a reasonable strength for such an establishment, which would in effect be a sort of rapid deployment brigade. A number of governments are studying the organization, training, and weapons and equipment requirements of such a rapid-reaction force.

As stated above, the availability of national units for such a force will depend on governmental decisions. Judging by experience, a rapid-reaction force based on national standby arrangements cannot be relied on to be available in all contingencies.

The alternative would be a volunteer rapid-reaction group as part of the

UN Secretariat. While a predominantly military group would be a great deal better than any arrangement currently available to the United Nations, the nature of present demands for action indicates that some new combination of skills and disciplines should be studied with a view to defining what mixture of military, police, civilian, technical, and other personnel would be more likely to provide maximum flexibility and effectiveness.

The Role of a Rapid-Reaction Group

The nature and training of such a group, whatever its composition or origin, will depend in large measure on the role it is to play and the tasks it is expected to perform. Here again much work needs to be done, but an outline of probable tasks might be:

- to provide a UN presence in the crisis area immediately after the Security Council has decided that the UN should be involved

- to prevent violence from escalating

- to assist, monitor, and otherwise facilitate a cease-fire

- to provide the emergency framework (arrangements, protection, etc.) for the UN's efforts to resolve the conflict and to get negotiations going

- to secure a base, communications, airfield, etc. for a subsequent UN force

- to provide safe areas for persons and groups whose lives are threatened by the conflict

- to secure essential humanitarian relief operations

- to assess the situation and provide firsthand information for the Security Council, so that an informed decision can be made on the utility and feasibility of further UN involvement

Obviously such a group must have first-rate logistical support, including airlift.

Rules of Engagement

Rules of engagement and for the use of force will be different from either peacekeeping operations or enforcement actions. The rapid-reaction group will never initiate the use of force but will be highly trained so that it can take care of its own security and mobility and have the ability and equipment to maintain its operations in the face of harassment and even opposition. It will in no circumstances have military objectives or be required to take sides in a civil war. It will be trained in peacekeeping and problem-solving techniques but will also have the training, military expertise, and esprit de corps to pursue those tasks in difficult, and even violent, circumstances.

Development of a Rapid-Reaction Group

Such a composite group could start relatively small and develop according to need and the results of experience. It might also prove more acceptable, and less intimidating, to governments than a purely military rapid-reaction force, as well as more acceptable to parties in conflict.

Some of the elements of a mixed-discipline rapid-reaction group already exist in different parts of the UN system. The UN Field Service, which has existed since 1948, is a uniformed service trained in security and communications functions and with a long and distinguished record of operating effectively in confused and violent situations all over the world. The United Nations Secretariat routinely supplies political, legal, and administrative officers for field missions. Many of these officials have developed skill and ingenuity in dealing with unexpected, and sometimes dangerous, situations. The High Commissioner for Refugees and UNICEF have long and varied experience in dealing at very short notice with emergency humanitarian situations. Outside the UN system, there is a wide range of nongovernmental organizations with a long record of dealing with humanitarian emergencies. Many of these elements could be brought together as the initial core of an established rapid-response group.

The present UN arrangements for rapid response are fragmentary, improvised, and understaffed. They lack the framework of security and convincing physical presence. They often do not, at the outset of a crisis, have the capacity for effective teamwork that only a standing group, training and developing together, can acquire. They do not have military and police elements, specially trained for the job, as part of a permanent establishment. They often lack the communications and other techniques that modern technology can supply. These are some of the shortcomings that need to be addressed in planning a rapid-response group.

Financing virtually any UN operational activity is now a problem. A rapid-response group, whatever its basis and nature, should be seen as a vital investment for the future and one that by its nature is designed to act at the point where action can be most effective, thus eliminating or reducing the necessity for later, larger, less effective, more costly action.

Conclusions

Whatever approach—standby national rapid-response contingents or some built-in UN rapid-response group—is followed, an intensive effort of study, organization, and experimentation will be required. At the present early stage, both basic approaches should be imaginatively explored so that the best aspects of both can eventually become part of a more effective and reliable system of international response to violent emergencies.

Response—*François Heisbourg*

First of all, I will not pretend to be a United Nations expert like most of the contributors to this volume. My experience with the UN goes back now some fifteen years, so I am badly out of date in terms of the inner workings of that body. Therefore I will examine the issues that Sir Brian Urquhart has so remarkably laid out in a wider framework and in the context of a broader strategic outlook.

The second remark I would like to make is that as a Frenchman I have few inhibitions about scaling up the nature of UN operations. That one should move away from the traditional forms of peacekeeping toward some of the tasks laid out in Urquhart's portion of this chapter does not in the slightest disturb me in the philosophical sense, although I will have some remarks to make in terms of the political difficulties that this entails.

What I would like to do is to pose three questions concerning the volunteer UN rapid-response capability. The first: Is it desirable? The second: Is it feasible, militarily, politically, financially? And last: What are the alternatives? Notably, what are the interim alternatives, if one assumes that such a force, such a capability, is desirable?

On the issue of desirability: On the face of it, the case is quite strong, and it suffices to cite the case of Rwanda. If a sizable force had been immediately available, if it had been able to act expeditiously in the framework of the tasks that Brian Urquhart has defined, indeed, many deaths would have been avoided. If some of those tasks—seizing the airport; securing Rwanda's communications (I think here in particular of seizing "Radio Mille-Collines," which was one the most egregious agents of the genocide in Rwanda)—had been done, no doubt Rwanda would be a better place than it became. I note en passant, as others have already, that a UN force was present in Rwanda ab initio, as a UN force was also present ab initio in Somalia. And that obviously raises some questions.

My comments therefore will not be on desirability. They will rather be more on the feasibility aspects from the military viewpoint, first of all. The objectives that are set out in the earlier part of this chapter are extremely challenging. The United Nations force would know no geographical bounds. It would also have to perform a combination of tasks, some of which are essentially forceless and others that could well turn out to be forceful—seizing safe havens, safe areas, airports, bases, and so on. In effect we would be putting together a brigade-sized force with administrative, police, and military functions. It's an unusual combination, much broader than that of national intervention forces, even those with a multinational composition, such as the Foreign Legion.

Now if one adds to this the challenge of the UN building up its own army, as it were, on a stand-alone basis, with its own esprit de corps, with its own discipline, I would simply say that this is extremely difficult to do. To create a force that would be as effective as the Foreign Legion while performing a wider range of tasks than the Foreign Legion—that is not a small order.

A Difficult-Enough Undertaking

I have a greater problem with reconciling some of the force's objectives as laid out in Urquhart's discussion with the simultaneous imperative of not taking sides. And this is a point that was made in a different context by my friend John Roper. Seizing an airport in the midst of genocide in Rwanda would have resembled the Foreign Legion's operations in Kolwezi in 1979 rather than a UN peacekeeping operation. Nor could one say that seizing the airport, creating safe areas, would have been "impartial." It would have been an extremely partial operation. That does not mean that I would be uncomfortable with it. I would have been delighted if this had happened. But I do not think that it is possible, if one extends the UN's role to those types of tasks, to maintain impartiality. Therefore I would consider that this is in the realm of the feasible if at least two conditions are fulfilled. One is that we are clear about what we are doing; that is, that we should not pretend that certain tasks can be done without de facto taking sides. The second, and more fundamental, point is that we have to be ready to bear the consequences of such a policy of pursuing what are in effect coercive and partial objectives.

This has been done in the past by the UN, and Brian Urquhart is more qualified than anyone else to talk about accepting such consequences. Indeed, in the Katanga, back in the early 1960s, this is in effect what the UN did. It was not an impartial operation in the sense that the UN was changing a status quo in a given way. And it was done in a manner that was rather different from what we now call the "traditional" peacekeeping operations of subsequent years. But I would also argue that it is not entirely by chance that after the Congo operations a clear distinction eventually emerged between peacekeeping operations, on the one hand, and enforcement operations, on the other hand—whether those forcible operations are under UN aegis or not. We see that in Bosnia it is exceedingly dangerous, politically and militarily, to blur the line. Talking about "Chapter 6 1/2" operations does not make things easier for those who are caught between the hammer and the anvil in Bosnia. And I am not sure that there would be many contingencies in which a force of about ten thousand men and women would escape the dangers of, as it were, blurred objectives. That does not mean that there will never arise contingencies where "6 1/2" operations can be implemented with success. And if such contingencies were to arise, Urquhart's formula would obviously come very much into its own.

Let me turn now to political feasibility. The assumption behind the proposal for a standing rapid-response force is that the United Nations Security Council will be ready to adopt in a timely fashion resolutions that will trigger the use of that force. If one looks in retrospect at the Rwandan crisis, I don't know whether the United Nations Security Council would have authorized the dispatch of such a rapid-response force in April or May 1994, when the genocide was in full swing. Maybe it would; maybe it would not have. But given the procrastination, if I may put it that way, that was manifest vis-à-vis a well-documented genocide in Rwanda between April and July 1994, I am not at all sure that the answer would have been positive. I would add here that, at least in France—and I think it was the same in other countries—not only was the genocide well documented, but also there actually was a lot of television footage concerning it.

I would add that some of the objectives that Urquhart ascribes to the reaction capability appear to require a redefinition of UN operations, whether by extending the definition of peacekeeping in support of humanitarian operations or by extending the meaning of "Chapter 6 1/2." Seizures of bases, airports, and communications are not exactly acts that are readily encompassed (and Urquhart mentions this) in traditional peacekeeping. To come back to the Rwandan case, I would have been delighted if a UN force, or a force operating under the UN aegis, as was the case of the French, had seized the transmitter of Radio Mille-Collines, but that was not in the cards because that was not in the mandate provided by the UN Security Council.

Moving to the financial aspects, I see that our calculations are pretty close. Working on French cost and pay scales, I came up with a figure of somewhat more than $300 million a year for a ten-thousand-person rapid-reaction force; that would include training, equipment renewal, maintenance, other life-cycle costs, and pay. This would not include the specific costs engendered by the multinational character of such a force nor would it include logistical elements (notably the airlift). I would add that the plan to have precontracted airlift arrangements, is, I think, an entirely workable one. The French have had a good deal of experience in using such precontracted arrangements in order to be able to use nonmilitary lift when circumstances required them to do so for interventions in Africa.

Now I come to the last question: What are the alternatives, and more particularly, what are the interim alternatives? Let me begin by reiterating that the alternative of maintaining the status quo is clearly not as desirable as Brian Urquhart's rapid-reaction proposal. But let's look at things from a different angle. First, as I noted, a number of the tasks that Urquhart listed are essentially peaceful and nonforceful in nature, or, at most, they belong to peacekeeping in the most traditional sense of that expression—assisting a cease-fire, assessing the situation with monitors, and so forth. I wonder whether we shouldn't focus initially on this first category of tasks and think of setting up a standing cadre, a rapid-reaction group of rather smaller dimensions than that suggested by Urquhart; maybe a few thousand, with a mix of civilians, administrators, monitors, field officers, and Blue Helmets, restricted to these peaceful—or peacekeeping, in the traditional sense of the word—sets of objectives. Among those objectives one could include preventive action as long as it was not forceful.

Here I would like to say a few things about preventive action. This is, as we all know, a very popular theme nowadays. Politicians of all stripes and colors will tend to emphasize the need for preventive diplomacy, preventive action, and so on and so forth. However, what strikes me is the discrepancy between resources that are made available, however grudgingly, to military operations, even UN military operations, and the resources that are actually allotted to preventive action. Now some of this no doubt has to do with bureaucratic realities in the member states; that is, that defense ministries, which are not responsible for preventive diplomacy or preventive action more generally, tend to be rather more heftily endowed than foreign ministries. But we would all be well served if the United Nations' preventive capability in financial, political, and practical terms were enhanced. The UN needs a standing capability not only for

rapid reaction but also for rapid action, as it were, for preventive operations. Such action is what may well be called for to cope with a contingency such as that which may emerge in Burundi. One of the things that
probably holds us back in terms of preventive action is that it does not
make as "good" television as military operations tend to do. Helicopters
strafing rooftops in Mogadishu make good television, whereas successful
preventive deployments do not make good television. But I would also
add that when the helicopter crashes over Mogadishu, that also makes
excellent television, but the political results are rather awful; so I would
argue that not having a CNN spinoff can also have positive value, and
preventive action can help in that respect.

Now, as for the second category of tasks that Urquhart outlined (i.e.,
those tasks that may imply forceful action going much beyond traditional
peacekeeping, such as the expeditious creation of safe areas or the seizure
of air bases and communications), I suspect that current political and
financial realities will continue to force us to rely on the willingness and
the ability of a number of states—so-called coalitions of the willing—to
provide the necessary troops and firepower. In the short run, improving
standby capabilities and arrangements may be our best bet, even though
I would easily recognize that the best is unfortunately not good enough.
And I will readily acknowledge that the world would be a better place if
we had Brian Urquhart's fully fledged fire brigade at the beck and call of
the United Nations.

Part IV

Humanitarian Protection

9

Humanitarian Action and Peacekeeping

Jan Eliasson

The humanitarian imperative is now clearly in the center of UN activities. Dealing with urgent crises and disasters, assisting people in immediate need, is now one of the main preoccupations of the United Nations. The organization is like a fire brigade rushing from one crisis to another, putting out flames, but with very little time to assess the root causes of disasters or to find the arsonists. Responding to man-made disasters is one of the most important challenges to the United Nations in the post–Cold War era.

Early action and identification of the root causes of humanitarian disasters have become primary objectives. In order to prevent crises, political, economic, social, and environmental factors must be addressed. The instruments available to the United Nations for peacemaking, peacekeeping, and peacebuilding can all be utilized. If well coordinated, early multifaceted UN operations will save lives—and money.

A New Generation of Peacekeeping Operations

The end of the Cold War has seen the introduction of new kinds of more active and comprehensive peacekeeping operations. The UN has engaged in multifunctional operations in conflicts that are mainly of an internal character.

These operations have exposed peacekeepers and aid workers to much more danger than previously, with the possible exception of the Congo operation in the 1960s. The front lines are not as clear as in traditional operations. The parties are not easily identified. They often consist of militias or armed civilians with lax discipline and unclear chains of command. The consent of the parties is not always apparent. There is a certain fatigue among UN member states and a growing reluctance to provide troops or financial contributions to new operations.

UN operations have combined peacekeeping with political and humanitarian activities, including supervising elections, establishing civilian institutions, training local police, and providing relief. The UN role has involved assistance in the very reconstruction of state and society in El Salvador, Cambodia, and Somalia. These operations have encountered multiple difficulties due to unclear mandates and insufficient political support and resources. The media have quickly depicted some of them as outright failures, putting the blame on the UN system. Other operations have, however, worked remarkably well away from the media spotlight and provide valuable lessons. The UNTAG operation in Namibia, UNTAC in Cambodia, and ONUMOZ in Mozambique could even fairly be described as UN success stories.

Negative perceptions and experiences in Somalia, the former Yugoslavia, and Rwanda have put in doubt the capacity of the United Nations to address such complex situations. In these cases, imperfect mandates and the reluctance of member states to provide adequately trained troops have seriously handicapped UN operations. UN mandates, which have introduced elements of enforcement with reference to Chapter VII of the Charter authorizing the use of force beyond self-defense, have further complicated these efforts. The role and impartiality of the United Nations have been questioned, and troops have been repeatedly humiliated. The absence of a functioning state authority in Rwanda and Somalia has presented the UN with additional difficulties in carrying out its mandate.

Preventive Action

A lesson drawn from all these cases is that the United Nations must pay much more attention to the imperative of prevention. The international community must improve its capacity to anticipate crises before they erupt into open violence. The United Nations must strengthen its ability to identify warning signals and take early action. More resources must be allocated to gathering and handling information at an early stage. Nongovernmental organizations and UN organs and programs as well as specialized agencies all have a particular role in this regard.

The UN Development Programme (UNDP), for example, has identified six indicators of a high degree of risk of conflict: food shortage, high unemployment and decreasing wages, violations of human rights, ethnic violence, regional imbalances, and excessive military expenditure. Humanitarian organizations respond rapidly to crises. Early presence and proximity to people in the field enable humanitarian organizations to provide early warning.

The international community is generally reluctant, however, to engage in operations before conflict has erupted. It has been difficult to mobilize the necessary resources in terms of personnel or money for early action. Not until "the CNN factor" has created public pressure—after gruesome pictures of disaster and human suffering—have governments been willing to spend larger sums to intervene. This points to the need for a special fund for early measures of prevention.

Newly independent countries are often suspicious of early warning systems and early UN action. They often fear that the big powers, through decisions in the Security Council as a response to early warning, might impose themselves on less powerful states. For these countries it is often more acceptable to give a role to regional organizations in the early stages of a conflict. As has been shown by the Organization for Security and Cooperation in Europe (OSCE, formerly CSCE), a regional organization can do much in the area of confidence-building and early action. The OSCE fact-finding missions to Estonia, Latvia, and the former Yugoslav Republic of Macedonia (FYROM) are cases in point. Should tensions appear between the Russian-speaking population and Estonians or Latvians, or should the conflict in Bosnia start to have spillover effects in the region, the OSCE—through its monitors in place—would immediately be informed. In cases of preventive action by regional organizations, close coordination with the United Nations is of great value. The UN may need to follow up the action taken by the regional organization and may provide advice and logistical assistance.

The cooperation in Central America between the Organization of American States (OAS), the Contadora Group, and the United Nations is an excellent example of the benefits of joint efforts, as is the UN cooperation with ASEAN in Cambodia and with the OAU in Somalia and Rwanda. The UN has also worked closely with the OSCE in the former Yugoslavia and in the CIS area.

A Ladder of Action

Several possibilities for preventive action could be listed as steps on a ladder, ranging from early warning and fact-finding missions through dispute settlement and peacekeeping to enforcement actions. The report of January 1995 by the Commission on Global Governance, cochaired by Sir Shridath Ramphal and Prime Minister Ingvar Carlsson of Sweden, describes such a ladder.

After the early warning signal, a fact-finding mission could be dispatched without delay and some kind of international presence could be established on the ground. Such a presence could have a stabilizing effect. The need for assistance from the international community could be assessed through such a presence. In agreement with the host country, the UN Commissioner for Human Rights could dispatch monitors, who might help reduce tension.

The fact-finding mission or a special representative of the secretary-general could start a process of reconciliation and suggest confidence-building measures. They could report on the need for humanitarian relief or development efforts and suggest measures to come to terms with social and environmental degradation. All this can take place on the initiative of the secretary-general without the involvement of the Security Council.

Member states should be ready to provide the secretary-general with candidates who possess political and diplomatic skill and knowledge of certain regions. These persons could serve, at short notice, in fact-finding missions or as special representatives of the secretary-general in emergency situations. Furthermore, the secretary-general should have more latitude in deciding on fact-finding missions. In some cases, such missions should be discreet and, if successful, not necessarily lead to further action. On the basis of the report of a fact-finding mission, the secretary-general can bring an issue to the Security Council in accordance with Article 99 of the UN Charter.

Peacemaking

Early involvement would make it possible to address the root causes of conflict and provide sufficient information on the situation, if later military involvement should ensue. In most cases, early humanitarian relief and suitable development assistance would be essential. Very often, this should be combined with peacemaking efforts.

In Chapter VI of the UN Charter, On Peaceful Settlement of Disputes, a number of instruments for peacemaking are mentioned, such as negotiation, inquiry, mediation, conciliation, arbitration, judicial settlement, and resort to regional agencies or arrangements. As a further step a peace-keeping force could be deployed on the ground. In FYROM, preventive deployment of a UN peacekeeping force has been carried out along the borders with Serbia and Albania, in order to contain the escalation and proliferation of the conflicts in the former Yugoslavia.

Enforcement action, in accordance with Chapter VII of the UN Charter, should be contemplated only as a last resort. In that chapter different enforcement measures are suggested, including economic sanctions. The use of military force should be an alternative only when all other measures have been exhausted.

Internal Conflict

Over the years, armed conflicts between states have become less frequent. The strong and effective reaction of the UN and the international community to the Iraqi invasion of Kuwait served as an important lesson to potential aggressors. If other aggressors are not met with equal firmness, however, this lesson may be lost.

Crises in recent years have more often been of an internal character. Although the UN Charter refers to internal conflicts as not subject to UN interference, there are important exceptions. Humanitarian action within a state has become a generally accepted UN response to conflicts. Through General Assembly Resolution 46/182 of December 1991, governments have committed themselves to provide access to people in need and have accepted the responsibility for the well-being of their own populations. In complex emergencies—civil wars and other conflicts—the UN during the past few years has provided humanitarian assistance to around forty countries, helping millions of people.

Humanitarian action may enable broader UN engagement in internal conflicts. It can play a role as a catalyst both to help people in need and to develop a new, dynamic form of diplomacy. Humanitarian diplomacy is increasingly recognized as a dynamic means of gaining access to people in distress. In Sudan and Angola, humanitarian corridors, which are almost the equivalent to local, temporary cease-fires, have been negotiated.

The concept that solidarity does not end automatically at a border but rather it should include all human beings in need has gained acceptance with regard to humanitarian assistance. In the area of human rights, however, such a broad definition of solidarity is considered by some as an infringement on state sovereignty.

Peace Enforcement

States are often reluctant to consent to intervention by the United Nations in an internal conflict. Governments fear that this would infringe upon their sovereignty and give the impression that they cannot handle the situation themselves. Intervention may also allow opposition groups to obtain international recognition and be seen as legitimate parties to the conflict. A balance must be sought between sovereignty and solidarity with people in need.

In principle, UN peacemaking and peacekeeping activities require the consent of the parties, in particular the acceptance of the host government. Enforcement action in an internal conflict without the consent of the parties is, of course, possible if the Security Council decides that such a conflict constitutes a threat to international peace and security. In the case of Haiti, a flow of refugees into neighboring countries motivated a Security Council decision in accordance with Chapter VII of the UN Charter.

Yet such cases are exceptions. The United Nations nevertheless has responsibility for the security of individuals and not only for states. The question is whether the UN should be able to act in some way without the consent of the host government in extreme cases, where human security is threatened on a mass scale. It should then be kept in mind that such action can be very dangerous, demand large resources, and put in jeopardy the humanitarian activities of the United Nations and nongovernmental organizations (NGOs). In situations of complete anarchy, as in Somalia and Rwanda, the UN's responsibility to intervene has been recognized by practically all member states.

Most UN humanitarian action can and should take place without decisions or involvement of the Security Council. The Security Council needs to get involved only if there is a strong security or military component and where council action is required for peacekeeping or sending observers or for protection of a humanitarian operation. Preferably, humanitarian action should take place without resorting to protection or military assistance.

Sometimes, NGOs or prominent, independent individuals can play peacemaking roles in internal conflicts. Their contributions can be useful for governments that are not ready to accept political UN intervention.

The presence of such organizations or individuals can play an important role in prevention, such as in Burundi. In these cases, close coordination with ongoing UN activities is of paramount importance. Major NGOs have already been included in the UN Inter-Agency Standing Committee, which coordinates policy for humanitarian action. But the formal links between UN operations and NGOs should be formed on a case-by-case basis and in the early planning of an operation.

NGOs rightly need to maintain independence and distance from political issues in order to have access to the victims and to preserve their humanitarian credibility. They would otherwise risk becoming hostages to political games and making humanitarian assistance a bargaining chip. They must avoid suspicions of collusion between humanitarian and political efforts.

The NGOs are crucial to UN relief efforts. They bring their own perspective and knowledge to relief operations, often in the form of early warning signals. They are a constant reminder that UN efforts must translate into greater support for those working in the field. Furthermore, they are operational partners, who bring substantial resources and people to field activities.

The Use of Force

In the more complex UN operations with humanitarian relief, peacemaking, peacekeeping, and peacebuilding activities, it is essential that the impartiality and neutrality of UN action be respected. The consent of the parties is a crucial factor.

Impartiality means helping victims on all sides of a conflict and behaving evenhandedly in relation to all parties. The UN emblem and other humanitarian symbols must be respected in humanitarian operations as representing fundamental legal and ethical values. If the guiding principles of humanity and impartiality are compromised, the legitimacy and utility of the UN action are placed at risk, as is the security of relief organizations and their personnel. In addition, humanitarian access may be restricted.

In traditional peacekeeping operations the troops have been equipped with light arms and authorized to use force only in self-defense. Peacekeeping should be a diplomatic endeavor closely linked to peacemaking, laying the groundwork for peaceful solutions of conflicts. The use of force other than in self-defense should be avoided. The peacekeeping force should act with firmness and determination but be very careful not to use excessive force and risk being perceived as not treating the parties evenhandedly. Otherwise, the peacekeeping force might become part of the problem instead of part of the solution.

In some cases, as in the former Yugoslavia, the peacekeeping troops have had to act more forcefully. This should be seen as compatible with the concept of self-defense and should not be deemed to fall under Chapter

VII of the UN Charter. A firm stance will not be seen as partial as long as the peacekeepers react in the same way to violations regardless of who is committing them. Not to resist harassment may have a negative effect on the credibility of the UN force, in particular if such unacceptable harassment makes it possible for a party to flagrantly take over weapons and vehicles from the peacekeepers.

The former special representative of the UN secretary-general in Cambodia, Yashushi Akashi, has explained that UNTAC interpreted self-defense in a very strict manner at the beginning of the UN operation in that country. As a result, UNTAC troops did not resist severe harassment from Khmer Rouge elements. Later, when these incidents became a serious impediment to the accomplishment of its duties, UNTAC started to actively defend itself, with Khmer Rouge casualties as a result.

It is, however, not easy to decide what level of self-defense may be justified. Countries sending troops to peacekeeping operations must have a precise understanding in advance of what level of force should be permitted, and the troops must be trained and equipped accordingly. Such issues must be dealt with pragmatically—and in detail—in the initial planning phase of a peacekeeping operation.

It should be recalled that protection of the humanitarian operations could be provided on a smaller scale, without the expense and potentially grave security implications of a larger peacekeeping operation. UN guards, as in northern Iraq, could be used in some cases. Civilian police or military observers may also protect a humanitarian operation. These may be seen as weaker alternatives from the military point of view, but a symbolic presence of the United Nations and the international community could be sufficient in some situations.

At any rate, such alternatives should be routinely considered. They may provide us with less expensive solutions—and diminish the risks as well. Full-scale peacekeeping operations are very costly; in Somalia, for example, for every dollar spent on humanitarian assistance in 1993, ten dollars was paid for military protection—and this in a massive humanitarian crisis situation. As under-secretary-general for humanitarian affairs at the time, I found this hard to accept.

Coordination of Humanitarian, Peacemaking, Peacekeeping, and Peacebuilding Activities

The United Nations is basically an organization for people as well as for states. It is natural for the United Nations to care for the welfare of individual human beings. Yet humanitarian efforts should never be seen in isolation. Apart from bringing relief, humanitarian action could be an element in peacebuilding—one of the three pillars of UN action, along with peacemaking and peacekeeping. These areas of activity could be more effective by being made more mutually reinforcing.

Humanitarian action can serve as a dynamic force for peace. It can create momentum toward restoring security and promoting reconciliation. Through its peacemaking activities, the United Nations could take advantage of this momentum in order to help parties reach peaceful solutions to their disputes. Humanitarian action and diplomacy can buy time and space for political action and can create an environment that is conducive to negotiations. Likewise, political action in the field of peacemaking could greatly assist humanitarian endeavors to reach prisoners of war, facilitate distribution of relief, etc. In Cambodia, El Salvador, and Mozambique, political initiatives often helped resolve serious refugee problems.

In complex emergency situations, where there is a need for security and a military component, the various UN roles should be developed simultaneously. Efforts in the military, political, and humanitarian areas should be seen as complementary (and mutually reinforcing). They should not be put on a time axis starting with the role of the military and ending with development programs. Building roads, schools, and bridges; taking away land mines; and creating jobs for young people constitute substantial contributions to military security. This was proven in Mozambique. In Somalia, unfortunately, these humanitarian aspects were not sufficiently emphasized.

UN humanitarian action may also create goodwill and confidence in the United Nations, with positive effects on UN peacekeeping and peacemaking activities. Even the peacekeepers themselves could contribute to confidence building through their humanitarian activities. Many UN troops have had the experience of building roads for the local population or admitting patients for medical treatment in UN field hospitals. UNPROFOR in the former Yugoslavia, for example, helped in repairing schools, hospitals, and roads, as well as in providing electricity, gas, and water to Sarajevo and operating the Bosnian capital's airport.

Conversely, the presence of UN peacekeeping forces may secure a suitable environment for humanitarian activities. These forces provide protection for relief workers and protect distribution of aid. The UN operation in the former Yugoslavia was an example of peacekeeping in support of humanitarian activities. The primary role of the United Nations in Bosnia was to assist in the delivery of humanitarian assistance to over four million people in need.

Coordination is crucial in the initial stages of a UN operation. The early planning phase should involve all humanitarian agencies and programs, as well as NGOs. In peacekeeping operations, troop contributors should also be invited to present their concerns and advice. The UN Department of Humanitarian Affairs (DHA) should take part in the early planning of peacekeeping operations to assess the need for humanitarian action. Preferably, the person responsible for coordination in the field should be involved in the early planning stages.

It is particularly important to strengthen coordination in the field, beginning at the stage of training peacekeeping troops and relief workers. Joint training programs should be encouraged. The extent of formal linkages between the various UN activities in the field must be decided in the early phase through close consultation and coordination.

In cases of traditional peacekeeping requiring the consent of the parties, the combinations of humanitarian, political, and military efforts are dynamic and complementary. On the other hand, during military enforcement operations or when UN sanctions are applied against one of the parties, UN action may not be perceived as neutral and impartial. The impartiality of UN efforts in the humanitarian field will undoubtedly be put to a test.

Military enforcement action should always be the very last resort and should be carried out with overwhelming strength, well-trained troops, and effective equipment. In enforcement cases, parties may argue that the humanitarian efforts should be separated from military action. Since it is difficult to envisage the UN abandoning its humanitarian role in a conflict, a credible delinking of the different UN roles would then have to be sought.

Conclusions

Unclear mandates, often the outcome of political compromises, create confusion, not least in relation to the parties, as does a blurred borderline between peacekeeping and peace enforcement. A particular danger is involved when a peacekeeping operation gradually turns into peace enforcement.

In Rwanda, changing political objectives and mandates made it difficult to sustain the linkages between peacemaking and peacekeeping on the one hand and humanitarian activities on the other. Humanitarian space became severely constrained—with deeply tragic consequences.

Somalia (where I personally was involved), the former Yugoslavia, and

Rwanda are examples of complex UN operations that have faced particular difficulties in linking humanitarian activities, peacemaking, and peacekeeping. The problems facing the operations in Cambodia, Namibia, and Mozambique were fewer and less serious. This may be partly because there were fewer political complications. Partly, however, coordination in these cases was done in a more effective manner and the dynamic interplay was allowed to follow its positive course.

Lessons were learned in the process. It is important to absorb and digest both the positive and negative experiences in order for the UN to be prepared to take on the demanding and difficult tasks ahead.

10

Humanitarian Responses to International Emergencies

Sadako Ogata

The fiftieth anniversary of the United Nations and the approach of the third millennium provide an ideal opportunity to reflect upon the challenges confronting the international community. While the direction that history is taking may not be very clear, it is now quite evident that the United Nations is confronted with an international environment that is very different from the one that existed just a decade ago, let alone that which prevailed when the organization was established in 1945.

One of the predominant characteristics of the contemporary world is the prevalence of armed conflict. According to most estimates, around thirty wars are currently being fought around the globe, as well as seventy low-intensity conflicts and sixty disputes in which one or more of the parties has threatened the use of force. More than 4 million deaths can be attributed to armed conflict since the end of the 1980s, with civilians representing as much as 90 percent of the casualties. The number of people who have been uprooted by persecution, violence, and human rights abuses now stands at some 50 million, of whom some 27 million are being protected and assisted by the United Nations High Commissioner for Refugees (UNHCR). Humanitarian organizations have struggled to keep pace with the demands of each new displacement, while governments around the world are becoming increasingly reluctant to offer refuge to these victims of violence. The international community must devise effective responses and solutions to the growing problem of human displacement. It is morally repugnant that so many millions of people have had to abandon their own homes, communities, and countries in order to survive.

At the same time, the world has a more pragmatic interest in averting and resolving refugee problems. Mass population displacements and the forces that provoke them represent an increasingly important dimension of the quest for global security. As recent events in regions such as the Balkans, the Caucasus, and West and Central Africa have demonstrated, refugee movements frequently have destabilizing consequences, particularly when they involve countries of asylum that have weak economies, fragile ecologies, and a delicate balance of ethnic groups. The difficulties experienced by countries of asylum do not justify the closure of borders to threatened populations nor the forcible return of refugees to countries where their lives might be at risk of regrettably common occurrences, both in the industrialized states and in the developing world. The burden imposed by large-scale refugee influxes does, however, provide the international community with an incentive to address the root causes of forced displacement with much greater political will.

The following pages discuss the nature of the complex emergencies witnessed in recent years and examine the way in which UNHCR and other humanitarian organizations have sought to strengthen their capacity to respond to such events. This chapter analyzes the evolving role of UN-mandated military forces in complex emergencies and concludes with a discussion of the need for a proactive and preventive approach to the problem of human displacement, enabling people to live safely in their own homes. Complex emergencies include Armenia and Azerbaijan, Bosnia and Herzegovina, Burundi, Chechnya, Liberia, Rwanda, Sierra-Leone, Somalia, and Tajikistan. During the past few years, the world has witnessed a succession of vicious armed conflicts and massive population displacements. Variously described in the academic literature as "humanitarian emergencies," "international emergencies," and "complex emergencies," such crises have varied considerably in their scope, scale, and duration, as well as in the degree of international attention that they have attracted. Nevertheless, these emergencies share a number of characteristics that allow them to be grouped together for analytical purposes.

First, while external forces have played an important part in all the crises identified above, the complex emergencies of the 1990s have derived essentially from internal conflicts, marked in the majority of cases by strong ethnic (or, more accurately, communal) allegiances. During the Cold War, the world's more powerful countries might have used their influence to prevent such conflicts and to restore the authority of the state. In the 1970s and 1980s, for example, the leaders and ruling groups of many low-income countries were regularly removed from office in military coups and popular uprisings. But new governments were quickly established to replace them, often with the overt or covert support of the superpowers and their allies.

In the 1990s, however, with the demise of the bipolar system, the richer nations have a greatly reduced interest in countries that lack any real strategic or economic significance. States that were once very weak have effectively collapsed. In a number of countries, government structures have been replaced by warlords, local military leaders who normally lack any coherent ideology and whose activities blur the conventional distinction between the struggle for political power, social banditry, and organized crime. Such breakdowns in the rule of law have been accompanied in every case by grievous human rights violations.

Second, as the adjective "complex" suggests, many of the world's most recent emergencies have been multifaceted in nature, characterized not only by political conflict but also by a simultaneous process of social, economic, environmental, and even cultural disintegration.

In the case of Rwanda, for example, many commentators have drawn attention to the supposedly ancient enmity between the Hutu and Tutsi people and the way in which this ethnic tension was manipulated by the country's rulers. Far fewer commentators have recognized the other difficulties that have confronted Rwanda in recent years: an annual population growth of over 3 percent; the highest population density in the African continent; the exhaustion of the country's limited agricultural land; a 30 percent reduction in per capita food production since the early 1980s; a collapse in the international market price for coffee, Rwanda's main export crop; and the introduction of a rigorous structural adjustment program that led to an 80 percent devaluation of the local currency.

As a recent OECD-sponsored study of the Rwanda emergency concluded, "The present can be explained only as a product of a long and conflict ridden process, in which many factors contribute to the total picture." Similar observations could be made about the crises in countries such as Liberia, Somalia, and the former Yugoslavia. In the words of one relief official who attended a recent conference convened by UNHCR and the Organization of African Unity, analyses of the recent spate of internal conflicts have perhaps focused too much on the end of the Cold War. "Too little attention," he stated, "has been given to what in reality has been a 30 year trend in increasing disaster vulnerability, impoverishment and social unrest. What is being witnessed today under the rubric of complex emergencies is the continuation and intensification of radical social adjustment."

Third, recent emergencies in Africa, the former Yugoslavia, and the former Soviet Union have all entailed large-scale forced migrations, both within and across state borders. As recent experience in these regions suggests, in the volatile circumstances that accompany the fragmentation of states and the creation of new territorial entities, social and political conflict is liable to assume particularly violent forms, provoking unusually large and speedy population displacements.

Contrary to popular opinion, the number of internal wars and refugee-producing conflicts taking place throughout the world has not increased significantly since the end of the Cold War. But the number of people displaced in each conflict has become much larger, a trend that is directly linked to the large number of small arms, automatic weapons, and land mines that combatants now have at their disposal. In many situations, of course, even the notion of a "combatant" has become largely irrelevant, given the extent to which adults, adolescents, and even children have been armed.

In a number of recent emergencies, massive population displacements have not simply been an unplanned consequence of violence but have been the direct objective of one or more conflicting groups. In the former Yugoslavia alone, where the terrible notion of "ethnic cleansing" originated, more than three million people have been uprooted during the past four years. Forced to leave their own community by physical threats, sexual violence, and other human rights violations, many of the people displaced by this process have also been required to sign a supposedly legal document formally handing over their property to the people responsible for their expulsion.

Fourth, and as a direct consequence of such mass population displacements, recent humanitarian emergencies have tended to be international in nature, drawing in neighboring and nearby countries, regional organizations, and the international community as a whole.

Liberia provides a striking example of this tendency. Beginning in 1989 as a relatively localized insurrection in the northeast of the country, the conflict swiftly engulfed the whole of Liberia, provoking massive internal displacements and an exodus of refugees into half a dozen West African states. Within two years the conflict had spilled across the border into Sierra Leone, contributing to the deepening political and economic crisis in that country. At the same time, the collapse of the Liberian state triggered the intervention of a multinational military force under the auspices of the Economic Community of West African States, as well as the deployment of a much smaller UN observer mission.

As the following sections of this chapter suggest, the consequences of such large and complex disasters have been twofold. First, humanitarian organizations have been placed under mounting pressure, requiring them to strengthen their operational capacity and to devise new emergency preparedness and response arrangements. Second, refugee problems and humanitarian issues have been pushed to the top of the international agenda, attracting much greater attention from states and the political organs of the UN system. These trends have converged in a series of large-scale relief operations, involving both humanitarian organizations and military forces mandated by the Security Council.

Emergency Response Arrangements

Since the Persian Gulf crisis of 1991, a humanitarian disaster that revealed a number of weaknesses in the international relief system, some important steps have been taken to improve the UN's response to complex emergencies. During an Economic and Social Council (ECOSOC) debate in July of that year, UNHCR pointed to the need for "a mutually reinforcing stand-by emergency response capacity, and a well defined standing mechanism for interagency cooperation." Five months later, the General Assembly passed Resolution 46/182, which appointed an emergency relief coordinator and paved the way for the establishment of the Department for Humanitarian Affairs.

More recently, the question of relief capacity and coordination within the UN system has again been raised by an ECOSOC resolution calling for a comprehensive review of the world body's emergency response arrangements. At the same time, a number of donor states have made no secret of their belief in the need for a restructuring of the UN system to eliminate the duplication of effort, to make the best use of scarce resources, and to enhance the linkage between relief and longer-term development activities.

As well as contributing to this debate, UNHCR has in recent years made systematic and practical efforts to improve the speed and effectiveness with which it can respond to emergencies. Experienced staff members with skills in areas such as protection, programming, logistics, and communications are now on permanent standby, ready to leave their regular duties when a crisis erupts. Within seventy-two hours, a completely operational and largely self-sufficient UNHCR emergency team can be deployed anywhere in the world. Special emergency guidelines, training programs, and contingency plans have also been established in association with governments and nongovernmental organizations (NGOs), further strengthening the organization's emergency response capacity.

Such initiatives have been complemented with a variety of other arrangements. These include, for example, the conclusion of agreements with the UN volunteers and a number of NGOs enabling UNHCR to call upon the services of trained emergency staff at short notice; the establishment in strategic locations of emergency stockpiles consisting of vehicles, telecommunications equipment, and computers, as well as essential relief items; an increase in the size of UNHCR's emergency fund, enabling the organization to commit up to US$6 million to an operation while a formal appeal is being launched; and the implementation of an agreement between UNHCR and the World Food Programme defining respective responsibilities for the procurement, delivery, and distribution of emergency rations.

The Use of the Military for Humanitarian Purposes

Recent efforts to enhance the emergency response capacity of the UN system and the international community as a whole have been characterized by the growing involvement of the military, especially UN-mandated forces, in emergency relief activities. Until the end of the 1980s, when the Cold War was drawing to a close, there were few direct linkages between the UN's efforts to protect and assist displaced populations and the world body's endeavors to maintain peace and security. During this period, the peacekeeping operations launched by the Security Council were almost exclusively deployed in situations where a conflict had arisen between two states and where the protagonists agreed on the need to end a military confrontation.

Such operations were generally quite small in scale, limited in the dangers to which they were exposed, and predominantly military in composition and function. Of the thirteen UN peacekeeping operations deployed before 1989, only three involved humanitarian assistance activities, and in none of those cases was the delivery of relief the original or primary purpose of the UN force. Peacekeeping units, operating under the supervision of the UN Security Council, and refugee relief organizations, functioning under the leadership of UNHCR, generally worked in different locations, with different objectives, and brought different skills to their task.

During that period, moreover, few if any voices were calling for a closer relationship to be established between the UN's political, military, and humanitarian functions. UNHCR and other relief agencies wished to distance themselves from the rivalry of the Eastern and Western blocs, while member states generally recognized that humanitarian organizations required a degree of autonomy if they were to function effectively. And the world's military establishments, their status protected by the Cold War and the particular notion of international security associated with that period, had no reason to seek an expanded role in the international relief arena.

In the past few years, this situation has changed dramatically. During the late 1980s, as relations warmed between the United States and the Soviet Union, it became possible to resolve a number of long-standing regional conflicts. In a number of these situations, such as Namibia, Cambodia, El Salvador, and Mozambique, large-scale UN operations were launched, designed to facilitate the transition from war to peace and from authoritarian to pluralistic political systems. Entailing a wide variety of different functions such as registering voters, organizing elections, demobilizing combatants, and repatriating refugees, for example, such operations also obliged the political, military, and humanitarian components of the UN system to work in closer cooperation than they ever had before.

This process was reinforced by the almost simultaneous appearance of the spate of internal conflicts and complex emergencies identified earlier in this chapter. Despite their inclination to look inward and focus on domestic and regional policy issues, the world's more powerful states have not been able to ignore these disasters. In some cases, particularly the former Yugoslavia and northern Iraq, national interests have been affected, not least by the movement of refugees and asylum seekers provoked by those conflicts. The intervention of the Western powers in northern Iraq, for example, was not only designed to protect the population of that area from the country's armed forces but also was intended to spare Turkey, a fellow NATO member, from a massive influx of Iraqi Kurds. In other situations, such as Rwanda and Somalia, the international community in general and the Western states in particular have been spurred into action by the sheer scale of the human suffering involved, coupled with the growing influence exerted by public opinion, the media, and the international relief community. In each of these cases, however, the international community was unable to mount an effective response by means of conventional relief operations undertaken by humanitarian organizations and civilian personnel.

In the case of Rwanda, the sheer speed and scale of the refugee exodus, as well as the threat that neighboring states would close their borders to the new arrivals, necessitated an alternative approach. In Somalia, regular relief efforts were jeopardized and in some areas rendered impossible by the collapse of state authority and the violence perpetrated by the warlords. In Iraq, a central government certainly existed, but it was not initially prepared to give humanitarian organizations access to the communities that it had attacked and displaced. It was not until the Security

Council had passed Resolution 688 and Operation Provide Comfort had been launched that the United Nations was able to sign a memorandum of understanding with the Iraqi government, authorizing UNHCR and other organizations to operate in the north of the country. And in the former Yugoslavia, the deliberate diversion of relief supplies and obstruction of aid convoys meant that the international community's initial humanitarian efforts had to be radically rethought. As in the preceding cases, the world's more powerful states concluded that the only appropriate response was to be found in the deployment of military forces.

As a result of these developments, UNHCR and other humanitarian organizations have been increasingly called upon to work in conflict zones and in close association with forces endorsed by the United Nations: UNOSOM and UNITAF in Somalia, Operation Turquoise and UNAMIR in Rwanda, UNPROFOR in the former Yugoslavia, and ECO-MOG in Liberia. Unsurprisingly, perhaps, the balance sheet of this new generation of peacekeeping operations is a mixed one, with a significant number of entries on both the credit and the debit pages of the ledger.

Military Involvement: Achievements and Limitations

Humanitarian organizations have traditionally been wary of the military—an understandable outlook, given the very different objectives and working methods of the two institutions. As far as most relief personnel were concerned, the world's armed forces and defense establishments were to a large extent responsible for the human suffering that they sought to alleviate. Cooperation with them was consequently neither feasible nor desirable.

During the past five years, such perceptions have undergone a profound transformation. With the end of the Cold War and the growing involvement of the military in complex emergency operations, humanitarian organizations have been obliged to acknowledge the military's unrivaled ability to deliver large amounts of relief at very short notice, irrespective of the difficulties of distance and terrain. Whether flying food into Sarajevo, safeguarding food supplies in Mogadishu, erecting tents in northern Iraq, or establishing water purification systems in Goma, the armed forces have demonstrated the important role that they can play in humanitarian activities.

Military involvement has also assisted in the effort to avert and resolve mass population displacements. The decision to launch Operation Provide Comfort, for example, was a controversial one at the time. But no one can doubt that the allied intervention in northern Iraq and a subsequent agreement with Baghdad that allowed humanitarian organizations to operate in the area enabled those people to go back to their homes in conditions of relative safety. Similarly, while questions have been raised regarding the motivation and impact of Operation Turquoise, there is considerable evidence to suggest that this initiative helped to limit the scale of the refugee exodus to Burundi and Zaire.

Despite these very real achievements, a number of important issues have arisen in situations where humanitarian organizations and the military find themselves working closely together. First, the degree of support available from the military in complex emergencies is unpredictable. As the experience of the past five years has demonstrated, the willingness of the Security Council to support the deployment of UN troops varies from one situation to another. Similarly, member states are not normally prepared to put their troops, equipment, and relief supplies at the automatic disposal of humanitarian organizations.

UNHCR has attempted to bring some order and predictability into the military-humanitarian relationship by developing the concept of "service package arrangements," whereby governments agree to assume responsibility for specific relief activities' logistics—water supply or air traffic control, for example—in the event of a new emergency. Ultimately, however, the decision to deploy a country's military assets will always be taken by military commanders and their political masters, not by the United Nations or any relief organization.

Second, even in situations where military support is available, difficulties can arise in the management of humanitarian activities. Who, for example, decides how much relief should be delivered and in what location, particularly in situations where there is insufficient assistance available to meet all of the needs? And who is responsible for determining when a situation is so hazardous that a relief operation should be suspended? Such issues are of particular pertinence in situations where there are no obvious national interests at stake. A government's decision to intervene in an emergency, taken at a time when the media are giving headline coverage to a crisis and when public feelings are running high, can just as quickly be reversed when soldiers are killed and their bodies are flown home.

Third, the assistance that the armed forces can provide is limited in nature. When it comes to airlifting heavy equipment into an inaccessible area, escorting relief convoys through a war zone, or repairing a broken bridge, the military has few if any rivals. But in situations where unaccompanied children have to be reunited with their parents or where the victims of sexual violence require counseling and support, military assets are clearly not a substitute for the work traditionally undertaken by humanitarian organizations. It is for this reason that UNHCR's efforts to strengthen its emergency response capacity will continue to build on the organization's established and vital partnership with other international organizations and NGOs.

Fourth, the involvement of the armed forces can be a threat to the traditional neutrality and impartiality of humanitarian assistance. This threat is of relatively little concern in UN peace plan operations of the type undertaken in Cambodia, El Salvador, Namibia, and Mozambique, where the conflicting parties have stopped fighting, where the terms of the settlement have been negotiated, and where there is a general consent to the UN's role and presence. In situations of active conflict, however, where one or more of the warring parties refuse to respect humanitarian norms, and especially when troops deployed under the UN flag are obliged to resort to the use of force, the risks are considerably greater.

Even so, such risks should not be exaggerated. In Bosnia and Herzegovina, for example, UNHCR always emphasized the impartiality of its activities and its willingness to assist all populations according to their needs. When NATO force was threatened or used, the organization's situation was undoubtedly complicated, especially in its relationship with the Bosnian Serb military, while the risk to UNHCR staff increased considerably. Nevertheless, the daily task of providing assistance and, where possible, protection to war-affected populations continued, thereby alleviating some of the dreadful human suffering created by the war. Even with UNPROFOR's assistance, conducting the humanitarian operation under these circumstances was very difficult. Without the support of the multinational force, it would have been impossible.

Humanitarian Action and Conflict Resolution

When states and other actors persist in violations of human rights and international humanitarian law, military action, endorsed by the international community, may prove to be both appropriate and necessary. As the preceding sections of this chapter have suggested, there may also be circumstances in which the deployment of the armed forces is required to ensure the protection and delivery of emergency relief, particularly in situations where food supplies and relief assistance are deliberately being used as weapons of war.

But it would be naive to ignore the political constraints on the deployment of UN-mandated forces, for in recent months, states have started to express a new degree of caution about the UN's expanded peacekeeping role. The era of "assertive multilateralism," as it was characterized by the U.S. administration in the early 1990s, may have already come to an end. As indicated by the international response to the genocide in Rwanda, governments may be wary about committing their armed forces to operations that are nonconsensual in nature and where their national interests are not perceived to be at risk.

There is also a need to acknowledge the human costs of the traditional, reactive approach to complex crises. However speedy and effective the international community's emergency response arrangements, the provision of humanitarian relief cannot spare refugees the physical and psychological suffering that inevitably occurs when people are forced to abandon their homes at short notice and to seek sanctuary elsewhere. Much greater efforts are required, therefore, to defuse social and political tensions before they assume a violent form and to bring stability to those societies that have already been shattered by protracted wars.

This emphasis on peaceful, preventive, and anticipatory action is not, of course, a new notion. Chapter VI of the UN Charter, for example, identifies a number of conflict prevention and resolution techniques—negotiation, inquiry, mediation, conciliation, arbitration, and judicial settlement—with the evident intention of avoiding the kind of coercive action that can be authorized under Chapter VII. More recently, in his 1992 report *An Agenda for Peace,* the secretary-general built upon the provisions of Chapter VI by exploring the notion of preventive diplomacy, which he described as "action to prevent disputes from arising between parties, to prevent existing disputes from escalating into conflicts and to limit the spread of the latter when they occur." Such action, the report explains, falls into five principal categories: confidence-building measures, formal and informal fact-finding, early warning, preventive deployment, and the creation of demilitarized zones.

The task of preventive diplomacy and the peacekeeping activities listed in Chapter VI of the UN Charter fall primarily within the competence of the secretary-general himself and other elements of the UN Secretariat, as well as the Security Council, General Assembly, and regional organizations. The role that humanitarian agencies can play in this area is inevitably limited, for preventive diplomacy is an intensely political activity, raising important questions of sovereignty and the involvement of the international community in domestic disputes.

But this is not to suggest that humanitarian agencies are excluded from the broader task of averting internal conflicts and resolving the complex emergencies that they provoke. Indeed, experience has demonstrated that humanitarian organizations, working in a neutral and impartial manner, can help to stabilize fragile situations, buy time and space for political negotiations, and reinforce the process of post-conflict reconciliation.

Humanitarian action and presence has a number of other advantages. As the following discussion of recent UNHCR activities suggests, it brings tangible benefits to the countries concerned and can be undertaken in a discreet manner. As such, it may be more acceptable to local people and political leaders than other forms of international intervention. Humanitarian action is immeasurably less expensive than the deployment of peacekeeping forces. It is able to draw upon the considerable expertise that UN and nongovernmental organizations have already gained in relief and development work. And it can be sustained over long periods of time, unlike the much shorter and sharper mode of intervention usually associated with the military.

UNHCR Activities in Countries of Origin

For almost four decades after the organization's establishment in 1951, UNHCR's activities were concentrated in the relatively safe and stable environment provided by countries of asylum. During the 1990s, however, the organization has increasingly been called upon to provide protection and assistance to uprooted populations and people who are at risk of displacement within their countries of origin.

Significantly, of the 27 million women, children, and men who were benefiting from UNHCR's services at the beginning of 1995, only 14.1 million were refugees in the conventional sense of the word: people who have fled from their own country and been granted asylum in another as a result of persecution, violence, and grave human rights abuses. The remaining 13 million consisted primarily of internally displaced populations, former refugees who had recently returned to their homeland, as well as besieged and war-affected populations in the former Yugoslavia.

As these statistics suggest, UNHCR's task is no longer limited to protecting the rights and welfare of exiled populations, although that remains a primordial task. Increasingly, the organization's concern is to promote the security of people in areas of past, potential, and actual instability, thereby enabling them to remain in, and return to, their homes in conditions of safety. This right to remain is inherent in Article 9 of the Universal Declaration of Human Rights, which states that no one shall be subjected to arbitrary exile.

As this concept suggests, people who are living within their own country—whether they are internally displaced people, returnees, or settled members of the population—depend ultimately on the willingness and ability of the state to ensure the welfare of its citizens. One of UNHCR's primary objectives, therefore, must be to assist government authorities, at both the national and the local level, in discharging this responsibility.

Achieving this objective is not easy. In some countries, civil institutions have been destroyed by years of armed conflict. In others, the central government controls only a part of the national territory, does not command the confidence of every minority group, or does not exist at all. And despite the process of democratization that has taken place throughout much of the world, there are still a good number of states that, with varying degrees of intent, fail to respect the rights of their citizens.

Despite these constraints, UNHCR has found that a wide range of measures can be taken to strengthen the protection that citizens receive from the state. Governments can be encouraged to establish amnesties and other formal guarantees for returning refugees and displaced people. International organizations can help national authorities draft equitable laws on issues such as nationality and citizenship, address the problem of statelessness, to recognize minority rights in their constitutional arrangements, and promote equitable participation in their political systems. In addition, resources and technical assistance can be provided to depoliticize and strengthen judicial systems, establish courts, train police and prison officials, and provide the population with proper identity documents.

Government structures, of course, do not function in a social or cultural vacuum. As can be demonstrated by the plight of the Roma people (Gypsies) in Eastern and Central Europe, official hostility toward minority groups both feeds and feeds upon broader public prejudices. Similar comments could be made about the ethnic Vietnamese population in Cambodia, the Muslim minority in Myanmar, and the Tuaregs of Mali and Mauritania, significant numbers of whom have been displaced in recent years. Efforts to support national protection capacities must therefore incorporate initiatives designed to enlighten public opinion, promote social tolerance, and combat notions of racial or ethnic supremacy. The institutions of what has become known as "civil society"—voluntary associations, community groups, nongovernmental organizations, churches, and the independent media—have a particularly important role to play in this area.

A second means of limiting conflict and averting population displacements is to be found in the establishment of an international civilian presence. Although this strategy has received far less attention than the deployment of UN peacekeeping forces, it has now been used in a number of conflict-affected countries. In Sri Lanka, for example, UNHCR staff have been stationed in a number of locations known as open relief centers, which are situated in areas inhabited by large numbers of returnees and internally displaced people and which provide a temporary refuge to those who do not feel secure.

In Somalia, UNHCR has established a cross-border program from Kenya, providing assistance and protection to people who might otherwise feel obliged to move into a neighboring country and encouraging the return of people who have already abandoned their homes. And in Tajikistan, UNHCR has, with the agreement of the government, been able to deploy mobile protection teams, working primarily in areas of the country where refugees returning from Afghanistan have settled.

From the experience gained in these and other situations, it is evident that international personnel can pursue a wide variety of valuable tasks in countries where there is a risk of human rights abuse and forced migration. These functions include, for example, intervening with local and national authorities when human rights violations take place, providing the international community with information concerning actual and potential abuses and population displacements, and encouraging conflicting parties to negotiate with each other and to establish codes of conduct regarding the treatment of civilian populations.

Ideally, international personnel should be deployed at a very early stage of a human rights or refugee problem, before attitudes have become intractable and conflicts have assumed a violent form. In an attempt to implement this principle, UNHCR has recently developed its own version of "preventive deployment": the posting of international staff to the former Soviet republics of Central Asia, all of which are experiencing serious tensions resulting from independence, democratization, and the transition to market-oriented economies.

The provision of material assistance represents a third form of "soft intervention." This activity serves a much wider range of purposes than simply keeping people alive. In the former Yugoslavia, for example, UNHCR's large relief distribution program has enabled the organization to establish a strong and accepted presence in the field and provided the organization with access to war-affected populations. UNHCR's role in the food distribution process, coupled with its efforts to treat all communities on the basis of needs, has also given the organization some bargaining power in its relationship with combatants and local authorities. This again has sometimes enabled the organization to moderate the behavior of the warring parties, although it has at times also made UNHCR a target of their hostility.

In other parts of the world, humanitarian assistance has played a useful role in the process of post-conflict reconciliation, thereby encouraging refugees to repatriate and to reestablish themselves within their country of origin. In Nicaragua, for example, UNHCR's rehabilitation program obliged supporters of the Contras and Sandinistas to work together if they wished to take advantage of the international resources that the organization had at its disposal. Similarly, in Cambodia, UNHCR was able to bring the leaders of different political factions together at the local level to discuss issues of mutual concern.

The task of post-conflict reconstruction and reconciliation is itself inseparable from that of conflict prevention. A country that has experienced one civil war may soon be confronted with another if efforts are not made to restart the development process, to develop a pluralistic political system, and to build new and effective institutions.

Donor states and aid organizations have too often concentrated their resources on relatively short-term activities in post-conflict situations. Cease-fires and peace agreements often attract large amounts of external assistance, as do high-profile activities such as refugee repatriation programs. But when large amounts of external assistance are pumped into weak states over short periods of time, there is an inevitable tendency for local structures to be bypassed and undermined. In the rush to establish programs and implement projects, it is often easiest for experienced international agencies to assume such responsibilities directly rather than working through weak indigenous institutions. As a result, local actors frequently have little or no voice in deciding what assistance a country receives, to which activities it is allocated, and how it is administered.

Finally, there is now recognition that post-conflict recovery is a multifaceted task, requiring coordinated action in the social, political, and economic fields. In this respect, it has become clear that the international financial institutions that play such an important role in determining the economic policy options of low-income and conflict-affected countries have not been drawn sufficiently into this process. As a growing number of analysts are now asking, can such states be expected to manage the transition from war to peace, from dictatorship to democracy, and from centralized to market economies without experiencing new forms of social conflict, political instability, and mass population displacement? Without a satisfactory response to this question, there is a real danger that countries that are struggling to shake off the effects of war will instead find themselves in the grip of another complex emergency.

Conclusions

Rather than focusing reactively on the tragic human consequences of armed conflict, the international community must attempt to address the causes of such phenomena and must do so in a truly comprehensive manner. As the world is belatedly recognizing, the problem of human displacement cannot be properly addressed without an integrated effort to resolve tensions within and between states, defend human rights, promote development, and conserve the natural environment.

Humanitarian action has an important but ultimately limited role to play in this challenging endeavor. Experience has shown that the presence of neutral and impartial humanitarian actors in situations of actual or potential conflict can help to foster a climate that is conducive to the resolution of disputes, the protection of human rights, and the prevention of refugee movements. Clearly, however, humanitarian action alone cannot avert complex emergencies or act as a substitute for the will of states. We must therefore urge the world's political leaders to desist from any action that creates the conditions for conflict and complex emergencies and encourage them to find speedy and lasting solutions to the crises that currently afflict our world.

Part V

Regional Dimensions

11

The Failed State and Political Collapse in Africa

Ali A. Mazrui

Issues of peacekeeping, peacemaking, and conflict management in Africa's experience are more likely to be within states than between states. Certainly the most deadly conflicts in post-colonial Africa have been within states. Since independence, hundreds of thousands of people have perished in African civil conflicts and civil wars. Out of every fifty war casualties Africa has sustained since independence, forty-eight were probably in civil conflicts within states. Those who died as a result of conflict between states were only a fraction of those numbers. We therefore need to understand the causes of internal conflicts more urgently than the causes of external war.

There are categories of these internal conflicts. Primary political violence occurs in disputes about the boundaries of the political community—groups who do not fully accept each other as fellow citizens of the same polity. Secessionist civil wars are in this case primary; they seek to redraw the boundaries of the political community. The Biafra war (Nigerian civil war, 1967–70) and the first Sudanese civil war (1955–72) were primary in this sense. So, of course, was the American Civil War in the 1860s.

Secondary political violence occurs when citizens are in disagreement about the goals of the political community without wanting to redraw the boundaries. The post-colonial civil war in Mozambique was secondary in this sense. So was the Spanish civil war of the 1930s. Is the second Sudanese civil war (since 1983) secondary if John Garang is sincere in not wanting the south to secede? Is it a war about the goals of the Sudanese political community rather than its boundaries?

Tertiary political violence is caused by the wider environment of the political community, both in the ecological sense of environment and in the sense of external factors precipitating internal tension:

- The drought and famine in Ethiopia in 1973 were among the causes of the creeping revolution in 1974. This was tertiary in the ecological sense.

- Did falling cocoa prices in the 1960s and the CIA contribute to Kwame Nkrumah's fall in 1966? This was tertiary in the global sense of political economy.

- How credible are the claims that Iran has had much to do with violent Islamic militancy in Egypt or Algeria? Iranian causation would be tertiary in the regional sense.

On balance, the deadliest civil conflicts in Africa are the primary ones, the separatist ones; three years of civil war in Nigeria probably cost half to three-quarters of a million lives.

On the other hand, the second Sudanese civil war (since 1983)—though less primary than the first—is outstripping the first both in number of casualties and in categories of suffering.

The conflicts between Muslim militants and the governments of Egypt and Algeria are secondary in our sense: they are concerned with the goals rather than the boundaries of the political community. The question arises whether religion generally in Africa is at worst a cause of secondary political violence (a conflict over goals), whereas ethnicity and tribalism can sometimes escalate to primary civil war.

It is arguable that none of the secessionist civil wars in Africa has been religious—not even the first Sudanese civil war. Much more divided North and South than just religion. Ethnicity and tribalism are, therefore, by far more powerful and more dangerous forces than religious sectarianism.

The Organization of African Unity (OAU) has firmly discouraged primary civil conflict by steadfastly refusing to countenance secessionism. It is one of the most consistent policies pursued by the OAU. There is reason to believe that Africa's firm policy against secessionism has helped to stabilize Africa's borders—for better or for worse.

Almost all spectacular armed secessionist bids were made in the 1950s and 1960s: the Anya Nya, Katanga, Biafra, and even Eritrea. On secessionism, the OAU's policy was not confidence building but confidence shaking. The confidence of would-be separatists was shaken and neutralized; mini-breakaway states would not be given pan-African recognition; a piece of Senegal here, a piece of Somalia there, were discouraged. Does this policy need reviewing? Or is it one of the OAU's successes in containing conflict? Primary political violence has been denied legitimacy through the organization's single-mindedness.

What about the OAU's record in containing secondary political violence—conflict arising out of disagreement about the goals rather than the boundaries of the political community? Here it is worth noting the paradoxical role of democracy in Africa; democracy has been both a cause of, and a cure for, conflict.

Certainly when defined as unregulated multiparty pluralism, democracy in Africa can even be disastrous. It is arguable that one of the causes of the Nigerian civil war (1960–66) was the multiparty system that preceded the war. Nigeria's First Republic helped to ignite Nigeria's civil war by arousing ethnic, regionalist, and religious rivalries to dangerous levels.

In other parts of Africa, one-party systems were a denial of democracy—but did they stabilize civilian rule and keep the soldiers out of politics? In the first quarter-century of Africa's independence, the longest-surviving civilian administrations were single-party regimes. These included Côte d'Ivoire, Zambia, Tanzania, Malawi, Kenya, and Guinea under Sekou Touré. In contrast, multiparty politics in Sudan, Ghana, and Nigeria repeatedly precipitated military intervention. Was the one-party system a better protection against military coups during the first quarter-century of Africa's independence?

On the other hand, prolonged denial of democracy and social justice can precipitate rebellion and demonstrations, if not revolution. Hence the costly revolution in Ethiopia in 1974 and its aftermath; hence the devastation in Liberia, Rwanda, and Somalia; hence the confrontations in Democratic Republic of the Congo (formerly Zaire and hereafter Congo-Kinshasa), Togo, Algeria, Cameroon, and elsewhere. Prolonged denials of social justice can lead to prolonged disorder and despair.

Africa needs to find a middle ground between democracy as a cause of conflict and democracy as a cure. Africa has to tilt the balance away from democracy as part of the problem to democracy as part of the solution.

Between Tyranny and Anarchy

Every African regime has continued to walk that tightrope between too much government and too little government. At some stage, an excess of government becomes tyranny; at some stage, too little government becomes anarchy. Either trend can lead to the failed state. Indeed, either trend may lead to the collapse of the state. The leviathan is at risk.

Somalia under Siad Barre was a case of tyranny finally leading to the collapse of the state; the Congo-Leopoldville (now Kinshasa) in 1960 was a case of anarchy nearly destroying the new post-colonial state. It was saved by the United Nations.

A major unresolved dilemma lies in civil-military relations. Perhaps in everybody's experience, military rule often leads, almost by definition, to too much government. On the other hand, civilian rule in countries like Nigeria and Sudan has sometimes meant too little government, with politicians squabbling among themselves and sometimes plundering the nation's resources. If military regimes have too much power and civilian regimes have too little control, countries like Nigeria and Sudan have to find solutions for the future.

Dr. Nnamdi Azikiwe, the first president of Nigeria after independence, once proposed a constitutional sharing of power between the military and civilians; it was called diarchy, a kind of dual sovereignty. At the time that Azikiwe proposed the dual-sovereign idea (part military, part civilian) in 1972, he was roundly denounced, especially by intellectuals and academics who were against military rule. But the dilemma has persisted in Dr. Azikiwe's own country, Nigeria, and elsewhere in Africa of how to bridge the gap between the ethic of representative government and the power of the military.

Has Egypt quietly evolved a diarchy since the 1952 revolution—a system of government of dual sovereignty between civilians and soldiers? Has Azikiwe's dream found fulfillment in Egypt, however imperfectly? Or is the Egyptian system still in the process of becoming a diarchy? Starting as a military-led system in 1952, has it become increasingly civilianized, yet still in the process of change towards full power-sharing?

Another dilemma concerning too much government versus too little hinges on the party system. There is little doubt that one-party states tend towards too much government. This has been the case in most of Africa.

On the other hand, multiparty systems in Africa have often degenerated into ethnic or sectarian rivalries resulting in too little control. This tendency was illustrated by Ghana under Hilla Limann, Nigeria under Shehu Shagari, and the Sudan under Sadiq El-Mahdi in the 1980s. The state was losing control in all three cases.

If one solution to the civil-military dilemma is diarchy, what is the solution to the dilemma between the one-party state and the multiparty system? How can the leviathan prevail?

Uganda is feeling its way towards one solution to the dilemma: a no-party state. Concerned that a multiparty system would only lead to a reactivation of Uganda's ethnic and sectarian rivalries, President Yoweri Museveni lent the weight of his name, office, and prestige to the principle of a Uganda without political parties for at least five years. In an election held in March 1994 to choose members of the Constituent Assembly, candidates in favor of a no-party Uganda seemed to have won a majority of the seats. The Constituent Assembly has yet to draw up the actual definitive provisions of Uganda's new constitution.

Under both Idi Amin (1971–79) and the second administration of Milton Obote (1980–85), Uganda experienced some of the worst excesses of both tyranny and anarchy at the same time. Although the state did not actually collapse, it lost control over a large part of the territory and was unable to perform many of its basic functions. Champions of a Uganda without political parties hope that their new partyless approach to politics may avert the type of situation that brought Idi Amin into power in the first place.

There are other possible solutions to the dilemma between multiparty anarchy and one-party tyranny. One possibility is a no-party presidency and a multiparty parliament. This could give a country a strong executive with extensive constitutional powers but one who is elected in a contest between individuals and not between party candidates. Parliament or the legislature, on the other hand, could remain multiparty. The president would not be allowed to belong to any political party. A system of a presidency without a political party may indeed give undue advantage to Africa's millionaires—the "Ross Perots" of Africa. That may be the price to pay for a no-party presidency in a multiparty society.

All of the above are situations where the state succeeds or fails in relation to the nature of the political institutions (military or civilian, multiparty or one-party or other). But in reality a state succeeds or fails in relation to wider societal configurations as well. In post-colonial Africa, ethnicity continues to be a major factor influencing the success or failure of the state.

Yet here, too, Mother Africa presents her contradictions. The road to state collapse could be either through having too many groups in the process or, paradoxically, too few. Previous failures of the state in Uganda were partly due to the very ethnic richness of the society: the striking diversity of Bantu, Nilotic, Sudanic, and other groups, each of which was itself internally diverse. The political system was not yet ready to sustain the immense pressures of competing ethnocultural claims. Ethiopia under Mengistu Haile-Mariam also drifted towards state failure, partly because the system was unable to accommodate its rich cultural and ethnic diversity. Mengistu's tyranny did not foster free negotiations, compromise, or coalition building among ethnic groups.

But how can a state fail or collapse because it has too few ethnic groups? At first glance it looks as if Somalia has been such a case. George Bernard Shaw used to say that the British and the Americans were a people divided by the same language. It may be truer and more poignant to say that the Somali are a people divided by the same culture. The culture legitimizes the clans that are among the central causes of discord. The culture legitimizes a macho response to interclan stalemates. The culture legitimizes interclan feuds.

Interclan rivalries among the Somali would decline if the Somali themselves were confronting the competition of other ethnic groups within some kind of plural society. The Somali themselves would close ranks if they were facing the rivalry of the Amhara and the Tigre in a new plural society. It is in that sense that even a culturally homogenous society can have major areas of schism if wise answers are not found for them.

In any case, Somalia even on its own could be studied as a plural society of many clans rather than of many "tribes." The single culture of the Somali people may be a misleading indicator. The pluralism of Somalia is at the level of sub-ethnicity rather than ethnicity. That disguised pluralism of Somalia was exploited by Siad Barre to play off one clan against another. Siad Barre's tyranny lasted from 1969 into the 1990s. It turned out to be the high road to the destruction of the Somali state.

The real contrast to the plural society as a threat to the state is the dual society. The plural society endangers the state by having more sociological diversity than the political process can accommodate. Paradoxically, the dual society endangers the state by having less sociological differentiation than is needed for the politics of compromise. It is to this understudied and even unrecognized category of the dual society that we must now turn.

The Dual Society and Political Tension

As we grapple with new levels of conflict in Africa, from Kigali to Kismayu, from Maputo to Monrovia, we ought at least to try to identify which sociopolitical situations are particularly conflict prone. To use the terms of Thomas Hobbes, when are we confronted with "a state of war"?

Quite a good deal of work has been done on the plural society in Africa—the type of society like Kenya or Tanzania that has a multiplicity of ethnic groups and plurality of political allegiances. What has yet to be explored adequately is the phenomenon of the dual society—a country whose fundamental divide is between two groups or two geographical areas. The state in a dual society is vulnerable in a different way from the state in a plural society. In a dual society two ethnic groups may account for three-quarters of the population.

Rwanda is a dual society. So is the Sudan. But they are dual societies in very different senses. Rwanda is an ethnically dual society; the fatal cleavage is between the majority Hutu and the minority Tutsi. Burundi is similarly bifurcated between majority Hutu and minority Tutsi. The Sudan is a regionally dual society, divided between a more Arabized northern Sudan and a Christian-led southern Sudan. But although the Sudan is regionally dual, it is ethnically plural. Both northern and southern Sudan are culturally diverse within themselves.

Cyprus is both regionally and ethnically dual between Greeks and Turks. There is a stalemate hovering between partition and confederation, which the United Nations is still trying to mediate. Czechoslovakia was also both ethnically and regionally dual between Czechs and Slovaks. In the post-communist era, the country has indeed partitioned itself into separate Czech and Slovak republics. In effect, the old Czechoslovak state has collapsed and split into two.

The riskiest situations are not those involving a convergence of ethnic duality and regional (territorial) duality, as in Cyprus or Czechoslovakia. It is true that when the two ethnic groups are concentrated in separate regions, the risk of territorial or political separatism and secession is increased. But, in human terms, that may not be the worst scenario. The riskiest form of duality for the leviathan is that of pure ethnic differentiation without territorial differentiation. It means that there is no prospect of a Cyprus-style stalemate, keeping the ethnic groups separate but peaceful. It also means that there is no prospect of Czechoslovakia's "gracious parting of the ways"—creating separate countries. Rather, the two groups are so intermingled in neighborhoods, at times so intermarried, that a soured ethnic relationship is an explosive relationship.

Rwanda and Burundi fall into that category—ethnic duality without regional duality. The two groups are intermingled from village to village, certainly from street to street. Rwanda also happens to be the most densely populated country on the African continent (estimated at 210 persons per square kilometer in the 1980s, or about 540 persons per square mile). Ethnic duality without regional separation can be a prescription for hate at close quarters. Rwanda's and Burundi's tragedies are a combination of ethnic duality, population density, geographic intermingling, and the legacies of colonial and pre-colonial relationships.

Northern Ireland is also a case of ethnic duality (Protestant and Catholic) with considerable intermingling within the north. There is no question of partitioning the north itself into a Catholic sector to be united with the Irish Republic and a Protestant section loyal to the United Kingdom. A second Irish partition is not in the cards, not least because the population of the north is too geographically intermingled for another partition. Intercommunal hate is therefore immediate and at close quarters.

Ethnically dual societies are vulnerable to the risk of polarization. The absence of potential mediating coalitions through other groups makes the Rwandas and Burundis of the world more vulnerable than ever to periodic ethnic convulsions. Cultural frontiers without territorial frontiers—a dual identity within a single country, a society at war with itself.

The Sudan is also a country at war with itself, but its duality is regional rather than ethnic. As previously indicated, both northern and southern Sudan are multiethnic, but the south is distinctive because it is culturally more indigenous, less Islamized, and led by Christianized Sudanese. There was a civil war between the two regions between 1955 and 1972, ending with the Addis Ababa accords of the latter year. In 1983 a second Sudanese civil war broke out and has raged ever since.

The first civil war was more clearly secessionist. The southern rebels wanted to pull out of the Sudan and form a separate country (the Czechoslovakia solution of later years). The second Sudanese civil war has been more ambivalent about secession. Indeed, southern military leader General John Garang has emphasized that he stands for democratization of the whole of the Sudan rather than for southern secession. There is indeed some nationwide intermingling between southerners and northerners, but on a modest scale. The real divide is region specific and can be territorialized—unlike the division between Hutu and Tutsi in Rwanda.

The speed of killing in Rwanda in April 1994 was much faster that almost anything witnessed in the Sudanese civil war—some two hundred thousand people were killed in Rwanda within barely a two-week period.

Of course, the state has not collapsed in Khartoum, though it has no control over parts of the south. Second, unlike the Rwandan national army, the Khartoum national army has not been seeking out helpless civilians for slaughter, from refugee camps to hospitals. However, over the long run, both civil wars have indeed been very costly in human lives and human suffering. The Sudan has yet to find a solution to its violent dualism. Its split cultural personality between north and south has so far been more deadly than its split ethnic personality among diverse tribes and clans.

The dual society continues to cast its shadow over plural Africa, from Zimbabwe (Shona versus Ndebele) to Algeria (Arab versus Berber), from Nigeria (north versus south), to the tensions in Kigali and Khartoum. The leviathan is at risk.

While Czechoslovakia was a case of both ethnic and territorial dualism (Czech versus Slovak) and Burundi and Rwanda are cases of ethnic dualism (Tutsi versus Hutu) without territorial dualism, Yemen has been a case of territorial dualism (north versus south) without significant ethnic dualism. Is the distinction between the self-styled Republic of Somaliland and the rest of Somalia a case of territorial dualism without ethnic dualism (as in the case of Yemen)? Or is there sub-ethnic dualism between the two parts of Somalia that makes it more like the case of Cyprus (Greek-Cypriot versus Turkish-Cypriot), which is both ethnically distinct and territorially differentiated? Alternatively, the two parts of Somalia may be an intermediate category of dualism, equally prone to internecine conflict.

The United Republic of Tanzania is a more artificial case of dualism between the much smaller member, Zanzibar, and the mainland of the old Tanganyika. There have indeed been heated political disputes between the two parts of the United Republic, with separatist sentiments sometimes manifested on the island of Zanzibar and sometimes, paradoxically, manifested among mainlanders. Is it a situation to which the present secretary-general of the Organization of African Unity (himself a Tanzanian) should pay special attention? Are there ominous ethnoreligious warning signs in Tanzania that we ought to monitor?

Conclusions

Because almost all African countries are unstable in varying degrees, we must not assume that they are unstable for the same reasons. Put differently, because all patients in a hospital are sick in varying degrees, we must not assume that they suffer from the same disease.

Conflict prevention requires greater and greater sophistication in diagnosing conflict-prone situations. Not all Hobbesian states of war are the same. Unfortunately, Africa is full of contradictions—conflict generated by too much government versus conflict generated by too little; conflict generated by too many ethnic groups, as distinct from conflict ignited by too few ethnic groups. It is dark outside. Africa is awaiting her real dawn. Let us hope the wait is not too long.

What is the solution in situations of acute state failure or political collapse? One option is unilateral intervention by a single neighboring power to restore order. There is the precedent of Tanzania's invasion of Uganda in 1979, when troops marched all the way to Kampala. Tanzania then put Uganda virtually under military occupation for a couple of years. Tanzania's intervention was very similar to Vietnam's intervention in Cambodia to overthrow Pol Pot, except that the Vietnamese stayed on in Cambodia much longer. The question arises whether Yoweri Museveni's Uganda should have intervened in Rwanda in April 1994 the way

Julius Nyerere's Tanzania intervened in Uganda fifteen years earlier.

Another scenario of intervention is that by a single power but with the blessing of a regional organization. There is no real African precedent, but there is an Arab one: Syria's intervention in the Lebanese civil war with the blessing of the League of Arab States.

A third scenario of intervention is inter-African colonization and annexation. In a sense, this is a kind of self-colonization. One precedent is Tanganyika's annexation of Zanzibar in 1964, partly under pressure from Lyndon B. Johnson of the United States and Sir Alec Douglas-Home of Great Britain. The West wanted to avert the danger of a kind of a Marxist Cuba on the clove island off the East African coast. Nyerere was persuaded that an unstable or subversive Zanzibar would be a threat to the mainland. He persuaded the dictator of Zanzibar at the time, Abeid Karume, to agree to a treaty of union—very much the way the British used to convince African chiefs to "accept" treaties by which they ceased to be sovereign. Nobody held a referendum in Zanzibar to see whether the people in the country wanted to cease being a separate independent nation. But the annexation of Zanzibar was the most daring case of what became, de facto, *Pax Tanzaniana*.

The fourth scenario as a solution to political collapse is regional integration. In the longer run, one solution to Rwanda and Burundi may well be a federation with Tanzania so that Hutus and Tutsis stop having de facto ethnic armies of their own but have those soldiers retrained as part of the federal army of the United Republic of Tanzania. German colonialism before World War I had leaned towards treating Tanganyika and Rwanda-Burundi as one single area of jurisdiction. Is a federal leviathan now needed?

Union with Tanzania for Rwanda and Burundi would, in the short run, be safer than union with Congo-Kinshasa, in spite of the shared Belgian connection with Congo-Kinshasa and the link with the French language. Tanzania is a less vulnerable society than Congo-Kinshasa, and a safer haven for Hutus and Tutsis. It is indeed significant that Hutus and Tutsis on the run are more likely to flee to Tanzania than to Congo-Kinshasa in spite of ethnic ties across the border in Congo-Kinshasa. Moreover, Hutus and Tutsis are getting partially Swahilized and should be able to get on well with "fellow" Tanzanian citizens. But why should Tanzania agree to such a federation? The international community would have to create a package of incentives for present-day Tanzania.

A fifth scenario for conflict resolution is the establishment of an African security council, complete with permanent members in the style of the United Nations Security Council. The permanent members could be

Egypt from North Africa, Nigeria from West Africa, Ethiopia from Eastern Africa, and the Republic of South Africa from Southern Africa. There should be some nonpermanent members, ranging from three to five. The principle of permanent members would be reviewed every thirty years. For example, in thirty years it may be necessary to add Congo-Kinshasa as a permanent member to represent Central Africa. In times of crisis, should the African security council meet at the level of African heads of state? Should each permanent member have a veto or not? These issues would also have to be addressed.

The sixth scenario of conflict resolution in times of political collapse is the establishment of a pan-African emergency force—a fire brigade to put out fires from one collapsed state or civil war to another and to teach Africa the arts of a *Pax Africana.* Should this pan-African emergency force be independently recruited and trained in a specialized manner? Or should it be drawn from units of the armed forces of member states? And how are the training, maintenance, and deployment of the emergency force to be paid for? Certainly the successes and failures of ECOMOG in Liberia should be studied carefully in preparation for this new venture.

The seventh scenario of conflict management would consist of ad hoc solutions from crisis to crisis, more in the tradition of mediation and search for solutions than in the tradition of the use of force. Such ad hoc efforts are definitely much better than nothing and could constitute a major part of Africa's search for *Pax Africana*—an African peace established and maintained by Africans themselves, to end a Hobbesian state of war.

In this more modest tradition of intervention is the Organization of African Unity's Mechanism on Conflict Prevention, Management and Resolution, which for the first time gives the regional organization a more active role in internal civil conflicts. Modest as the mechanism is, it signifies a qualitative shift in the orientation of African heads of state. To paraphrase Winston Churchill, this shift may not be the beginning of the end, but could it be the end of the beginning?

12

The OAU Role in Conflict Management

Salim Ahmed Salim

The escalation of civil strife and armed conflict in Africa has not only been worrying to Africa but has also constituted a serious impediment to the development process of the continent as a whole. Conflicts and domestic tension have had devastating effects on the lives of people in Africa, as well as on their efforts towards meaningful socioeconomic transformation, integration, and development.

It is true that as a result of greater understanding and cooperation between the various countries in Africa, especially since the end of the Cold War, a significant decrease in interstate conflicts has come about. This notwithstanding, there has been a rising tide of domestic tension and armed conflicts in many parts of Africa, with the most serious cases taking place in Liberia, Somalia, Rwanda, Burundi, and Sierra Leone. Furthermore, while some of the old conflicts have been successfully resolved, new ones, more devastating and more intractable, have emerged. As the world has continued to assume the dimensions of a global village, so too has it now become necessary that the world, as a community of nations, should rise to the challenge of conflicts. The Organization of African Unity (OAU) has taken this challenge seriously and is devoting considerable time, effort, and resources to it. In this task, the African countries have acted individually and collectively through the Organization of African Unity. The advantages of acting together have been obvious. The collective voice of Africa as the OAU has brought greater focus on the conflicts we face and helped to marshal resources to resolve them. Africa has given priority to collective action in the firm belief that the challenge of fostering peace in the continent is a task vested in OAU as our regional organization. Like the OAU, other regional organizations such as the Organization of American States, the League of Arab States, and the European Union, among others, have also taken this challenge seriously.

Regional organizations are the first line of defense in the search for solutions to conflicts. For one thing, the proximity of these organizations to the theater of conflicts gives them incisive knowledge into the genesis of those conflicts and of the key players involved. This proximity and knowledge are important if we are to have a head start in trying to forge a consensus for the resolution of a given conflict. Of course, there are factors of shared culture, geography, and history that play a critical function in conflicts and conflict resolution in any given region. We always see how these factors interplay both in determining the course of conflicts and in the means of resolving them. Invariably, it becomes necessary in any attempt at resolving conflicts to have a firm grasp of these factors and how to use them constructively in the process of consensus building that is so crucial in times of crisis.

At times, however, this proximity generates tension and undermines the spirit of impartiality between neighbors, sometimes to the extent that they become part of the problem. At any rate, a regional approach is most effective when the participation of neighbors sharing borders is managed properly and is best when these are excluded from certain conflict-management situations affecting each other. On the other hand, combining the principle of neighborhood with the principle of distant impartiality serves to address this issue to a considerable extent. This is critical because at times keeping neighbors entirely out of each other's problems carries the risk of fomenting suspicion and resentment.

Conflict management in its comprehensive form should be seen and appreciated as a system that at any one time and at every stage involves not only many actors reacting to one another but also a range of activities in the areas of conflict prevention, peacemaking, peacebuilding, and peacekeeping. It follows, therefore, that as we would like to see an effective partnership between the United Nations and the Organization of African Unity put into place, that partnership should extend to embrace also the sub-regional organizations that, in the case of Africa, would help to enhance OAU's conflict management capability. Sub-regional organizations such as the IGADD, COMESA, SADC, ECOWAS, ECCAS, and the Maghreb Union would provide a key link in a continent-wide strategy to deal with conflicts in a comprehensive manner if their capacities in the field were enhanced.

Between the United Nations and the sub-regional organizations lies the Organization of African Unity as a regional entity for conflict management. The biggest advantage of having the Organization of African Unity midway is that the organization is neither too far from, nor too near to, the theater of conflicts. In its direct involvement, the OAU is also in a position to coordinate all the activities relating to conflict management as performed by the various sub-regional entities.

For the OAU as a regional organization entrusted with the responsibility of promoting the unity and solidarity of the African states as well as ensuring peaceful settlements of disputes, the stage for promoting peace and security on the continent was set thirty-two years ago. Ad hoc arrangements were put in place to deal with interstate conflicts, although intrastate conflicts were left to each member state to handle. The OAU Charter itself provided for the establishment of the Commission of Mediation, Conciliation and Arbitration, which was set up as the official organ charged with the peaceful settlement of disputes among member states. It is true that these ad hoc arrangements, which included not only the use of ad hoc committees but also the use of elder statesmen, were not without limitations. Notable among them were the tendency of the newly independent member states to guard their sovereignty jealously and their corresponding preference of political to judicial means of settling interstate disputes. These limitations notwithstanding, the methods did have a positive impact on stabilizing conflict situations between states. Clearly, without those arrangements the history of Africa would have been different.

In response to the tensions and armed conflict on the continent, the Assembly of Heads of State and Government, in July 1993, in Cairo, Egypt, adopted a declaration establishing within the OAU a Mechanism for Conflict Prevention, Management and Resolution. This was a radical departure from all of the OAU's earlier ad hoc arrangements for conflict management. By creating the mechanism, the African leaders demonstrated their determined effort to work together in assuming greater responsibility for the prevention and resolution of all types of conflicts, be they interstate or intrastate, and for the maintenance of peace, security, and stability on the continent.

Since the adoption of the Mechanism, the OAU has expended a lot of energy in ensuring that the Mechanism takes off and becomes fully operational. In this process, we have received a lot of encouragement and material support from the international community with which we have worked in operationalizing the Mechanism.

One of the areas relating to the Mechanism in which the OAU has been the busiest has been observing elections. Even before the adoption of the Mechanism in 1993, the OAU had already started to respond to invitations from member states to send teams of people to observe elections. So far the OAU has been able to observe thirty-nine elections or referenda in twenty-five member states, including South Africa. This was a radical departure from the past. Prior to 1990, nobody ever imagined that any member state of the OAU would ever invite the OAU secretary-general to send a team of people to observe elections. Today, a growing number of member states are inviting the OAU not merely to observe elections but also to supervise them. I see this as a new disposition on the part of member states to rely on the OAU as a partner in sustaining the democratization process of the continent.

Conflict resolution has also been handled effectively by the OAU through preventive diplomacy, which has taken many forms, including the use of the good offices of the secretary-general, the use of eminent persons, the use of special envoys, representatives of the secretary-general, direct contacts between the OAU and the governments of the countries concerned, as well as of missions from the general secretariat to conflict areas. Such field missions as those that have been recently undertaken in the Congo, Gabon, Sierra Leone, Somalia, Rwanda, Burundi, Sudan, Nigeria, Cameroon, and Lesotho, to cite only a few, have been aimed at facilitating the mediation process between the parties in conflict or assessing the conflict situation on the ground.

Other African initiatives at mediation through the OAU can also be cited. In the case of Liberia, the OAU has been very supportive of the ECOWAS initiative to restore peace and stability in that country. Professor Canaan Banana, former president of the Republic of Zimbabwe, is my special envoy for the Liberian crisis assisting ECOWAS in resolving the conflict. In the Congo, when a crisis arose between the government and the opposition, the OAU moved in quickly and played a central role in the mediation process aimed at restoring normalcy to that country. In like manner, when a crisis developed between the government of Gabon and some members of the opposition party, the OAU was immediately called upon by the president of that country to help in defusing the crisis. Furthermore, SADCC played a leading and successful role in the Lesotho crisis of last year, as well as in the crisis that developed between the Frelimo government and RENAMO in Mozambique just before the elections were held.

We take cognizance of the fact that the bulk of the OAU activities within the realm of conflict management should be in the field of prevention, since it is cheaper to prevent than to put out the flames of war. At the same time, however, given the realities present in Africa, we also believe that the time has come for Africa to be prepared to take some degree of responsibility in peacekeeping. It was for that reason that during the recent summit in Addis Ababa, the African heads of state and government took a decision requesting member states of the OAU to earmark and train contingents from their national armies that can be called upon to perform duties relating to peacekeeping.

We in the OAU see our role as being an amalgam of facilitating negotiations between those at conflict, constructive involvement by way of diplomatic action and mediating conflicts, and peace observation, including preventive deployment of military observers. Ultimately, we see the organization expanding into peacekeeping to close the operational gap that the organization experiences from time to time.

In the function of facilitation, the OAU has given its services to those who are in conflict and who are willing to submit to negotiated settlements. The most successful example was in Rwanda before the breakdown that precipitated the horrendous massacres and genocide last year. The OAU, in cooperation with the countries of the region, had maintained a momentum for negotiation that culminated in the Arusha Peace Agreement of August 1993. Through the combination of the sponsorship of the negotiation and peace observation through the military observer group, the OAU was able to inspire the confidence of the negotiators enough to spell out the most minute details of the peace agreement. Of course, it remains a matter of deep regret that the momentum of peace could not have been maintained enough to avert the catastrophe that befell that country.

The OAU has undertaken preventive diplomatic action to contain potentially explosive situations in countries such as Congo and Gabon. This we have done as part of the preemptive involvement of the organization in lingering conflicts, intended to offer the protagonists an opportunity for dialogue and accommodation.

At another level, we have raised this constructive involvement in peace observation as a means of building confidence and creating an atmosphere for dialogue. In Burundi, the OAU is now involved in efforts at rebuilding confidence and helping the political forces in the country sustain the momentum for peace. The OAU observer mission in Burundi is composed of military and civilian components, both aimed at confidence building. These limited military missions of peace observation are in a sense low-level preventive deployment, which in the case of Burundi has acted in some considerable measure as a disincentive to generalized violence.

But at the same time, we have come to realize the difficulties of this limited preventive deployment, particularly when we have been called upon to join the United Nations in more manpower- and resource-intensive peacekeeping operations. This is why the OAU has now decided to look into how it can build an African capacity in peacekeeping that can be put at the service of the United Nations and, in case of need, the organization itself.

Beyond the task of helping in the resolution of active conflicts, regional organizations must also address the other issues that underlie the conflicts now facing the world. I have in mind here the role of regional organizations in fostering democracy, protecting human rights, and promoting economic development as a means of building secure foundations of peace. We in the OAU have taken this challenge seriously. The OAU has associated itself fully with the process of democratization in the continent, in part through the observation of multiparty elections in most of the countries. Through the instrumentality of the African Commission of Human and Peoples' Rights, the OAU has fostered the development and protection of human rights. And while human rights violations may still occur on the continent, we have made great progress in integrating a human rights agenda into the politics of Africa. Today, national human rights committees exist in many countries, acting as watchdogs of government performance in this field. Governments too have responded to this challenge, and increasingly they are voluntarily submitting to performance assessment in the field of human rights.

In economic development, the OAU member states signed the Abuja Treaty in 1991 as a blueprint for continental integration through the establishment of the pan-African economic community. Today, work is in progress on a variety of protocols to the treaty in such areas as money and finance, custom, transport, and telecommunications.

Ultimately, democratization, the observance of human rights, and economic development are collectively insurance against social chaos and instability that precipitate conflicts. As in the area of conflict resolution, regional organizations also need the partnership of the United Nations to address these issues fully. Naturally, the responsibility must remain primarily that of the regional organizations, with the United Nations bringing its political support and resources to their aid.

Regional organizations are, in my view, the pillars upon which the United Nations must anchor its global peace agenda. The UN needs the cooperation and, indeed, the partnership of regional organizations if it is to be fully effective in brokering peace and ending conflicts. This is why I believe that it will be necessary for the UN to seek to expand and deepen its consultations with regional organizations as well to help strengthen them. For this reason, the United Nations should, at the political and institutional level, begin to see regional organizations as partners in a shared agenda of peace.

In the process of strengthening regional organizations, which I believe is necessary, I see the strong need to overcome institutional rigidities that militate against limited devolution in the area of conflict prevention, management, and resolution.

There is the equally compelling need for these organizations to work with the United Nations to harmonize their processes of consultation and coordination so as to resolve the perennial difficulty, at least in the case of the OAU, of being on different wavelengths when dealing with the same problem. In this process, it may perhaps be necessary to look into the possibility of creating a mechanism within the UN to liaise with regional organizations, exchange information on conflicts, and coordinate responses to them.

Equally, the time may have come for the United Nations Security Council to support the function of regional organizations through expanding the present arrangements provided for in the UN Charter, so as to give regional organizations improved and more direct access to its machinery when circumstances dictate. Along with this improved access must come the financial, material, and human support of regional efforts through a self-triggering mechanism, rather than having to work through the often tedious legal and political procedures of the United Nations to secure funding for regional efforts at conflict resolution.

I speak of the need for improved mechanisms of liaison, coordination, and consultation between regional organizations and of their access to the resources of the UN because of the experiences we in the OAU have gathered in dealing with conflicts in Africa, particularly in Somalia, Rwanda, Liberia, and Burundi.

Sometimes the process of consultation has not been as smooth as we would have wished, and sometimes institutional limitations within the OAU as well as in the United Nations have not allowed for timely action. Many times we experience operational difficulties because of our limited resource base, and quite often the United Nations has equally been institutionally constrained in coming to our speedy assistance. All these problems could be resolved through an institutional adjustment that could give regional organizations improved access to the assistance of the Security Council and the resources of the United Nations system, as well as by the establishment of equally improved mechanisms for consultation, exchange of information, and coordination of joint action where necessary.

As conflicts increasingly assume regional characteristics, the role of regional organizations should also be enhanced so as to enable them to play a meaningful role in promoting peace. These organizations will have to be helped with resources so that they can devise regional solutions to regional problems. But with this imperative, I see the role of these organizations being built on the following considerations:

1. that the United Nations with its cumulative experience should remain the preeminent international body with overall responsibility for the maintenance of international peace and security

2. that the United Nations and regional and sub-regional organizations should form and maintain a partnership to act decisively and expeditiously in elaborating new approaches to crisis prevention, management, and resolution in the post–Cold War period

3. that those new approaches to international and regional peace and security should be structured in a manner that transcends the traditional politicomilitary considerations, embracing as they should economic, environmental, and humanitarian as well as human rights issues, as these play an important role in conflict situations

4. that there is pressing need for regional organizations to develop and maintain formal and explicit capacities to ensure that they pay attention to other matters with direct relevance to conflicts. Issues such as debt, democratization, management of transition, and economic transformation must be continually addressed as integral parts of the agenda of building foundations for long-term stability in those regions.

5. that regional organizations, on the one hand, and the United Nations system, on the other, should endeavor to evolve mechanisms for improved cooperation in the maintenance of peace and security

6. that regional organizations should realize that the need for them to take primary ownership of their own problems, especially those relating to peace, security, and stability, has never been more pressing than it is in the post–Cold War period. This is necessary because outsiders are becoming increasingly less enthusiastic about sharing in regional problems. At the same time, if regions do not take care of their problems as regional entities, they will, as in the case of Africa, continue to shoulder costly humanitarian problems such as refugees and internally displaced persons, as well as continue to bear witness to heavy losses of human lives and property, as was the case in both Somalia and Rwanda.

If regional organizations must take primary responsibility for taking care of their own problems, especially those relating to peace and security, then the strengthening of those organizations becomes imperative. Indeed, the strengthening of the regional organizations I spoke of will make the United Nations itself stronger and more relevant to world problems. In the effort to find resources to meet the challenges of the steadily growing number of regional conflicts, especially those relating to peace-keeping, examining how regional organizations can bring greater support to the United Nations must be a primary objective.

The end of the Cold War has precipitated the resurgence of old rivalries and conflicts. The threat of a generalized global nuclear war has subsided and has given way to many intrastate and regional conflicts. This multiplication of conflicts has tested the capability and resources of the United Nations almost to the limit. We now see a reassessment of the role of the United Nations in these intrastate and regional conflicts and a recognition that ultimately it will be necessary to devolve some of these tasks to the regions. We should be looking at how the UN can devolve some of its tasks while at the same time maintaining a strong operational link to regional organizations in the entire process of conflict resolution.

Note

This chapter draws on the keynote address I delivered at the Twenty-fifth Annual IPA Vienna Seminar on Peacekeeping and Conflict Resolution, Anton Hüber Haus, 9–19 July 1995.

13

The Contribution of Regional
Organizations in Europe

John Roper

The Range of Regional Organizations

The end of the Cold War, like the end of World Wars I and II, has brought about a renaissance of the multilateral imperative, the desire to find multilateral solutions to problems of international relations and security. It has also been, as pointed out by Professor Phil Williams,[1] the experience of the last five years that regional organizations, like world organizations, have found the post–Cold War world frustrating and the "multilateral imperative matched only by its elusiveness." That having been said, there is a need to examine ways in which regional organizations may be able to assist the United Nations in its functions in providing for world security. This chapter will examine a range of regional organizations and their potential contributions to the field of peacekeeping and peace enforcement and assess the costs and benefits of using regional organizations rather than the United Nations for peacekeeping and peace enforcement.

The focus of the chapter will inevitably be Eurocentric, partly as a result of the author's experience and partly because much of the use of regional organizations has been in Europe during the past five years. Regional organizations are far from homogeneous in their nature, and it is important first to examine the differences between them before examining their potential contributions to peace operations. The secretary-general's 1992 *Agenda for Peace* report makes this clear in paragraph 61:

> The Charter deliberately provides no precise definition of regional arrangements and agencies, thus allowing useful flexibility for undertakings by a group of states to deal with a matter appropriate for regional action which also could contribute to the maintenance of international peace and security. Such associations or entities could include treaty-based organizations,

whether created before or after the founding of the United Nations, regional organizations for mutual security and defense, organizations for general regional development or for cooperation on a particular economic topic or function, and groups created to deal with a specific political, economic or social issue of current concern.[2]

The discussion of regional organizations and arrangements in connection with the United Nations normally concentrates on Chapter VIII of the Charter and in particular Articles 52–54. It is, however, important to recall that Article 48.2 also deals with the way in which the members can carry out the decisions of the Security Council, either directly or through their action in appropriate international organizations of which they are part. It may therefore be more appropriate to think of regional agencies acting for the Security Council in these terms; and although there is no similar reference in Chapter VI, it would appear that what applies in Chapter VII would equally apply to the use of regional agencies as far as Chapter VI measures are concerned.

It is equally interesting to note that, in the discussions of the General Assembly in 1950 at the time of the question of the recognition of the Arab League as a regional body, a resolution was passed.[3] It is clear from this resolution that a wide interpretation was given to the term "regional" that took into account not only the geographic dimension but also the community and affinity of traditions and interests of the members of a regional organization. This wide interpretation could be of value if, for instance, the North Atlantic Treaty Organization (NATO), which, some would argue, has members in more than one geographic region, were to ask for formal status with the United Nations.

There are, however, three broad categories of regional organizations and arrangements; the distinction between the former and the latter appears to turn on the issue of whether or not the body has a treaty. A regional organization or agency is characterized by a treaty that creates permanent institutions that have an international legal personality, while this would not apply to regional arrangements.[4] In the first category are those one might call classical regional organizations; the second category includes collective self-defense organizations with a potential for peacekeeping; and the third includes regional groups that have been primarily created for more general functions rather than foreign and security policy issues.

The first category of organizations can be described as classical regional organizations that fit clearly within the structure of Chapter VIII. These are organizations covering a well-defined geographic region to which all members of the region are entitled to belong and for which the prototype seems to be the Organization of American States (OAS), which was discussed at length at the San Francisco Conference in 1945. The Arab League was also considered at the same time, although, as the earlier discussion has suggested, this was somewhat more controversial. Among organizations that would seem today to fall into this first category are the OAS, the Organization of African Unity (OAU), and the Organization for Security and Cooperation in Europe (OSCE). These are all, in a sense, mini–United Nations with structures in many ways paralleling that of the UN, although none has the power or the decision-making arrangements that exist in the Security Council. While the regional character may mean that there is slightly more homogeneity within the membership of these organizations, there is a wide range of social and political structures in their member states, and these states cannot be said to have significantly affected their sovereignty by becoming members of such regional organizations. All three of the organizations mentioned have now had some experience in taking measures to deal with security and related problems in their own regions, but the success of these has been relatively limited. Inevitably, however, when there have been successes, they have received little publicity, whereas the actions such regional organizations have taken that have not succeeded have been those to which the most public attention has been drawn.

The second group of organizations includes those designed initially for collective self-defense but that have a potential for peacekeeping in the post–Cold War world. Of these, NATO and the Western European Union (WEU) both existed during the Cold War; in addition, the Commonwealth of Independent States (CIS)—particularly those members of it who have agreed to the Tashkent agreement—has some similar characteristics.

It is perhaps worth noting that, at the time of their establishment, there was a debate as to how far both WEU and NATO were to be seen as regional organizations or purely as organizations for collective self-defense. The debate in the Belgian Chamber of Deputies in March 1948 at the time of the ratification of the Brussels Treaty (on which WEU was based) brought this out. The view, however, was taken that WEU should be based primarily on the provisions concerning collective self-defense in Article 51 of the Charter, rather than on Article 52 as a regional organization. Later, at the time of the ratification of the modifications to the Brussels Treaty in 1954, the debate in the French Parliament made it clear that France saw WEU as a body that could deal with aggression from outside as well as respond to challenges that came from a signatory to the treaty.

As far as NATO was concerned, during the negotiations on the treaty, Dean Acheson pointed out:

> There were two concepts which would have to be mutually exclusive, although it would be difficult to draw the line between them. One was collective self-defense—something that could be engaged in at any time without anybody's approval in the event of armed attack. The other concept was enforcement action, which was something done to somebody else not in self-defence.[5]

But Dean Acheson was aware that, without the authorization of the Security Council, the alliance could not undertake enforcement action but could take only self-defense measures. This argument was too subtle to be understood by public opinion. As a result, the negotiators agreed to the following statement, which reminded the parties to the treaty not to quote Chapter VIII of the Charter of the United Nations in public statements:

> It is the common understanding that the primary purpose of this Treaty is to provide for the collective self-defense of the Parties, as countries having common interests in the North Atlantic area, while reaffirming their existing obligations for the maintenance of peace and the settlement of disputes between them. It is further understood that the Parties will, in their public statements, stress this primary purpose recognized and preserved by Article 51, rather than any specific connection with Chapter VIII or other Articles of the United Nations Charter.[6]

This was not completely the end of the story as, during the discussions on ratification of the treaty in the U.S. Senate, the following statement was made by the Foreign Affairs Committee:

> The question has been raised as to whether the Treaty establishes a regional arrangement within the meaning of Chapter VIII of the Charter. As stated earlier in this report, the Treaty is intended primarily to establish a collective defense arrangement under Article 51. However, it is not necessary to define the organization of the North Atlantic Community as exclusively one or the other. The Treaty need not be departmentalized. Its purpose is to assist in achieving the great purposes of the [UN] Charter, primarily the maintenance of peace. It can be used as a regional arrangement under Chapter VIII or in any way, subject to the principles and all pertinent provisions of the Charter, which may be useful to accomplish these purposes.[7]

These issues about the double nature of NATO and WEU were not significantly discussed between the time of their inception and the 1990s. In

1992, both WEU (in the Petersberg Declaration of 19 June 1992) and the North Atlantic Council (at its Oslo meeting of 4 June 1992 and its Brussels meeting of 17 December 1992) indicated their availability for undertaking peacekeeping operations under the authority of the then Conference on Security and Cooperation in Europe (CSCE), now known as the Organization for Security and Cooperation in Europe (OSCE) and the United Nations. The Oslo communiqué of the North Atlantic Council stated that the CSCE should declare itself a regional arrangement under Chapter VIII of the United Nations Charter and that its potential for conflict prevention and crisis management should be strengthened. It is interesting that, in calling on the CSCE to declare itself a Chapter VIII organization without making any reference to its own position, NATO was perhaps implicitly suggesting that it still did not wish to be thought of as a "regional arrangement." A similar reference was made to the CSCE declaring itself a regional arrangement in the Petersberg Declaration of WEU Ministers issued two weeks later. It went on:

> As WEU develops its operational capabilities in accordance with the Maastricht Declaration, we are prepared to support, on a case-by-case basis and in accordance with our own procedures, the effective implementation of conflict prevention and crisis management measures, including peacekeeping activities of the CSCE or the United Nations Security Council. This will be done without possible prejudice to possible contributions by other CSCE countries and other organizations to these activities.[8]

The same declaration set out subsequently the basis on which WEU's operational role would be strengthened:

> WEU member states declare they are prepared to make available military units from the whole spectrum of their conventional armed forces for military tasks conducted under the authority of WEU. Decisions to use military units available to WEU will be taken by the WEU Council in accordance with the provisions of the UN Charter. Participation in specific operations will remain a sovereign decision of member States in accordance with national constitutions. Apart from contributing to the common defense in accordance with Article 5 of the Washington Treaty and Article V of the modified Brussels Treaty respectively, military units of WEU member States, acting under the authority of WEU, could be employed for:
> * humanitarian and rescue tasks;
> * peacekeeping tasks;
> * tasks of combat forces in crisis management, including peacemaking.[9]

The Western European Union therefore has a basis for its action and capacity to provide forces to the UN or OSCE for a wide range of military actions.

Although collective self-defense organizations have a limited impact on the sovereignty of their members as a result of the commitments to mutual self-defense (these being defined more rigorously in the modified Brussels treaty than in the Washington treaty), the practice of NATO in integrating its members' armed forces within an integrated command structure has been considered by some to be a form of pooling part of national sovereignty. It was indeed the extent of the restriction on national decision making that this imposed on France that led General de Gaulle to withdraw France from the integrated military structure of the alliance in 1966.

Both WEU and NATO are made up of groups of countries that are relatively homogeneous in terms of shared norms, principles, and common values. In the field of collective self-defense, they have demonstrated a common will to act and, in the case of NATO, have developed effective procedures for multilateral action. Although decision making in both cases requires unanimous agreement of all members (except, in the case of WEU, where other provisions are agreed to), they are generally assumed to have a greater probability of reaching a consensus on decisions to use their forces than are the larger regional arrangements such as OSCE.

The third group of organizations to be considered is made up of those regional groups that have been developed for general purposes and that may develop a function in the foreign and security policy area. The European Union is probably the most advanced of these, although the Association of South East Asian Nations (ASEAN) could be seen as an organization that may follow a similar route, and the same may be true in the longer term for the Gulf Cooperation Council. The European Union, which began as an economic community but which developed a clear political vocation with the Treaty of Maastricht, is therefore also playing a part in the development of the Common Foreign and Security Policy (CFSP) for its members. It has already involved a significant pooling of sovereignty in the economic area where decisions can be made that are binding on all members by a qualified majority vote. Although this applies to a lesser extent in the case of the CFSP and is explicitly excluded in the case of defense matters, there is a dynamic in the nature of the European Union that is likely to lead to increased responsibility for the union collectively compared with that of the member states. In the areas of CFSP, Article J.5 of the Maastricht treaty makes clear that "the presidency shall represent the Union in matters coming within the Common Foreign and Security Policy" and "shall be responsible for the implementation of common measures; in that capacity, it shall in principle express the position of the Union in international organizations and international conferences." As far as the United Nations is concerned, explicit reference is made in the Maastricht treaty to the position of the members of the European Union that are also members of the United Nations Security Council:

> Member States which are also members of the United Nations Security Council will concert and keep the other members fully informed. Member States which are permanent members of the Security Council will, in the execution of their functions, ensure the defense of the positions and the interests of the Union without prejudice to their responsibilities under the provisions of the United Nations Charter.[10]

The Maastricht treaty also made explicit the relationship between the European Union and WEU, which is described as being "an integral part of the development of the Union" with a responsibility "to elaborate and implement decisions and actions of the Union which have defense implications."[11] The European Union and WEU are both committed to reviewing their procedures and their relationship in 1996, and the intergovernmental conference of that same year may well increase the structural relationship between the two organizations.

It is perhaps useful to make a distinction between the nature of the military cooperation that occurs within alliances and that which can develop as part of the process of countries growing together towards a confederal/federal objective. The first form of military alliance is usually initiated as a result of an external threat or challenge. One could describe this as the exogenous motive for military cooperation. It is not necessarily the case that such cooperation will cease with the end of the threat or challenge, as the practice and habits of cooperation may persuade the states concerned to maintain a framework for military cooperation. This cooperation is, however, likely to be of a static kind. However, in the second form of military alliance, in which countries are gradually moving together towards a more unified structure, there may well be patterns of cooperation occurring as a result of that process. Some of these may cover all of the countries in the organization, while others may be restricted to a limited number of member states. This cooperation can be seen as *endogenous*; one could see as an example the way in which the various Swiss cantons gradually moved their armed forces towards a common unit while retaining cantonal responsibilities in some respects. This could be paralleled at the level of the European Union with the cooperation initially between France and Germany and subsequently involving Spain, Belgium, and Luxembourg in the European Corps, or the decisions by France and Britain to develop a common air staff. Such cooperation is not a function of an external challenge but is a response to the process of closer relations between the countries concerned. It can be argued that this sort of cooperation is likely to have a dynamic development of its own, irrespective of the external environment.

This discussion of the types of regional organizations has addressed those that are created on a permanent basis. It is, however, also worth considering those that are created on an ad hoc basis to deal with particular situations. These may be described as "coalitions of the willing" and may of course be created from within a regional organization on some occasions. They are referred to within the secretary-general's paper *An Agenda for Peace* in paragraph 62. It may well be that they have a particular role when there is a need for more substantial peace enforcement action.

The Contribution of Regional Organizations to Peace Operations

The earlier discussion of regional organizations has shown their variety and their different characteristics. It will now be useful to examine the range of activities that they can undertake in support of peace operations.

Regional organizations, in some cases, by their existence contribute to the elimination of the risk of conflict between their members. This is to the extent to which they form "security communities" in the sense defined by Karl Deutsch and his colleagues.[12] A security community is defined there as "one in which there is real assurance that the members of that community will not fight each other physically, but will settle their disputes in some other way. If the entire world were integrated as a security community, wars would be automatically eliminated." NATO and the European Community/European Union working together have effectively created a security community in Western Europe and, to that extent, have eliminated the need for peacekeeping or peace enforcement operations within that region. Such a process is not necessarily perfect and may have problems at its margins, as the experience of Cyprus demonstrates.

The European Union and the Atlantic Alliance may be able to effect stabilization in their own neighborhoods and therefore prevent the need for peacekeeping or peace enforcement by their gradual extension. The involvement of countries in Central and Eastern Europe with the European Union, WEU, and the Atlantic Alliance through Europe Agreements in the case of the European Union, Associate Partner status in the case of WEU, and Partnership for Peace in the case of NATO, can be seen as a way in which peacebuilding is accomplished in this region.

A third way in which the European Union, through its member states, makes a contribution to United Nations peacekeeping is through their contribution to the peacekeeping budget. The member states of the European Union contribute in total over 36 percent of the peacekeeping budget. In addition, of course, member states, through the costs of maintaining their own forces in peacekeeping operations, make, in total, a substantially larger contribution to the costs of peacekeeping and increasingly have given assistance to other states to ensure effective peacekeeping participation. The European Union as such has made one contribution to financing a peacekeeping operation: it paid the costs of the Belgian battalion initially serving in the UNOSOM operation in Somalia. This rather unusual example of a regional organization supporting peacekeeping activities by a member state is an interesting precedent. On the other hand, the initial offer of the European countries coming from WEU and NATO to make their forces available to UNPROFOR in Bosnia in 1992 at no cost to the United Nations was not considered to be a helpful precedent, as it directly challenged the United Nations practice of treating the core costs of peacekeeping as a regular expense of the organization. "At the time, a number of United Nations officials and governments such as Canada feared it would begin to erode the hard-won principle of collective financial responsibility for peacekeeping."[13] The view was also taken that if regional organizations were to pay for peacekeeping in their own neighborhoods, they might be less willing to contribute to peacekeeping operations in other parts of the world where the regional organizations would not have similar resources.

The members of regional organizations already contribute peacekeeping forces to United Nations activities, and within regions, subgroups are beginning to make collective contributions to such forces. Reference should here be made to the SCANBAT (Scandinavian Battalion) that operated in UNPROFOR and the development of BALTBAT (Baltic Battalion), bringing together companies from Estonia, Latvia, and Lithuania for training in preparation for deployment in peacekeeping functions. The member states of the European Union have among their numbers states that have long records of contributions to peacekeeping and in 1995 contributed some 40 percent of all UN peacekeeping forces. If the countries of Central and Eastern Europe that are associate partners of WEU and have Europe Agreements with the European Union are also included, the total of peacekeepers from this region rose to over 52 percent of all UN peacekeepers. The intensity of their contribution to peacekeeping can be seen in another way: on average, countries contributing to UN peacekeeping operations contribute eleven men or women per million of the population, while countries within the European Union contribute at a rate five times higher than this. There are, of course, individual countries within the union that have significantly higher contribution rates.

Europe as a regional organization has to some extent also served as a model for the development of regional security structures elsewhere. It thereby, by example, serves as a contributor to peacekeeping and peacemaking. Although, of course, the variations from region to region mean that structures cannot be directly borrowed, the success of the OSCE process and of the development of the European Community/European Union has been noted by those attempting to develop regional organizations in other parts of the world. Thus the model for confidence- and security-building measures within the CSCE has been examined within the OAS, and the development of the European Union has provided a model for discussion of common markets elsewhere. As has been seen earlier, these can lead to the development of Deutschian security communities.

It may be argued that this discussion to date has involved indirect contributions by European regional organizations or merely grouped the contributions by member states of the United Nations who are also members of European regional organizations. There are also the direct contributions to peacekeeping and peacemaking that have been undertaken by European regional organizations. These are discussed below.

CSCE/OSCE. The High Commissioner for National Minorities has undertaken a great deal of preventive diplomacy, and in addition the CSCE, through its observer missions, has played a constructive role as a regional organization in Moldova, Georgia, Macedonia, Kosovo, Estonia, Slovakia, and Nagorno-Karabakh.

WEU. The Western European Union in 1987–88 coordinated the activities of those of its member states that were involved in mine clearance operations in the Persian Gulf at the time of the Iran-Iraq war. It was the first application by the member states of WEU following their declaration in Rome in 1984 to "consider the implication for Europe of crises in other regions of the world" and the statement in The Hague Platform of 1987 to concert their respective policies on crises outside Europe "in so far as they may affect our security interests."

WEU acted in 1990 in support of UN Security Council Resolutions 661 and 664 following Iraq's invasion of Kuwait. It instructed a group of representatives from the foreign and defense ministries of its member states to coordinate the contributions of member countries to naval operations in the Gulf in support of those UN resolutions and, in addition, to Resolutions 665 of 25 August 1990 and 678 of 29 November 1990. These actions were all reported to the United Nations secretary-general, as provided for under Article 54 of the Charter.

In autumn of 1991, the WEU Council and an ad hoc group examined the consequences of the implementation of UNSC Resolution 713 of 25 September 1991 on the former Yugoslavia for WEU member states. It provided the secretary-general with contingency planning work undertaken by WEU experts and supported the initiatives of members of WEU who were also members of the Security Council in order to get Resolution 743, creating UNPROFOR, adopted on 21 February 1992.

Subsequently, at a meeting preceding that of the North Atlantic Council and held in the margins of the CSCE Helsinki Summit, the WEU Council of Ministers decided to assist in surveillance of the embargo imposed on the former Yugoslavia by UNSC Resolutions 713 and 757 by making available air and naval elements deployed in international waters off the Yugoslav coasts. They agreed to make available to the United Nations a list of contributions that WEU member states could make to implement new decisions by the Security Council to provide humanitarian relief to regions within Bosnia. Security Council Resolution 770 of 13 August 1992, which called upon states "to take nationally or through regional agencies or arrangements all measures necessary to facilitate in coordination with the United Nations the delivery by relevant UN humanitarian organizations and others of humanitarian assistance to Sarajevo and wherever needed," responded to some extent to this initiative.

Later in the month, at the London conference on the former Yugoslavia, the WEU countries considered what could be done, and the ministerial council meeting in London on 28 August expressed the view that support for humanitarian organizations, including the protection of convoys, should be organized by the United Nations and expressed the collective will of WEU members to contribute to this initiative. Following the adoption of UNSC Resolution 776, which authorized the extension of UNPROFOR's mandate to Bosnia, six WEU countries made forces available to the UN. At the same time, in August 1992, the WEU ministerial council said that it was ready to help the Danube riparian states in maintaining sanctions along the Danube. This was reaffirmed by UNSC Resolution 787 of 16 November 1992, and later in November the WEU ministers declared that they were prepared to provide assistance to the countries concerned. This action was undertaken from 1993 to 1995, and ensured cooperation with Bulgaria, Hungary, and Romania.

NATO. In the same period, NATO agreed on action to enforce the embargo on the Adriatic, and while the NATO and WEU operations were initially run in parallel, they were subsequently organized on a cooperative basis. In addition, NATO provided military force to impose a "no-fly zone" and to provide support for "safe areas." This latter activity, referred to as "conflict mitigation," is an innovation for UN peacekeeping, and some problems have arisen in terms of NATO-UN cooperation. These will be examined later. The no-fly zone also involved aerial surveillance of Yugoslavia by NATO AWACs aircraft.

A final way in which regional organizations in Europe could assist peacekeeping, and possibly peace enforcement, would be to support other regional organizations. These proposals have been discussed informally with the Organization of African Unity and were mentioned by the then secretary-general of the Western European Union, Dr. Willem van Eekelen, when he took part in the meeting of secretaries-general of regional organizations convened by the secretary-general of the United Nations on 1 August 1994. Subsequently, French and British leaders meeting in Chartres in November 1994 supported the idea that European countries should find ways of supporting peacekeeping operations in Africa. The idea would be that if the Organization of African Unity were to accept a mandate from the UN to undertake a specific peacekeeping operation, individual African countries might have difficulty equipping and transporting battalions of peacekeepers to fulfill this mandate. A European regional organization could provide logistic and other support to this OAU activity, either on a regional-organization-to-regional-organization basis or by arranging for different member states to partner those African countries considering providing peacekeeping battalions. This was done to a limited extent in the deployment of UNAMIR II to Rwanda in 1994 but could clearly be developed. While this has been discussed so far in the case of the Organization of African Unity, it could presumably be developed to apply to other regional organizations as well.

A Cost-Benefit Analysis of Regional Organizations in Peacekeeping and Peace Enforcement

This discussion so far has outlined a variety of ways in which regional organizations could be involved to a greater extent in peacekeeping and peace enforcement. Before deciding on the desirability of an increased role for regional organizations vis-à-vis the world organization, it is probably useful to try to analyze such a shift from the point of view of the United Nations, the regional organizations, and member states. In each case, there will be advantages and disadvantages of such a shift, and it is only by making an overall analysis that a judgment can be made about the value of such a development.

At the level of the United Nations, faced at the moment with a problem of more demands for its peacekeeping services than it can meet, the attractiveness of a devolution of peacekeeping, and perhaps peace enforcement, to regional organizations would be the immediate relief on budgetary pressures, the availability of additional manpower through regional organizations, and the argument that regional organizations might have a greater coherence in operating in common in some of the more difficult peacekeeping/peace enforcement situations that have arisen since the end of the Cold War. A regional organization such as NATO, and perhaps in the future the Western European Union, could be expected to have greater experience of working together as a force, and member states might be more prepared to transfer forces to the operational control of a force commander whom they knew from his activities in a regional organization than to a UN force commander from a country with which they had previously not had any combined military activities. This might also permit the force commander to take a greater degree of responsibility for the overall action and reduce the regrettable tendency of contingents contributed to UN peacekeeping activities to remain to a significant extent under the command of their national authorities.

On the other hand, the use of a regional organization could lead to problems of loss of control by the UN Security Council and secretary-general of an operation. The then secretary-general of NATO made it clear that while the Security Council resolutions spoke of NATO acting "in support of UNPROFOR in the performance of its mandate," he does not consider NATO to be a "sub-contractor" of the United Nations.[14] Regional organizations are concerned about their own "credibility" and do not like to be in situations where they appear to be subject to an external body. Increased use of regional organizations would also mean the loss of the "United-Nationsness" of the operation.[15]

Turning to the regional organizations, the problem immediately arises that these are, as has been seen, not homogeneous. There is a wide range of organizations, and the advantages and disadvantages to them vary according to their nature. In most cases, however, the post–Cold War world has tended to give them a greater vocation for regional security activities. This can be seen in the case of the OAS and the OAU as well as the European organizations. There is also a clear distinction between those in the second category of organizations discussed earlier, which were established as collective defense organizations and which, in the view of some, are now looking for new roles in the post–Cold War world, and the traditional regional organizations of a Chapter VIII type. The advantages and disadvantages of regional organizations also clearly vary depending upon the type of peace operation being considered.

Regional organizations feel that they have a particular knowledge of, and responsibility for, their region and that therefore they will have an advantage in undertaking work there. They could argue that they are likely to be more militarily effective than UN forces because of the greater coherence that they provide and because of their proximity to the country in which the peacekeeping force is being deployed. They would probably be less expensive as well.

When it comes to the disadvantages to a regional organization of undertaking military action under a United Nations mandate, these seem to be that the regional organization may be so constrained by the mandate that it is not able to operate successfully and that therefore its credibility as an effective organization will be reduced. There have been indications of this in some complaints made in NATO countries about the relationship between the UN and NATO in Bosnia-Herzegovina. A further disadvantage, in the view of some, is that peace operations may be a diversion from an organization's remaining collective defense function; some feel that peace operations should therefore be undertaken only when they are of such military complexity as to require the equipment, training, and command structures that regional organizations such as NATO possess. There may also be political costs to a regional organization taking part in peacekeeping if by doing so its position in the world becomes challenged.

Looking finally to the benefits and costs of regional organizations rather than the United Nations undertaking peace operations, from the point of view of member states, one again has a range of positions. There is of course a distinction between states in the region and those outside it, and a distinction between the states undertaking the peacekeeping operation and those to whom it is applied. Even within a member state there are sometimes differences of approach, with different positions being taken up by the diplomatic representatives of the same state at discussions of peacekeeping operations in UN bodies and in regional organizations.

An increased role for regional organizations in peace operations would certainly provide an opportunity for countries in which UN peacekeeping forces were deployed to use the option of the replacement of a UN force by a regional force as a bargaining lever. The attempts—ultimately successful—by President Tudjman of Croatia to propose that NATO or WEU forces should replace UNPROFOR were an example of this. It is not clear whether a recipient country feels that it would have more political leverage with a regional organization than it would with the world organization or whether it feels that the regional organization would have more sympathy for its position.

There is, however, linked to this the possibility that in the view of countries receiving peacekeeping or peace-enforcement operations, a regional organization might be seen as less impartial; there is always the risk of the perception of domination by a regional hegemon. This could be Nigeria in the case of the ECOMOG operation in Liberia, the United States in the case of some OAS actions, and Russia in the case of CIS actions. To that extent, the member state receiving a peace operation might see a considerable disadvantage in a regional approach rather than a United Nations approach.

For states that provide troops for the peacekeeping operation or that are members of the regional organizations, the benefits are presumably those of coherence and efficiency, of greater political understanding, and of cost effectiveness.

The disadvantages may be that a regional organization, even when it possesses a United Nations mandate for its operations, might be considered to have less legitimacy than a UN operation. The military effectiveness might therefore be outweighed by some reduction in political effectiveness.

Conclusions

The debate on all of these issues is still too open for anything more than very tentative conclusions or suggestions to be made. It may be that regional organizations as such will have a most important role in the future in relieving the United Nations of the need to undertake directly some of the traditional peacekeeping activities, namely "the presence in the field (normally including military and civilian personnel) with the consent of the parties to implement or monitor the implementation of arrangements relating to the control of conflicts (cease-fires, separation of forces, etc.)."[16] They would not necessarily operate as far as the resolution of disputes is concerned, and the issue of the protection of the delivery of humanitarian relief seems to require a good deal further study. As far as traditional peacekeeping activities are concerned, Chapter VIII organizations such as the OAS, the OAU, and OSCE might very well be able to undertake them in future. In other cases, it might be that regional organizations either of a formal or informal kind could develop their role of providing packages of forces to a UN force. References have already been made to the role of SCANBAT and BALTBAT in this regard, but a body like WEU could provide packages of forces of brigade or possibly divisional level to a UN peace operation.

At the other end of the scale, when it is necessary to have a peace-enforcement action under Chapter VII in response to interstate aggression, it might be possible in the future to see a regional organization take the lead in this activity. The regional organization might therefore provide from within its own members a "coalition of the willing" that could also include some participation from outside its membership. The discussion of the Combined Joint Task Force concept in NATO and WEU already gives some indication of how this could be done in the future. It is, however, recognized that such actions by regional organizations would require a United Nations mandate.

The difficulties arise with actions that fall between these two cases. This is the gray area where the military effectiveness of a regional organization should ideally be combined with the political impartiality and judgment of the United Nations in order to provide an ideal solution. There is no doubt that this presents very serious problems of politicomilitary interface as well as the difficulties of coalition warfare in general. Military effectiveness requires clear lines of command and a well-ordered structure, but the political reality of two or three layers of political decision making, at the level of the Security Council, the regional organization, and the contributing states, suggests that this will be very difficult to attain.

Notes

1. Phil Williams, "Multilateralism: Critique and Appraisal," in *Multilateralism and Western Strategy*, ed. Michael Brenner (New York: St. Martin's Press, 1994), 209 ff; quote on 210.

2. Boutros Boutros-Ghali, *An Agenda for Peace*, United Nations, 1992, para. 61.

3. A/Res/477 (V), 1 November 1950. I am grateful to Luisa Vierrucci for this reference. A fuller discussion of these and related issues appears in Luisa Vierucci, "WEU: A Regional Partner of the United Nations?" Chaillot Paper 12, WEU Institute for Security Studies, December 1993.

4. United Nations, Office of Legal Affairs, *Manual of the Pacific Settlement of Disputes between States* (New York: United Nations, 1992).

5. Reid Escott, *Time of Fear and Hope: The Making of the North Atlantic Treaty, 1947–49* (Toronto: McClelland, Stewart, 1977).

6. Escott, *Time of Fear and Hope*, app. 3, 268.

7. W. Eric Beckett, *The North Atlantic Treaty, the Brussels Treaty, and the Charter of the United Nations* (London: Stevens & Sons, 1950), 34.

8. Petersberg Declaration: WEU Council of Ministers, Bonn, 19 June 1992, para. I.2.

9. Ministers Declaration, WEU Council of Petersberg, Bonn, 19 June 1992 para. II. 2–4.

10. Treaty on European Union, Maastricht, 1991, Article J.5(4).

11. Treaty on European Union, Article J.4 (2).

12. Karl W. Deutsch et al., *Political Community and the North Atlantic Area* (Princeton, N.J.: Princeton University Press, 1957).

13. Enid C. B. Schoettle, in *Keeping the Peace in the Post–Cold War Era: Strengthening Multilateral Peacekeeping,* report to the Trilateral Commission, 1993. Schoettle refers to the statements by the Canadian foreign minister before the United Nations General Assembly on 24 September 1992 and the statement by the Australian ambassador to the UN on 12 November 1992.

14. Statement quoted by Reuters, 27 October 1994.

15. Shashi Tharoor, "United Nations Peacekeeping in Europe," *Survival* (Summer 1995): 125.

16. *Improving the Capacity of the United Nations for Peacekeeping, Report of the Secretary-General,* 14 March 1993, A/48/403, para. 4 (c).

Part VI

Peacebuilding

14

A Holistic Approach to Building Peace

Thomas M. Franck

The task of this chapter is to address the role of the UN in developing a political, social, and economic infrastructure of peace. This requires reflection on the lessons of some recent UN operations; specifically, those that have tried to address as a threat to the peace the problem of states in social upheaval. The emerging doctrine of these operations manifests a new, as yet but sketchy, holistic approach to the civic restructuring of societies destroyed by civil war. The pursuit of such a holistic approach has involved UN personnel in addressing a broad range of tasks including the protection of human rights, conducting of democratic elections, and multidimensional economic rehabilitation.

It is not the mission of this chapter to evaluate the effectiveness of such operations as UNTAG, ONUSAL, UNTAC, UNAVEM, ONUMOZ, and UNOSOM II. To do so in one chapter is impossible and to do so at all is to ignore a basic obstacle to judgment: namely, compared to what can each operation be judged? For example, an endeavor like UNO-SOM II in Somalia would rank low as an exercise in utopian civic reconstruction but quite high as an example of global willingness to save lives and give a nation a second chance. It surely ranks high when compared to the traditional alternatives: colonial domination and "benign" neglect.

Vacuous operational assessment is not a useful exercise. It is, however, a valid mission to analyze the experience of the past in terms of a different standard: the options that may be offered by the new century. This is plainly an invitation to imagine alternate futures, and to do so with the freedom to assume—and it is an assumption validated by the events of the past decade—that in the twenty-first century, momentous changes are more probable than is status quo stasis.

The Origins of Peacebuilding Operations

The operations that make up the history of UN attempts at civic reconstruction are all quite recent and include those in Namibia (UNTAG, 1989–90), El Salvador (ONUSAL, 1991–95), Cambodia (UNTAC, 1992–93), Angola (UNAVEM I, II, and III, 1989–97), Mozambique (ONUMOZ, 1992–94), and Somalia (UNOSOM II, 1993–95). These operations have little in common. Although each was authorized by the Security Council, only one, UNOSOM II, was authorized by the Security Council under Chapter VII, using the council's power to enforce a settlement in a civil dispute found to be causing a "threat to the peace." Some of the others, however, at their peak also involved large military deployments: in particular, UNTAG, UNTAC, and ONUMOZ.

What these operations had in common, besides their varying scale of deployment of security-enhancing forces, was their search for a holistic approach. Each had a mandate that incorporated a broad range of security-restoring and nation-building activities.

These mandates were selected, as appropriate, from the following: disarming warring factions; integrating militias into a national military force; reorganizing and retraining the police; monitoring human rights conditions; recreating or reforming the judiciary; writing or rewriting the constitution; investigating past human rights abuses; assisting land reform; providing food, clean water, sanitation, medical services, housing, and road repairs; repealing noxious and oppressive laws; overseeing transitional national ministries; compiling electoral rolls; securing agreement on electoral laws and practices; conducting or observing national elections; ensuring the transition to elected government; and coordinating and facilitating the work of nongovernmental organizations (NGOs). Deliberately omitted from the ensuing survey are the UN's more traditional single-purpose operations, in which the sole objective is to establish and maintain a cease-fire or (more recently) to observe an election.

Four Lessons of Peacebuilding

Of the holistic operations that are included in this look at recent experience, not all consisted of exactly the same building blocks; but in each case various UN services were combined to provide a full-service approach. It is safe to say that such full-service operations will grow in importance. That makes these early operations of particular interest to futurologists. It also makes them roughly comparable in the sense that each manifests a belief that the disintegration of a civil society must be addressed by inter-venors, if at all, on a broad front, involving many different forms of recon-structive assistance. These holistic operations are in keeping with the UN secretary-general's emphasis, reiterated in his September 1994 Report to the General Assembly on "a comprehensive approach to a peaceful inter-national order," one that offers "a broad range of means toward this goal."

Such holistic full-service operations are new. They respond to a set of needs that probably predated the end of the Cold War but that only its ending made operationally necessary and feasible. By this two things are meant.

First, recent events have made the holistic approach necessary. The end of the Cold War has unleashed a wave of previously repressed tribalist conflict that has rent the social fabric of many states. Of course, the surge of post-modern tribalism dates not from 1986 but from 1960, with the end of the unifying shackles of colonialism. After 1986, however, the super-powers—lacking either the means or the motive to keep iron regimes in place—stopped supporting their authoritarian clients in Eastern Europe, Asia (the momentum began in the Philippines), Africa, and Latin Amer-ica. With that release, new forces came to the fore that battled one another for turf and resources. This aroused a brutal lust that has persisted, almost independent of territorial aims, and that soon destroyed fragile civiliza-tions and their infrastructures. These could not be rehabilitated by addressing only the symptoms of conflict. A holistic approach became necessary.

Second, the end of the Cold War meant that new approaches became possible. The UN became the accepted vehicle for addressing these crises. The superpowers, and other states with global interests, which had been burnt trying to shore up their dictatorial client regimes, became decidedly reluctant to step in alone to glue together the shards of civil society scat-tered about in the wake of their clients' downfall. Thus the ending of the Cold War created an unaccustomed vacuum of opportunity, yet one that no state or group of states rushed to fill. In that sense, the UN's holistic role was facilitated by the default of more traditional geopolitical actors.

It is a very recent role, and any deductions from its performance would have to be ventured from a very narrow database. Nevertheless, some of the record at least suggests tentative hypotheses that are worth dis-cussing. As the UN began to assume its new burden, each operation was undertaken only after an agreement—usually brokered by a representa-tive of the secretary-general—with the "parties concerned" (i.e., the armed antagonists) and "interested parties" (adjacent or sponsoring states). The sole exception to this common thread is the operation in

Somalia, where the multiplicity of clan factions and absence of any governing authority, or even of regional "interested parties," made the search for such prior agreement illusory.

That UNOSOM II, among these operations, has encountered by far the most difficulty in achieving its holistic mission therefore might be attributed, in part, to this difference between it and the other comparable operations. It is certainly possible to deduce that a UN operation that launches a full-service project of civil reconstruction without previously having concluded negotiations with the parties on the steps necessary to achieve such an ambitious goal is likely to encounter greater problems than operations—such as those in Namibia, El Salvador, Cambodia, and Mozambique—where a detailed step-by-step blueprint for social reconstruction (and the UN's role in it) had first been developed.

The trouble with this deduction—potentially our "first lesson"—is that it is both obvious and rather lacking in practical value. Of course, one's instinct growls, prior agreement to a blueprint is likely to enhance the prospects of a holistic UN operation.

True, there are instances where multinational UN operations have succeeded in the absence of any such prior road mapping. The swift, overpowering use of force in Operation Desert Storm achieved much, despite lack of prior agreement among the parties on what might follow Iraq's capitulation. The truce observation and military disengagement operation of UNFICYP, in Cyprus, required only very limited agreement: to a cease-fire and monitored disengagement. These, however, were single-purpose operations based on military deployment. The holistic operations of recent years, in sharp contrast, deployed a mix of civilian and military personnel in a broad range of activities that are intended to enhance, but also assume some prior commitment to, cooperation among previously hostile forces: not merely to stop fighting but to reconstruct a state. In the absence of detailed agreement at the outset, the prospects for these new operations are indeed dimmer.

But (1) what if, as in Somalia, thousands of persons are starving while negotiations for a framework agreement and blueprint founder or do not take place at all? And (2) what if, as in Cambodia, an agreement hammered out over years of negotiation, while the fighting continued, breaks down as soon as one of the "parties concerned" realizes that, at the end of the day, it is going to lose the crucial election? Should the lesson of UNOSOM II dictate nonengagement in the absence of a blueprint? Should a UN engagement be terminated when one or more of the affected parties tears up the blueprint on which it was based?

Just such a question is addressed by the most recent Security Council resolution (S/RES/976 of 8 February 1995), which envisages the deployment of a new multinational force of seven thousand UN military personnel plus additional police, human rights specialists, mine removers, radio station operators, and others in operation UNAVEM III. This resolution adopts the blueprint for ending the civil war negotiated by the parties under UN auspices as the "Accordos de Paz"; but it also sets a series of standards, requires that the secretary-general report regularly as to whether they are being adhered to in accordance with an agreed schedule terminating in February 1997, and implies that a report of significant noncompliance will lead to the nonrenewal of the operation at the end of each six-month authorization. Moreover, the triggering mechanism for the council's approval of UNAVEM III was an extremely detailed description of the objectives, concepts, costs, and prospects of that operation in a formal report by the secretary-general (S/1995/97 of 1 February 1995).

It is worth asking whether, in the event of the failure of the parties to agree to such a blueprint, an operation should simply not be launched at all. Or should the Security Council instead draw up its own detailed blueprint and schedule, imposing it on the parties to a civil conflict under Chapter VII? And, if a blueprint is agreed to and an operation is launched, what should be the consequence of noncompliance of one or all parties to a breach of its terms or its implementation schedule? Should such violators be forced back into compliance, or be ignored, or should the operation be disbanded? Should the council, the contributing states, and the parties to the civil reconstruction know beforehand which is the probable consequence?

In fact, in the case of Somalia, the secretary-general did secure an agreement by Interim President Ali Mahdi and General Aidid, his principal opponent, at the end of March 1992, on the mechanisms for monitoring a cease-fire and on arrangements for the distribution of humanitarian assistance. Only thereafter, in April, did he recommend to the Security Council the establishment of UNOSOM I. It is true, however, that the agreement achieved in March was both very limited, leaving reconciliation and reconstruction untouched, and quite vague.

But what does this prove? Knowing that an operation launched with less than optimal blueprinting is more likely to encounter difficulties does not make unwise the decision to proceed, notwithstanding the greater difficulties. It all depends on the available contextual alternatives. In the Somali case, the alternative to an ill-blueprinted operation would have been either an operation extensively blueprinted by agreement among the members of the Security Council and the contributor states, which would scarcely have eased the operation's troubled relations with the clans, or else no operation and the deaths of hundreds of thousands of civilians—persons who were saved, even if by a less-than-textbook effort.

UNTAC proved in Cambodia that even the most excruciatingly negotiated and exquisitely detailed blueprint does not guarantee against breakdown at the moment of truth. Thus, there is something to be said for getting a UN operation under way even under less-than-ideal circumstances, not only because time is of the essence when there are lives to be saved, but also because a UN operation (when of sufficient size), once on the ground, changes the local power equation and may make further agreement more likely.

This Heisenbergian effect was demonstrated when the Mozambique insurgent party, RENAMO, tried to "do a UNITA" by pulling out of elections just as they were being held. The difference between UNITA's effective sabotage of the previously agreed UN-monitored elections in Angola and RENAMO's compelled withdrawal of its threat to do the same in Mozambique was the powerful UN presence at all levels of the latter's security system and infrastructure. Such a powerful presence does not ensure agreement—the huge deployment of UNOSOM II failed to broker an agreement among the warring clans—but it increases negotiation's prospects. It does this not only by virtue of the UN personnel deployed but also by arousing what would otherwise be, at best, only a latent interest of the international community in bringing the parties to closure. In Mozambique's instance, the Security Council members demonstrated their power, when united, to influence RENAMO not to back out of the long, laborious process just as the ballots were being counted. The very dimension of the global investment in Mozambique became a force for impelling the parties to allow the project to proceed to its conclusion.

Breakdown in the blueprint is a frequent occurrence. It happened in Cambodia, when the Khmer Rouge withdrew from the interim regime and boycotted the elections and when the losing party insisted on remaining in the government. It happened in Namibia when armed SWAPO forces began to infiltrate from Angola and the South African Defense Force (SADF) responded. In both instances, the UN was able to defuse the threat without resorting to arms. In Namibia this was facilitated by a minor addition to the agreement between the interested and concerned parties. In Cambodia it was achieved by largely ignoring the Khmer Rouge and proceeding with the agreed step-by-step plan essentially unaltered. Both operations were able to carry their mandate to successful conclusions.

When Cambodia is compared with Somalia—where UNOSOM II and American forces sought to compel the clans of General Mohamed Farah Aidid and Ali Mahdi Mohamed in Mogadishu to disarm and move to the

Security Council's prescribed beat—the latter operation does not fare well. There were substantial UN casualties in Somalia, a perceived failure on the part of the large UN deployment to effect the desired outcome, and some resultant disenchantment with UN operations in general. This has suggested—notably to authorities in Japan, which led, and contributed so much to, UNTAC—that there is a "second lesson" to be derived from a comparison of operations. It is this: that UN operations should never use military force to impose the blueprint for a holistic operation. To do so will bog the UN down in tribal war and must render the rest of the holistic approach, dependent as it is on civil cooperation, largely nugatory.

Whether this is a general lesson to be drawn from a comparison of UNOSOM II and the other holistic operations, and whether such a lesson should guide future operations, is a subject worthy of discussion. An informed evaluation, however, must begin by recognizing the essential differences between operations. In Cambodia, the Khmer Rouge's challenge came primarily in remote border regions where it could be ignored without compromising the main direction and timetable of the holistic enterprise. Ministries could continue to operate, services were maintained, voters were enrolled. So, too, in Namibia, where the armed clash between SWAPO and SADF was brief, occurred early in the operation, and was primarily localized at the Angolan frontier. In Somalia, by way of sharp contrast, the two principal contending clans were the occupiers of most of Mogadishu, which served not merely as the political and economic capital but also as the hub of railroads, highways, shipping, and communications. The challenge they posed to UNOSOM thus was of a quite different order from the challenges to UNTAC or UNTAG. For the UN in Somalia to ignore the clan challenges—as, indeed, UNOSOM II eventually was forced to do when its offensive against Aidid had failed—carried quite different implications for the holistic mission than did UNTAC's decision to ignore the Khmer Rouge. In Somalia, to ignore the defiance of the armed clans meant the virtual abandonment of the full-service enterprise. Nevertheless, an argument is made that the UN failed in Somalia—to the extent its success was limited to humanitarian relief—because it chose confrontation rather than a Cambodian-style avoidance of confrontation.

If UNOSOM II's failed use of force tempts us to this broader conclusion, it does so only ambiguously. It could as well be argued that the Somalia experience also permits the opposite conclusion, one at least for a time favored by the secretary-general; that is, that force should have been used earlier, more determinedly, and in an effort to disarm the factions hindering full implementation of the holistic civil reconstruction. In this view, a Cambodia-style nonconfrontational approach demonstrably had already failed when tried by the predecessor Somalia operation, UNOSOM I (1992–93). In that phase, meager UN forces, eschewing confrontation, proved largely unable to prevent the wholesale looting of relief supplies. Meanwhile, more than 300,000 Somalis died and more than 1 million fled the country. With the clans still fully armed, all efforts at negotiated civil reconciliation fell on stony ground. Only thereafter did the Security Council, at the secretary-general's urging, move to Chapter VII enforcement and confrontation. It did so first on 3 December 1992, by accepting the U.S. government's offer to undertake, with council authorization, Operation Restore Hope: 28,000 U.S. personnel, augmented by 17,000 troops from other countries. That operation (the Unified Task Force, UNITAF) aimed, with considerable success, at securing the principal ports, airports, and major relief centers, thereby permitting humanitarian relief to be distributed nationwide. Security operations also took place in the principal provincial towns and the capital, meeting little resistance. The lesson might be drawn that a holistic operation is more likely to be successful when civil cooperation is mandated by overwhelming force.

At this brief moment of opportunity, however, the decision was made by the U.S. government not to deploy forces to disarm the clan armies. That decision was opposed by the secretary-general, who, as early as 19 December 1992, two weeks after the initiation of UNITAF, called for it to control all heavy weapons, disarm lawless gangs, and assist in the creation of a new police force. This was to little avail. The United States and its UNITAF partners were understandably reluctant to sustain the casualties that might have resulted from an arms sweep.

The secretary-general also repeatedly called for applying to the Somalia factions the principle of "cantonment" to provide for storage of heavy weapons and the transitional accommodation of factional forces while they turned in small arms and registered for retraining and absorption into civilian or national military employ. In other holistic operations, in El Salvador, Cambodia, Namibia, and Mozambique, such cantonment had been agreed ab initio and, by and large, had worked. In Somalia, agreement to such measures was sought only after the operation had begun, and it generated insufficient momentum either to persuade or to compel the factions to cooperate.

When Operation Restore Hope was replaced by UNOSOM II, with an even broader Chapter VII mandate to bring together the military, political, legal, economic, and social elements of peace, the clans were still as armed as ever.

The tasks of UNOSOM II, assigned it by the Security Council, included disarmament and reconciliation; the restoration of peace, stability, law and order; assistance in reconstructing the Somali economic, social, and political life; reestablishment of the country's institutional structure; promotion of the means of democratic governance; and rehabilitation of the nation's economy and infrastructure. By March 1995, UNOSOM II ended its mandate with none of these tasks accomplished. A belated effort during the summer and fall of 1993 to capture General Aidid and disarm the Mogadishu factions proved a particularly poignant failure. Despite repeated distortion of the facts in the media and by politicians, however, this failure was primarily that of U.S. forces operating independently and not of the UN operation. (On the other hand, thanks to this very imperfect operation, starvation had been largely eradicated; immunization programs had reduced death by disease; schools, closed for three years, had mostly reopened; many district councils had been organized and were beginning to assume responsibility for local governance; five thousand police had been hired and trained by the UN; and numerous rehabilitation schemes sponsored and staffed by UN agencies and NGOs had been launched.)

A subsidiary lesson that some (the secretary-general, among them) have drawn from this discrepancy between the tasks assigned to UNOSOM II and the means available for their fulfillment is that the tasks members assign should better take the measure of the means they are willing to provide. Robert Browning has urged that "a man's reach should exceed his grasp, or what's a heaven for?" But perhaps this sentiment should not excessively move the Security Council. We must avoid a situation in which Security Council resolutions become vehicles not for action but only for posturing, as was so often the case with General Assembly resolutions during the Cold War and has sometimes been the case when the council has issued empty ukases with respect to the wars in the former Yugoslavia.

Perhaps this lesson has been learned. In recommending the dispatch of seven thousand troops to Angola as UNAVEM III, the secretary-general has stated that the "Angolan parties would be expected to keep in mind that the international community will not entertain delays in the fulfillment of their obligations under the Lusaka Protocol or extension of the mandate of the Mission" (S/1995/97, 1 February 1995). In other words, if the deadlines of the peacemaking blueprint are not met, the UN will leave. Given the limited size of the deployment, this may be wisdom as the better part of valor, but it is a renunciation, ab initio, of UN peace enforcement, although UNAVEM III does have the authority to "use . . .

force in self-defense, including against forcible attempts to impede the discharge of the operation's mandate" (S/1995/97). This weak military mandate, however, is balanced by the fact that the operation's very first task is to create and monitor the cease-fire, "quarter" and disarm the UNITA insurgents, and verify the return of the Angolan army to its barracks. All further UN activities to promote civil reconstruction, including election supervision, are made dependent upon the successful conclusion of this demobilization phase.

The more important (and more elusive) lesson of UNOSOM II, however, has to do with the use, or non-use, of force against the blocking clans. It is thus arguable that the failures—or flawed successes—of UNOSOM II derive from that important decision by UNITAF not to follow up its initial success in restoring order with a determined policy of disarming the factions. A study of UNOSOM II, perhaps the least evidently successful of the holistic operations, paradoxically could thus demonstrate both that its "failures" were due to a decision to use Chapter VII force against an indigenous faction and also that they were due to a decision, at the critical moment, not to use Chapter VII forces sufficiently. Both lessons are possible; neither is self-evident. It is also just possible that the two contradictory lessons may both be true: that no force should be deployed unless enough of it is committed to ensure success. And, moreover, it may be that if the UN is to engage in "full-service" operations, these should commence only after the militias have been disarmed or relocated out of harm's way, an effort that requires a substantial military deployment with authority to use force, at lease in defense of the operations' limited mandate.

Alas, what also emerges with some clarity is a "third lesson": that the states with the forceful means to protect and propel peacebuilding are extremely reluctant to engage in them if to do so might entail significant casualties. It is the prospect of such casualties that caused UNITAF to demur, and which, somewhat later, caused the United States to pull its contingent out of Somalia in March 1993. By March 1994, the UNOSOM II military contingent, authorized at 32,000, stood at under 20,000 owing to withdrawals. As a given of peacemaking, this third lesson is considerably more persuasive than the other two, and it will be considered further in the next part of this chapter. Can the UN count on commitments by members, in the words of the secretary-general's 1994 Report to the General Assembly, "that are willing to stay the course . . . under pressure"? The answer, in the present UN military configuration, is probably not! Some African and Asian states have taken casualties without complaint. The same cannot be said of some Western developed nations.

Adjunct to that lesson is a corollary: that holistic humanitarian, full-service operations are far less likely to achieve their objectives if they have no means to raise the cost to factions that are sabotaging UN peacebuilding measures. What does that lesson teach? While it may be true that peacebuilding cannot be compelled, the deliberate deconstructing of peace can be met with disincentives, which can range from the interdiction of the gem and mahogany trade in eastern Cambodia by an international force on the Thai border to the sort of land-settlement scheme for disarmed insurgents that is a feature of civil reconstruction in El Salvador and Mozambique. The problem is to find an appropriate mix of incentives and disincentives: fiscal, infrastructural, and military. Nowhere has an entirely successful formula been discovered and applied. It remains a critical task for the future, to which we will return.

There may have been more progress on incentives than on disincentives. ONUSAL, the UN operation in El Salvador, is an example of a UN operation designed to have both the length and the breadth of commitment necessary to constitute a formidable offer that parties to a prolonged costly civil war could not lightly refuse. The civil war in El Salvador left 75,000 persons dead and 1 million displaced. ONUSAL was launched only after a detailed blueprint had been painstakingly negotiated under the secretary-general's auspices between April 1990 and December 1991. That agreement made the UN operation the key factor across a wide spectrum of El Salvador's civil rehabilitation. Its tasks included not only peace negotiation but also promoting respect for human rights, reforms in the military and judiciary, the investigation of assassinations and disappearances by a truth commission, the creation of a new police force, integration of former insurgents into democratic politics, jump-starting the shattered civilian economy and agriculture through land redistribution, the holding of free and fair elections, and, in the words of El Salvador's ambassador at the 23 November 1994 meeting of the Security Council, enabling "the beginning of a new order of economic and social justice." In his words, "ONUSAL has been one of the most successful peacekeeping operations in the history of the United Nations. The Organization had played a central role in the peace accords from start to finish and had remained engaged in peacekeeping and in post-conflict peacebuilding."

ONUSAL, when it completed its mission in April 1995, had been in operation for four years. In the words of the secretary-general (speaking to the Security Council on 31 October 1994), its role was "innovative" in that it played a central role in the negotiation of the peace accords from start to finish and has overseen a multidimensional peacekeeping and peacebuilding operation in whose design it played a key part. It remains engaged in the transition from peacekeeping to post-conflict peacebuilding. This involves not only security-related aspects such as the abolition of the old military-controlled National Police and the creation of a new National Civil Police, following the reform of the Armed Forces in a role confined to defense against external threat, but also key institutional reforms designed to entrench the rule of law and provide a solid framework to guarantee respect for human rights. Last but not least, the United Nations supports a complex set of programs for the reintegration into society of former combatants of both sides and of the rural populations who occupied land in conflict zones during the years of armed confrontation.

At its inception, ONUSAL deployed a modest military and police contingent of approximately one thousand personnel, together with supporting civilian staff. (It should be noted in passing that even so modest an operation involved a cost of some $100 million a year.) Individual donor states and the United Nations Development Programme provided additional support for economic development that, on a per capita basis, far exceeded that put at the disposal of the other countries in which comparable UN operations have taken place. By ONUSAL's end, economic growth was averaging 5 percent a year, reflecting foreign aid but also reflecting the benefits of stability. Cynics might argue that El Salvador proves that having a civil war gets you the foreign aid needed for civic renewal. The same has been said, with reference to Germany and Japan, about losing a world war. But the sobering fact is that the cases of postwar international assistance for Germany, Japan, and perhaps El Salvador are more indicative of what is needed to do the job than of typical international response to most cases of civic disintegration.

Perhaps this does warrant generalization. If there is a "fourth lesson," it is that the success of a holistic UN approach to peacebuilding is more likely to succeed when there is a willingness on the part of the international community—bilaterally, regionally, and through the UN family of fiscal, refugee-assisting, health-enhancing, feeding, lending, and development-promoting institutions (IMF, UNHCR, WHO, WFP, IBRD, and sUNDP)—to underwrite in concert the structural changes to the economy that make peace possible. These usually include such financially intensive measures as land reform, start-up credits for agricultural and small business enterprises, water and vaccination programs, aid to schools, and occupational retraining programs.

It is worth noting that these kinds of foreign or multilateral assistance programs are generally regarded as "soft" in the sense that they do not promise the kind of direct economic return of a hydroelectric dam or a lumber mill. In even the most promising circumstances, such as prevailed in El Salvador, this may cause some important aid donors to march to a different drummer than the peacebuilders. The secretary-general's representative heading ONUSAL at its inception, Assistant Secretary-General Alvaro de Soto, has written (in *Foreign Policy* 94 [Spring 1994]) that while he was negotiating the terms of the political settlement to end El Salvador's civil war, the International Monetary Fund and the World Bank were imposing fiscal stringencies on El Salvador's government that made much more difficult the land reform, military demobilization, and restructuring that were key elements of the cease-fire. He wrote: "It was as if a patient lay on the operating table with the left and right sides of his body separated by a curtain and unrelated surgery being performed on each side."

The most appropriate formulation of this fourth lesson may be that a successful peacebuilding operation is likely to require a significant shift in priorities pertaining to global resource allocation. There may be excellent reasons in theory why the World Bank or the Security Council should not allow an obdurate civil war to induce a shift in its well-conceived institutional indicators and priorities. In that case, however, an operation may best be deferred. If, on the other hand, there is the political will to proceed, then issues of primacy must be faced at the outset. Whether political primacy succeeds in practice in setting the fiscal agenda inevitably will become a major determinant of any holistic operation's success.

The Future

As Secretary-General Boutros Boutros-Ghali said in his *Agenda for Peace,* the authority of the UN to provide a holistic, full-service approach to situations of civil disintegration "would rest on the consensus that social peace is as important as strategic or political peace. There is an obvious connection between democratic practices—such as the rule of law and transparency in decision making—and the achievement of the peace and security in any new and stable political order."

The experience of several holistic operations has demonstrated that, under favorable circumstances, the UN, in the words of Australia's foreign minister Gareth Evans (in *Cooperating for Peace*), can "meet the special needs of countries and peoples shattered by warfare." To accomplish this more consistently, he adds, "there is a need for much more integration of activities within the whole UN system, so that the pursuit of peace and security is seen to include the satisfaction of basic human needs as well as the prevention, containment, and settlement of violent conflict. This will inevitably require linkages between visions of a more peaceful world and greater integration within the system, particularly in relation to program planning, the application of resources, and the development of smooth functioning coordination mechanisms."

Of course, this is easier said than done. The UN system increasingly is having to practice a sort of disaster triage. In Somalia, the UN, led by its under-secretary-general for humanitarian affairs and working with UN agencies, the International Committee of the Red Cross and various non-governmental organizations, put together the blueprint for a relief and rehabilitation program that was approved at the UN Conference on Humanitarian Assistance to Somalia held from 11 to 13 March 1993 in Addis Ababa. It was also attended by representatives of Somalia, donor governments, and regional organizations and established agreed-upon priority programs with an initial price tag of $166 million, of which $130 million was pledged by international donors. In 1994, the Somali Aid Coordination Body (SACB) began to integrate donor and recipient activities. The similarly instituted International Committee on the Reconstruction of Cambodia operates as follow-up to the terminated UNTAC operation. Whether such coordinated planning and execution are effective will depend largely on the degree of security and stability in post–UNOSOM II Somalia and post-UNTAC Cambodia as well as on the extent to which successful implementation is able to counter a clearly discernible and growing donor fatigue.

Donor fatigue may explain, in part, the short attention span of the international community. Once an operation has gone on for two or more years, there is a growing desire, even if the operation is successful, to wind it up. A major General Assembly–authorized UN effort was mounted in October 1990 (in cooperation with the OAS) to ensure the fairness of the Haitian elections, not only by providing police security during the election campaign, but also by assisting in the drafting and implementation of the electoral law, organizing voter registration, and massive poll watching. Once elections were held and certified as free and fair, the operation was quietly disbanded. The military coup 30 September 1991 verified the secretary-general's warning, issued immediately after the withdrawal of United Nations Observer Mission for the Verification of the Elections in Haiti (ONUVEH), that elections are not a cure-all for underlying structural dysfunction.

It is to the credit of the UN system, however, that beginning with a

General Assembly resolution of 11 October 1991—which "strongly condemns both the attempted illegal replacement of the constitutional President of Haiti and the use of violence, military coercion and the violation of human rights" and "demands the immediate restoration of the legitimate Government"—the international system has worked fairly consistently and single-mindedly to reverse the situation created by Haiti's military coup, ordering sanctions in 1993 and finally resorting, in 1994, to military measures approved by Security Council Resolution 940. That resolution authorizes "Member States to form a multinational force . . . to use all necessary means to facilitate the departure from Haiti of the military leadership, consistent with the Governors Island Agreement, the prompt return of the legitimately elected President and the restoration of the legitimate authorities of the Government of Haiti, and to establish a secure and stable environment."

In its early phase, this second Haitian operation involved 21,000 troops in a multinational force. Although constituted primarily of U.S. forces, there were also more than 1,000 Bangladeshis, some 600 police from Caribbean nations, and contingents from CARICOM (the Caribbean Community), Guatemala, and elsewhere. This time, in contrast to Operation Restore Hope, these forces were deployed to raid, disarm, and arrest recalcitrant armed elements. In the words of the October 1994 report presented to the Security Council by then ambassador Madeleine Albright, the raid on the headquarters of Front révolutionnaire pour l'avancement du progrès en Haiti (FRAPH), with its military's clandestine terror squad, "appears to have modified FRAPH's behavior and ability to operate and influence." Leaders of these militia groups who had not fled were detained, investigated, and turned over to the civil authorities where charges appeared warranted. An active weapons search, buyback program, and policy of weapons destruction were effective in sharply reducing the firepower of these elements. This contrasts with the missed opportunity of the international system to disarm the parties in Somalia and builds on the Mozambique experience of ONUMOZ, which also quickly collected 150,000 weapons from rival forces while implementing a proactive program of cantonment and training a new, integrated 30,000-person Mozambican defense force composed equally of government and RENAMO troops.

In the case of Haiti, with violence thus curbed, the operation launched in 1994 was freed to assist in the training of a new police force in cooperation with the International Criminal Investigative Training and Assistance Programme (ICITAP) and international police monitors. A new police academy training program was inaugurated as the multinational force essentially replaced the dissolved military and police units of the former regime. At the same time, civil affairs teams in Haiti focused on such projects as restoring drainage; erosion control; rebuilding firefighting systems; landfill operations; market repair and construction; power generation; distribution facilities; school repair; street repair; water collection, treatment, and distribution; public health; public works; and utilities (S/1994/1208 of 24 October 1994). These activities closely followed the successful experience of ONUMOZ and may be a measure of the future.

In due course, when the UN assumes direct responsibility for ONUVEH II, the operation should be far better positioned to continue this holistic approach to Haiti than was UNOSOM II in Somalia when it took over from UNITAF. If so, it will be in part because lessons have been learned. It is premature, however, to calibrate the system's proven ability to learn and adapt. UNOSOM II cost (not counting the Relief and Rehabilitation Programme, which is funded separately) $1 billion annually. Here the donor fatigue and short attention span of members can become crucial factors in snatching defeat from the jaws of victory. By mid-1994, the assessment levied on members was a half a billion dollars undersubscribed, and the UN had to borrow internally to pay the program's expenses.

If there is a shortfall in carrots, there is an even more serious shortage of sticks. As the secretary-general pointed out in his 1994 Report to the General Assembly, it is not only a shortfall in the payment of assessed contributions that threatens the ability of the organization to apply the lessons learned in recent years; there is also a decline in states' willingness to contribute the personnel necessary to create the preconditions of security necessary for a holistic operation. He pointed out that it took an entire year to find and deploy the 7,600 additional troops authorized by the Security Council in June 1993 for service with UNPROFOR in Bosnia and two months to deploy the 5,500 troops authorized by the council in May 1994 for Rwanda. The secretary-general has also commented on the fact that if forces deployed in such operations sustain casualties, "public support may be rapidly undermined. Such circumstances may tempt troop-contributing countries to withdraw their contingents or to direct them to adopt an overly cautious attitude, avoiding risks, even though this may further jeopardize the mission." An example is the refusal of an Italian contingent of UNOSOM II to undertake a rescue mission ordered by General Bir, the UN commander. More significant is the introduction of the egregiously misnamed National Security Revitalization Act into the newly elected U.S. House of Representatives with over one hundred cosponsors. In sixty-seven pages, it seeks to seriously curtail U.S. participation in UN military operations by restricting deployment of American forces under foreign command without congressional authorization, requiring fifteen-day advance notification to Congress of expected Security Council votes to authorize new operations, and resolving to lower U.S. fiscal support for future peacekeeping.

In other words, the underlying, fundamental challenges to future UN peacekeeping operations are funding and personnel. Both problems evidence a lack of will. That this is likely to be manifest in future operations is the most irrefutable of lessons derived from the recent past.

Holistic operations are particularly prone to failure as a result of a shortage of funds and personnel. They necessarily assume high, long-term risks implicit in ventures that seek to penetrate to the very marrow of the societies being rehabilitated. While further improvements may result from yet a further restructuring of headquarters' command structure, with yet another revision of the channels of coordination between agencies, donors, host countries, and NGOs, even radical administrative and programmatic reconfigurations can have only limited effect. The question of resources—financial and personnel—and of will cannot be addressed without profound changes in the way these UN operations are funded and staffed. Exhortation, proposals to charge interest on unpaid assessments, etc., are feeble palliatives. The anticipatable dimensions of the problem call for a rethinking of the fundamental assumptions that have shaped the organization's activities in the past. Such reconsideration is a necessary part of thinking about the future of peacebuilding, because the experience of holistic operations during the past decade has made inescapable two salient lessons.

The first of these is that if the UN is to remain the principal executor of holistic peacebuilding missions, it will sooner or later need to recruit and train the basic integrated components of such missions on a permanent professional basis. This does not mean that some particularly personnel-intensive operations may not still need to be performed ad hoc, at least initially, by states franchised by the Security Council (as the United States and others were franchised to perform the UNITAF operation in Somalia or the multinational force operation in Haiti). It does imply, however, that the staffing of future full-service operations like ONUSAL or ONUMOZ should proceed around the deployment of a permanent volunteer UN military and civilian cadre. As the secretary-general told the members in January 1995: "I have come to the conclusion that the United Nations does need to give serious thought to the idea of a rapid reaction force. Such a force would be the Security Council's strategic reserve for deployment when there was an emergency need for peacekeeping troops" (*Supplement to An Agenda for Peace*, S/1995/1, 3 January 1995).

Of course, their deployment and terms of engagement would still need to be subject to Security Council authorizations. But the service would consist of specialists who had trained together for such tasks, had developed an experiential history and traditions, were ready for immediate posting, and whose availability would not be dependent upon the political climate within a particular state.

Such an integrated peacebuilding force might initially consist of twenty thousand military personnel and ten thousand peacebuilding specialists: engineers, human rights specialists, public health experts, accountants, lawyers, police instructors, school administrators, agronomists. Some, but not most as at present, might be on secondment from UN specialized agencies or NGOs. A tough core of the service ought to be crafted of career servants. Only such a core of career officers specializing in peacebuilding can provide a dependable professional culture to absorb the lessons of experience and create a dependable basis for the difficult and sensitive task of engaging disintegrating civil societies in their own rehabilitation.

Sir Brian Urquhart, the "father of peacekeeping," has recently proposed the creation of a volunteer militia. In his opinion, there "is one overwhelmingly good reason for this: the conditions of the post–Cold War world and the new challenges faced by the United Nations urgently demand it." The same is true of a professional nonmilitary component of holistic operations. At present, these staffs are pulled together with offers of short-term contracts from among persons of diverse levels of qualification, commitment, and experience who happen to be available on short notice, and from civil servants borrowed temporarily from various parts of the UN Secretariat or from governments. This is not good enough, if such full-service operations are to be a permanent and growing part of the organization's agenda.

The second salient—and even more controversial—lesson is that creating, training, and maintaining such a professional holistic peacebuilding service will not come cheaply. It is possible to argue that the cost of maintaining a professional service would be less than the ad hoc approach of recruiting anew for each operation; whether this is true or not, the cost would be substantial (perhaps $2 billion to $3 billion per year) and continuous. There could be no mandated sunsets. Unlike the ad hoc approach to operations, a professional peacebuilding staff would not operate under the guillotine of rapid termination; the commitment to a level of expenditure would have to be permanent. Moreover, the cost of a permanent allocation for a professional holistic peacebuilding establishment would not account for more than a portion of the funds necessary for rehabilitation, funds that would still have to derive in part from bilateral and multilateral aid projects. And the very largest operations would still require additional logistics, personnel, and funding from states able to mount an emergency operation.

This fiscal prognosis suggests the need for fundamental rethinking of the way such operations are funded. Such rethinking must begin by facing immutable facts. It is simply folly to expect the needs of strife-torn and disaster-prone parts of the world to be met indefinitely at the expense of the social, economic, security, or cultural programs of the contributor states. In democracies—the political condition, nowadays, of most UN members—there is little constituency for these expenditures except fleeting bursts of generosity, generated in response to harrowing media pictorialization of extreme human tragedy. A coherent holistic peacebuilding program cannot be built on the momentum created by CNN's decision to portray, or to stop portraying, starving children, here, there, or nowhere. If the world opts to take responsibility for approaching such extreme crises before they reach such a point, it must be willing to bear the cost of planning, training, and executing anticipatory operations that can respond in timely fashion, perform with seasoned skill, and, to emphasize again the secretary-general's phrase, that will "stay the course."

This can only be done by a different system of funding. But all systems of funding are manifestations of a weltanschauung. A new Weltanschauung is urgently overdue. It would begin with the dawning realization that not all persons are equal users of our proliferating global regimes. Those who are—for example, those who travel abroad, or deal in international trade and finance, or beam TV images abroad—benefit disproportionately from the stability these regimes create, as compared, for example, to the peasants of Chad or, for that matter, of Mississippi. The principal users of these regimes have a special obligation to support certain high-priority global peacebuilding endeavors. Selective and minuscule taxation of their profitable transnational activities can generate the funds necessary to ensure planned, long-term performance in operations designated and designed by the appropriate political organs of the UN system. We do not cavil at airport security taxes; we should not cavil at comparable taxes to secure other globalized activities.

Economists have little difficulty in devising a formula. James Tobin, for example, has proposed a .01 percent tax on speculative currency transfers, which amount to a market of $1 trillion daily. Such a tax could yield $100 million daily, enough to meet both the peacebuilding expenses of the UN and many of its other activities. It could do so with no measurable dislocation of the affected international activity.

Some new thinking along these or comparable lines is overdue. A coherent, holistic peacebuilding program cannot depend indefinitely upon the ephemeral, episodic support generated by television-targeted sympathy. If the world opts to bear the cost of planning for, training, and deploying professional peacebuilders, it must develop means of financing that do not force each operation to live hand-to-mouth, borrow from other UN budgets, or engender crippling deficits. What is needed is a reliable, predictable source of funding.

Moreover, this source should not be in the form of contributions from member states. It is folly to expect the needs of disaster-prone nations to be met indefinitely out of strained national budgets. Just as governments of many rich nations find their citizenry increasingly unwilling to tax themselves to support their own nation's residual poor—what Germans have come to call the "two-thirds nation" phenomenon—so national governments reflect the greater fatigue of their citizens with providing relief out of their pockets for nations that cannot resolve their tribal animosities in a civilized fashion. They may vaguely understand that in many instances these nations are beyond redeeming themselves; that they need help to help themselves; and that, if such help is not forthcoming, floods of refugees, disruptions of trade, and terrorist violence will in time affect the quality of life of everyone. Still, it is a clear lesson of the past decade's operations that all this does not add up to a willingness to make the necessary fiscal commitments to sustain even ad hoc operations, let alone a coherent professional peacebuilding service. Needed is some system of direct financing through a revenue-raising measure to be directed at the principal users of the sinews of the international system and, thus, the chief beneficiaries of its stabilization. These will also be the parties best able to bear what can be analogized to a minuscule "value-added" tax.

Conclusions

In the post–Cold War era, forces of civil conflict have been unleashed in almost all multinational states. This is a situation likely to become worse in the next millennium if it is not carefully managed. Whereas, in the past, such disintegrative tendencies were suppressed by dictatorial governments and their great power sponsors, today it falls on the UN to use a range of services—military, diplomatic, rehabilitative—to mitigate crises that, unmitigated, are likely to have a wider effect in flows of refugees, disruption of trade, impoverishment, and terrorism.

The holistic, full-service operations that are most likely to succeed in meeting this challenge are those that begin only after a step-by-step blue-print for peacebuilding has been carefully negotiated among all "inter-ested" and "concerned" parties. The success of such operations usually depends, in varying degree, upon the availability of the military resources needed to disarm the antagonists at an early stage and upon each opera-tion's ability—in terms of professional and fiscal resources—to take a broadly longitudinal and latitudinal approach to reforming the affected society's civic infrastructure. This service may range from electoral reform to land reform and may require restructuring the legislative and judicial branches, as well as retraining the police and military. It includes the pro-vision of emergency food supplies, repatriation of refugees, agricultural training and provisioning, water engineering, school construction, and much else.

The ad hoc approach to staffing and paying for these operations is inef-ficient and unreliable. If holistic, full-service peacebuilding is to become a feature of the UN agenda, the operation should be staffed by both a trained, coordinated professional core of experts and a volunteer military force operating under the authority of the Security Council and the direc-tion of the secretary-general. Such a professional core of peacebuilders should be financed by an equitable user or value-added-type tax on cer-tain commercial international activities that benefit from the stability in the international system that peacebuilding operations facilitate.

Such proposals for fundamental reform, or better ones, are not likely to eventuate at once, but come they must. They require a full-scale rethink-ing of ontological questions involving evolving loyalty systems, notions of shared responsibility, and the structure of perpetual peace. That, at least, can begin now.

Conclusion

The Peace-and-Security Agenda of the United Nations: From a Crossroads into the New Century

Olara A. Otunnu

The peace-and-security agenda of the United Nations has developed gradually in phases. In a period spanning some forty years, from the first mission that was established in 1948 to supervise the truce in Palestine (UNTSO) to just before the launching of the first major multidimensional peacekeeping operation in Namibia (UNTAG) in April 1989, the UN organized fifteen peacekeeping operations. Most of these operations were concerned with conflicts between states. The mandates of the missions consisted principally of monitoring or supervising truces, cease-fires, troop withdrawals, and buffer zones. Significantly, these were consent-based operations, marked by adherence on the part of the peacekeepers to the principles of cooperation, impartiality, and non-use of force except in self-defense.

This generation of operations defined what many commentators now call "traditional peacekeeping." The development of this mechanism in itself represented a major innovation by the UN. Indeed, the very idea of peacekeeping is not mentioned at all in the UN Charter, although the practice was developed in the spirit of Chapter VI of the Charter. During the same period, and corresponding to the explicit provisions of Chapter VI of the Charter concerning pacific methods of settling disputes, the UN also developed the use of fact-finding, good offices, and mediation as part of its repertoire of peacemaking activities.

This situation underwent a significant change in the late 1980s and early 1990s. The end of the Cold War, the success of an ambitious operation in Namibia, and a certain sense of triumph emanating from the Gulf War all injected a new feeling of confidence in the UN, thereby creating enlarged expectations about what the organization could accomplish. Responding to this new mood, the UN embarked on a more ambitious program of peace activities, with its operations growing in number and complexity. In a space of only six years (1989–95), the UN established twenty new peacekeeping operations.

Unlike in the previous era, most of these missions (seventeen) were inserted in the context of conflicts within nation-states. The tasks of peacekeepers now expanded to include implementation of complex peace agreements; overseeing the transition to democratic governance through supervision and observation of elections; demobilization and integration of previously opposing armed factions; rehabilitation of collapsed state structures; provision of broader support to humanitarian missions, including protection of "safe areas" and escort of relief convoys; and removal of antipersonnel mines from contaminated countrysides. This development represented the second phase of peacekeeping, whose high points were marked by the successful completion of the operations conducted in Namibia, Nicaragua, El Salvador, Cambodia, and Mozambique.

In spite of these remarkable achievements, the evolution of the peace-and-security agenda of the UN is caught at a difficult crossroads today. The rapid expansion of complex operations has generated serious political and financial stresses on the organization. These stresses, combined with the tragic failures in Somalia, Rwanda, and Bosnia-Herzegovina, have produced a mood of retrenchment for the present and serious uncertainties about future directions. They have also encouraged a reexamination of the UN's role in dealing with internal conflicts, with the intent of developing future options.

As we look to the future, what indeed are some of the principal lessons to be derived from almost fifty years of multilateral peacemaking and peacekeeping? This is a time for stocktaking by the United Nations; it must also be a time for sketching, however tentatively, the outlines of a future peace-and-security role into the new century. I am concerned that the UN should not swing from one extreme to another, from being committed to too much to undertaking too little. In charting this path, there are major challenges that will need to be addressed. The purpose of this chapter is to highlight some of these challenges.

Restoring a Sense of Perspective

Peace operations, including humanitarian relief, have increased by leaps and bounds in recent years. This dramatic development is leading to an increasing loss of perspective. Significant areas of imbalance are beginning to emerge in the overall vision and conduct of the UN peace-and-security agenda. Three such areas need to be examined with a view to restoring a sense of perspective.

The first area of imbalance has to do with the growing tension between peacekeeping operations and development activities. A serious disequilibrium is beginning to emerge between resource allocations for peacekeeping and relief operations, on the one hand, and resources available for long-term peacebuilding, on the other. The resources devoted by the UN, other international organizations, and donor governments to peacekeeping and emergency humanitarian activities are beginning to outstrip the resources for long-term peacebuilding—in other words, resources for development. In fact a number of governments and other donor institutions have diverted resources from their development budgets to peacekeeping operations and humanitarian relief in recent years.

As the UN budget for peacekeeping increased from $230 million in 1987 to $3.6 billion in 1994, the aggregate development assistance expenditure of OECD countries (albeit a larger absolute amount) witnessed a stagnation. In 1993, OECD members' Official Development Assistance (ODA) declined by 6 percent (in real terms) from the previous year; in contrast, the proportion of OECD spending on emergency assistance has risen sharply in recent years. In general, there has been a notable decline in funding for development activities within the UN system in contrast to funding for emergency relief operations. In recent years, for example, there has been a 15 percent reduction in the core resources of the UN Development Program (UNDP) as compared to an almost doubling of resources for the World Food Programme (WFP), the bulk of which is devoted to relief food assistance.

This trend needs to be reexamined. Investing in social and economic development is one of the surest ways to build a solid foundation for long-term peace within and between societies. This in turn means that development strategies must seek to address the roots of conflict; an example of this is a situation where a pattern of gross imbalance in the allocation of development resources is bound to provide a fertile ground for conflict. There is therefore a need to consciously build a capacity to respond to conflicts into the design of development projects, especially in countries where the potential for conflict or its escalation is high.

The second area of imbalance concerns the imperative for preventive action. The UN and other international actors need to invest a great deal more in preventive measures. Successful preventive action can be highly cost effective, saving lives and sparing general destruction. In addition, it is considerably cheaper than an operation to restore a broken peace.

It may be useful to clarify what is meant by preventive action here.

First, by preventive action I am referring to a broad spectrum of activities, going well beyond the traditional notion of preventive diplomacy and the new mechanism of preventive deployment. Preventive action must encompass a broad range of political, economic, social, and humanitarian measures aimed at averting or de-escalating the development of conflict. This is a project for long-term peacebuilding. It is for this reason that preventive action should be viewed as the link between an agenda for peace and an agenda for development. In this context, Senator Gareth Evans discusses in his contribution to this volume the concept of preventive peacebuilding, whereby, in order to ensure that conditions for conflict do not develop, attempts are made to meet people's crucial needs for security, a reasonable standard of living, and a sense of identity and worth.

Second, conflict prevention should not be viewed as the abolition of all conflicts in society. After all, conflict—by which I mean competition for power, resources, and prestige—is entirely natural to society. Indeed, it constitutes the essence of the political process. The challenge of preventive action is different. It is about how to manage this competition without plunging a society into a spiral of violence. It is about how to build equitable patterns of development, democratic institutions, and political cultures that can mediate such competition peacefully and routinely. In his contribution to this volume, Professor Al Mazrui uses examples from Africa to explore how failure to build such institutions and cultures can lead to a collapse of societies and the states that preside over them.

Third, preventive action must encompass the consolidation of peace in the aftermath of violence or following a political settlement. Unless systematic political, social, and economic measures are taken to consolidate the peace and rebuild confidence, a conflict can recur, thereby leading to a cycle of violence. The examples of Burundi and Rwanda illustrate this latter danger. Both countries have been caught in the throes of cyclical pogroms, in large measure because after each tragedy little or no effort was made to address the underlying causes of the conflicts or to embark on a serious project of national reconciliation. On the other hand, Cambodia, El Salvador, Guatemala, Liberia, Mozambique, and South Africa have just emerged from years of protracted conflicts. After achieving negotiated political settlements, they each now face a tenuous period of transition. It is in this post-conflict phase that internal and external measures must be taken to consolidate their newfound peace and avert a possible recurrence of violent conflicts in the future. In this respect, the evolution of Franco-German relations since World War II provides an example of a successful strategy of peace consolidation. Over the last fifty years, a deliberate process of political confidence building and economic cooperation has transformed these erstwhile historic enemies into partners in the construction of European unity, so much so that today it seems all but inconceivable that the two countries could ever again go to war against each other.

It is in this context that we should note that the evolution of conflict often follows a circular rather than a linear path. Thus, a political settlement should not be viewed as an end in itself, but rather as the beginning of a new political process. To build enduring peace, this process must lead to a credible project of reconciliation and overall peace consolidation. In its absence, there is a real danger that a political settlement will fracture, thus leading to the outbreak of another cycle of violence. External actors can play an important facilitating role in the process of peace consolidation by encouraging reconciliation and providing material incentives, but the impetus for a new beginning must ultimately germinate from the local soil.

Fourth, while we must probe the boundaries of preventive possibilities to the utmost, we should not lose sight of some serious constraints inherent in this enterprise. How, for example, shall we overcome the shield of national sovereignty or quite simply a country's sense of national pride, the temptation for brinkmanship, asymmetry of response amongst the parties in conflict, the tendency to misread a developing situation until it is too late, or the lack of interest or will on the part of international actors at critical moments? Indeed, efforts to intervene at the earlier stages of a conflict situation are likely to prove particularly frustrating for outside actors. For it is during this phase in particular that they are likely to come up immediately against the wall of national sovereignty. This is especially so when dealing with a strong state, a state that is itself the instrument of repression or is a major party to the conflict in question. In such cases, the challenge is how to induce the "opening of the door" sufficiently to allow for preventive initiatives.

Finally, it is critical that a body of both serious knowledge and serious practice be built in the area of preventive action, through systematic preventive engagement in specific situations of actual or potential conflict. This will require innovation and long-term commitment. The ambition must be to develop in the area of preventive action something akin to what has been built over the last fifty years in the peacekeeping sector. Unless this is done, I fear that preventive action will remain an easy but largely empty slogan.

The third area of imbalance is about the preoccupation with humanitarian action in a conflict situation vis-à-vis the need for a political process. It is important that humanitarian action be located within an overall vision of a society in conflict. This means, in particular, that humanitarian action should move in parallel with a political process aimed at addressing the underlying causes of a conflict and achieving a political settlement and national reconciliation. Otherwise I fear that the tremendous efforts being deployed on the humanitarian front will inevitably count for very little.

In this volume, Jan Eliasson and Sadako Ogata present two perspectives on the question of humanitarian action.

Building Institutional Capacities

Toward a Division of Labor

It is apparent that the UN presently lacks the capacity and resources to perform well all the peace-and-security tasks that it has come to assume in recent years. An appropriate division of responsibilities between the UN and other international actors in the spheres of preventive action, peacemaking, peacekeeping, enforcement action, and peacebuilding must therefore be developed to enable a more effective and comprehensive international response to conflict situations around the world. Such a division of labor could take advantage of the different capabilities and interests of regional organizations, national governments, and non-governmental organizations. The idea should be to identify areas of comparative advantage and build around them a system of complementarity. A possible division of labor may be developed along the following areas of comparative advantage.

United Nations. In the light of recent experience, it would seem most effective for the UN to concentrate its efforts on preventive action, traditional peacekeeping, humanitarian missions, mediation and peacebuilding activities through its various agencies.

In their contributions to this volume, Ismat Kittani and Thomas Franck focus on developing UN capacities in the areas of peacemaking and peacebuilding respectively. Kittani gives a detailed account of the UN's numerous innovations to enhance its capacities in the area of preventive diplomacy and peacemaking and provides recommendations for the future. Franck draws lessons from recent UN experience in Namibia, Cambodia, Angola, and elsewhere to argue in favor of, and provide specific recommendations for, a "holistic" approach to peacebuilding, whereby the implementation of a peacebuilding blueprint is accompanied by close coordination among all actors involved.

Regional Organizations. In time, regional organizations must come to assume greater responsibility for peace and security. In their contributions to this volume, OAU Secretary-General Salim A. Salim and John Roper draw upon the experiences of the Organization of African Unity and a number of European organizations—the Western European Union, the European Union, and the Organization of Security and Cooperation in Europe—as well as NATO, to explore the limits and possibilities of regional roles in conflict management.

Despite their promise, most regional organizations are still far from able to play the role envisaged for them in Chapter VIII of the UN Charter, mainly because of their lack of relevant tradition, financial resources, political prestige and credibility, impartiality, and operational capacity. This places a particular responsibility on the United Nations, the major powers, traditional peacekeeping countries, and other bilateral and multilateral donors to work in a more concerted way to help build the capacities of regional organizations. Until then, however, we must guard against exaggerated expectations. For the time being, the areas of comparative advantage for regional organizations would seem to be preventive action, peacemaking, and confidence building at the regional and sub-regional levels, while allowing for a more gradual development of peacekeeping capabilities.

In discussing a scheme of division of labor, there is a tendency to concentrate on the roles of the more established and traditional regional institutions, such as the Organization of American States, the League of Arab States, the Organization of African Unity, the European Union, and the Organization for Security and Cooperation in Europe. This is a mistake. We must not overlook the increasingly significant and innovative roles being played by less traditional regional arrangements. In particular, three types of formations deserve more attention: sub-regional organizations such as the ASEAN Regional Forum (ARF) or the Southern Africa Development Community (SADC); international political-cultural associations based on shared historical affinities, such as the Commonwealth or la Francophonie; and ad hoc or neighborhood self-help arrangements put in place for the purpose of undertaking particular regional projects, such as the Economic Community of West African States Monitoring Group (ECO-MOG) in relation to pacification in Liberia, the former Frontline States (FLS) in the context of the liberation of southern Africa, the former Contadora Group in relation to the Central American peace process, or the Intergovernmental Authority on Development (IGAD) Committee constituted by the countries of Eastern Africa for promoting a peace process in Sudan.

The comparative advantages of these associations and arrangements lie in part in their flexibility and informality and a certain quality of relations and affinities that tend to characterize their internal rapport. In addition, they are often able to move more lightly and respond more quickly to unfolding events than the UN or larger regional organizations. These features can translate into distinct advantages, especially for the purposes of undertaking preventive initiatives, mediation, and confidence building among their members.

But the emphasis on the role of regional organizations must not lead to a tribalization of peacekeeping activities, whereby, for example, conflicts in Europe are viewed as the responsibility of the Europeans or African conflicts as the domain of the Africans. This notion goes against the grain of the UN—its universality and its worldwide responsibility for maintaining peace and security. Moreover the problem is compounded by the uneven spread and varying capacities of regional organizations in different parts of the globe. Clearly member states from a particular region should be encouraged to spearhead an international response to a conflict situation within their region, but this must not detract from the importance of wider international participation in these efforts. This is necessary for reasons of broader legitimacy and solidarity, as well as for practical reasons of capacity.

Subcontracting to Ad Hoc Coalitions. For the foreseeable future, enforcement action will have to be "farmed out" to "coalitions of the willing and able." Inevitably this option is viable only when the national interests of key countries are sufficiently engaged by a particular development. In such a situation, the Security Council should, however, not simply authorize the action in question but also be more closely associated with the execution and the conclusion of the operation. When it is envisaged that the UN should take over a situation following the completion of enforcement action, as was the case in Somalia and Haiti, early and adequate preparation should be made for assuming that responsibility. In this context, particular attention needs to be given to formulating and organizing clear transition arrangements for this purpose.

Independent Actors. We are witnessing the emergence of independent actors in the field of peacemaking and peacekeeping. Drawn from the ranks of international civil society, these actors are increasingly making direct contributions to peace processes. On account of its informal and flexible character, this sector can often complement official efforts, particularly in the areas of early warning, preventive activities, peacemaking, humanitarian action, and peacebuilding. Different independent organizations tend to specialize in various aspects of these activities.

Peacekeeping and the Challenge of the "Gray Zone"

Traditional peacekeeping remains the most developed of all UN response mechanisms to conflict situations. In general, peacekeeping works best when there is an agreed peace to keep and when an operation is based on the consent of the parties in conflict, while observing the principles of cooperation, impartiality, and non-use of force except in self-defense.

The UN operation in Namibia marked the beginning of several innovations in the realm of peacekeeping carried out with the consent of the parties on the ground. In his contribution to this volume, Kofi Annan draws upon the recent UN experience of peacekeeping to suggest means for effectively implementing the two kinds of consent-based peacekeeping operations that the United Nations is most likely to be called upon to launch in the near future: preventive deployment, as seen in Macedonia; and "multidimensional" peacekeeping of the kind first seen in Namibia and subsequently in Cambodia, Angola, Haiti, and elsewhere.

At the other end of the spectrum from consent-based peacekeeping in its various forms, a more radical mode of response is available to the UN in the form of collective enforcement action. Enforcement action may be defined as a forcible collective military operation, authorized by the Security Council under Chapter VII of the Charter, for the purpose of restoring compliance with international norms following a major breach of the peace or an act of aggression. Although it involves war fighting, enforcement action should be viewed and conducted in a different way from a war waged primarily to achieve national objectives. In its fifty-year history, the UN has so far sanctioned the prosecution of two full-fledged enforcement operations, namely, in Korea in 1950 and against Iraq in 1991. In this regard, the reader may wish to refer to Edward Mortimer's contribution to this volume, where he uses John Stuart Mill's writings on intervention as a reference point to suggest the kinds of forceful responses to humanitarian crises that might be considered legitimate by the international community, the circumstances under which these interventions might take place, the form of these interventions, and who might intervene.

Before enforcement action is begun, at least three prerequisites need to be in place: adequate political will, including the will to bear the human cost of military operation; the will and capacity to assume the necessary financial cost; and the availability of troops adequately prepared and equipped for the task. This is a tall order. It is for this reason that, for the foreseeable future, it is more practical for the UN to continue to farm out such operations to coalitions of the willing and able. In practice, it is difficult to mobilize the requisite political will to commit national forces for enforcement action against a party in gross breach of international norms unless such a development also impinges in a crucial way on the national interests of the major powers. Recent experience, especially in Liberia, Somalia, Rwanda, and the former Yugoslavia, has demonstrated that on the ground there is a growing "gray zone" between these two well-defined modes of response. The gray zone is in effect the thin end of the enforcement wedge—it is the space between traditional peacekeeping (including an appropriate application of force for self-defense) and all-out war fighting. Situations encountered in the gray zone often require responses that are neither traditional peacekeeping nor full-blown enforcement action, but something in between.

Confusion between peacekeeping and enforcement action, including the tendency to slide from peacekeeping to enforcement action and then back again, has proved to be very dangerous. This is essentially what we witnessed in the operations in Somalia, Liberia, and the former Yugoslavia, with disastrous consequences in all three cases. This confusion has arisen precisely because no effective mechanisms have yet been devised for responding to the challenge of the gray zone.

The following scenarios are examples of the contingencies that may arise in the gray zone:

- when an armed faction in a conflict unilaterally blocks the way, preventing a relief convoy from gaining access to a population in distress

- when a "safe area" under the protection of the UN is attacked or overrun by a party in conflict

- when a peacekeeping contingent comes under a massive attack from a faction with superior firepower

- when peacekeepers are taken hostage

- when a "no-fly zone" is violated

- when a conflict suddenly escalates to a dramatic point but short of generalized large-scale violence, as, for example, in Rwanda in April 1994, following the presidential plane crash, when the massacres started but before they swelled into a genocidal tide

The above scenarios illustrate the range of worst-case situations that may develop in the gray zone. These situations tend to arise typically in the context of an ongoing armed conflict within a state in which several factions are contending for control and when there is no general agreement about the role of peacekeepers or when initial cooperation has collapsed.

These developments in the gray zone place peacekeepers in an untenable position in various ways. At the practical level, because they are lightly armed, peacekeepers usually lack the capacity for escalated armed response. The effectiveness of peacekeepers is dependent, not on the ability to impose their will by overwhelming force, but rather on the moral authority conveyed by their multilateral presence. From a political perspective, peacekeepers are supposed to remain impartial vis-à-vis the warring parties. For peacekeepers to engage in a military confrontation with a particular faction is to compromise their impartiality and thereby forfeit their political usefulness in the conflict situation.

The predicament of peacekeepers in the gray zone is further compounded by the sentiment of public opinion, which does not always appreciate why peacekeeping military contingents seem powerless to respond to force by force, even in the face of aggressive actions or atrocities. The fact that peacekeepers are there to play an essentially diplomatic rather than a military role is little understood by the public. In his contribution to this volume, General J. M. Sanderson draws upon his critical experience as force commander of UNTAC in Cambodia to highlight these difficulties.

All this underscores the need for a less ad hoc and more systematic response to contingencies arising in the gray zone. But this will require that at least two projects be explored more fully. In the immediate term, the UN should develop clear guidelines regarding the conditions for a more forceful response, whenever necessary, including a determination of decision-making responsibilities between the contingent commander on the scene, the overall mission commander, and UN headquarters in New York.

But more fundamentally, this may require the development of a third mechanism, separate from both traditional peacekeeping arrangements and massive enforcement actions. In particular, the UN should examine more seriously the various ideas that have been put forward for creating some form of rapid response capability. A rapid response force could be dispatched immediately to a conflict theater to avert or minimize the deterioration of the situation to crisis proportions. Intervention of this kind would go beyond traditional peacekeeping but still fall short (by its scope and duration) of a full-scale enforcement action. And being the thin end of the enforcement wedge, actions in the gray zone should necessarily be mandated by the Security Council under Chapter VII of the Charter.

In his chapter in this volume, Sir Brian Urquhart explores in detail the possibilities of rapid response by a standing UN volunteer force. He discusses the political, financial, logistical, and operational aspects of the assembly and deployment of such a force, and issues relating to its mandate and rules of engagement. In his critique of Sir Brian's proposals, François Heisbourg suggests that, given some inherent difficulties in the deployment and use of such a force, the UN's rapid response needs will be best served through strengthening the current standby arrangements system. Better still, timely and adequately funded preventive action conducted under the principles of traditional peacekeeping would obviate the need for a forceful response later.

In exploring the prospects for a rapid response capability, several questions will need to be examined more fully. To begin with, how should the proposed force be organized? Ideas range from an autonomous volunteer force recruited directly by the UN, to a force assembled on an as-needed basis from national contingents earmarked for that purpose, to an ad hoc coalition force organized outside the UN but acting with the authorization of the Security Council. Given the proliferation of crises worldwide, how many situations could be covered simultaneously by a rapid-reaction force? And how would the fact that deployment of such a force is authorized by the Security Council affect the perception of impartiality of the UN in relation to its other functions, particularly its mediation and traditional peacekeeping roles? Most important, are governments prepared to accept either the creation of an autonomous force at the disposal of the UN or, alternatively, the exposure of their own national contingents to the risks in the gray zone?

These are important but not insurmountable problems, provided sufficient political will can be generated for responding to them. For without an adequate response to the challenge of the gray zone, the peacekeeping role of the UN risks being seriously discredited. This could well be part of the lasting legacy of the combined failures in Somalia, Rwanda, and Bosnia-Herzegovina.

Seeking Additional Revenue Sources

The dramatic growth in peacekeeping activities has simply not kept pace with the flow of financial resources, as the present arrangements based on national contributions have come under increasingly severe stress. Three issues need to be addressed in this regard: the obligation of member states to fully and promptly meet their assessed contributions, an eventual reconfiguration of the present scale of assessments, and the possibility of seeking additional revenues from extragovernmental sources. The first two issues, which are the most critical at present, are currently under review by an official working group within the UN. Our concern here is to highlight the last issue, which has so far not received the attention it deserves.

The time may have come to think more innovatively about ways to generate additional revenues for multilateral peace-and-security activities. The idea of receiving direct contributions from sectors of the international community whose activities tend to benefit disproportionately from a more stable and peaceful international situation should be considered more seriously. There are several possibilities that deserve to be explored more fully in this context.

First, there are activities that benefit in a general way from a peaceful international environment. These include international air travel, telecommunications, international financial transactions, and the activities of the transnational corporations. Over the years, various schemes for direct surcharges or fees on these activities have been proposed. Some of these proposals seem quite practical, while others may appear somewhat far-fetched. A surcharge on international air travel, which is regulated by the International Air Transport Association (IATA), or on international communication, which is regulated by the International Telecommunication Union (ITU), could generate considerable revenue that would be relatively easy to collect in either case. The levels of surcharges do not have to be exorbitant. In fact, a contribution of $1 per international air ticket (which is less than a traveler might pay today for a cup of coffee at most international airports) could yield $315 million annually. A direct surcharge on international financial transactions has also been suggested as another possibility in this category; a surcharge rate of 0.5 percent on foreign exchange transactions could generate $1.5 trillion a year, at the same time dampening speculation in the foreign exchange markets. The above schemes are indicative of a wide variety of proposals that deserve more serious and systematic consideration than they have received so far in order to test their practical viability.

Second, there are corporate sectors that benefit in a particular way from access to certain facilities, whose use depends on the restoration of peace in a zone of conflict. Such was the situation with the Suez Canal during the Suez crisis of 1956. In the aftermath of the crisis, at the suggestion of the then UN Secretary-General Dag Hammarskjöld, the cost of clearing the canal was partly met through a surcharge on the normal tolls levied on ships using the waterway. The Panama Canal toll is an analogous arrangement that has existed in a peacetime context. Following the opening of the Panama Canal in 1912, a toll was levied on all international vessels navigating the canal, a practice that continues today. More recently, the use of the sea lanes and seaports in the Persian Gulf was greatly affected during the Iran-Iraq war of 1980–88 and the Gulf crisis of 1990–91. Why not consider the feasibility of obtaining a contribution to the UN from the commercial users of these facilities?

A third category could be special contributions that may be sought from some of the peacekeeping recipient countries, which after all are the direct beneficiaries of the peace operations. This category may also include states that, for reasons of special historical, political, or economic association, have a particular interest in the restoration of peace in a conflict area. There have already been some ad hoc examples of this kind of contribution. The cost of the United Nations Yemen Observer Mission (UNYOM) of 1963–64 was borne by Egypt and Saudi Arabia. Similarly, Indonesia and the Netherlands shared the cost of mounting the United Nations Temporary Executive Authority in West New Guinea (West Irian) in 1962–63 (UNTEA). Today Cyprus contributes one-third of the operational cost for the UN peacekeeping force in the country (UNFICYP), while Kuwait is responsible for two-thirds of the cost of the UN military observer mission on its border with Iraq (UNIKOM). These ad hoc arrangements need to be developed into a more systematic framework for seeking special contributions from some of the beneficiary countries, especially those with a strong revenue base.

In order to explore more fully the various options on extragovernmental funding, member states should first be prepared to modify a kind of ideological prejudice that has conditioned discussions of this matter; I refer to the view that the financing of UN peace operations should be an exclusive affair of governments. I do not believe that this position can be sustained in the long run. However, it must be recognized that member states have some legitimate concerns that need to be addressed in any discussion of extragovernmental sources of revenue. Of particular significance in this regard are the concerns about possible loss of control over decision making and derogation from collective intergovernmental responsibility for peace-and-security activities.

The recent experience of the OAU may be of some relevance here. Traditionally all the activities of the OAU have been supported through a system of assessed contributions from member states. In the period 1992–93, in the discussion leading to the establishment of the new OAU Mechanism for Conflict Prevention, Management and Resolution, a controversial issue arose as to whether the OAU should solicit and accept financial contributions from funding sources outside Africa for the operation of the Mechanism. Was there not a danger that outside contributions would compromise the independence of the OAU and expose its agenda to external manipulation? After a difficult debate, the decision was made in favor of accepting such contributions. This decision was accompanied, however, by a carefully defined policy to ensure transparency and control over contributions by the OAU. So far this innovation has worked well, affecting neither the primacy of member states in these matters nor their control over the new Mechanism.

The OAU experience would seem to demonstrate that it is at least possible, through clearly designed policies and procedures, to meet the legitimate concerns of member states. It must be emphasized, moreover, that the idea of extragovernmental funding is not meant to supplant, but rather to supplement, governmental sources of revenue. It is appropriate that governments should bear the primary financial responsibility for the peace-and-security activities of the UN; this corresponds with their political responsibility in this area.

Reforming the Security Council

Any discussion of the evolving peace-and-security agenda of the UN must take account of the growing demand for reform of the Security Council. Although there is so far no agreement on the scope, formula, and timetable for reform, there is no doubt about the strength of the movement for change. Any reform project should seek to achieve four main objectives: clarification of the role and mandate of the council; recomposition of its membership; broadening of the base of participation and transparency in the work of the council; and strengthening of the effectiveness and credibility of the council. These objectives translate into several themes of reform.

The first is the need to clarify the scope of the Security Council's mandate. Under the UN Charter the Security Council is entrusted with primary responsibility for the maintenance of international peace and security. In the immediate aftermath of World War II, the dominant concern was understandably over threats of cross-border aggression. This concern translated directly into the central mandate of the Security Council. In the past, therefore, the notion of a "threat to international peace and security" was generally understood to encompass an act of aggression or a breach of the peace, usually in the context of an interstate or regional conflict.

By contrast, the preoccupation of the international community today is with the rampant breakdown of peace and security within national borders. A survey by the Stockholm International Peace Research Institute (SIPRI) in 1995, for example, recorded thirty major armed conflicts in the world in that year, all of them situations of internal strife. In response to this development, a trend has emerged of a more expansive interpretation of the concept of a threat to international peace and security, with a number of measures being adopted by the Security Council, most of them aimed not so much at interstate conflicts as at violent struggles within countries.

Recent examples of situations that have been determined by the council to constitute threats to international peace and security include the internal repression of the civilian population in northern Iraq, including the cross-border flow of refugees (Resolution 688 of April 1991); the failure of the Libyan government to extradite the suspects in the bombing of the Pan American jetliner that exploded over Lockerbie in Scotland in 1988 (Resolution 748 of March 1992); the magnitude of human suffering caused by conflict within Somalia (Resolution 794 of December 1992); and the reluctance of the military junta in Haiti to restore power to the democratically elected government of President Jean-Bertrand Aristide (Resolution 940 of July 1994). It remains open to debate whether all of these situations fall truly within the meaning of a threat to international peace and security as envisaged in the Charter.

If the Security Council is to remain relevant, it must adapt to this new reality by developing a more progressive interpretation of what constitutes a threat to international peace and security. This is the path of pragmatic response. But the legitimacy of the Security Council would suffer if its practice in the long term was seen as departing too radically from the explicit stipulations of the Charter. For the immediate future, this dilemma underscores the importance of the need for the Security Council to seek to build broad-based international support for its decisions. If the present trend continues indefinitely, however, it may well raise the issue of amending the UN Charter to take account of this new phenomenon, the preponderance of intrastate conflicts and their ramifications.

Another issue relating to the scope of the Security Council mandate concerns nonmilitary aspects of security. A broader understanding of threats to security is emerging; this includes economic, social, and environmental concerns. In this connection, at its first summit meeting on 31 January 1992, the Security Council declared: "The absence of war and military conflicts amongst States does not in itself ensure international peace and security. The non-military sources of instability in the economic, social, humanitarian and ecological fields have become threats to peace and security. The United Nations membership as a whole, working through the appropriate bodies, needs to give the highest priority to the solution of these matters" (S/23500, 31 January 1992). The question arises as to whether all these issues of security belong to the agenda of the Security Council. This has implications for the division of labor between the Security Council, on the one hand, and the other organs of the UN on the other, particularly the General Assembly and the Economic and Social Council (ECOSOC).

The second theme of reform concerns the restructuring of the membership of the Security Council. Two developments in particular have given impetus to this movement: the dramatic growth in UN membership, from 51 in 1945 to 185 in 1995; and the emergence of a new power structure in the world of today, compared to the situation that obtained in 1945 when the UN was founded. In this context, there is broad agreement that the reemergence of Japan and Germany as major powers deserves some special recognition. But there is less common ground as to what constitutes appropriate recognition. Should they assume permanent seats on the council? And, if so, with or without the right of veto?

It would be difficult, however, to accord a special status to Japan and Germany without at the same time addressing the issue of an overall balance in the composition of the council. This may entail the creation of a new category of membership; they may be called "tenured" or "standing" members. Such members would occupy their seats for an extended period of time, but less than permanently (say, five to seven years), with provision for reelection or rotation. The crucial point here is that the selection of tenured members should combine the need for both regional and global representation. Regional representation would in the first place be a response to the concern about "northern" dominance of the present council, a situation that would be further compounded by any dispensation for Japan and Germany. Equally important, this would provide a constructive opportunity for promoting good "regional citizenship," since election to a tenured regional seat would necessarily depend on the goodwill and support of members of a particular region. Although this in itself would not stop the emergence of regional hegemonies, it could provide a powerful incentive against overbearing behavior.

Selection to global tenured seats, on the other hand, would be through direct election by the General Assembly from an open slate of candidates. This exercise would be designed to promote good citizenship at a broader level, by recognizing significant contributions to the work of the United Nations and, in particular, to its peace-and-security activities.

Whatever formula for recomposition may be adopted in the end, it is important that the composition of the Security Council not be set in stone. It will be necessary to review any new arrangement on a periodic basis, perhaps every ten to fifteen years, to ensure that council membership reflects the evolving power relations in the world.

The third theme of reform is about the right and use of veto power. There is a general reluctance to extend veto entitlement to new members. In addition, there is disquiet about the unbounded use of existing veto powers. A formal move to curtail this power would lead to a direct confrontation with the five permanent members, all of whom are likely to oppose any formal modification of their present prerogative.

For the foreseeable future, therefore, it would be more practical to encourage self-restraint, while exercising peer pressure. Already in recent years a trend has set in for an occasional use of the veto rather than the trigger-happy use that was prevalent during the Cold War era. Whereas in the decade between 1976 and 1985 a total of sixty vetoes was cast in the Security Council, the figure had nearly halved to thirty-seven in the decade between 1986 and 1995. By 1991, the percentage of resolutions that were vetoed had fallen to nearly zero from 30 percent in 1986.

This is a positive trend that needs to be encouraged and strengthened through peer pressure by the general membership of the UN. One such device could be a declaration by the General Assembly expressing concern about the use of the veto and providing a guideline to narrow the range of issues to which the veto may apply. The veto should be a defense mechanism to be used in extremis, only when a truly vital interest of a permanent member is at stake.

The fourth theme of reform relates to the need for more transparency and broader participation in the work of the council. The challenge is how to achieve this objective without compromising the equally important goal of ensuring prompt and effective action by the council. There are two areas where the work of the council could be improved in this respect.

The first area of concern relates to the fact that the Security Council remains the only major decision-making body of the UN that does not have a channel of communication for receiving information, ideas, and proposals from independent nonofficial sources. In other sectors of the activities of the UN, notably in the humanitarian, economic, environmental, social, and cultural spheres, the input of NGOs is now well developed and accepted. There is no reason why the peace-and-security sector should remain an exception. The presidency of the council could be the initial focal point of communication. The president could receive information from, and hold informal audience with, representatives of civil society and independent public figures. To avoid opening a floodgate, the interaction would have to be selective, restricted initially to organizations and public figures with known track records and credibility and who have specific contributions to make to issues under consideration by the council. This arrangement could be extended gradually, by invitation, to include informal audiences with the council as a whole, whenever this is judged to be useful.

The other area of concern in this regard is the need to broaden the base of participation by the wider UN membership in the decision-making process of the council. After all, the authority of the Security Council derives from the special responsibility conferred upon it by the membership of the UN as a whole; thus the 15 members of the council act on behalf of the entire 185 members of the organization. Several measures could help reduce the present sense of exclusion felt by the general membership.

First, more opportunities should be accorded to the wider UN membership to provide substantive inputs before final decisions are made by the Security Council on important questions. This means that in addition to the frequent informal consultations, which are private and held behind closed doors, the council should make it a practice to schedule some special open sessions for this purpose. A better balance should be struck between the need for informal consultations and the need for some open sessions that can serve as a means for wider consultations. Second, the Security Council needs to develop a more systematic method for consulting member states that are likely to be especially affected by measures under consideration. Recently a process of consultation with troop-contributing countries has been instituted, but this practice needs to be broadened and deepened. Third, there is a need to develop a better briefing system that would provide all members of the council, especially some of the nonpermanent members with limited independent means, the essential elements they need for making informed decisions. This could be organized by the secretariat. It is also necessary to improve the briefing system between the council and the rest of the UN membership. The idea here is to ensure that relevant information is readily available to all concerned.

The fifth theme concerns the credibility of the Security Council in relation to its own decisions. There is a growing dissonance between the flow of resolutions from the council and developments on the ground. The work of the council is driven by the speed of events, public pressure to "do something," and contradictory pulls from different political quarters. This sometimes results in a lack of coherence and inadequate attention to the provision of resources and means necessary for the implementation of the council's resolutions.

The experience in the former Yugoslavia has particularly highlighted this problem. Between 1991 and 1995, the Security Council adopted some ninety resolutions concerning the situation in the former Yugoslavia. Some of the resolutions appeared to contradict each other, others did not relate well to developments on the ground, and few were accompanied by the necessary means and resources for implementation. This placed the UN Secretariat, and the peacekeeping and peacemaking missions in the field, in a very difficult situation.

Because it is a political organ, it is inevitable that the Security Council should respond politically to the competing pressures on its decision-making process. On the other hand, if the present trend continues, it could seriously erode the credibility of the council. The authority of the Security Council ultimately depends on its capacity to adopt measures that are credible, carry weight, and have prospects of implementation.

Generating Collective Will

Building Domestic Support for International Action

A critical challenge faces the international community as a whole today. In the face of pressing domestic preoccupations, budgetary constraints, low tolerance for risks of casualties, and a creeping sense of crisis fatigue, how can we build domestic political constituencies in support of collective international action? In part this is the challenge of relating what has hitherto been a narrow concept of national interest to the broader imperatives of an increasingly interdependent world. Traditionally, national security was organized to respond to a particular conception of threats, usually military and territorial in nature or relating to strategic and geopolitical interests. These threats emanated from particular sources, with country-specific targets. This vision of national security may have worked well in the past, especially during the Cold War era, but is today rendered too narrow and inadequate against emerging global realities.

Today there is a growing list of transnational threats that are generalized in scope and unpredictable in their evolution. This list includes the spread of nuclear weapons and materials, as well as other weapons of mass destruction; terrorism, both domestic and cross-border; the production and consumption of narcotic drugs; life-threatening epidemics; high population growth relative to diminishing resources; mass migration of peoples; and natural as well as human-caused humanitarian catastrophes. These problems stand out in part because they defy the traditional logic of national boundaries and national solutions. To tackle them effectively requires concerted international response. Global interdependence has come to stay—it is an inescapable fact of modern international life. This basic reality needs to be articulated more clearly and consistently.

But beyond the general reality of interdependence, there are specific interests that tend to shape national responses to international crises. Among the interests at play are the following.

Direct Interests of Major Powers. When the vital interests of the major powers are at stake, as was the case in the Gulf crisis, international action is easier to mobilize because of the highly motivated leadership on the part of the countries directly affected.

Regional Interests. The interest in avoiding instability in a regional neighborhood as well as the desire to demonstrate good regional citizenship can often provide a strong incentive for countries to contribute to peace initiatives and operations within their region. Australia, Japan, and the ASEAN countries, for example, played a leading role in the Cambodian peace process. France and the United Kingdom contributed the largest peacekeeping contingents for the former Yugoslavia, while the United States and several Latin American countries spearheaded the operation in Haiti. In a similar way, the countries of West Africa were propelled by the force of events in neighboring Liberia to mount the ECO-MOG operation; this was in effect a sub-regional self-help project.

Indirect Impact. Civil wars may rage for the most part within the borders of particular countries in remote corners of the globe, but it is impossible to throw a cordon sanitaire around them. Local conflicts have a tendency sooner or later to walk across national borders, spreading violence and refugees in their paths and destabilizing entire regional neighborhoods. Thus the war in Rwanda caused instability in, and imposed a major humanitarian burden on, the neighboring countries of Burundi, Tanzania, and Zaire. The conflict in Liberia shook a large zone of West Africa, and directly contributed to civil strife in Sierra Leone and instability in the Gambia. Similarly, the conflict in the former Yugoslavia could have spread to engulf most of the Balkan region, and the effects of the war in Chechnya have affected stability in the Russian Federation as well as some of the neighboring former Soviet republics. It is sometimes the case that the fate of a particular country in conflict is unable initially to arouse much external concern, but the stakes soon change when the same conflict expands to affect neighboring countries whose stability has greater impact on international relations.

Burden Sharing. Collective international action provides a framework for sharing the political, financial, and human costs of an operation. The enforcement action against Iraq, the peacekeeping operations that restored peace to Cambodia (U.S.$1.65 billion) and Mozambique (U.S. $541.7 million) or UNPROFOR in the former Yugoslavia (annual cost U.S. $1.1 billion)—the burden of each of these operations would have been difficult to bear without broad-based international cooperation. It is also important to emphasize that from the point of view of a cost-benefit analysis, the earlier collective action is engaged, the lower is the cost in all respects.

Humanitarian Concern. There are some situations where the primary impetus for international action remains humanitarian concern. Such was the case in Somalia in 1992–93 or in Rwanda in the aftermath of the genocide in 1994. The pressure of public opinion, especially in democratic societies, often makes it difficult for governments to abstain altogether from some measure of response to major humanitarian tragedies. That being said, public opinion is by nature unpredictable and sways both ways, providing at different times either a spur or a brake on international action. Leaders' perceptions of public opinion also play a role in defining policy. These factors are, in turn, influenced by access to information, the facility with which information and images are transmitted across the globe, and the extent to which they can stir public reaction.

Umbrella of Legitimacy. A multilateral response can also serve the purpose of providing internal as well as external legitimacy for difficult and politically risky undertakings. In 1990 and 1991, for example, then U.S. President George Bush invoked United Nations actions and resolutions in his efforts to mobilize American congressional and public support for the Gulf War. Both Japan and Germany have also invoked the legitimacy conferred by the United Nations to allay public disquiet about their involvement in any military-related engagements abroad. Yet there is a need for vigilance here. The broader legitimacy of the United Nations would suffer if the organization were viewed too much as a vehicle for providing multilateral blessing for "pre-cooked" national projects.

Moral Imperatives. The question needs to be asked whether there are any situations of radical transgression of international norms or massive human suffering for which the international community is prepared to undertake enforcement action as a matter of collective obligation. Examples of such radical breaches might include an act of aggression or a campaign of genocide. It is one thing to express moral outrage but quite another to translate such sentiment into concrete action. It remains very difficult to mobilize sufficient collective will to take action primarily on the basis of a moral imperative, without a compelling coincidence of direct national interests being at stake as well, as was the case in the Gulf crisis. However, in the case of Somalia, international action was mobilized on humanitarian grounds. Ironically, it is in no small part the disastrous experience of Somalia that has led to a retreat from such engagements. This is also what we have witnessed in the cases of Rwanda and Bosnia-Herzegovina.

Role of Information. Another important factor in shaping national response is the role of information and the part played in it by the media. Wars and scenes of mass suffering tend to attract extensive media coverage. But averting, mediating or ending a conflict is not nearly as news-creating. Yet public awareness and reaction are largely dependent on what is received through the media. This underscores the importance and responsibility of the media in providing a more balanced coverage of conflict situations. It also highlights the responsibility of the United Nations to convey a clearer picture of peacekeeping, its possibilities and constraints, its successes and failures, as well as its objectives and costs.

Providing Leadership

At a given moment, any of the factors outlined above can combine to define national response to particular international crises. But these factors do not operate independently. Their function and impact are in turn shaped by political leadership.

To provide an adequate multilateral response to the growing peace-and-security agenda will require political imagination and leadership at the national as well as the international level. At the domestic level, leadership needs to articulate the nexus between national interest, broadly conceived, and international responsibility, by explaining to its constituents the ways in which national well-being can ultimately be affected by seemingly faraway dangers. This is a new reality being driven by the fact of growing interdependence. Furthermore, we believe that there exists a largely untapped reservoir of humanitarian concern in many societies. The question is whether national leaders are prepared to galvanize this resource and channel it in support of international action.

The end of the Cold War and the collapse of the Soviet Union have thrust the United States into a position of unparalleled preeminence, having left it on the world stage with no other obvious center of power to provide a countervailing weight. The United States is presently perhaps the only nation in a position to project its power in a sustained fashion on a global scale. This raises the challenge of the stewardship of this power. To what political ends is the United States prepared to project this considerable influence? What kind of leadership is the United States prepared to offer the world today? The United States acting alone cannot lead the world. But the role of the United States, acting in concert with others, providing leadership through engagement and the force of ideas, is crucial to the viability of any major multilateral enterprise today.

But a general mood of political reticence seems to have descended on the remaining superpower. There appears to be little political support in the United States for the financial costs or human risks of international engagement, except when American vital national interests are clearly involved. Fundamentally, this is a debate about the international vocation of the United States, now that the Cold War is over. This national debate is likely to continue for the foreseeable future. In the meantime, however, we must not overlook other levels of contributions that the United States could provide right away in support of multilateral peace-and-security activities. These might include contributing to the development of a system for preventive action; helping to build the capacities of regional organizations for conflict management; in the context of burden sharing, paying its fair share of the costs of peacekeeping and peacemaking; providing logistical and other support systems to countries in need of assistance in deploying their contingents in peace operations; and playing a leading role in humanitarian relief operations.

Selecting Priorities for UN Engagement

The proliferation of conflicts in many parts of the world, all of which call for some form of UN involvement, stands in sharp contrast to the limited capacity and resources of the organization. In view of these contradictory pressures, the UN will have to determine more systematically where, when, and to what degree to get involved. These are questions concerning the breadth, the depth, and the stage of UN engagement, which are distinct from the issue of functional priorities (such as investment in preventive action, mediation, traditional peacekeeping, and peacebuilding activities) discussed earlier.

In general, the UN should invest its political and material resources where they are needed most and where they are likely to make the greatest difference. Yet political realities, combined with the difficulty of formulating any objective criteria for applying such a policy, mean that decisions will in practice be made on a case-by-case basis. Is there not a danger, then, that such an ad hoc method of decision making could become entirely hostage to the fortunes and vagaries of the political process? The challenge for the Security Council in this regard is to apply, and be seen to apply, similar policies in similar situations.

While selective engagement is perhaps a necessary response to the present realities, it also poses a serious moral predicament as a long-term policy. Under selective engagement, conflicts will inevitably fall into two categories: on the one side, those "adopted" by the UN or other international organizations and, on the other, the ones that are allowed to fall between the cracks of the international system. These latter conflicts would be left to run their course and would effectively constitute the forgotten tragedies of the world. This moral predicament provides a poignant reminder of the necessity to develop, as a matter of priority, two measures discussed earlier, namely, investing in preventive action and building the capacities of regional and other organizations to assume more responsibility for peace and security in the world.

A Regime of International Norms

Evolution of Sovereignty

The issue of national sovereignty will continue to be both central and controversial. When and how can international action be reconciled with the principle of noninterference in matters deemed to be essentially within the domestic jurisdiction of states (Article 2.7 of the UN Charter)? This question becomes acute when a country is faced with a massive humanitarian crisis that begs for some form of international response.

International response to a human rights or humanitarian catastrophe can take several forms. These may be divided into five broad categories: multilateral peer pressure, as in denunciation of human rights abuses in a given country by the UN Commission on Human Rights or the UN General Assembly; use of bilateral and multilateral conditionalities that have become increasingly common, if controversial, means of promoting human rights, democratization, and structural economic reforms; humanitarian relief; provision of a relatively benign international presence on the ground, such as human rights monitors or military observers; and, finally, a radical insertion of an international presence under Chapter VII of the UN Charter.

The issue of interference is rendered moot as long as an operation is being conducted with the consent and ongoing cooperation of the competent national authorities. But in the absence of consent, two principles come into competition. On the one hand, the stability of the present international system depends in large measure upon accepting and respecting the sovereign rights of states. On the other hand, there is a major evolution in thinking at the level of international public opinion that can no longer accept that massive suffering should go unchallenged behind the walls of national sovereignty.

The search here is for an acceptable threshold. When is the level of human suffering within a given country of such magnitude as to warrant an energetic international response? This problem cannot be resolved through a juridical design. The appropriate threshold is more likely to emerge slowly over a period of time, through judgment on a case-by-case basis. This judgment needs to be informed by some general considerations.

First, national sovereignty has always been a relative rather than an absolute principle. The growth of global interdependence, human rights standards, and humanitarianism in general have further accentuated the relative quality of this principle. In effect, the very notion of what constitutes the domestic affairs of a state is shrinking. Furthermore, sovereignty is under pressure simultaneously from forces of both integration and fragmentation. The movement towards globalization and regional integration is chipping away at sovereignty from above, while devolutionist pressures, internal fragmentation, and collapse undermine it from below.

Second, the concept of national security has traditionally been confined to the narrow sphere of the security of the state. In nondemocratic polities, there has developed a perverse situation whereby the security of the state has often been organized at the expense of the security of the very people whose protection and welfare constitute the raison d'être of the state in the first place. Because of this contradiction, there is need for a broader concept of security, one that encompasses the well-being of the citizens of a country as well as the legitimate security needs of a democratic state.

Third, there is need for a sense of measure here. It is not just any incident of human rights violation or act of petty repression that must give rise to a dramatic international response. Forceful international intervention is a drastic move; it should be applied as a measure of last resort, only when all other means of inducing change have failed to yield results.

Fourth, there continues to be a North-South cleavage on this issue. This cleavage arises in part because the Security Council, as the principal decision-making organ on these questions, is dominated by the major Western powers, while the "recipient countries" are predominantly located in the south. One way to counter this imbalance is to ensure that greater efforts are made to arrive at decisions that command broad support within as well as outside the Security Council.

Finally, there is a growing paradox surrounding the question of intervention today. In the past, this issue was marked by apprehensions of unilateral intervention by the major powers of the West and the East. Although this tendency has not disappeared altogether, the greater danger today may come from the opposite direction—the prospect of too much disengagement, if not outright indifference. This is due in part to the sheer proliferation of apparently intractable armed conflicts, particularly those raging within nation-states. Another reason is the fact that, with the end of the Cold War, the major powers have redefined their interests and shifted their focus to domestic preoccupations.

Building a Community of Values

It is difficult to build an effective and sustainable framework for preserving peace and security without some kind of normative underpinning. In the past this was less apparent because everything was subordinated to the logic of the Cold War. Today the task of constructing appropriate peace-and-security mechanisms needs to be related to the challenge of building a community of values at various levels of the international system.

At the global level, the UN has been instrumental in the development and dissemination of a core of normative standards covering such areas as human rights, environmental ethics, peaceful settlement of disputes, women's rights, and minority rights. These universal principles can best be taken seriously when translated into a context of application at lower levels of the international system. A regional organization or a subregional arrangement can provide a more concrete and local framework for the application of universally accepted principles of governance. The core principles might comprise the following: the general observance of universal human rights standards; the practice of democracy; the peaceful settlement of internal and interstate conflicts; and the protection of minorities and other structurally disadvantaged groups.

A formal and common commitment to these principles would then become the basis for assessing good citizenship within a particular region or subregion as well as the criteria for participation in the regional association. The idea here is to create a form of regional political code of conduct by which the actions and policies of member governments can be judged. Unless translated into regional commitments of this kind that can give rise to regional discipline and neighborhood peer pressure, universal norms can seem remote and abstract and, at times, compromised by overtones of great-power hegemony.

Today the experience of Europe represents the most advanced efforts at building a community of values at the regional level. The Helsinki Final Act of 1975 led to a long political process that culminated in the Charter of Paris of November 1991. This sets out a common pan-European commitment to certain basic principles of democratic governance and a regime of rights. In Western Europe, with its well-rooted democratic tradition, this may not be breaking any new ground. But more important is the fact that the states that have just emerged from the former communist bloc of Europe should accept to be judged by these same standards, even as they struggle to put them into practice.

In Latin America, an important beginning has been made on the issue of democracy. A common regional commitment contained in the Santiago Declaration of June 1991, to change governments only through democratic elections, has already been successfully invoked to delegitimize and resist the military junta in Haiti that had toppled the democratically elected government in September 1991.

On the other hand, the regions of Africa, Asia, and the Middle East by and large have not yet joined in this process of building a community of values at the regional and sub-regional levels. In order to respond effectively to the rising incidence of conflicts, especially at the intrastate level, that beset those regions, it will be necessary to address this issue more directly.

Everything I have said argues for exploring the full potential of the UN. Yet in doing so, we must not lose sight of some of the objective political and material limitations under which the organization must operate. It is for this reason that the UN should always strive to identify its comparative advantages in any given sphere of activity in relation to other actors on the international scene. This is particularly pertinent today as the UN contemplates the future evolution of its peace-and-security agenda.

Moreover, the UN is not a world government; it is an association of sovereign states. As such, the effectiveness of the organization depends largely on the role that the constituent governments are willing to entrust to it. In this regard, the UN cannot operate solely on the basis of ideals and principles, divorced from the realities of the world of power politics. On the other hand, the UN should not become merely an instrument of Realpolitik. The UN should be the place where power relations are recognized but mediated by ideals and principles. It is within this context that the UN must formulate a credible peace-and-security agenda for the new century. It is our hope that from the present crossroads, there will emerge an important, balanced, and sustainable role for the UN in fulfilling its mission of preserving international peace and security.

Index

Abkhazians, 134
Abuja Treaty, 250
Accordos de Paz, 279
Acheson, Dean, 258
Addis Ababa accords, 240
ad hoc arrangements, 303; for funding, 310; subcontracting to coalitions, 304
administration, international, 45–46
Afghanistan, 10, 113; refugees from, 98; USSR in, 124
Africa, xi, 218; European contributions to peacekeeping operations in, 266; failed state and political collapse in, 233–43; French intervention in, 122, 124; IPA programs, xi–xii; scenarios for conflict resolution, 241–43. *See also* Central Africa; West Africa; specific countries.
African Commission of Human and People's Rights, 250
African National Congress (ANC), 74
An Agenda for Peace (UN), 2–6, 33, 62–63, 73, 84, 86, 102, 225, 255–56, 262, 287; concept of preventive deployment, 79–80; definition of peacemaking, 90; definition of preventive diplomacy, 90; recommendations about ICJ, 82; *Supplement to An Agenda for Peace*, 89, 91, 99–100, 105, 138, 212, 290
aggression: definition of, 29; enforcement against, 18n7; use of armed force to reverse, 124
Agreement on Refugees and Displaced Persons (Dayton accords), 42

Aidid, Mohammed Farah, 132, 279–81, 283
Akashi, Yashushi, 104, 210
Albania, 66
Albright, Madeleine, 289
Algeria, 234–35, 240
Amin, Idi, 120, 237
anarchy, 235–38
ANC (African National Congress), 74
ancient ethnic hatred, 29, 35
Angola, 113; humanitarian corridors in, 207; Observer States in, 97; training experiments, 182; União Nacional para a Independência Total de Angola (UNITA), 284; United Nations Angola Verification Mission (UNAVEM), 24, 52, 180, 183, 276, 279, 283
Annan, Kofi, xii
Annual Report of the Secretary-General on the Work of the Organization (UN), 90, 94–95
Aouzou Strip dispute, 66
Arab League, 73, 245, 256–57, 303; and Iraq's invasion of Kuwait, 67
Arabs, 240
ARF (Association of South East Asian Nations Regional Forum), 78, 303
Argentina, 65–66, 97
Aristide, Jean-Bertrand, 312
armed forces. *See* military
Armenia, 36–37, 216
Arms Control and Regional Security multilateral track, 78
arms embargoes, 46–47
Arusha Peace Agreement, 249

ASEAN. *See* Association of South East Asian Nations
Assembly of Heads of State and Government, 247
assertive multilateralism, 4, 225
Association of South East Asian Nations (ASEAN), 260; joint efforts with, 205; responses, 317; Spratly and Paracel Islands dispute, 65
Association of South East Asian Nations Regional Forum (ARF), 78, 303
Australia, 69, 74, 317
authority: in international peace and war, 10–11; to override domestic sovereignty, 3–4; United Nations Secretary-General, 91; United Nations Security Council, 90–91; United Nations Temporary Executive Authority in West Guinea (West Irian) (UNTEA), 310; United Nations Transitional Authority in Cambodia (UNTAC), 128–29, 149, 153–56, 158, 161–63, 171, 204, 210, 213, 224, 276, 278, 280–82, 298, 318
authorization for intervention, 134–35
autogenocide, 17n6
Azerbaijan, 36–37, 216
Azikiwe, Nnamdi, 236

Bahrain, 92, 94
Balkans, 27–28, 34, 216
Baltic Battalion (BALTBAT), 263
Banana, Canaan, 248
Bangladesh, 120, 289
Beagle Channel dispute, 65–66
Belgian Congo, 127
Belgium, 119, 134–35, 263
Berbers, 240
Biafra war, 233–34
Bosnia-Herzegovina, 7–8, 10, 23, 119, 216; coordination of activities in, 211; diplomatic recognition of, 48; ethnic v. communal conflict in, 30; genocide in, 141; humanitarian intervention in, 126, 265; international administration of, 45, 56; mediation in, 39–40; moral impera-

tives, 319; NATO intervention in, 124, 151; peacekeeping in, 32, 35, 37, 43–45, 267; population exchange, 42; refugees from, 98; UN intervention in, 23, 25, 97, 132–33, 140; United Nations Protection Force (UNPROFOR), 43–44, 53, 56n31, 57n35, 139, 164, 211, 222, 224, 263, 265, 267, 289, 298. *See also* former Yugoslavia; Herzegovina; Bosnian Muslims, 42
Boutros-Ghali, Boutros, xii, 4, 8, 21–26, 33, 287; and East Timor dispute, 103–4; importance of international administration, 45–46; restructuring, 72; as Secretary-General, 91; types of action for addressing conflicts, 37. See also *An Agenda for Peace, Supplement to An Agenda for Peace*
Bretton Woods institutions, 95
Brindisi, Italy: UN equipment depot, 183
Britain. *See* United Kingdom
Browning, Robert, 283
Brussels Treaty, 257–58
brutality, 18n10
Bubiyan Island, 67
Bujumbura, 96
Bunche, Ralph, 92
burden sharing, 318
Burundi, 216; conflict management in, 245; dual society of, 239–40; fact-finding missions, 96; OAU field mission in, 248–49; peace enforcement in, 45, 208; preventive deployment in, 66, 102–3
Bush, George, 34, 114, 116, 129, 318

Cable News Network (CNN), 170, 199, 205, 293
Cambodia, xi, 6–7, 11, 113, 280; autogenocide, 17n6; humanitarian intervention in, 221; International Committee on the Reconstruction of Cambodia, 288; peace process, 124, 150–51, 160–63, 205, 317; post-UNTAC, 288; preventive action in,

300; UNHCR activities in, 229; United Nations Transitional Authority in Cambodia (UNTAC), 128–29, 149, 153–56, 158, 161–63, 171, 204, 210, 213, 224, 276, 278, 280–82, 298, 318; Vietnamese intervention in, 120, 124; Vietnamese population in, 227

Cameroon, 235, 248

Canada, 23, 97, 263

cantonment, 282

Cardenas, Emilio, 10

Caribbean, 122

Caribbean Community (CARICOM), 289

Carlsson, Ingvar, 206

Carrington, Lord, 47–48

Carter, Jimmy, 69, 92, 97

Carter Center, 66, 74, 103

Caucasus, 216

Central Africa: refugee movements in, 216

Central America, xi; joint efforts in, 205; U.S. intervention in, 122

Central Intelligence Agency (CIA), 234

CFSP. *See* Common Foreign and Security Policy

Chad, 66

"Chapter 6 1/2 " operations, 197

Charter of Paris, 324

Chechnya, 37, 116, 216, 317

Chile, 65–66

China, 4; and Korean nuclear activity, 69–70, 74; and military intervention, 114; Spratly and Paracel Islands dispute, 65

Christopher, Warren, 34

CIA (Central Intelligence Agency), 234

CIS (Commonwealth of Independent States), 205, 257, 303

citizenship, regional, 313

civic action, 175–77

Civilian Police Unit (DPKO), 182

civilians, unarmed: humanitarian action by, 126

civil rights, 85

civil society: institutions of, 227

civil war, conflicts: in Africa, 234; definition of, 29. *See also* specific countries

Clausewitz, Carl von, 167

Clinton, Bill, 4, 115; Presidential Decision Directive 25, 49

CNN factor, 170, 199, 205, 293

coalitions of the willing, 199, 262, 270

co-citizenship, 36

coercive inducement, 174; limits of, 175

Cold War, 17n3, 216; end of, 128–29, 217, 277; military intervention during, 112–13; peacekeeping during, 17n5, 92–94; UN intervention in Congo during, 127–28

collaboration, 97–98

collective will, generating, 316–21

Colombia, 96

colonialism, 9

Combined Joint Task Force, 270

COMESA, 246

command, 157–60; levels of, 158; operational level, 159–60; strategic level, 158–59; tactical level, 160

command and control systems, 163–66

Commission of Mediation, Conciliation and Arbitration, 247

Commission on Global Governance, 136–37, 140, 206

Commission on Sustainable Development, 25

Common Foreign and Security Policy (CFSP), 260

Commonwealth of Independent States (CIS), 205, 257, 303

communal conflict, 31–35

community of values, 323–24

Concert of Europe, 142

Conference on Security and Cooperation in Europe (CSCE), 259, 264

conflict(s): civil war, 29, 234; communal, 29–35; ethnic, 29–30, 33; evolution of, 301; indicators of high degree of risk of, 205; internal, 207, 312; military intervention in, 111–44; techniques for addressing, 37–47 conflict management. *See* conflict resolution

conflict mitigation, 265–66

conflict prevention, 59–107, 123

conflict resolution, 123, 146–47; humanitarian action and, 224–26; OAU role in, 245–53; preventive action and, 61–87; scenarios for, 241–43

Congo, 8; anarchy in, 235; OAU intervention in, 248–49; United Nations Operation in the Congo (ONUC), 17nn4–5, 124, 127–28, 139, 203

consent inducement, 172–77

Contact Group for the former Yugoslavia, 38, 97

Contadora Group, 205, 303

Contras, 229

control systems, 163–66

Convention against Torture and Other Cruel, Inhuman or Degrading Treatment or Punishment, 85

Convention on the Elimination of All Forms of Discrimination Against Women, 85

Convention on the Elimination of All Forms of Racial Discrimination, 85

Convention on the Prevention and Punishment of Genocide, 114, 131, 136

Convention on the Rights of the Child, 85

cooperation: in Cambodia, 160–63; between UN and others, 21–22

coordination: of activities, 210–12; framework for, 96

core group, 162

costs, 101; of early prevention, 65; of peacekeeping, 58n45, 263; of peacekeeping operations, 204; of preventive diplomacy practitioners, 78–79; of rapid-response group, 191–92; of regional organizations, 266–69; Relief and Rehabilitation Programme, 289; UNOSOM II, 289

Côte d'Ivoire, 235

Crimea: preventive diplomacy in, 66

Croatia, 37, 119; conflict in, 30; diplomatic recognition of, 48; and former Yugoslavia, 32; mediation in, 39–40; United Nations Confidence Restoration Operation (UNCRO), 23–25, 44–45, 57n35, 97, 124

CSCE. *See* Conference on Security and Cooperation in Europe

cultural pluralism, 36

cultural rights, 85

Cyprus, 38; dual society of, 239, 241; military intervention in, 113; United Nations Peace-keeping Force in Cyprus (UNFICYP), 6, 23, 50, 123, 171, 278, 310

Czechoslovakia, 41, 124, 239–40

Czech Republic, 66

Czechs, 239–40

Dallaire, Romeo, 174

Dayton accords, 27, 35, 39–40, 97; Agreement on Refugees and Displaced Persons, 42

Declaration of Fact-Finding, 64

de Gaulle, Charles, 260

Delors, Jacques, 33–34

Demining Unit (DPKO), 182–83

democracy, ix, 84, 122

Democratic People's Republic of Korea (DPRK), 68–70, 74

Democratic South Africa, ix

democratization, 250

Department of Administration and Management (UN), 179, 183

Department of Humanitarian Affairs (DHA) (UN), 95, 179, 219; coordination of activities by, 212; framework for coordination, 96

Department of Peace-keeping Operations (DPKO) (UN), 95, 177–79, 178f; capacity of, 177; Civilian Police Unit, 182; Demining Unit, 182–83; Field Administration and Logistics Division (FALD), 183; financial resources, 72; framework for coordination, 96; Lessons-Learned Unit, 181; Medical Support Unit, 183; Military Adviser's Office,

184; military expertise, 184; situation center, 99; strengthening of, 186; Training Unit, 182
Department of Political Affairs (DPA) (UN), 72, 85, 94, 179; centralization of, 105; financial resources, 72; framework for coordination, 96; policy analysis team, 100; responsibilities in support of preventive action and peacemaking, 94–95
deployment: preventive, 79–81; trip wire, 79–80
de Soto, Alvaro, 287
development, 299; economic, 250
devoir d'ingérence (duty to interfere), 130
DHA. *See* Department of Humanitarian Affairs
diarchy, 16, 236
diplomacy: multitrack, 75; policy dilemmas, 47–48; preventive, 2, 63–75, 89–107; second track, 75
diplomats: available personalities, 100; skills training for, 75–79
displaced persons, 42. *See also* refugees
disputes: internationalization of, 101, *See also* specific disputes
domestic crises, 207. *See also* civil war; military intervention in, 111–44
domestic sovereignty, 3–4
domestic support, 316–19
Dominican Republic, 56n29, 124
DOMREP. *See* Mission of Representative of the Secretary-General in the Dominican Republic
double key approach, 22
Douglas-Home, Alec, 242
DPA. *See* Department of Political Affairs
DPKO. *See* Department of Peace-keeping Operations
DPRK. *See* Democratic People's Republic of Korea
dual society, 238–41
duty to interfere (devoir d'ingérence), 130

East Pakistan, 119–20, 124
East Timor dispute, 101, 103

ECCAS, 246
ECOMOG. *See* Economic Community of West African States Monitoring Group
Economic and Social Council (ECOSOC), 85–86, 313
Economic Community of West African States (ECOWAS), 218, 246, 248
Economic Community of West African States Monitoring Group (ECOMOG), 222, 303, 317
economic development, 250
economic rights, 85
economics, 37
economic sanctions, 46–47, 124
ECOSOC. *See* Economic and Social Council
ECOWAS. *See* Economic Community of West African States
education, 37
Egypt, 8, 119, 139, 310; government in, 236; Islamic militancy in, 234
El-Mahdi, Sadiq, 236
El Salvador, xi, 6–7, 11, 113, 124, 171; civil war, 17n6; financial aid to, 286–87; Friends of the Secretary-General for, 98; humanitarian intervention in, 221; peacemaking and peacekeeping in, 96; preventive action in, 300; United Nations Observer Mission in El Salvador (ONUSAL), 204, 224, 276, 278, 282, 285–86, 290, 298
embargoes, arms, 46–47
emergencies: complex, 216–17; humanitarian, 216; humanitarian responses to, 215–30; international, 216; response arrangements, 219–20
emergency relief coordinator, 219
enforcement, 124, 207; in context, 150–52; peace, 2, 109–99, 208–9, 266–69. *See also* peacekeeping
engagement: priorities for, 320–21; rules of, 193–94
EP5 (expanded permanent five), 162
equipment depot (Brindisi, Italy), 183
Eritrea, 66, 74, 113, 234
Estonia, 66, 205, 263–64

Ethiopia, 66, 74, 234–35, 237
ethnic cleansing, 41–42, 116, 133, 218
ethnic conflict, 29–30, 33
ethnic hatred, ancient, 29, 35
ethnicity, 234
EU. See European Union
Europe: community of values in, 324;
    contribution of regional organiza-
    tions in, 255–71; contributions to
    peacekeeping operations in Africa,
    266
Europe Agreements, 262
European Community (EC), 38; diplo-
    matic recognition policy, 48; inter-
    vention, 119; as model, 264; security
    community, 262
European Corps, 261
European Union (EU), 245, 260, 303;
    Common Foreign and Security Pol-
    icy (CFSP), 260; contribution to
    peace operations, 263–64; contribu-
    tion to UNOSOM, 262–63; as medi-
    ator, 41; as model, 264; security
    community, 262; Stability Pact
    framework, 123; and United
    Nations, 261; and WEU, 261
Evans, Gareth, 287, 300
evolution: of conflict, 301; and innova-
    tion , 5–10; of sovereignty, 321–23
expanded permanent five (EP5), 162

fact-finding missions, 96, 206; Declara-
    tion of Fact-Finding (1991), 64;
    OSCE, 205
failed states, 141; in Africa, 233–43
FALD (Field Administration and
    Logistics Division) (DPKO), 183
Falklands/Malvinas Islands dispute,
    64
Federation of Bosnia and Herzegov-
    ina, 40. See also Bosnia-Herzegovina
federations, 35–37
Field Administration and Logistics
    Division (FALD) (DPKO), 183
Field Operations Division, 183
financial aid, 286–87
financial constraints, 101. See also costs;
    funding

FLS. See Frontline States
force: dynamics of, 149–50; use of,
    109–99, 209–10
Foreign Legion, 196
former Soviet Union, 217; conflicts in,
    42–43; and Iraq's invasion of
    Kuwait, 67; UNHCR activities in,
    228
former Yugoslavia, 7, 217–18; arms
    embargoes against, 46–47; conflict
    in, 29, 42–43; Contact Group for, 38,
    97; criteria for involvement in, 49;
    humanitarian intervention in,
    221–22; joint efforts in, 205; media-
    tion in, 38–40; NATO and WEU in,
    124; peacekeeping in, 27–28, 43–45,
    265–66, 317–18; perspectives on,
    31–35; terminology, 29; UNHCR
    activities in, 228–99; UN interven-
    tion in, 22, 97, 116, 119, 150, 316;
    United Nations Protection Force
    (UNPROFOR), 23–25, 43–44, 49–54,
    56n31, 57n35, 139, 164, 204, 211,
    222, 224, 263, 265, 267, 289, 298; UN
    resolutions, 56n32; use of force in,
    209–10
Former Yugoslav Republic of Macedo-
    nia (FYROM), 37; dispute with
    Greece, 65; OSCE fact-finding mis-
    sion, 205; peacemaking in, 207, 264;
    United Nations Preventive Deploy-
    ment Force (UNPREDEP), 18n7, 44,
    66, 79, 102, 123, 171
"four plus one" formula, 96
France, 8; available personalities, 100;
    intervention, 115; intervention in
    African states, 124; intervention in
    Rwanda, 135, 138, 149; intervention
    in sub-Saharan Africa, 122; and
    Iraq's invasion of Kuwait, 67;
    peacekeeping, 23, 46, 97; responses,
    317; and UN intervention in Congo,
    128
FRAPH. See Front révolutionnaire
    pour l'avancement du progrès en
    Haiti
friendly regimes, 124
Friends of Haiti, 97

Friends of the Secretary-General, 96, 106; for El Salvador, 96, 98

Front for the Advancement and Progress of Haiti. *see* Front révolutionnaire pour l'avancement du progrès en Haiti (FRAPH)

Frontline States (FLS), 303

Front révolutionnaire pour l'advancement du progrès en Haiti (FRAPH), 289

funding, 101, 290. *See also* costs; additional, 306–11

FYROM. *See* Former Yugoslav Republic of Macedonia

Gabon, 248–49

Galbraith, Peter, 97

Gambia, 317

Gamsakhurdia, Zviad, 134

Garang, John, 233, 240

General People's Defense (Yugoslavia), 47

Geneva Conventions, 114

genocide, 140–41; autogenocide, 17n6; Convention on the Prevention and Punishment of Genocide, 114, 131, 136; definition of, 131, 141; protection against, 124

Genscher, Hans-Dietrich, 57n40

Georgia, 6, 9, 36–37; humanitarian intervention in, 118; peacekeeping in, 22, 134, 264

Germany: aid to, 286; and former Yugoslavia, 32; legitimacy, 318; peacemaking, 97; Security Council membership, 313

Ghana, 235–36

Gladstone, W. E., 121

global human values, 4

global neighborhood, 135–37, 145–46

globocop, 4

Golan Heights, 23, 123, 171

Gorbachev, Mikhail, 4, 34

Goulding, Marrack, 94

gray zone, 305–8

Greece, 32, 41, 65, 119

Grenada, 120, 124

Guatemala, 95, 124, 289

Guiccardi, Vittorio Winspeare, 92

Guinea, 235

Gulf Cooperation Council, 260

Gulf States, 67

Gulf War, 7, 119, 148, 297, 317–19; prevention of, 64–65

Gypsies, 227

The Hague Platform, 264

Haiti, 7, 312; coercive inducement in, 174; Friends of Haiti, 97; peace enforcement in, 208; training experiments, 182; United Nations Observer Mission for the Verification of the Elections in Haiti (ONUVEH), 288–89; UN operations in, 22, 133–34, 180, 288–90; U.S. intervention in, 124

Hammarskjöld, Dag, 91, 128, 309

Handbook on the Peaceful Settlement of Disputes between States, 62

hatreds, ancient ethnic, 29, 35

Heisbourg, François, 195–99

Heisenbergian effect, 280

Helsinki Final Act, 324

Herzegovina, 39–40, 45, 56. *See also* Bosnia-Herzegovina

High Commissioner on National Minorities (OSCE), 66, 123, 264

High-Level Task Force on UN Operations, 180

Hobbes, Thomas, 238

holistic approach, 275–95

humanitarian action, 203–13, 301–2; concern, 318; and conflict resolution, 224–26; coordination of, 210–12; emergencies, 216; intervention, 118, 126, 139–40; military for, 220–22; preventive, 98–99; protection, 201–30; responses to international emergencies, 215–30; safe areas, 133, 265–66, 298, 306; secure areas, 135; United Nations Conference on Humanitarian Assistance to Somalia, 288

human rights, 3, 37, 84; OAU initiatives, 250; United Nations Center

human rights *(continued)*
for Human Rights, 85; United Nations High Commissioner for Human Rights, 95, 103; Universal Declaration of Human Rights, 114, 226–27; Vienna Conference on Human Rights, 3–4
Hungary, 66, 118, 124
Hussein, Saddam, 5, 9, 114, 141
Hutu, 217, 239–40

IAEA. *See* International Atomic Energy Agency
IASC (Inter-Agency Standing Committee), 208–9
IATA (International Air Transport Association). 309
ICITAP (International Criminal Investigative Training and Assistance Programme), 289
ICJ (International Court of Justice), 66, 82, 141
IFOR (Implementation Force), 40
IMF (International Monetary Fund), 286–87
impartiality, 196
Implementation Force (IFOR), 40
in-country peacebuilding, 81, 83–86
independent actors, 304–5
India, 119–20, 124
Indonesia, 101, 103–4, 310
inducement, 172–77; coercive, 174–75; operations, 173; positive, 175–77
information, 319; United Nations Information Centers, 64; United Nations Office of Research and the Collection of Information, 71–72
innovation, 5–10
institutional capacities, 302–11
Inter-Agency Standing Committee (IASC), 208–9
interdependence, ix
Interim Mekong Committee, 85
internal strife, 207. *See also* civil war; military intervention in, 111–44
International Air Transport Association (IATA), 309

International Atomic Energy Agency (IAEA), 68, 70; safeguards verification measures, 69
International Committee of the Red Cross, 288
International Committee on the Reconstruction of Cambodia, 288
International Conference on the Former Yugoslavia, 97
International Court of Justice (ICJ), 66, 82, 141
International Covenant on Civil and Political Rights, 85
International Covenant on Economic, Social and Cultural Rights, 85
International Criminal Investigative Training and Assistance Programme (ICITAP), 289
international crises: indirect impact of, 317–18; national responses to, 317–19
international emergencies, 216; humanitarian responses to, 215–30
internationalization of disputes, 101
International Monetary Fund (IMF), 286–87
international norms, regime of, 321–25
International Peace Academy (IPA), xi–xii
International Police Task Force (IPTF), 45
international political-cultural associations, 303
international regimes, 81–83
International Telecommunications Union (ITU), 309
intervention, 125; arguments for, 138; authorization for, 134–35; building domestic support for, 316–19; criteria for, 49, 135–37; devoir d'ingérence (duty to interfere), 130; framework for, 164; humanitarian, 118, 126, 139–40; justification for, 120, 137–43; military, 9, 37, 111–44; nonintervention, 116–23, 321; in practice, 127–33; scenarios, 241–42; strategic objectivity and, 148–49; strengthening, 156–57; in theory,

123–27; typology, 123–24; UN, 156–57
IPA (International Peace Academy), xi–xii
Iran, 92–94, 234
Iran-Iraq war, 93–94, 113, 264
Iraq: genocide in, 141; Gulf War, 7, 64–65, 119, 148, 297, 317–19; humanitarian intervention in, 221–22; international administration, 45; invasion of Kuwait, 66–68, 114; Iran-Iraq war, 93–94, 113, 264; Kurdish refugee crisis, 114–15; military intervention in, 115; northern, 312; Operation Provide Comfort, 129, 131, 222–23; United Nations Iraq-Kuwait Observation Mission (UNIKOM), 6, 124, 310; UN operations in, 129–31, 305, 318
Islamic militancy, 234
Israel, 8
Israel-Palestine conflict, 50
Italy, 97
ITU (International Telecommunications Union), 309

Japan, 281; aid to, 286; and Korean nuclear activity, 69–70, 74; legitimacy, 318; responses, 317; Security Council membership, 313
Johnson, Lyndon B., 242

Karume, Abeid, 242
Kashmir, 50
Katanga, 127–28, 197, 234
KEDO (Korean Peninsula Energy Development Organization), 70
Keeping the Peace (International Peace Academy), ix
Kenya, 122, 235, 238
Khmer Rouge, 129, 153–54, 210, 280–81
Kim Il-Sung, 69
Kolwezi, 196
Korea, 7, 124, 305
Korean peninsula, 68–70, 74
Korean Peninsula Energy Development Organization (KEDO), 70
Korean War, 148

Kosovo, 37, 264
Kouchner, Bernard, 130
Krajina, 44
Kurdistan, 9–10
Kurds, 9, 114–15, 130, 141
Kuwait: Iraq's invasion of, 66–68, 114; United Nations Iraq-Kuwait Observation Mission (UNIKOM), 6, 124, 310

labor, division of, 302–5
Latin America, 182, 324. *See also* specific countries
Latvia, 66, 205, 263
leadership, 319–20; Security Council, 4
League of Arab States. *See* Arab League
League of Nations, 27–28, 45
League of Nations Council, 41
Lebanon: military intervention in, 113; Multi-National Force in Lebanon, 10; peacekeeping in, 46, 124; Syrian enforcement in, 124; UN inaction in, 26; United Nations Interim Force in Lebanon (UNIFIL), 139
legitimacy, 318
legitimate governments, 124
Lesotho, 248
Lessons-Learned Unit (DPKO), 181
Liberia, 216–18, 235; arms embargoes against, 46; civil war, 317; conflict management in, 22, 46, 245; Economic Community of West African States Monitoring Group (ECOMOG), 222, 303, 317; ECOWAS initiative in, 248; humanitarian intervention in, 118; preventive diplomacy in, 92; refugees from, 98
Libya, 66, 312
Lie, Trygve, 91, 191
Lithuania, 263
Lumumba, Patrice, 127–28
Lusaka Protocol, 24, 283

Maastricht treaty, 260–61
Macedonia. *see* Former Yugoslav Republic of Macedonia
Maghreb Union, 246

Mahdi Mohamed, Ali, 279–80
Malawi, 235
Malaya, 122
Mali, 227
Mandela, Nelson, ix–x
Mauritania, 227
media, 204; CNN factor, 170, 199, 205, 293
mediation, 37–41; IPA programs, xi
Medical Support Unit (DPKO), 183
Mengistu Haile-Mariam, 237
Mexico, 96
Military Adviser's Office (DPKO), 184
military intervention, 9, 37; achievements and limitations, 222–24; during Cold War, 111–13; in domestic crises, 111–44; for humanitarian purposes, 126, 220–24; as peacekeeping, 113; post–Cold War, 113–16; types of cooperation, 261–62
Military Staff Committee (UN), 114, 165; roles and responsibilities, 167n1
Mill, John Stuart, 116–20, 125, 138
mines: clearance of, 264; Demining Unit (DPKO), 182–83
minorities: High Commissioner on National Minorities (OSCE), 66, 123, 264
mission creep, 127
Mission of Representative of the Secretary-General in the Dominican Republic (DOMREP), 56n29
Mission Planning Service, 180–81
Mitterrand, François, 115, 130–31, 140
Moldova, 36–37, 264
Montenegro, 46
moral imperatives, 318–19
motivation, 65
Mozambique, 7, 248, 280, 289; civil war, 233; humanitarian intervention in, 221; preventive action in, 300; United Nations Operation in Mozambique (ONUMOZ), 124, 171, 204, 213, 224, 276, 278, 282, 289–90, 298, 318
multilateralism, assertive, 4, 225

Multi-National Force in Lebanon, 10
multiparty systems, 236
Museveni, Yoweri, 236, 241–42
Muslims, 42, 227
Myanmar, 227

Nagorno-Karabakh, 264
Namibia, 6–7, 113, 280; humanitarian intervention in, 221; United Nations Transition Assistance Group (UNTAG), 17n4, 124, 171, 204, 213, 224, 276, 278, 281–82, 297–98
nation(s): definition of, 29–30; v. state, 30–31
nationalism, 31; suicidal, 34
national minorities: High Commissioner on National Minorities (OSCE), 66, 123, 264
national responses to international crises, 317–19
National Security Revitalization Act, 289–90
nation-state, 30
NATO. *See* North Atlantic Treaty Organization
Ndebele, 240
neocolonialism, 18n10
neo-imperialism, 138
Netherlands, 310
New World Order: end of, 132; return to spheres of influence after, 133–35; UN intervention in Bosnia under, 132–33; UN intervention in northern Iraq under, 129–31; UN intervention in Somalia under, 131–32
NGOs. *See* nongovernmental organizations
Nicaragua, 113, 124, 229, 298
Nigeria, 235; administration by, 56; civilian rule in, 236; civil war, 233–35; dual society in, 240; First Republic, 235; multiparty system in, 236; OAU field mission in, 248; UN inaction in, 26
Nkrumah, Kwame, 234
no-fly zones, 124, 265–66, 306

nongovernmental organizations (NGOs), 74–75, 77; coordination of activities by, 212; emergency response arrangements, 219; peace enforcement by, 208–9

nonintervention, 116–23, 321; justification for, 121

Nonproliferation Treaty (NPT), 68

no-party systems, 16, 236–37

Nordic countries, 182

North Atlantic Council, 259, 265

North Atlantic Treaty Organization (NATO), 224, 257–60; contributions to peace operations, 263, 265–68; cooperation with UN, 22; intervention in Bosnia-Herzegovina, 124, 151; Partnership for Peace, 262; security community, 262

northern Iraq, 312; humanitarian intervention in, 221–22; Operation Provide Comfort, 129, 131, 222–23; UN intervention in, 124, 129–31. *See also* Iraq

Northern Ireland, 29, 239–40

North Korea, 68–70, 74, 112

NPT (Nonproliferation Treaty), 68

nuclear weapons development, 68–70, 74

Nyerere, Julius, 242

OAS. *See* Organization of American States

OAU. *See* Organization of African Unity

objectivity, 157–60

Obote, Milton, 237

observer missions, 218; United Nations Observer Mission for the Verification of the Elections in Haiti (ONUVEH), 288–89; United Nations Observer Mission in El Salvador (ONUSAL), 204, 224, 276, 278, 282, 285–86, 290, 298; United Nations Yemen Observer Mission (UNYOM), 310

Observer States in Angola, 97

ODA. *See* Official Development Assistance

OECD. *See* Organization for Economic Cooperation and Development

Office of Legal Affairs, 95

Office of Operations, 179

Office of Planning and Support (DPKO), 179–80, 183

Office of Research and the Collection of Information (UN), 71–72

Office of the Military Adviser, 179

Office of the Security Coordinator, 179

Official Development Assistance (ODA) (OECD), 299

OIC. *See* Organization of the Islamic Conference

Oman, 122, 124

ONUC. *See* United Nations Operation in the Congo

ONUMOZ. *See* United Nations Operation in Mozambique

ONUSAL. *See* United Nations Observer Mission in El Salvador

ONUVEH. *See* United Nations Observer Mission for the Verification of the Elections in Haiti

Operation Desert Storm, 278

Operation Lifeline Sudan, 126

Operation Provide Comfort, 129, 131, 222–23

Operation Restore Hope, 282

Operation Turquoise, 174, 222–23

Organization for Economic Cooperation and Development (OECD): Official Development Assistance (ODA), 299

Organization of African Unity (OAU), xi–xii, 73, 217, 234–35, 241, 303; and Burundi, 103; Charter, 247; contributions to peace operations, 257, 266–67, 269; field missions, 248; funding arrangements, 310–11; initiatives, 248; joint efforts with, 205; Mechanism for Conflict Prevention, Management and Resolution, 243, 247, 310–11; partnership with United Nations, 246; preventive diplomacy, 66; role in conflict management, 245–53

Organization of American States (OAS), 73, 134, 245, 257, 303; contributions to peace operations, 267, 269; joint efforts with, 205

Organization of the Islamic Conference (OIC), 73

Organization on Security and Cooperation in Europe (OSCE), 98, 205, 257, 259, 303; contributions to peace operations, 264, 269; High Commissioner on National Minorities, 66, 123, 264; preventive diplomacy, 66

organizations: and former Yugoslavia, 33–35; nongovernmental, 74–75, 77, 208–9, 212, 219; regional, 73–75, 77, 245–46, 252, 255–71, 303–4; subregional, 303

OSCE. *See* Organization on Security and Cooperation in Europe

Owen, Lord David, 38

Palestine, 45; United Nations Special Committee on Palestine (UNSCOP), 38

Panama Canal, 310

Pan American, 312

Paris Agreements, 153, 155, 161

Partnership for Peace, 262

PDD (Presidential Decision Directive), 25, 49

peace, ix; cooperating for, 160–63; threats to, 312; UN authority in, 10–11

peacebuilding, 98–99, 273–325. *See also* peacemaking; concept of, 81–86; coordination of activities, 210–12; future directions, 287–94; holistic approach to, 275–95; in-country, 81, 83–86; with international support, 85–86; lessons of, 276–87; through national effort, 83–85; post-conflict, 3, 62; preventive, 13; strategies of, 62

peace enforcement, 2, 109–99, 208–9; regional organizations in, 266–69. *See also* peacekeeping

peace-enforcing fatigue, 9

peace-enforcing missions, 7

peacekeepers, 177; available personalities, 100; players and methods, 71–75; principal actors, 90–92; skills training for, 75–79; special envoys, 101

peacekeeping, 3, 19–58, 109–99. *See also* specific operations; and challenge of gray zone, 305–8; challenges of, 169–70; classic model of, 123; coordination of activities, 210–12; costs of, 263; vs development, 299; end-of-Cold-War model of, 123–24; ethos of, 152–53; "four plus one" formula, 96; humanitarian action and, 203–13; implications for Secretariat, 177–85; improvements, 177–85; limits of, 1–18; military intervention as, 113; multidimensional, 305; new, 169–87; potential of, 1–18; regional organizations in, 266–69; requirements, 177–85; spending on, 58n45; strategies, 61–62; traditional, 17n5, 297; UN, 27–58

peacekeeping operations, 5–6, 220; annual costs, 204; consent for, 172–77; contribution of regional organizations to, 262–66; failure of, 24; first-generation, 6; full-service, 284; generations of, 5, 203–4; origins of, 276; perspective on, 298–302; second-generation, 6, 17n4; second-generation multidimensional, 6–7; third-generation, 7, 17n4; types of, 170–72; withdrawal from, 22–24

peacemaking, 2–3, 19–58, 89–107, 206–7; Cold War cases, 92–94; constraints on, 99–101; coordination of activities, 210–12; definition of, 90; DPA responsibilities in support of, 94–95; "four plus one" formula, 96; modalities, 94–99; observations on, 104–6; political obstacles, 101–2; principal actors, 90–92; recent cases, 102–4. *See also* peacebuilding

Peacemaking and Peacekeeping for the Next Century (International Peace Academy), xii

Pérez de Cuéllar, Javier, 47, 57n40, 93
Perot, Ross, 237
Persian Gulf, 9, 66–67, 310
personnel, 290, 295
pluralism: cultural, 36; tribal, 238
police: Civilian Police Unit (DPKO), 182; International Police Task Force (IPTF), 45
political collapse, 233–43
political-cultural associations, 303
political obstacles, 101–2
political personalities, 100
political rights: International Covenant on Civil and Political Rights, 85
political tension, 238–41
political violence: primary, 233; secondary, 233; tertiary, 233–34
population exchange, 41–42
Portugal, 97, 101, 103–4
positive inducement, 175–77
post-conflict peacebuilding, 3
Presidential Decision Directive (PDD), 25, 49
prevention, 59–107; early, 63, 65; late, 63
preventive action, 61–87, 198–99, 204–5; delivering, 86–87; DPA responsibilities in support of, 94–95; humanitarian, 98–99; imperative for, 299–301; ladder of, 205–6; peacebuilding, 13; scope of, 61–63
preventive deployment, 18n7, 86, 123; concept of, 79–81; force tasks, 81; legal basis for, 80
preventive diplomacy, 2; in action, 65–66; Cold War cases, 92–94; concept of, 63–65; constraints on, 99–101; costs, 78–79; definition of, 90; early and successful, 68–70; failure to use, 66–68; first track, 65; modalities, 94–99; observations on, 104–6; players and methods, 71–75; political obstacles, 101–2; principal actors, 90–92; recent cases, 102–4; second track, 65, 75; UN experience, 89–107
protected zones, 155; safe areas, 133, 265–66, 298, 306; secure areas, 135

protection: against genocide, 124; humanitarian, 201–30; of war victims, 114

Quakers, 74

Radio Mille-Collines, 195
Ramphal, Shridath, 206
rapid deployment initiatives, 185
rapid deployment units, 190–91
rapid response: alternatives to, 192–93, 198; case against, 195–99; case for, 189–95; desirability of, 195–96; feasibility of, 197–98; options, 190–92; prospects for capability, 189–99; rules of engagement, 193–94
rapid response group, 191–92, 194–95; nature of, 192; role of, 193; tasks for, 193
recognition policy, 47–48
reconciliation, 166
reform: Security Council, 311–16; UN, 25–26
refugee camps, 155
refugees, 221, 312; Agreement on Refugees and Displaced Persons (Dayton accords), 42; Kurdish crisis, 114–15, 130; movements of, 216. *See also* United Nations High Commissioner for Refugees (UNHCR)
regimes: friendly, enforcement of, 124; international, 81–83; of international norms, 321–25
regional citizenship, 313
regional dimensions, 231–71
regional interests, 317
regional organizations, 73–75, 77; categories of, 256–61; classical, 257; conflict management, 245–46; considerations for, 252; contributions in Europe, 255–71; contributions to peace operations, 262–66; cost-benefit analysis of, 266–69; credibility of, 267; possible division of labor for, 303–4; range of, 255–62. *See also* specific organizations
religious sectarianism, 234

RENAMO (Resistência Nacional
    Moçambicana), 280, 289
Republic of Bosnia and Herzegovina,
    40. *See also* Bosnia-Herzegovina
Republic of Korea (ROK), 69–70, 74
Republic of Serb Krajina, 39
Republic of Somaliland, 241
Republika Srpska, 40
Resistência Nacional Moçambicana
    (RENAMO), 280, 289
retrenchment, 10–12
revenue sources, 101, 290; additional,
    306–11. *See also* costs
Rhodesia, 46
rights: Convention on the Rights of the
    Child, 85; human, 3, 37, 84, 250;
    International Covenant on Civil
    and Political Rights, 85; Internation-
    al Covenant on Economic, Social
    and Cultural Rights, 85; of petition,
    136; United Nations Center for
    Human Rights, 85; United Nations
    High Commissioner for Human
    Rights, 95, 103; Universal Declara-
    tion of Human Rights, 114, 226–27;
    Vienna Conference on Human
    Rights, 3–4
ROK. (Republic of Korea), 69–70, 74
Romania, 84
Roma people (Gypsies), 227
Roper, John, 196
RPF (Rwandese Patriotic Front),
    134–35
Ruanda-Urundi, 45
rules of engagement, 193–94
Rumaila oil field, 67
Russia, 36; administration by, 46, 56;
    and former Yugoslavia, 32; and
    intervention in Haiti, 134; interven-
    tion in Tajikistan, 122; as mediator,
    39, 97; national self-determination,
    37; peacekeeping, 23, 134; preven-
    tive diplomacy in, 66
Russian Federation, 116
Rwanda, 9, 216–17, 235; arms embar-
    goes against, 46; and Burundi, 103;
    civil war, 240, 317; conflict manage-
    ment in, 147, 245; dual society of,

238–40; French intervention in, 138,
    149; genocide in, 141; humanitarian
    intervention in, 221, 318; interna-
    tional administration of, 45, 56;
    joint efforts in, 205; military inter-
    vention in, 116; moral imperatives,
    319; OAU intervention in, 248–49;
    Operation Turquoise, 174, 222–23;
    peace enforcement in, 208; refugees
    from, 98, 164; United Nations Assis-
    tance Mission for Rwanda
    (UNAMIR), 52, 134–35, 163–64, 191,
    195–96, 204, 213, 222, 289, 298; Unit-
    ed Nations Assistance Mission for
    Rwanda (UNAMIR II), 266
Rwandese Patriotic Front (RPF),
    134–35

SACB (Somali Aid Coordination
    Body), 288
SADC (Southern Africa Development
    Community), 246, 303
SADCC, 248
SADF (South Africa Defence Force),
    281
safe areas, 133, 265–66, 298, 306
sanctions, economic, 46–47, 124
Sandinistas, 229
Santiago Declaration, 324
Saudi Arabia, 67, 310
Scandinavian Battalion (SCANBAT),
    263
sectarianism, religious, 234
secure areas, 135
security communities, 15, 262
Sekou Touré, 235
self-defense, 155; political imperative
    for, 155–56
self-determination, 7, 9; national, 37
Senegal, 74
Serbia, 32, 36, 46
Serbs, 30, 35, 119
settlements: enforcement of, 124
Shagari, Shehu, 236
Shaw, George Bernard, 237
Shevardnadze, Eduard, 134
Shona, 240
Siad Barre, 8, 235, 238

Sierra Leone, 216, 218; civil strife, 317; conflict management in, 245; humanitarian intervention in, 118; OAU field mission in, 248

Sinai, 113, 123; United Nations Emergency Force (UNEF I), 139

SIPRI (Stockholm International Peace Research Institute), 312

skills training, 75–79

Slavonia, 44

Slovakia, 66, 264

Slovak Republic, 66

Slovaks, 239–40

Slovenia, 37

Socialist Federal Republic of Yugoslavia, 30–31; end of, 36–37; General People's Defense, 47. *See also* former Yugoslavia

social rights, 85

Somalia, 7–8, 10, 216–17, 235, 288; arms embargoes against, 46; conflict in, 29; conflict management in, 245; dual society of, 241; humanitarian intervention in, 118, 126, 221, 318; military intervention in, 115, 210; moral imperatives, 319; OAU field mission in, 248; peace enforcement in, 56, 205, 288; post-UNOSOM II, 288; Resolution 794, 115, 312; tyranny in, 235, 237–38; UNHCR activities in, 228; UN intervention in, 9, 22, 52, 131–33, 136, 140, 149, 204, 213; United Nations Conference on Humanitarian Assistance to Somalia, 288; United Nations Operation in Somalia (UNOSOM), 181, 222, 262–63, 277–78, 281, 298; United Nations Operation in Somalia (UNOSOM I), 279, 282; United Nations Operation in Somalia (UNOSOM II), 132, 275–76, 278, 280–84, 289; United Task Force (UNITAF), 131–32, 174–75, 222, 282, 284, 290; U.S. withdrawal from, 23

Somali Aid Coordination Body (SACB), 288

Somali National Alliance, 9

South Africa, 46, 300

South Africa Defence Force (SADF), 281

South China Sea dispute, 74

Southern Africa Development Community (SADC), 246, 303

South Korea, 112

South Pacific Forum, 73

South West Africa People's Organization (SWAPO), 280–81

sovereignty, 7, 115, 301; evolution of, 321–23; UN authority to override, 3–4

Soviet Union. *See* Union of Soviet Socialist Republics (USSR)

Spain, 96

special envoys, 100–101; skills training for, 75–79

special representative of the secretary-general (SRSG), 161–62

spending. *See also* costs: on peacekeeping, 58n45

spheres of influence, 133–35

Spratly and Paracel Islands dispute, 65

Sri Lanka, 228

SRSG. *See* special representative of the secretary-general

stabilization, 134–35

staffing, 290, 295

standby arrangements, 181, 185

Starovoitova, Galina, 37

states, 30–31

Stockholm International Peace Research Institute (SIPRI), 312

Stoltenberg, Thorvald, 97

strategic objectivity, 148–49

subcontracting: to ad hoc coalitions, 304; to NATO, 267

sub-regional organizations, 303

sub-Saharan Africa, 122

Sudan, 235; civilian rule in, 236; dual society of, 238–40; first civil war, 233–34, 240; humanitarian corridors in, 207; intervention in, 115, 130; multiparty system in, 236; OAU field mission in, 248; Operation Lifeline Sudan, 126; second civil war, 233–34, 240

Sudan Council of Churches, 115
Sudeten Germans, 41
Suez Canal, 309
Supplement to An Agenda for Peace, 89,
    91, 99–100, 105, 138, 212, 290
SWAPO (South West Africa People's
    Organization), 280–81
Syria, 46, 124

Tajikistan, 6, 36–37, 216; humanitarian
    intervention in, 118; international
    administration of, 46; Russian inter-
    vention in, 122; UNHCR activities
    in, 228
Tanganyika, 242
Tanzania, 235; and Burundi, 103; inter-
    vention in Uganda, 120, 124, 241;
    pluralism in, 238
Task Force on Peace Operations, 95–96
terminology, 29–31
Tibet, 116
Tito, 34
Togo, 235
tolls, 309–10
training assistance teams (UNTATs),
    182
Training Unit (DPKO), 182
tribalism, 234, 238
trip wire deployment, 79–80
Tuaregs, 227
Tudjman, Franjo, 25, 44, 57n35, 267
Turkey, 41, 121
Tutsi, 141, 217, 239–40
tyranny, 235–38

Uganda: and Burundi, 103; no-party
    system, 236–37; Tanzanian inter-
    vention in, 120, 124, 241
Ukraine, 66
UNAMIR. *See* United Nations Assis-
    tance Mission for Rwanda
UNAVEM. *See* United Nations Angola
    Verification Mission
UNCRO. *See* United Nations Confi-
    dence Restoration Operation
UNDP. *See* United Nations Develop-
    ment Programme
UNEF. *See* United Nations Emergency
Force
UNFICYP. *See* United Nations Peace-
    keeping Force in Cyprus
UNHCR. *See* United Nations High
    Commissioner for Refugees
Uni:pa Nacional para a Independência
    Total de Angola (UNITA), 284
UNICEF (United Nations Children's
    Fund), 194
UNIFIL. *See* United Nations Interim
    Force in Lebanon
UNIKOM. *See* United Nations Iraq-
    Kuwait Observation Mission
Union of Soviet Socialist Republics
    (USSR), 10, 112–14; fall of, 36–37,
    116; intervention in Afghanistan,
    124; intervention in Czechoslova-
    kia, 124; intervention in Hungary,
    124; and UN intervention in Congo,
    128. *See also* former Soviet Union
UNITA. *See* União Nacional para a
    Independência Total de Angola
UNITAF. *See* United Task Force
United Kingdom, 4, 8; and Bahrain,
    92–94; conflict in, 29; intervention,
    115; intervention in Iraq, 124; inter-
    vention in Malaya, 122; interven-
    tion in Oman, 124; national policy,
    121; peacekeeping, 23, 97; respons-
    es, 317; and UN intervention in
    Congo, 128
United Nations, 259; advantages, 51;
    agenda for peace, 2–5; authority,
    3–4, 10–11; budget, 3, 21, 299; col-
    laboration with, 97–98; colonialism,
    9; command and control problems,
    8–9; constraints on, 99–101; cooper-
    ation with others, 21–22; coordina-
    tion of activities in, 211; criteria for
    involvement, 49; developments
    within, 94–97; diplomatic recogni-
    tion policy, 48; enforcement opera-
    tions, 305; European Union (EU)
    and, 261; Fiftieth General Assembly,
    72; framework for involvement in,
    164; General Assembly, 90–91, 256,
    313; inaction in Lebanon and Nige-
    ria, 26; institutional defects, 50–51;

intervention, 9, 127–33, 145–57; intervention in Cambodia, 160–63; intervention in domestic crises, 111–44; joint efforts with, 205; mandate in Croatia, 25; mediation, 37–41; Military Staff Committee, 112, 114, 167n1; and nonintervention, 121–23; partnership with Organization of African Unity (OAU), 246; peace-and-security agenda, 297–325; peacekeepers, 177; peacekeeping, 3, 5–7, 27–58, 153–55, 177–85, 203–4, 220; peacemaking, 19–58, 89–107; possible division of labor for, 302–3; preventive diplomacy, 66, 71–72, 89–107; principal actors, 90–92; priorities for engagement, 320–21; rapid response capability, 189–99; reason for, ix; reform, 25–26; Resolution 43/131, 130; Resolution 46/182, 130, 207, 219; Resolution 598, 113; Resolution 661, 264; Resolution 664, 264; Resolution 665, 264; Resolution 678, 114, 130, 264; Resolution 688, 114–15, 130, 312; Resolution 713, 265; Resolution 743, 265; Resolution 748, 312; Resolution 757, 265; Resolution 770, 265; Resolution 776, 265; Resolution 787, 265; Resolution 794, 115, 312; resolutions on former Yugoslavia, 56n32; restructuring, 72; strategic level organization, 159; strategic problems, 10; use of force by, 145–68; war-making, 8–10; withdrawal from former Yugoslavia, 24–25; withdrawal from peacekeeping operations, 22–24. *See also* specific departments, operations

United Nations Angola Verification Mission (UNAVEM), 24, 52; UNAVEM I, 276; UNAVEM II, 276; UNAVEM III, 180, 183, 276, 279, 283

United Nations Assistance Mission for Rwanda (UNAMIR), 52, 134–35, 163–64, 191, 195–96, 204, 213, 222, 289, 298; UNAMIR II, 266

United Nations Center for Human Rights, 85

United Nations Charter, 111–12, 146–48, 165–66, 258; Article 2.7, 121–23; Article 29, 96; Article 33, 62–63; Article 36, 64; Article 46, 167n1; Article 47, 167n1; Chapter VI, 63; Chapter VII, 148; command and control systems and, 163–66

United Nations Children's Fund (UNICEF), 194

United Nations Conference on Humanitarian Assistance to Somalia, 288

United Nations Confidence Restoration Operation (UNCRO), 23–25, 44–45, 97, 124; mandate, 57n35

United Nations Development Programme (UNDP), 204–5, 286; core resources, 299

United Nations Emergency Force (UNEF I), 139

United Nations Field Service, 194

United Nations High Commissioner for Human Rights, 95, 103

United Nations High Commissioner for Refugees (UNHCR), 41, 95, 98, 194, 215–17, 222, 224, 286; activities in countries of origin, 226–29; and Burundi, 103; emergency fund, 220; emergency response arrangements, 219–20; preventive deployment, 228; primary objectives, 227; service package arrangements, 223

United Nations Information Centers, 64

United Nations Inter-Agency Standing Committee (IASC), 208–9

United Nations Interim Force in Lebanon (UNIFIL), 139

United Nations Iraq-Kuwait Observation Mission (UNIKOM), 6, 124, 310

United Nations Observer Mission for the Verification of the Elections in Haiti (ONUVEH), 288; ONUVEH II, 289

United Nations Observer Mission in El Salvador (ONUSAL), 204, 224, 276

United Nations Observer Mission in El Salvador (ONUSAL) *(continued)* 278, 282, 285, 298; role, 285–86; staffing, 290

United Nations Office of Research and the Collection of Information, 71–72

United Nations Operation in Mozambique (ONUMOZ), 124, 171, 204, 213, 224, 276, 278, 282, 289, 298, 318; staffing, 290

United Nations Operation in Somalia (UNOSOM), 181, 222, 277–78, 281, 298; costs, 289; EU contribution to, 262–63; UNOSOM I, 279, 282; UNOSOM II, 132, 275–76, 278, 280–84, 289

United Nations Operation in the Congo (ONUC), 17nn4–5, 124, 127–28, 139, 203

United Nations Peace-keeping Force in Cyprus (UNFICYP), 6, 23, 50, 123, 171, 278, 310

United Nations Preventive Deployment Force (UNPREDEP), 18n7, 44, 66, 79, 102, 123, 171

United Nations Protection Force (UNPROFOR), 43–44, 53, 139, 211, 222, 224, 289, 298; BALTBAT (Baltic Battalion), 263; command and control systems, 164; European contributions to, 263, 265; mandate, 57n35; NATO's contributions to, 267; personnel and fatalities, 56n31; SCANBAT (Scandinavian Battalion), 263

United Nations Secretariat: capacity of, 177–85; improvements, 184; roles and responsibilities, 165

United Nations Secretary-General, 90–91, 284; *Annual Report of the Secretary-General on the Work of the Organization,* 90, 94–95; authority, 91; and East Timor dispute, 103–4; and former Yugoslavia, 32–33; Friends of the Secretary-General, 96, 106; Friends of the Secretary-General for El Salvador, 96, 98; good-offices role, 38, 91; High-Level Task Force on UN Operations, 180; as mediator, 38; Mission of Representative of the Secretary-General in the Dominican Republic (DOMREP), 56n29. *See also* specific secretaries-general

United Nations Security Council, 3–4, 90–91, 111; activity, 3; authority, 90–91; cooperation with others, 22; credibility of, 315; criteria for intervention, 49, 135–37; improvements, 184; leadership, 4; membership, 313; participation in, 314–15; preventive diplomacy and peacemaking, 96; reforming, 311–16; roles and responsibilities, 165; veto power, 314

United Nations Special Committee on Palestine (UNSCOP), 38

United Nations Temporary Executive Authority in West Guinea (West Irian) (UNTEA), 310

United Nations Training Assistance Teams (UNTATs), 182

United Nations Transitional Authority in Cambodia (UNTAC), 128–29, 149, 153–56, 161–63, 171, 204, 210, 213, 224, 276, 278, 280–82, 298, 318; levels of command in, 158

United Nations Transition Assistance Group (UNTAG), 17n4, 124, 171, 204, 213, 224, 276, 278, 281–82, 297–98

United Nations Truce Supervision Organization (UNTSO), 297

United Nations Yemen Observer Mission (UNYOM), 310

United Republic of Tanzania, 241

United States, 8, 10; and breakup of Yugoslavia and Soviet Union, 37; contribution to UN, 23; intervention, 112, 114–15; intervention in Central America and Caribbean, 122; intervention in Dominican Republic, 124; intervention in Grenada, 120, 124; intervention in Guatemala, 124; intervention in Haiti, 124, 133–34; intervention in

Iraq, 124; intervention in Nicaragua, 124; intervention in northern Iraq, 124; intervention in Somalia, 132; intervention in Vietnam, 124; and Iraq's invasion of Kuwait, 67; and Korean nuclear activity, 69–70, 74; leadership, 320; legitimacy, 318; as mediator, 38–41; National Security Revitalization Act, 289–90; peacekeeping, 96–97, 282, 284, 317; policy on former Yugoslavia, 34–35; power of, 4; spending on peacekeeping, 58n45; and UN intervention in Congo, 128; withdrawal from Somalia, 23

United Task Force (UNITAF), 131–32, 174–75, 222, 282, 284, 290

Universal Declaration of Human Rights, 114, 226–27

UNOSOM. *See* United Nations Operation in Somalia

UNPREDEP. *See* United Nations Preventive Deployment Force

UNPROFOR. *See* United Nations Protection Force

UNSC. *See* United Nations Security Council

UNSCOP. *See* United Nations Special Committee on Palestine

UNTAC. *See* United Nations Transitional Authority in Cambodia

UNTAG. *See* United Nations Transition Assistance Group

UNTATs. *See* United Nations Training Assistance Teams

UNTEA. *See* United Nations Temporary Executive Authority in West Guinea

UNTSO. *See* United Nations Truce Supervision Organization

UNYOM. *See* United Nations Yemen Observer Mission

Urquhart, Brian, 92–93, 189–95, 292

U Thant, 92

value-added tax, 293

values: building community of, 323–24; global human, 4

Vance, Cyrus, 38, 65

van den Broek, Hans, 47

van Eekelen, Willem, 266

van Zyl Slabbert, Frederik, 74

Vatican, 65–66

Venezuela, 96–97

veto power, 314

Vienna Conference on Human Rights, 3–4

Vienna Seminar, xii, 1, 12

Vietnam, 120, 124

Vietnamese, 227

Vojvodina, 37

volunteer militia, 292

war(s), 145–68, 238; civil, 29, 234; of federal secession, 119; UN, 8–10; UN authority in, 10–11. *See also* specific countries, conflicts

Warba and Bubiyan Islands, 67

War Crimes Tribunal, 56n32

weapons: arms embargoes, 46–47; nuclear, 68–70, 74; prevention of, 124

West Africa: Economic Community of West African States (ECOWAS), 218, 246, 248; Economic Community of West African States Monitoring Group (ECOMOG), 222, 303, 317; refugee movements in, 216

Western Europe, 33–35, 262

Western European Union (WEU), 257, 260; Associate Partners, 262; contributions to peace operations, 263–65, 267, 269; Council of Ministers, 259, 265; European Union (EU) and, 261; intervention in former Yugoslavia, 124; nature of, 258–59

West Guinea (West Irian): United Nations Temporary Executive Authority in West Guinea (West Irian) (UNTEA), 310

Westphalian order, 142

WEU. *See* Western European Union

WFP. *See* World Food Programme

Whig theories, 122

WHO (World Health Organization), 286

Wilson, Woodrow, 28

World Bank, 287

World Court. *See* International Court of Justice

World Food Programme (WFP), 103, 220, 286, 299

World Health Organization (WHO), 286

world order, 115; New World Order, 129–33; post–Cold War, 146; post–New World Order, 133–35; Westphalian model of, 142

Yeltsin, Boris, 37

Yemen, 240–41; United Nations Yemen Observer Mission (UNYOM), 310

Yugoslavia. *See* former Yugoslavia; Socialist Federal Republic of Yugoslavia

Zagreb agreement, 39

Zagreb Four, 97

Zaire, 103, 135, 235

Zambia, 74, 235

Zanzibar, 241–42

Zimbabwe, 240

About the Contributors

Kofi A. Annan was elected secretary-general of the United Nations on 17 December 1996 to serve a five-year term of office. A national of Ghana, he took up the post after more than three decades of high-level service with the world organization. He was under-secretary-general for Peace-Keeping Operations from 1993 to 1996 and assistant secretary-general in that department from 1992 to 1993. He has also served as controller of the United Nations and assistant secretary-general for human resources management. He has held UN posts away from UN headquarters in New York with the Office of the High Commissioner for Refugees, Geneva, and the Economic Commission for Africa, Addis Ababa. He has also served in Zagreb, as special representative of the secretary-general to the former Yugoslavia and special envoy to NATO, and he led the first negotiating team to initiate discussions with the Government of Iraq on the "oil for food" formula to ease the humanitarian crisis. He is honorary chairman of the IPA Board of Directors.

Boutros Boutros-Ghali was secretary-general of the United Nations from 1992 to 1997. From May 1991 until he became secretary-general, he was Egypt's deputy prime minister for foreign affairs; previously, he served as minister of state for foreign affairs (1977–91). He has had a long association with international affairs, as a diplomat, jurist, scholar, and widely published author. He was a member of the International Law Commission from 1979 until 1991 and is a former member of the International Commission of Jurists. In September 1978 he attended the Camp David summit conference and had a role in negotiating the Camp David accords between Egypt and Israel, which were signed in 1979. From 1949 to 1977, he was professor of international law and international relations at Cairo University. He is a former honorary chairman of the IPA Board of Directors.

Michael W. Doyle is director of the Center of International Studies and professor of politics and international affairs at Princeton University; he was the senior fellow (1995–97) and vice president (1993–94) of the International Peace Academy. He is the author of *Empires* (1986), *UN Peacekeeping in Cambodia: UNTAC's Civil Mandate* (1995); and *Ways of War and Peace* (1997) and coeditor with Ian Johnstone and Robert Orr of IPA's *Keeping the Peace* (1997). He is chairman of the Committee of Editors of *World Politics* and a member of the IPA Board of Directors.

Jan Eliasson is state secretary for foreign affairs of Sweden. He entered the Swedish Foreign Service in 1965 and has served as foreign policy adviser on Asian and African affairs in the Political Department (1980–82); foreign policy adviser, Prime Minister's Office (1982–83); ambassador, under-secretary for political affairs, Stockholm (1983–87); and Sweden's permanent representative to the UN (1988–92). He was under-secretary-general for humanitarian affairs at the UN from 1992 to 1994 and from 1988 to 1992 was personal representative to the secretary-general in Iran-Iraq. He is a member of the board of directors of the Institute for East-West Security Studies and of the IPA.

Gareth Evans is former foreign minister of Australia and now deputy leader of the opposition. He was a lecturer in law at the University of Melbourne (1971–76) and barrister-at-law (1977–78). Within the government, he has served as attorney-general (1983–84); minister for transport and communications (1987–88); minister for foreign affairs (1988–96); and leader of government in the Senate (1993–96). He is a member of the Carnegie Commission on Preventing Deadly Conflict and the author of *Cooperating for Peace: The Global Agenda for the 1990s and Beyond* (1993), from which part of his chapter is drawn. He was awarded the 1995 Grawemeyer Prize for Ideas Improving World Order.

Thomas M. Franck is the Murry and Ida Becker Professor of Law and director of the Center for International Studies at New York University School of Law. He is the author of numerous books and articles covering international law, international organization, international relations, national security law, the foreign policy process, and ethics and has five times received the American Society of International Law Certificate of Merit for publications, including his most recent work, *Fairness in International Law and Institutions* (1995). Professor Franck is currently counsel to the Government of Bosnia and Herzegovina in the Case Concerning Application of the Convention on the Prevention and Punishment of the Crime of Genocide before the International Court of Justice (ICJ). He has been counsel in several cases before the ICJ and adviser to various governments on international legal questions. From 1980 to 1982 he was director of research at the United Nations Institute for Training and Research. He was editor-in-chief of the *American Journal of International Law* from 1984 to 1993. In 1993, he was invited to give the general course in public international law at the Hague Academy of International Law. He has twice been a Guggenheim Fellow and is a member of the Institut de Droit International.

*

François Heisbourg is senior vice president, Matra Défense/Espace in Paris. He served as assistant to the director of economic affairs, Ministry of Foreign Affairs (1977–78), and was a member of the ministry's policy planning staff from 1978 to 1979. He served as first secretary, Permanent Mission of France to the UN (1979–81); international security adviser to the minister of defense (1981–84); vice president, Thomson International (1984–87); and director, International Institute for Strategic Studies, London (1987–92). He is the author of *La Puce, les hommes, et la bombe; Les Volontaires de l'an 2000*; and numerous articles in international media and scholarly journals.

Ismat Kittani is special adviser to UN Secretary-General Kofi Annan and formerly special adviser to UN Secretary-General Boutros Boutros-Ghali. He was under-secretary-general for UN Peace-keeping Operations and chairman of the Secretary-General's Steering Committee for the World Summit for Social Development. Mr. Kittani has had a long and extensive career at the UN. A former under-secretary for foreign affairs of Iraq, he was elected president of the UN General Assembly in 1981, the first person to hold that post who had been both a UN delegate and a member of the secretariat. After service as Iraq's permanent representative to the UN in both New York and Geneva, Mr. Kittani was secretary of the Economic and Social Council and chief of specialized agencies in the Department of Economic and Social Affairs. He was the UN secretary-general's special representative to Somalia (1992–93) and special envoy to Tajikistan (1993). He is a member of the IPA's Board of Directors.

Nelson Mandela has been president of the Republic of South Africa since May 1994. He was a lawyer and national organizer for the African National Congress. He was on trial for treason from 1956 to 1961 and was sentenced to five years' imprisonment in 1962. From 1963 to 1964, he was on trial for further charges and in June 1964 was sentenced to life imprisonment. He was released in February 1990. He received the Jawaharlal Nehru Award in 1979; in 1993 he was awarded the Liberty Medal (USA) and shared the Nobel Prize for Peace. His publications include *No Easy Walk to Freedom, How Far We Slaves Have Come: South Africa; Cuba in Today's World* (with Fidel Castro), *Nelson Mandela Speaks: Forging a Non-racial Democratic South Africa,* and *Long Walk to Freedom.*

Ali A. Mazrui is director of the Institute of Global Cultural Studies and Albert Schweitzer Professor in the Humanities at State University of New York at Binghamton and also Senior Scholar at Cornell University and the Albert Luthuli Professor-at-Large at the University of Jos in Nigeria. He has published over twenty books, including *Cultural Forces in World Politics* (1990), and was editor and coauthor of *Africa since 1935: Volume VIII of the UNESCO General History of Africa* (1993). He is also author and narrator of the BBC/PBS television series *The Africans: A Triple Heritage* (1986).

Edward Mortimer is foreign affairs editor of the *Financial Times.* He was previously assistant Paris correspondent for the *Times* (1967–70) and then foreign specialist and leader writer (1973–85). He was a fellow of All Souls College, Oxford, from 1967 to 1972 and again from 1984 to 1986 and senior associate at the Carnegie Endowment for International Peace in 1980–81. His books include *France and the Africans* (1969), *Faith and Power: The Politics of Islam* (1982), *The World That FDR Built* (1989) and an Adelphi Paper for the International Institute of Strategic Studies, *European Security after the Cold War* (1992).

Sadako Ogata has been United Nations High Commissioner for Refugees since 1991. She was envoy extraordinary and minister plenipotentiary for Japan's mission to the UN in 1978–79 and was the UN special emissary investigating problems of Cambodian refugees on the Thai-Cambodian border in 1979 . She served as the representative of Japan on the UN Commission for Human Rights from 1982 to 1985. She is a former chair of the Executive Board of UNICEF and a former director of the Institute of International Relations, Sophia University, Tokyo, where she also was dean of the Faculty of Foreign Studies.

Olara A. Otunnu is president of the International Peace Academy and Special Representative of the UN Secretary-General for Children and Armed Conflict. He practiced law in New York prior to teaching law at Albany Law School. He served as secretary-general of Uganda Freedom Union and member of Uganda National Consultative Council (Uganda's interim parliament) before becoming Uganda's permanent representative to the UN from 1980 to 1985. During his tenure at the UN, he served as president of the Security Council, chairman of the Contact Group on Global Negotiations, and vice president of the General Assembly. Returning to Africa in 1985, Mr. Otunnu became his country's minister of foreign affairs, during which time he played a leading role in the Uganda peace negotiations that culminated in the Nairobi Peace Agreement of December 1985. From 1987 to 1989, he lived in Paris, where he was Visiting Fellow at Institut Français des Relations Internationales and Visiting Professor at the American University. Mr. Otunnu has served on several commissions, including the Commission on Global Governance, the Carnegie Commission on Preventing Deadly Conflict, and the Club of Rome. He serves on the boards of several organizations, including the Carnegie Endowment for International Peace, the Aspen Institute, Hampshire College, the International Crisis Group, and the Advisory Committee of the Stockholm International Peace Research Institute.

Adam Roberts has been the Montague Burton Professor of International Relations at Oxford University and Fellow of Balliol College since 1986. He is a Fellow of the British Academy. He is the author of *Nations in Arms: The Theory and Practice of Territorial Defense* (1986); and editor, with Benedict Kingsbury, of *United Nations, Divided World: The UN's Roles in International Relations*

John Roper is a professor at the College of Europe in Bruges and has been an Associate Fellow of the Royal Institute of International Affairs, London, since 1995. From 1990 to 1995, he was the first director of the Institute for Security Studies of the Western European Union in Paris. He was a member of Parliament (1970–83), an opposition spokesman on defense (1979–81), and chief whip of the Social Democratic Party from 1981 to 1983. From 1983 to 1990 he was a senior member of the staff of the Royal Institute of International Affairs, where he edited the institute's journal, *International Affairs* (1983–88). A founding member of the European Strategy Group, he is the author and editor of a number of published works on the problems of UK and European defense and Western security.

Salim Ahmed Salim was reelected secretary-general of the Organization of African Unity (OAU) for a third term in June 1997. His initial term began 19 September 1989. Prior to his election as secretary-general, Dr. Salim held public office in his country, the United Republic of Tanzania, where he served in various capacities for twenty-seven years. He was prime minister from 1984 to 1985 and then served as deputy